Intelligence services form an important but controversial part of the modern state. Drawing mainly on British and American examples, this book provides an analytic framework for understanding the 'intelligence community' and assessing its value. The author, a former senior British intelligence officer, describes intelligence activities, the purposes which the system serves, and the causes and effects of its secrecy. He considers 'intelligence failure' and how organization and management can improve the chances of success. Using parallels with the information society and the current search for efficiency in public administration as a whole, the book explores the issues involved in deciding how much intelligence is needed and discusses the kinds of management necessary. In his conclusions Michael Herman suggests a strategy for optimizing intelligence's national value in the post-Cold War world. He also argues that it has important contributions to make to international security, but that some threat-inducing activities should be kept in check.

Intelligence services form an important but controversial part of the modern state. Drawing mainly on British and American examples, this book provides an analytic framework for understanding the 'intelligence community' and assessing its value. The author, a former senior British intelligence officer, describes intelligence activities, the purposes which the system serves and the causes and effects of its secrecy. He considers 'intelligence failure' and how organization and management can improve the chances of success. Using parallels with the information society and the current search for efficiency in public administration as a whole, the book explores the issues involved in deciding how much intelligence is needed and discusses the kinds of management necessary. In his conclusions Michael Herman discusses intelligence's national value in the post-Cold War world. He also argues that it has important contributions to make to international security, but that its threat-inducing activities should be kept in check.

Intelligence power in peace and war

Intelligence power
in peace and war

Michael Herman

THE ROYAL INSTITUTE OF
INTERNATIONAL AFFAIRS

CAMBRIDGE
UNIVERSITY PRESS

Published by the Press Syndicate of the University of Cambridge
The Pitt Building, Trumpington Street, Cambridge CB2 1RP
40 West 20th Street, New York, NY 10011-4211, USA
10 Stamford Road, Oakleigh, Melbourne 3166, Australia

First published 1996

Printed in Great Britain at the University Press, Cambridge

A catalogue record for this book is available from the British Library

Library of Congress cataloguing in publication data
Herman, Michael, 1929–
Intelligence power in peace and war / Michael Herman.
p.   cm.
Published in association with the Royal Institute of
International Affairs.
Includes bibliographical references.
ISBN 0 521 56231 7 (hc) ISBN 0 521 56636 3 (pb)
1. Intelligence service. 2. Intelligence service – Great Britain.
3. Intelligence service – United States. I. Title.
JF1525.I6H47 1996 327.1241 – dc20   95–48112   CIP

ISBN 0 521 56231 7 hardback
ISBN 0 521 56636 3 paperback

WD

Contents

IV – Accuracy

V – Evaluation and management

VI – The 1990s and beyond

VII – Summary

Figures

Preface and acknowledgements

This book has dual origins. One is in the thirty-five years I spent as a professional intelligence practitioner, after two earlier ones as a national serviceman in the British Intelligence Corps just after the Second World War. This career coincided almost exactly with the Cold War. It was spent mainly as a member of a collection agency, with spells in other intelligence jobs in the Cabinet Office and the Ministry of Defence. Over the years I became increasingly interested in how big intelligence institutions operated, and in the way they fitted together into a national 'system'. By accident or inclination my viewpoint came to be that of an Organization Man.

The second origin is in the contact I was free to make after retirement with the world of scholarly 'intelligence studies' (mainly in the United States and Canada but now developing in Britain), and with the academic faculties in which it is based. I was able to do some writing and teaching about intelligence and explore its literature. My base in Nuffield College Oxford also helped me to make some forays into social science's studies of organizations and their transmission and use of information.

From these origins has come this attempt to add to existing theory about intelligence power and the institutions through which it works. By 'theory' I mean nothing more than concepts and generalizations that seek to explain things. I have always been struck by the attention paid to concepts of war, both in academic 'war studies' and in practical military education, and have felt that intelligence studies and practitioners' vocational training both lack a corpus of this kind. There is some good North American work on intelligence concepts of various kinds, but it is incomplete; and outside a small academic circle is not as well known in Britain as it should be.

Hence this work, which tries to evaluate and extend the existing literature and merge it with my own experience and reflection. It is intended neither to attack intelligence nor to defend it; my object is simply that it should be better understood. This writing is directed at anyone interested in the subject, inside and outside official circles, critics as well as defenders.

The case for writing in this way is easily stated. Intelligence is now big business, with a legal status and a public persona; it is no longer sensible to pretend that it does not exist. Democracies have to recognize it, and public opinion and those who form it need some basis for informed views. Governments have to judge what to expect of it, how much to spend on it, and how to control it. Academically the disciplines of modern history, war studies (and peace studies), international relations and political science are incomplete without some literacy in the subject. Practitioners, especially those just coming into the profession, need to learn something from books; intelligence is now so diverse that after a working lifetime one realizes the great gaps in one's understanding of it. All those involved with intelligence in these various ways need some idea of its special features and how it relates to the rest of the world. Retired diplomats and service officers produce useful insights about their own professions, and former intelligence practitioners can contribute in the same way.

The plan for doing so here is set out in the Introduction, but two preliminary comments are needed. The first is that I do not deal with the controversial issues of intelligence's democratic accountability, legal status and implications for individuals' rights. These are important, and merit the extensive attention that they have received in US literature, and in recent British books by Gill and (jointly) by Lustgarten and Leigh. Sensible discussion of these matters depends on knowing what intelligence does, without either demonizing or romanticizing it, and I hope that this book will contribute in that way. But to deal specifically with this mixture of political, moral and legal issues would need separate and different treatment.

The second concerns the effect of secrecy. Even though this is no work of autobiography, security considerations have formed a constant background to what I have written. Intelligence is now no longer a forbidden subject, and the flow of official US releases and authorized publications by retired senior professionals has been accompanied by recent British moves towards greater openness. But the need for reticence about some operational secrets is still genuine enough. Moreover real secrets must in practice be surrounded by a wider glacis of secrecy if they are to be successfully defended; there are gradations rather than black-and-white distinctions between what is damaging and what is not. Opinions differ considerably (and change over time) on where security lines should be drawn. But few would deny that formal defences have to be erected somewhere.

Hence this book has been written from the beginning on the under-standing that it would be submitted for official scrutiny. Like other retired intelligence officers I have undertaken not to communicate certain types of information without authorization, and am bound by the special restrictions of the current Official Secrets Act. In any case I am a believer in having an official scrutiny procedure, provided that it is driven by reasonable interpretations of national security: for intelligence, mainly the protection of current and future sources. (It would be better if the procedure included arrangements of some kind for appeals against official rulings; but that is a separate matter.) I am glad to say that, subject to some deletions and changes, security clearance has been given for the text of this book, as it was for my earlier articles and lectures on which it draws. Nevertheless I am conscious that observant readers will find some deliberate obscurities and circumlocutions, and a lower level of proof for some assertions than they might expect in a normal academic work. I must of course add that this official clearance carries with it no official responsibility for any of the contents, or approval for them.

I hope that, despite the security limitations, this combination of personal experience with ideas developed in an academic milieu will be found useful. My main regret over the rather abstract treatment is that it has precluded describing why modern intelligence appeals to those engaged in it, in peace as well as in war. My time as a practitioner coincided almost exactly with the Cold War, in a period in which the USSR was continually improving its information defences, and Western intelligence was always running hard to keep up and draw ahead if possible. Methods were revolutionized by computers, and parts of intelligence production were transformed into rather special, high-technology factories. I saw intelligence become in some ways like a large-scale, multinational news agency, constantly seeking to handle more information more quickly to meet an ever-increasing demand for authentic world news. Part of the fascination and challenge of this enterprise was in promoting efficiency and job satisfaction, and in the wealth of human contacts this entailed. In these respects there was nothing unique about intelligence. What gave the work its special flavour was the profound conviction that, if done properly, it was helping Western governments to manage East–West conflict sensibly and avoid the disaster of nuclear war.

I touch on these aspects of intelligence management in Part V, particularly chapter 18. I have also made suggestions elsewhere about some practical matters of organization and effectiveness. But on the whole this book is safely distanced from personal impressions, and distils them as abstractions rather than recollections. It is not intended to provide any original source material for intelligence history. The aim is to provide generalized ideas of what intelligence is for and how it does it. These may help historians, but I hope will also have some direct bearing on the present and future.

So if I am criticized for producing an unscintillating book on an absorbing subject I plead extenuating circumstances. But 'theory' has its place if things are to be properly understood. And intelligence has had enough titillating revelations already.

In this work I have had help from many people and much kindness. In the official world I was indebted to Sir Peter Marychurch, Director GCHQ, when I first began it. His successor Sir John Adye has been characteristically open-minded and helpful in important ways; he may not wish to be labelled as encouraging a practitioner's book about intelligence, but I must express gratitude for a distinctly benevolent neutrality. Other former colleagues still in official service have had the labour of scrutinizing successive versions of this draft as well as my earlier articles; I am glad to say that arguments over security clearance have been conducted in civilized terms, on the whole with tolerable conclusions.

For my return to Oxford and the eight years spent there I owe much to Sir Michael Howard, and to the Warden and Fellows of Nuffield College for making me a Gwilym Gibbon Research Fellow in 1987–8 and an Associate Member for six years thereafter. I received special encouragement in the college from Byron Shafer and the late John Vincent, and from others in Oxford including Robert O'Neill, Adam Roberts and David Robertson. I am grateful to those who allowed me to try out ideas in papers at various British, American and Canadian universities; at meetings of the International Studies Association; and in teaching intelligence courses at Birmingham University and King's College London. An earlier version of chapter 15 was given to the Canadian Association for Security and Intelligence Studies in October 1994 and has been published in *Intelligence and National Security* for October 1995. Nick Woodward and others at Templeton College introduced me to management theory; Blaise Cronin, now at Indiana University, opened my eyes to 'informatics' and other writing about the information age; and Kevin Cunningham of the United States Army provided hospitality at West Point and frequent insights into US thinking. I apologize to the many others whose help I have failed to acknowledge here.

As a Chatham House project the book originated in the enthusiasm of

Sir James Eberle and John Roper, and I gratefully acknowledge the support provided in 1988–9 by the Leverhulme Trust. John Roper conducted negotiations with Whitehall at a time when the Peter Wright case seemed to be blighting the prospect of any serious intelligence writing, and subsequently chaired a Chatham House study group which considered early drafts. His successor Trevor Taylor patiently prodded me to decide what I was trying to say. In more recent years Jack Spence and Margaret May have kept faith in the work and arranged publication.

Chapters have been read in various forms by Geoffrey Best, Ken Booth, John Ferris, Andrew Hurrell, Sheila Kerr, Ken Robertson, Maurice Scott and Maxwell Taylor, from all of whom I have had helpful comments. Philip Barton provided great help with early versions and word processing, at times when help was much needed. I am also specially grateful to Robert Lane, who combined the roles of model Oxford landlord, social science sage on his summer sabbaticals from Yale, and friend and mentor to this fugitive from my less reputable, non-academic profession.

I owe even more to my wife Ann's constant tolerance and support for this way of spending retirement years, and to her eventual insistence that writing had to come to an end; that the shipbuilder had to stop endless carpentry, painting and polishing, and get the ship into the water. Katy Cooper, as copy-editor, then helped to make the vessel seaworthy, and showed exemplary patience with my last-minute finishing touches as it went down the slipway, while Barbara Hird coped with the complications of the index.

However my greatest debt is to Michael MccGwire – naval officer, rugby player, intelligence expert on the Soviet navy, academic, convivial talker, and friend of long standing in all these guises – who first encouraged me to write about intelligence and was generous with his time thereafter. To complete the nautical image: without MccGwire's motivating, this book would have remained yet another dream-ship, safe in the imagination, never exposed – at long last – to the practical test of seeing whether it floats.

December 1995

Glossary of terms and abbreviations

Abbreviations and acronyms are included only if repeated without expansion in the text. Professional intelligence terms are limited to those I have used. I have given notes on those that have variable meanings, often reflecting transatlantic and service–civilian differences, and have explained where I have chosen particular meanings. Some new terms, without any previous use, have been suggested and explained in the text but have not been included here.

As elsewhere, 'intelligence' in the abbreviations, acronyms and terms listed here denotes knowledge, organization or activities (or all three), the meaning depending on the context.

Acoustint	Acoustic intelligence: tracking and identification from underwater sound; minor above-water source. Sometimes also Acint.
Analysis	Used here mainly for all-source work; though single-source work also has its analysis components, for example 'traffic analysis' in Sigint.
ASAT	Anti-satellite systems.
Assessment	Used here for definitive all-source product written for executive users, often with policy implications; for example JIC assessments.
Assessments Staff	Small Cabinet Office group producing JIC reports.
Bletchley Park	British Second World War Sigint centre.
CDI	Chief of Defence Intelligence. Head of DIS; now also with responsibilities for armed forces' intelligence as a whole.
CDS	Chief of Defence Staff.
CIA	Central Intelligence Agency.

CIGs	Current Intelligence Groups producing assessments in the JIC system.
Codes and ciphers	Sigint targets. The semantic difference between the two is unimportant here.
Combat information	Military term. Used here to denote military information obtained in combat by forces under operational control, and not by intelligence-controlled collection.
Comint	Communications intelligence; Sigint from intercepting and exploiting communications.
Counterespionage	Used here as the detection of espionage, not for passive defensive measures designed to make it more difficult.
Counterintelligence	Humint professionals use the term to denote the targeting of opponents' Humint agencies and attempts to penetrate them by Humint means. Some US usage equates it with information security of all kinds. The term is used here (atypically) to denote intelligence on *any* foreign intelligence agency, obtained by *any* means.
Cryptanalysis	Sigint attempts to break codes and ciphers.
CSBMs	Confidence- and Security-Building Measures.
C^{3}I	Command, control, communications and intelligence/information. Now also C^{4}I, including computers.
DCI	Director of Central Intelligence.
DEA	Drug Enforcement Administration.
DF	Radio direction finding to locate transmissions.
DGI	Director-General of Intelligence. Now CDI.
DIA	Defense Intelligence Agency.
DIS	Defence Intelligence Staff.
DMI	Director of Military Intelligence.
DNI	Director of Naval Intelligence.
DoD	Department of Defense.
Electronic Warfare	(1) The use of electronic interception directly, immediately and locally for threat detection, warning, avoidance, target acquisition and homing, and (2) jamming,

	deception and other electronic means, used directly to prevent or reduce an enemy's effective use of radio and other electronic emissions.
Elint	Sigint on 'non-communications' emissions, such as radars, which do not convey messages.
Estimate	US and military term for definitive all-source report. 'Assessment' usually preferred here.
EW	See Electronic Warfare.
FBI	Federal Bureau of Investigation.
FCO	Foreign and Commonwealth Office (formerly Foreign Office).
Finished intelligence	Used here for all-source reports.
Foreign intelligence	On foreign targets, including external threats.
GCHQ	Government Communications Headquarters.
GRU	Soviet military intelligence organization.
Hacking	Unauthorized access to computers.
Humint	Intelligence from human sources.
IAEA	International Atomic Energy Authority.
Imagery	Intelligence from photographic and other images. Also sometimes Imint and Photint.
Imint	Imagery.
INR	Bureau of Intelligence and Research.
Intelligence Coordinator	Senior member of JIC.
IT	Information technology
JARIC	Joint Air Reconnaissance Interpretation Centre.
JCS	Joint Chiefs of Staff.
JIB	Joint Intelligence Bureau.
JIC	Joint Intelligence Committee (now also used for US Joint Intelligence Centers).
JIS	Joint Intelligence Staff (serving wartime JIC).
KGB	Soviet intelligence and security organization.
MoD	Ministry of Defence.
National	Mainly used here for intelligence agencies serving all parts of government, not individual departments. Also used,

	particularly in Sigint, for control at a central ('strategic') level rather than at lower ('tactical') levels.
National Assessment	Used here for important reports for top-level users.
NFIP	National Foreign Intelligence Program; budget for 'strategic' intelligence.
NHS	British National Health Service.
NIC	National Intelligence Council.
NIE	National Intelligence Estimate: formal interdepartmental report for top level.
NIO	National Intelligence Officer.
NPM	New Public Management. Term coined to cover the sweeping changes in Britain and many other countries in 1980s and 1990s.
NRO	National Reconnaissance Office.
NSA	National Security Agency.
NTMs	National Technical Means of collection.
Nucint	Technical collection on nuclear targets.
ONE	Office of National Estimates.
OSS	Office of Strategic Services.
Photint	Imagery.
POW	Prisoner of War. POW intelligence is gained by interrogation, bugging, and similar methods.
PSIS	Permanent Secretaries' Committee on the Intelligence Services.
Radint	The product of radars used for intelligence purposes; also information available for intelligence as a by-product of surveillance by operational radars.
Security	Information security. Also national security; security intelligence; and security agencies.
Security intelligence	Intelligence on 'internal' threats. Contrasted here with foreign intelligence.
Sigint	Signals intelligence; electronic interception and (all) cryptanalysis. Comprises Comint and Elint; see also Telint. For other interception for

immediate, local use see Electronic
Warfare.

Single-source reports   Produced by one collection agency and
based on its own kind of intelligence
material.

SIS   Secret Intelligence Service.

SNIE   Special NIE.

Strategic   High-level intelligence control and
budgeting (see also 'national'). Also used
for a high level of users and decision-
taking served by intelligence. (Note
therefore that the level of control does not
necessarily equate with the level of
intelligence produced; 'strategic'
collection can be tasked to produce
'tactical' intelligence.) 'Strategic' also
used to denote intelligence of long-term
rather than immediate value.

Sweeping   Search for bugs and other eavesdropping
devices.

Tactical   Compare with 'strategic'. Tactical
collection is under devolved control and is
normally geared to produce intelligence
for use at the command level to which it is
devolved. 'Tactical' intelligence also has
general connotations of short-term rather
than long-term use. It is used here, for
example, in 'tactical support' for
diplomatic negotiations.

Technical base   A body of knowledge that is not usable
intelligence but is the basis for attacking
and exploiting targets.

Technical collection   By Sigint, imagery and other non-human
sources.

Technical intelligence   Intelligence (irrespective of source) on
technical subjects.

Telemetry   Radio transmissions carrying
measurements from missiles under test;
intercepted and analysed during the Cold
War.

Telint   US term for Sigint from interception and
analysis of telemetry transmissions.

| TIARA | Tactical Intelligence and Related Activities budget. |
| Ultra | Wartime codeword for high-grade Sigint decrypts. |

Introduction

Governments collect, process and use information. Part of statecraft is what a writer on war has called 'the central importance of *knowing*, both in general and in particular'.[1] In Deutsch's phrase, systems of knowing are part of the 'nerves of government'.[2] Modern government has many such systems, most of them geared to routine functions: taxation, law-and-order, social security, vehicle licensing, and so on.

Other organizations also have their own information systems; and 'intelligence' is sometimes employed to describe them all, governmental and non-governmental, and the information they produce. 'Business intelligence' and 'competitor intelligence' are established parts of the private sector; 'racing intelligence' is designed to predict horse-racing results; other commercial information services have similar labels. Intelligence within large organizations has been called 'the information – questions, insights, hypotheses, evidence – relevant to policy'.[3] Even more broadly it has been argued that 'social intelligence . . . is the process whereby a society, organization or individual acquires information in the widest sense, processes and evaluates it, stores it and *uses* it for action'[4] (emphasis added).

But 'intelligence' in government usually has a more restricted meaning than just information and information services. It has particular associations with international relations, defence, national security and secrecy, and with specialized institutions labelled 'intelligence'. Intelligence in this sense was described in 1949 by Sherman Kent – an American academic who had seen wartime intelligence service and was to become a leading member of CIA's Office of National Estimates – as

---

[1] J. Keegan, *The Mask of Command* (London: Penguin, 1987), p. 325.
[2] K. W. Deutsch, *The Nerves of Government* (New York: Free Press, 1963).
[3] H. L. Wilensky, *Organizational Intelligence* (New York/London: Basic Books, 1967), preface p. ix.
[4] B. Cronin and E. Davenport, 'The Compound Eye/I: an Introduction to Social Intelligence', *Social Intelligence* vol. 1 no. 1 (1991), pp. 1–2. For the etymology of intelligence and its eight meanings see A. Durant, ' "Intelligence": Issues in a Word or in a Field?', *Social Intelligence* vol. 1 no. 3 (1991), and P. Baumard, 'Towards Less Deceptive Intelligence', same issue.

'a kind of knowledge ("What intelligence have you turned up on the situation in Columbia?")'; 'the type of organization which produces the knowledge ("Intelligence was able to give the operating people exactly what they wanted")'; and 'the activity pursued by the intelligence organization ("The [intelligence] work behind that planning must have been intense")'.[5] Although this threefold definition is often used, the key element is Kent's second, organizational one. 'Intelligence' in government is based on the particular set of organizations with that name: the 'intelligence services' or (sometimes) the 'intelligence communities'. Intelligence activity is what they do, and intelligence knowledge what they produce.

Organized intelligence of this kind has been a twentieth-century growth industry, and most governments now have it as a permanent institution. It is a significant part of the modern state and a factor in government's success and failure. It consumes sizeable if not massive resources; US expenditure on it at the end of the Cold War was about a tenth of the cost of defence, and the current British effort costs rather more than diplomacy. It has even had some direct economic effects, as in its influence on early computers and subsequently on the development of space satellites and miniaturized electronics. It constitutes its own particular kind of state power: *intelligence power*. This book is about this power and the institutions that provide it.[6]

Intelligence of this kind now has a serious literature which has developed over the last twenty years. It includes excellent historical writing, with particular emphasis on the Second World War, and a growing body of analytic work, mainly American. As a discrete subject 'intelligence studies' has become a recognized part of history and political science courses at universities and colleges in the United States and Canada; at the last count some 130 of them were identified at 107 institutions.[7] Britain has its modest counterpart in academic courses now approaching double figures.[8]

---

[5] S. Kent, *Strategic Intelligence for American World Policy* (Hamden, Conn.: Archon Books, 1965 edition), introduction p. xxiii. All references are to this edition.

[6] The concept of intelligence power used here draws on Professor Freedman's definition of power as the 'capacity to produce effects that are more advantageous than would otherwise have been the case' (L. Freedman, 'Strategic Studies and the Problem of Power' in Freedman, P. Hayes and R. O'Neill (eds.) *War, Strategy, and International Politics* (Oxford: Clarendon Press, 1992), p. 291). For discussion of its effects see chapters 8–12.

[7] J. M. Fontain, *Teaching Intelligence in the 1990s* (Washington D.C.: National Intelligence Study Center, 1989).

[8] British universities with intelligence courses and options in 1995 included King's College London, Cambridge, Salford, Edinburgh, Birmingham, Aberystwyth and St Andrew's.

Nevertheless the analytic part of this work still has the marks of a young subject. Reliable information is still shrouded in official secrecy. The literature is heavily weighted towards US intelligence seen through US eyes, with much less that draws on other national arrangements and perspectives.[9] The terminology is confused by transatlantic and military–civilian differences. Intelligence power has not yet received anything like the prolonged attention given to military power, or to the diplomacy with which intelligence is connected. Military men have long recognized the need, as put in 1994 by the then British Chief of Defence Staff, for military doctrine which teaches people 'not what to think but how to think about going to war and war fighting'.[10] Intelligence has still relatively little of this, either in government or outside it. An American academic has recently argued that it is 'the least understood and most undertheorized area of international relations'.[11] A leading intelligence historian has commented that the analytic literature on the subject 'is dominated (and thus distorted) by works of opposition or apology'.[12]

This book therefore seeks to add to the existing analysis. Most writing of this kind about intelligence has been centred on its output and its interaction with policy-making; here I move rather further back into it and start by examining it as a system and a set of processes, with special attention to the big, computer-based agencies which are an important part of the modern community. I go on to consider its purposes, the issues that arise over evaluating its performance, and its post-Cold War importance for the 1990s and beyond. I try to draw on other studies, particularly of organizations and the use of information, when these seem to illuminate intelligence.

The study falls into seven parts. Part I (chapters 1–3) describes how the modern system has evolved and provides an outline model of it and the subjects with which it deals. Part II (chapters 4–7) takes the model to pieces and looks in more detail at its components and their boundaries with each other and other government activity. Part III (chapters 8–12)

---

9 For a statement of differences between the British and US 'schools' see K. Robertson, 'An Agenda for Intelligence Research', *Defense Analysis* vol. 3 no. 2 (1987). For other surveys and critiques of intelligence literature see S. Farson, 'Schools of Thought: National Perceptions of Intelligence', *Conflict Quarterly* vol. 9 no. 2 (spring 1989), and G. Hastedt, 'Towards a Comparative Study of Intelligence', *Conflict Quarterly* vol. 11 no. 3 (summer 1991).

10 Field Marshal Sir Peter Inge, 'The Capability Based Army', *RUSI Journal* vol. 139 no. 3 (June 1994), p. 2.

11 J. Der Derian, *Antidiplomacy: Spies, Terror, Speed, and War* (Oxford: Blackwell, 1992), p. 19.

12 J. Ferris, 'The Historiography of American Intelligence Studies', *Diplomatic History* vol. 19 no. 1 (winter 1995), p. 92. This is a comprehensive and sympathetic critique of American intelligence studies.

outlines intelligence's effects. Part IV (chapters 13–15) deals with the problems of intelligence judgment, and suggests some principles for improving performance. Part V (chapters 16–18) deals in the same way with the search for efficiency. Part VI (chapters 19 and 20) tries to estimate intelligence's national and international importance in the post-Cold War world. Conclusions about intelligence as a whole are summarized as Part VII (chapter 21). Notes on terminology are included in the glossary.

Some explanation is needed here of the intelligence model set out in the first part of the book and used thereafter; whether it is intelligence worldwide, or the British or US national systems, or some kind of hybrid. I have a British viewpoint, and the descriptions are drawn mainly from the British and US examples. However the study is not intended to be narrowly focused on one or both of these two. Its basic assumption is that there are some regularities about intelligence organizations and operations which warrant generalizations about intelligence's nature, not limited to particular times and places, in the same way as it is possible to write on the principles of military operations or law enforcement or (on a wider canvas) about the 'nature' of the state.

But the regularities do not apply to all systems with equal force. The image behind the use of the model here is of a series of different national systems arranged in something like a set of concentric circles, whose contents have some things in common but differ increasingly as one moves from the centre to the periphery. At the centre is the UK–US model, most of whose characteristics are shared by the British Old Commonwealth countries. Some differences between British and US practices are noted as the book proceeds. But the predominant feature is of common dynamics and problems. The Second World War influence of the British example and the close contact subsequently between the two systems explain this closeness. For most purposes here it is unnecessary to distinguish between the different national elements of this UK–US (and Commonwealth) model. For convenience the term 'intelligence community' – found in Anglo-Saxon countries but not elsewhere – is used to refer specifically to it.

However there is also much in common between this community and a wider circle of systems embracing Western intelligence as a whole. ('Western' here means, loosely, Western Europe. Israeli intelligence resembles the Western pattern though with its own special priorities. It is probably still too early to say whether intelligence in Eastern Europe is yet 'Western' in this general sense.) The effects of similar origins, Second World War alliances, military relationships under NATO and other kinds of transnational cooperation have produced considerable commonality. Most of the generalizations offered here apply in some degree to this 'Western' circle.

Lastly there is a much wider circle embracing intelligence everywhere else. Here these generalizations have much less force. Soviet intelligence had its own characteristics intimately bound up with the nature of the Soviet state; the forms of intelligence differ everywhere between despotisms and democracies. But some regularities still apply, at least where states have more than rudimentary arrangements. Military intelligence has some world-wide features common to other military thinking.[13] Equivalents of the Western intelligence building blocks can usually be discerned somewhere in intelligence systems elsewhere, rearranged in individual national ways. Some features and problems, like the complexities of intelligence–policy relationships, have a universality about them.

Nevertheless this work is not a comparative study of intelligence everywhere. The basis for its generalizations remains the UK–US model, itself an amalgam of the two separate ones. Descriptions and conclusions apply mainly to these two communities and the related Commonwealth ones, with some validity in 'the West' as a whole, and some more limited application elsewhere.

A final point to be established about the approach used here is whether it deals with how intelligence actually appears, warts and all, or is based on its role when doing its job properly. The conclusions draw on historical experience and give some attention to failures. But they are more normative than descriptive; the main concern is with intelligence's functions and how they should be carried out, rather than the variations in its actual performance. Military forces, police forces and states themselves may be incompetent or corrupt, but this does not invalidate generalizing about what they are *for*, and about the principles on which they should work.[14] Generalizations about intelligence are offered here in the same way.

---

[13] There was, for example, a strong resemblance between Soviet military doctrine on intelligence (or reconnaissance) and the Western equivalent; see D. A. Ivanov, V. P. Savel'yev and P. V. Shemanskij, *Fundamentals of Tactical Command and Control* (Moscow, 1977, translated and published by the US Air Force in the series 'Soviet Military Thought'), chapters 4 and 7. Types of reconnaissance are described at pp. 155–61.

[14] Compare for example Weber's use of 'ideal' types to understand organizations: 'In Weber's work the concept of "ideal type" is used as a methodological tool for understanding many aspects of society. He believed that in order to understand the social world it was necessary to develop clear-cut concepts against which one could compare empirical reality. All of the ideal types he developed were intended to serve this end . . . By using different ideal types to discern different forms of organization, he believed that one possessed a powerful method for understanding the social world' (G. Morgan, *Images of Organization* (London: Sage, 1986), p. 349).

Part I

Evolution and outline

1   Antecedents

Intelligence as news

Intelligence as a set of permanent institutions dates back only to the second half of the nineteenth century. But as information and news – in the dictionary meaning used in English since the middle of the fifteenth century, of 'knowledge as to events, communicated by or obtained from another, especially military' – it has always been collected as part of warfare. Roman armies had their information-gathering *speculatores* or scouts. Spies, informers, the interception of messages and the use of captured or surreptitiously copied documents can all be seen in early medieval warfare; 'the political and military intelligence services of the Norman and Angevin kings were not run on the basis of gossip in the market-place or the camp.'[1] English armies in the sixteenth and seventeenth centuries had their 'scoutmasters', responsible for collecting intelligence in the field.[2] In eighteenth-century campaigns field intelligence of this kind was one of the many jobs of quartermasters general, while generals' secretaries handled political and strategic intelligence.[3]

Collecting and using 'intelligence' in this same sense has always been equally important in peacetime. Rulers from the earliest times tapped the knowledge of merchants and other travellers, and specialist collectors or 'intelligencers' appeared under Elizabeth I in peace as well as war. Diplomacy evolved in Renaissance Italy for information gathering as well as for negotiation: 'one of the chief functions of the resident ambassador came to be to keep a continuous stream of foreign political news flowing

---

[1] J. O. Prestwich, 'Military Intelligence under the Norman and Angevin Kings' in G. Garnett and J. Hudson (eds.), *Law and Government in Medieval England and Normandy: Essays in Honour of Sir James Holt* (Cambridge: Cambridge University Press, 1994), quotation from p. 11.

[2] B. A. H. Parritt, *The Intelligencers: the Story of British Military Intelligence up to 1914* (Ashford, Kent: Intelligence Corps Association, 2nd edition 1983), pp. 1–12.

[3] M. Van Crevald, *Command in War* (Cambridge, Mass.: Harvard University Press, 1985), pp. 35–8.

to his home government.'[4] The diplomatic system which became institutionalized in Europe in the sixteenth and seventeenth centuries was largely a response to nation states' need for information.[5]

States have always also had their systems for handling and recording the 'intelligence' thus collected. For foreign affairs they developed their chanceries in fits and starts, with variable results. 'Until about the middle of the seventeenth century, none of the three great Western powers [England, France and Spain] possessed diplomatic archives as orderly and usable as those of the Florentines and Venetians two hundred years before.'[6] England had one of these fits of enthusiasm for information handling after the Restoration. 'The most important function vested in the Secretaries of State in the seventeenth century was the management of "the intelligence". The term denoted not only the provision of extraordinary information concerning enemy countries or domestic plotters, but also a regular, settled supply of every kind of news from abroad.'[7] The modern British Cabinet has origins in the 'Intelligence Committee' of the Privy Council which existed briefly after 1660.[8] The present-day *London Gazette* was founded in the same period to disseminate home and overseas news of every kind for government; this staid document now has some claim to be a precursor of the present-day British Joint Intelligence Committee's weekly summary of foreign intelligence, the so-called Red Book.[9]

Secret intelligence

This mass of 'intelligence' has always contained some more than usually sensitive information, or 'secret (or covert) intelligence'. Spies and informers ('human intelligence' or *Humint* in modern US terminology)

[4] G. Mattingly, *Renaissance Diplomacy* (London: Cape, 1955), p. 67.
[5] Mattingly, *Renaissance Diplomacy*, pp. 242–4. There were of course many earlier diplomatic systems, to which Raymond Cohen is now drawing attention; see R. Cohen, *Diplomacy 2000 B.C.–2000 A.D.* (paper delivered to the British International Studies Association annual conference, 1995); *On Diplomacy in the Ancient Near East* (Leicester: Leicester University Centre for Diplomacy Discussion Papers, 1995); 'All in the Family: Ancient Near Eastern Diplomacy', *International Negotiation* vol. 1 no. 1 (1996, forthcoming).
[6] Mattingly, *Renaissance Diplomacy*, p. 229.
[7] P. Frazer, *The Intelligence of the Secretaries of State and their Monopolies of Licensed News 1660–1688* (Cambridge: Cambridge University Press, 1956), p. 1.
[8] P. Hennessy, *Cabinet* (Oxford: Blackwell, 1986), p. 1, quoting J. P. Mackintosh, *The British Cabinet* (London: Stevens and Son, 1962 edition), p. 37.
[9] Frazer, *The Intelligence of the Secretaries of State*, pp. 1–5. The same claim can be made for the *Oxford Gazette*, now the official university news-sheet. The modern 'Red Book', like these predecessors, is not restricted to information from secret sources.

were part of the earliest kinds of government; as an English term spying or 'espial' goes back to Chaucer. Intercepting messages (nowadays part of 'Signals Intelligence' or *Sigint*)[10] is as old as governments' use of writing and their protection of it by 'secret writing' or cryptography. The first surviving document on cipher-breaking is said to be an Arabic one from the ninth century.[11] But it was the development of European diplomacy and mail services after the Renaissance that encouraged regular encipherment and the complementary art of cryptanalysis. By the eighteenth century most of the European powers – including Britain – had arrangements for clandestine mail-opening, with 'Black Chambers' to decipher the codes and ciphers encountered. Most diplomatic ciphers were regularly or occasionally readable by other powers,[12] a situation that recurred in the first half of the twentieth century.

Then as now, secret intelligence was never clearly separated from other kinds of government information. Before the emergence of private newspapers and press freedom, governments tended to see all information as their property, secret to some extent; the distinction between information 'in the public domain' and 'classified' official information is a modern one. Diplomats themselves made little distinction between overt and covert methods. By 1600 most embassies used secret agents, and in the century that followed ambassadors were regarded as licensed spies.[13] A French commentator wrote in 1790 that 'The ablest ambassador can do nothing without spies and he would achieve even less if he chose them from the gutter. Taken from the higher ranks of society they are necessarily more expensive. To fulfil his mission worthily, an ambassador must be ready to buy anyone from the secretary to the valet, from the serving-maid of the favourite mistress to the lady-in-waiting of the Queen.'[14] The much later separation of legitimate diplomacy from secret collection was never complete. As late as 1939 the French Ambassador in Berlin had secret funds for buying information.[15]

---

[10] *Signals* Intelligence is also described as *Signal* Intelligence. Usage varies.
[11] It has been accepted that the earliest work was an Arab manual dated 1412. See D. Kahn, *The Codebreakers* (London: Sphere [Books], 1973), p. 80. But in 1992 it was claimed that similar Arab work could be identified in the ninth century (Ibrahim A. Al-Kadi, 'The Origins of Cryptology: the Arab Connection', *Cryptologia* vol. 16 no. 2 (April 1992).
[12] History from Kahn, *The Codebreakers*, chapters 1–6.
[13] Mattingly, *Renaissance Diplomacy*, p. 267; for 'licensed spies' see D. Ogg, *Europe in the Seventeenth Century* (London: Black, 1925), p. 29.
[14] A. Cobban, *Ambassadors and Secret Agents* (London: Cape, 1954), p. 117, quoting from *Coup d'Oeil Sevère Mais Juste Sur Le Livre Rouge*.
[15] R. J. Young, 'French Military Intelligence and Nazi Germany, 1938–1939' in E. R. May (ed.), *Knowing One's Enemies: Intelligence Assessment before the Two World Wars* (Princeton: Princeton University Press, 1986), pp. 273–4.

Nevertheless in this pre-nineteenth-century period some kinds of intelligence were more connected than others with what the British called Secret Service. Well-placed spies were more secret than casual informants. Decipherment had its early suggestions of occult skills, and remained surrounded by special secrecy. Deciphered diplomatic dispatches in eighteenth-century Britain were referred to as 'The Secrets', and handled with much the same security precautions as are used today.[16]

Early organization

Diplomacy evolved as governments' institution for gathering foreign intelligence, with its conduct, privileges and ceremonial recognized in the seventeenth century; and there were glimmerings of other 'intelligence' organizations and institutions. Diplomacy was supplemented by governments' networks of overseas correspondents, with varying degrees of clandestinity. In Britain Walsingham's network of agents and interception under Elizabeth I was followed by Thurloe's internal and external networks under the Protectorate. Their successors in the seventeenth and eighteenth centuries developed their continental coverage through espionage and postal interception and deciphering. The Admiralty covered the naval bases of France and Spain for early warning of naval preparations, through London-controlled agents, Embassy and consular networks, and the debriefing of merchant ship captains returning from abroad.[17] (This British system for reporting selected foreign movements survived, incidentally, late into the Cold War.) Of the period 1715–41 it has been said that 'perhaps at no other time in English history, save in wartime, was so much time and energy devoted to the securing of intelligence.'[18]

In particular the interception of foreign letters and dispatches needed slick organization. In the period 1736–52 the instructions from the King of Prussia to his ambassador at the court of the Elector of Saxony were abstracted for cipher-breaking there as follows:

[16] K. Ellis, *The Post Office in the Eighteenth Century* (Oxford: Oxford University Press, 1958), appendix 7.
[17] F. P. Renaut, *Le Secret Service de l'Admirauté Britannique 1776–83* (Paris: Editions Graouli, 1936), p. 30. For background see also J. Black, 'British Intelligence and the Mid-Eighteenth Century Crisis', *Intelligence and National Security* vol. 2 no. 2 (April 1987).
[18] P. S. Fritz, 'The Anti-Jacobite System of the English Ministers 1715–1745', *Historical Journal* vol. 16 (1973), p. 280.

As soon as the postal courier from Berlin arrived on Saxon territory, at Grossenhain, his bag was picked during the changing of horses, the official letters abstracted and sent by swift horse-rider to Dresden, where the Black Cabinet unsealed, copied and resealed them, and returned them to the post, which delivered them at the same time as the rest of the mail, which had arrived in the interval.[19]

The equivalent British machinery showed similar sophistication over interception and copying, forging seals, solving codes and ciphers, forwarding results to kings and ministers and protecting secrecy.[20] There was professional liaison with Hanover, and a wide network of other continental 'interceptions'.[21] In the eighteenth century, British money was available to buy continental intelligence, in the same way as it bought political and military support in the way emphasized by Paul Kennedy in his account of 'the winning of wars' in this period.[22]

Nevertheless these arrangements differed from modern intelligence in two crucial respects. First, though diplomacy was well established, other information collection and handling was largely *ad hoc*, without permanent institutions; and, second, nowhere was the control of collection and the evaluation of results a specialized activity, separated from policy-making and action. For kings and ministers 'intelligence' in all its aspects was part of statecraft, inseparable from the exercise of power. Walsingham first established himself as an 'intelligencer', but his intelligence system became subsumed within his apparatus as Secretary of State. In the same way the responsibilities of his post-Restoration successors for 'the intelligence' soon became overlaid by executive responsibilities.

The same applied in military and naval operations. For centuries the rudimentary headquarters of generals sufficed for handling information in war, and the same applied even more to war at sea. Great captains like Marlborough used intelligence to the full, and Frederick the Great wrote about spies and even classified them (as common spies, double spies, spies of consequence, and forced spies).[23] But organizing and using intelligence was a very personal matter, like other aspects of generalship;

[19] A. Langie (trans. J. C. H. Macbeth), *Cryptography* (London: Constable, 1924), p. 24.
[20] For British postal interception and deciphering in the eighteenth century see Ellis, *The Post Office in the Eighteenth Century*, chapter 6.
[21] Ellis, *The Post Office in the Eighteenth Century*, pp. 74–5; Black, 'British Intelligence and the Mid-Eighteenth Century Crisis', p. 213.
[22] P. Kennedy, *The Rise and Fall of the Great Powers: Economic Change and Military Conflict from 1500 to 2000* (London: Fontana, 1989), chapter 3.
[23] R. G. Rowan with R. G. Deindorfer, *Secret Service* (London: Kimber, 1969 edition), p. 91.

there was no standard wartime organization, and no perpetuation of wartime experience in peacetime. Eighteenth-century intelligence was still set in a military framework described by one writer as the 'stone age of command', slowly changing but still in transition through the Napoleonic Wars.[24] Despite the Roman precedent, battlefield reconnaissance did not become a full-time speciality until both the French and the British formed Corps of Guides during the Napoleonic Wars.[25] These wars did something to modify eighteenth-century intelligence. Napoleon's mobile headquarters included a Statistical Bureau which provided him with collated strategic intelligence, but Napoleon, like Wellington, interpreted the data himself.[26] The wars demonstrated the use of intelligence, but did little to institutionalize it.

The same applied to the element of secret intelligence. There were no permanent government espionage bureaus; Walpole as Prime Minister ran his own agents among his Jacobite enemies, meeting them in person in taverns.[27] The eighteenth-century Admiralty network was run personally by the Admiralty Secretary. The Black Chambers stand out as professional secret intelligence-providing organizations, but their scale was still quite small; the combined British Secret Office of the Post Office and Deciphering Branch at their height in the eighteenth century employed a total of nine people.[28]

Changes

The forty years or so after the Napoleonic Wars saw some changes, but these did not greatly affect the earlier situation. There was some regular continental interest in peacetime military intelligence, and the development of printing and gradual liberalization of press and publication laws made books and newspapers increasingly available as sources of foreign information. Reports from military attachés became another; the first of them was appointed by Prussia in 1817, and British attachés' appointments began after the Crimean War.[29] 'By 1830, the Prussians and Russians were producing objective intelligence summaries containing strengths and dispositions, published openly.'[30] In Britain a Depot of

---

[24] Van Crevald, *Command in War*, pp. 38–9.
[25] Parritt, *The Intelligencers*, pp. 36–45.
[26] Van Crevald, *Command in War*, pp. 66–8.
[27] Fritz, 'The Anti-Jacobite Intelligence System', pp. 279–80.
[28] Ellis, *The Post Office in the Eighteenth Century*, pp. 66, 76, 129.
[29] P. Towle (ed.), 'Introduction', *Estimating Foreign Military Power* (London: Croom Helm, 1987), p. 86.
[30] Towle, *Estimating Foreign Military Power*, p. 54.

Military Knowledge was created in 1803 and lingered on for half a century.[31]

But there was little fundamental change. In the Crimean War the contestants' intelligence was as improvised and abysmal as the rest of their command arrangements. Interception and deciphering remained among governments' weapons, but the increased use of government couriers rather than postal services had made the interception of diplomatic dispatches less rewarding. Postal interception was used mainly against internal revolutionary threats, and (except in Russia) fell foul of liberal sentiment; the British organization was closed down in 1844, and the French and Austrian ones after the revolutions of 1848.[32] Except for diplomacy, intelligence remained substantially uninstitutionalized.

Changes came from around the middle of the century onwards. 'Intelligence' still remained in one sense just a synonym for information, as it still does. Newspapers for a long time remained 'intelligencers', and diplomats continued to speak of 'political intelligence'. But the term also gradually came to be associated for the first time with government institutions established specifically for 'intelligence' purposes, separated from decision-taking and policy-making, and distinct from the machinery of embassies and foreign offices which continued (and continue) to combine information-gathering with these executive functions. Intelligence became for the first time a specialized lens for viewing parts of the world. This development is outlined in the next chapter.

Summary

Intelligence as information is as old as government; so too is secret intelligence. But until the mid-nineteenth century there was little in the way of specialized, permanent intelligence institutions. Controlling collection and evaluating the results were integral parts of statecraft and military command. Intelligence as an institution was a Victorian innovation.

[31] Parritt, *The Intelligencers*, pp. 41–3.   [32] Kahn, *The Codebreakers*, p. 111.

2   Organizations

Military intelligence

The change in intelligence's status came from the new military technology of the second half of the nineteenth century and its effects on command. Armies acquired improved weapons and the use of railways and telegraph communications; navies came to have iron construction, steam propulsion, big guns, explosives and armour, and (much later) the introduction of radio. Warfare involved bigger armies over bigger areas, with more opportunities for strategic surprise and victory by rapid movement and concentration. Command had to adapt itself to this new scale and complexity.

The response was to create permanent military and (later) naval staffs, charged with mobilization, war planning and support to commanders' decision-taking and control. Their raw material in peace and war was information about their own and foreign forces, topography, the railways and other factors relevant to battle. They depended on regular reports, organized information and effective communications; in modern jargon, effective C^3I, or command, control, communications, and intelligence/ information.[1] The influential model was the Prussian General Staff, which had been slowly taking shape after 1815 and acquired great prestige after the victories over Austria and France in 1866 and 1870. By about the turn of the century most countries had adopted some version of it.[2]

Part of the staff's duty was the study of enemies and potential enemies, and the continental Statistical Bureaus evolved into the 'Foreign Armies' sections of the new staffs. In Britain a new War Office Topographical and Statistical Department was created after the Crimean War but did not have much impact. The decisive moves towards 'intelligence' in the staffs began when a new War Office Intelligence Branch was formed in 1873 and an Indian Intelligence Branch in 1878. The

---

[1] Now often expanded to C^4I, to include computers.
[2] M. Van Crevald, *Command in War* (Cambridge, Mass.: Harvard University Press, 1985), p. 149.

Admiralty created its Foreign Intelligence Committee in 1882; and the first War Office and Admiralty Directors of Intelligence (DMI and DNI) were both appointed in 1887.[3] Around the same time a standard British army doctrine was evolved for field intelligence.[4] In the United States the Navy and Army Intelligence Departments were founded in 1882 and 1885.[5]

Initially this 'intelligence' was associated with a range of staff functions, not just the study of foreign forces. A British officer addressing the Royal United Services Institute in 1875 on 'The Intelligence Duties of the Staff Abroad and at Home' included information about British forces and territory when he described the need for 'the collection, sifting and arrangement of all information required by governments and military authorities to enable them to take such measures in peace as will insure the rapid commencement and vigorous prosecution of any war whether at home or abroad'.[6] A lecturer in the same forum some years later on naval intelligence and trade protection joined proposals for the surveillance of foreign warships with an ingenious scheme for information on the movements of the friendly merchant shipping that had to be protected.[7] When the British Intelligence Departments were introduced, their responsibilities included mobilization planning and matters of strategy; the absence of a British General Staff and Naval Staff meant that they were the nearest things to information-gathering and 'thinking' functions. 'The early DMIs and DNIs were powerful figures' with wide influence.[8] When a proper General Staff was created after the Boer War, the DMI post was amalgamated with the new Director of Military Operations, not to be restored until 1915.[9]

Continental thinking had initially been similar. The Prussian example discouraged rigid specialization; in the campaigns of 1866 and 1870 the Prussian Headquarters 'was not so much a formal structure in which each member had his well-entrenched niche and sphere of responsibility

[3] F. H. H. Hinsley with E. E. Thomas, C. F. G. Ransom, and R. C. Knight, *British Intelligence in the Second World War* vol. I (London: HMSO, 1979), p. 7.
[4] T. G. Fergusson, *British Military Intelligence 1870–1914* (London: Arms and Armour Press, 1984), chapter 3, especially pp. 129 and 139–41 for colonial wars.
[5] R. Jeffreys-Jones, *American Espionage: From Secret Service to CIA* (London: Free Press, 1977), p. 24.
[6] Major C. B. Brackenbury, 'The Intelligence Duties of the Staff Abroad and at Home', *RUSI Journal* vol. 19 no. 80 (1875), p. 242.
[7] J. C. R. Colomb, 'Naval Intelligence and Protection of Commerce in War', *RUSI Journal* vol. 25 no. 112 (1881).
[8] Hinsley, *British Intelligence in the Second World War* vol. I, p. 7.
[9] P. Gudgin, *Military Intelligence: the British Story* (London: Arms and Armour Press, 1989), pp. 37–8.

as an informal gathering of friends, meeting once a day and taking their meals together whenever possible'.[10] As late as September 1914 the famous car journeys by one of Moltke's staff around his Western Front armies, and the crucial assessments about pulling back the German right wing, were made by his intelligence officer, not his operations staff.[11]

Yet intelligence departments had come by then to concentrate overwhelmingly on foreign forces. This was partly just a result of staffs' growth and specialization, in armies if not navies. But it also reflected the increasing need before 1914 for knowledge about potential opponents and the development of their weaponry. Military and naval threats and balances were studied everywhere, with anxious guesses about others' plans for new forces and equipment. By 1914 foreign forces were recognized as intelligence's speciality.

It had by then received the permanent imprint of staff methods, by which the new commanders drew on their staffs instead of relying on their own first-hand assessments. Staff work had developed as part of the new idea of war by railway timetables, logistics and the telegraph rather than inspirational leadership amid the battle.[12] From the middle of the nineteenth century the commander's 'traditional *coup d'oeil* with its implications of immediate personal observation gave way to the German-derived "estimate of the situation," implying map study and written reports'.[13] Intelligence retained this 'scientific' character. Its method was not the *ad hoc* search for secrets, but the methodical collection and assimilation of all relevant information, and its presentation in military 'appreciations' for rational command decisions.

The pace of this development, was patchy. The British doctrine for field intelligence evolved earlier than intelligence's separation from policy and planning at the top level.[14] Intelligence appreciations in the British Admiralty in the First World War continued to be mixed with

---

[10] Van Crevald, *Command in War*, p. 142.

[11] Van Crevald, *Command in War*, p. 155; Major-General Sir Kenneth Strong, *Men of Intelligence: a Study of the Roles and Decisions of Chiefs of Intelligence from World War I to the Present Day* (London: Cassell, 1970), pp. 13–18.

[12] Van Crevald, *Command in War*, pp. 103–47.

[13] Van Crevald, *Command in War*, p. 57.

[14] See for example Lt-Col. J. S. Rothwell (ed.) *Staff Studies: A Series of Lectures for the Use of Officers at the Staff College* (Staff College, Camberley, 1890), quoted by Fergusson, *British Military Intelligence 1870–1914*, p. 29: '[In the field] the Staff Officer for intelligence is the recipient of all information bearing on the force, positions and organisation of the enemy, as well as any changes in his *Ordre de Bataille*. All information collected by spies, and any journals and dispatches etc. captured from the enemy, are examined by him. He questions all prisoners. The department under his orders supplements by reconnaissance in the theatre of war the information gathered by the Intelligence Division of the War Office, and the maps prepared by it in time of peace.'

operational decisions, and signals intelligence was insulated from other information until after Jutland.[15] Even until Pearl Harbor the Operations Branch of the US Navy Department claimed that on important matters *it* should assess the Japanese Navy; intelligence existed just to supply the data.[16]

Nevertheless the army and navy intelligence departments provided by 1914 the pattern of modern armed forces' intelligence. Since then most countries have moved towards some amalgamation of the separate armed services' departments. Thus the United States created the all-service Defense Intelligence Agency (DIA) in 1961, though it left the powerful single-service agencies in place. Britain amalgamated the three service intelligence staffs and its Joint Intelligence Bureau (JIB) to become the central Defence Intelligence Staff (DIS) in the defence reorganization of 1964. But the original military idea of analysing foreign targets by using all data about them, with a role of providing information rather than decision-taking, continues to be the basis not only of what is now often called *defence intelligence*, but also of other intelligence on foreign targets, or *foreign intelligence*.

Internal security and secret police

Alongside this military study of foreign forces a more inward-looking intelligence specialism also developed, at varying rates over roughly the same period. This originated in the nineteenth-century 'secret policing' which appeared on the Continent in the first half of the century through the widespread fear of repetitions of the French Revolution. Police forces developed arrangements for surveillance, informers and mail interceptions.[17] The earliest separate institution for this purpose was the Russian Third Section of the Imperial Chancery founded in 1826, which was later succeeded by the Okhrana and its eventual communist descendant, the KGB.[18] After 1848 the fear of mass revolution declined, but communism and anarchism continued to present threats at a time when all policing was becoming more professional, with 'the emergence of the criminal investigation department, the application of scientific

---

[15] P. Beesly, *Room 40: British Naval Intelligence 1914–18* (London: Hamish Hamilton, 1982), pp. 177–83.

[16] R. Wohlstetter, *Pearl Harbor: Warning and Decision* (Stanford: Stanford University Press, 1962), pp. 317-19.

[17] R. J. Goldstein, *Political Repression in Nineteenth-Century Europe* (London: Croom Helm, 1983), pp. 69–72.

[18] C. Andrew and O. Gordievsky, *KGB: the Inside Story of its Foreign Operations from Lenin to Gorbachev* (London: Hodder and Stoughton, 1990), chapter 1.

techniques to the problems of the detection, apprehension, surveillance of and storage of information about criminal areas and populations'.[19] As part of this process secret policing became more institutionalized and more international; as early as 1870 the French force had sixty agents stationed abroad, and the Okhrana's Foreign Agency was established in Paris in 1882.[20] By the early years of this century some of these agencies overlapped with collectors of overseas intelligence: thus before 1914 the Okhrana and the French Sûreté both ran secret sources in foreign embassies in their capitals, and engaged in diplomatic codebreaking.[21]

Britain had no organized policing until 1829, and a structure of local forces thereafter. Central government maintained occasional informers and interceptions of private mail, even after the interception of diplomatic material had ceased in 1844. But there was no specialized policing over internal threats until the Metropolitan Police's Special [Irish] Branch was established in 1883 (and reformed in 1887) to counter Fenian bombings in Britain.[22] When the fear of foreign espionage after the turn of the century produced a demand for counterespionage, the separate Secret Service Bureau (also responsible for conducting espionage overseas) was formed in 1909. Initially an offshoot of military intelligence, the home (counterespionage) section eventually evolved into the independent Security Service.[23]

The First World War intensified the Europe-wide need for counter-espionage and counter-sabotage, and Soviet activities and world communism after 1917 provided new threats of subversion and ideological espionage. After bureaucratic battles with the Metropolitan Police these internal intelligence functions in Britain were concentrated in the Security Service in 1931 (except for intelligence on the IRA threat to the mainland, which had to wait another sixty-two years before being given formal coordinating responsibility in 1992). The Second World War produced the British successes in detecting and 'turning' German agents. Countermeasures to Soviet espionage and other clandestine Soviet activities then became a major Western theme everywhere. The

[19] C. Dandeker, *Surveillance, Power and Modernity: Bureaucracy and Discipline from 1700 to the Present Day* (Cambridge, England: Polity Press, 1990), p. 122. See his pp. 119–33 on general developments in nineteenth- and twentieth-century policing.

[20] Goldstein, *Political Repression in Nineteenth-Century Europe*, p. 72; Andrew and Gordievsky, *KGB*, p. 6.

[21] C. Andrew, 'France and the German Menace' in E. R. May (ed.), *Knowing One's Enemies: Intelligence Assessment before the Two World Wars* (Princeton: Princeton University Press, 1986), pp. 130-1.

[22] C. Andrew, *Secret Service: the Making of the British Intelligence Community* (London: Sceptre edition, 1986), pp. 42–7.

[23] Hinsley, *British Intelligence in the Second World War* vol. I, pp. 3–7.

British also had their prolonged experience of internal intelligence in decolonization campaigns, and their experience in Palestine and Malaya established counter-insurgency techniques which they then drew on elsewhere. Like most other nations they subsequently experienced prolonged terrorist campaigns against domestic targets.

Thus in the West these distinctive internal security institutions emerged alongside military intelligence. Currently the British Security Service, the Canadian Security Intelligence Service (CSIS), the German Bundesamt für Verfassungsschutz (BfV), the French Direction de la Surveillance du Territoire (DST) and the Israeli Shin Beth exemplify the pattern. A less common alternative has been for internal security to remain a specialized part of national policing, as in the FBI's Intelligence Division. The Royal Canadian Mounted Police had similar powers in Canada before the formation of CSIS in 1984. Whatever the precise organizational form, Western countries now have this *security intelligence* as a complement to foreign intelligence. It should be added that most armed forces also have their own security units and staffs, for wartime as well as peacetime use; but these are separate from intelligence (though very close to it), and need not be discussed here.

'National' collection

Military and security intelligence grew up conducting most of their own information collection. For mid-Victorian military intelligence the foreign targets were not deeply secretive; Europe was a relatively open continent, and Reuters and the telegraph increased the volume and speed of overseas news. Until towards the close of the century, intelligence departments could rely mainly on newspapers, books and attachés' reports, supplemented by officers' travelling.[24] As late as the Russo-Japanese War the European powers had observers with both sides, even with the Japanese fleet at sea.[25]

Of course there was some covert intelligence collection. There was the long-lasting British and Russian Great Game in Central Asia, though with little restriction on publishing the results.[26] The British Foreign

---

[24] For a brief summary of Victorian collection see A. Clayton, *Forearmed: a History of the Intelligence Corps* (London: Brassey's, 1993), p. 6.

[25] For examples see D. and P. Warner, *The Tide at Sunrise: a History of the Russo-Japanese War 1904–1905* (London: Angus and Robertson, 1975), pp. 184, 288.

[26] For details of the Indian Government's intelligence collection see J. Ferris, 'Lord Salisbury, Secret Intelligence, and British Policy toward Russia and Central Asia, 1874–1878' in K. Neilson and B. J. C. McKercher (eds.), *Go Spy the Land: Military Intelligence in History* (London: Praeger, 1992), pp. 121–3.

Office obtained Russian documents by bribery; Salisbury wrote in 1875 that 'we receive pretty constantly copies of the most important reports and references that reach the Foreign Office and War Office at St Petersburg'.[27] Prussian agents played some part in monitoring Austrian deployments by rail in the war of 1866.[28] Espionage varied from country to country, but secret intelligence collection was not the main preoccupation of the new military intelligence organizations.

This changed in the later years of the century and early years of the new one. The trends that made military and naval intelligence more important also increased secrecy, and hence gave more emphasis to the covert collection needed to penetrate it. Technological innovation stimulated technical intelligence on new *matériel*, for example in the Anglo-German naval rivalry, and produced a commensurate growth in secrecy.[29] The 'timetable war' on land, based on mobilization and deployment by rail, put a premium on acquiring the opponent's plans; the Redl case, in which a senior Austrian officer was a Russian source for eight years up to 1912, illustrated the new importance of covert sources of this kind.[30]

Thus by 1914 military espionage was on an increasing scale. Coincidentally the use of the telegraph for diplomatic telegrams had stimulated virtually all major powers to acquire copies of them from their telegraph offices and revive their Black Chambers for cipher-breaking. French cryptanalysis was revived in this way in the 1880s.[31] Britain before 1914 was not deciphering in London, but was breaking Russian and other telegrams in India.[32]

This gradual growth of covert collection was followed by its explosion in the First World War. This was partly in the extensive use of human sources, as in 'railway watching' by inhabitants of occupied France for

---

[27] J. Ferris, 'Penny Dreadful Literature: Britain, India and Strategic Intelligence on Russia and Central Asia, 1825–1947', p. 21. (Paper given at US Army War College Conference on Intelligence and Strategy, May 1989.)

[28] Van Crevald, *Command in War*, pp. 296–7, refers to intelligence in 1866.

[29] In Britain 'from 1885 on, greater attention was paid to official secrecy about naval affairs' (C. Dandeker, 'Bureaucracy, Planning and War', *Armed Forces and Society* vol. 11 no. 1 (fall 1984), p. 138). For later examples see H. H. Herwig, 'Imperial Germany' and P. M. Kennedy, 'Great Britain before 1914', in May, *Knowing One's Enemies*, pp. 70, 179.

[30] W. C. Fuller Jr, 'The Russian Empire' in May, *Knowing One's Enemies*. See also H. C. Deutsch, 'Sidelights on the Redl Case', *Intelligence and National Security* vol. 4 no. 4 (October 1989), pp. 827–8.

[31] Andrew, 'France and the German Menace', p. 129.

[32] For British codebreaking in India in 1905 and 1906 see J. Ferris, 'Before "Room 40": the British Empire and Signals Intelligence, 1898–1914', *Journal of Strategic Studies* vol. 12 no. 4 (December 1989), pp. 431–57.

evidence of German troop concentrations. But even more striking was the war's stimulation of the two new 'technical' sources. One was radio interception, following the introduction of radio communications; naval radio and radio interception added what Sir Michael Howard has described as 'virtually a fourth dimension of war'.[33] The other was airborne photography, now known as *imagery*, or sometimes Imint or Photint. Both these technical sources remained in existence after 1918, and the Second World War saw them developed again, on a vastly larger scale. 'The most successful generals tended to be those whose radio-interception services were able to bring them the promptest and most accurate information about the intentions of their opponents',[34] and the same applied at sea. The Allies' ability to conduct photo-reconnaissance over the whole of Germany was of almost equal importance. After 1945 the Cold War gave intelligence a quite new peacetime status; the USSR was wedded to covert intelligence gathering which was also the West's only means of penetrating Soviet secrecy. Out of these requirements came massive investments in Sigint and imagery, culminating in US and Soviet satellite surveillance.

Part of this twentieth-century development of collection was the evolution of Western specialist 'national' collection agencies, each concentrating on particular kinds of collection and meeting the needs of all parts of government. The 1909 British Secret Service Bureau's component for espionage overseas emerged as the Secret Intelligence Service (SIS) in 1921.[35] The French Service de Renseignments re-established its position as the principal French collection agency of this kind in 1936, though it remained a military service.[36] Amid the kaleidoscope of German intelligence organization in the Third Reich almost the only consistent feature was the position of the Abwehr as the main espionage agency, though by no means the only one.[37] After 1945 the separation of covert human collection organizations from service intelligence became fairly general, as in surroundings as varied as France, Israel and Australia. US Humint developed in CIA's Operations Directorate; though not a separate Agency, this Directorate developed with much of the self-contained character of one.

[33] M. Howard, *War in European History* (Oxford: Oxford University Press, 1976), p. 127.
[34] Howard, *War in European History*, p. 134.
[35] Hinsley, *British Intelligence in the Second World War* vol. I, pp. 16-17.
[36] For references to it see Andrew, 'France and the German Menace' and R. J. Young, 'French Military Intelligence and Nazi Germany' in May, *Knowing One's Enemies*, pp. 135 and 274–8; also J. T. Richardson, *Foreign Intelligence Organizations* (Cambridge, Mass.: Bellinger, 1988), p. 153.
[37] M. Geyer, 'National Socialist Germany' in May, *Knowing One's Enemies*, pp. 317-18.

Much the same has applied in Sigint. First World War radio interception was conducted everywhere by army and naval intelligence, though in some countries the civilian successors of the Black Chambers shared cipher-breaking. In Britain, with no extant Black Chamber in 1914, all Sigint was done by the services; decrypted German diplomatic material was handled by the navy, as when the DNI personally handled the Zimmerman telegram whose decryption by the British helped to bring the United States into the war.[38] However, after the war the civilian Government Code and Cypher School was established, under the head of SIS, as a separate national codebreaking organization, with some coordinating responsibilities over the services' radio interception.[39] But the doctrine of a strong single organization received a special impetus through the Second World War British successes in breaking Axis ciphers, particularly the concentrated Bletchley Park attack on the Enigma cipher used by all the German services. After 1945 British Sigint became firmly centred on Government Communications Headquarters (GCHQ), a separate, largely civilian organization with service contributions.

Other countries conducted Sigint in the Second World War with much less central control. The United States had its separate Army and Navy organizations. German Sigint was even more fragmented. However the prestige of the wartime British successes caused its pattern to be copied fairly widely after 1945. The separate US service organizations were put under the National Security Agency (NSA) formed in 1952.[40] Commonwealth countries also adopted the British pattern. Almost all Western countries now conduct Sigint with some centralization and civilian staffing, with varying degrees of service participation and independence.

The British also developed this concept of 'national' agencies in developing their Second World War organizations for imagery interpretation and long-term POW interrogation, with US participation in both cases. After 1945 strategic imagery interpretation in Britain remained concentrated on a single, joint-service organization, the Joint Air Reconnaissance Interpretation Centre (JARIC). The main development of 'national' institutions for imagery has however been in the United States, where the National Reconnaissance Office (NRO) was developed for the programmes for satellite imagery collection, and a central agency (now the Central Imagery Office) for some of the interpretation.

---

[38] See B. Tuchman, *The Zimmerman Telegram* (London: Constable, 1959); summarized in Andrew, *Secret Service*, pp. 169–76.

[39] Hinsley, *British Intelligence in the Second World War* vol. I, pp. 20–4.

[40] J. T. Richelson, *The US Intelligence Community* (Cambridge: Ballinger, 1985), p. 15.

Specialist national agencies of these kinds developed partly through the sheer growth of collection, but avoidance of inter-service duplication and the development of specialist skills were other factors. Political sensitivity was another: in establishing the SIS in 1921 the British Foreign Office and the three services all wanted the results of espionage, but did not want to run it themselves or let the others do it. For these mixed reasons the Victorian military intelligence departments' control of collection was gradually eroded in favour of the national, mainly civilian agencies for governments' biggest intelligence-collection investments.

National assessment

Thus between the two wars Britain had specialist intelligence agencies and departments; but these arrangements still presupposed that knowledge of foreign countries could be organized in segments, not as a totality. The First World War had indeed shown that total war needed total intelligence; foreign military power had come to depend on factors of industrial capacity, demography and morale which fell outside the analysis of normal military and naval intelligence. But it took many years for this to be translated into intelligence responsibilities.

The impetus came in peacetime, as central planning for defence slowly took shape. British national defence decisions in the 1930s needed intelligence on German capabilities as a whole, particularly its capacity for military production and its dependence on imported raw materials. A further strand was the need, realized after the war scares of early 1939, for some means of bringing together all evidence of immediate German intentions; the lack of any central assessment machinery had provoked the precipitate British guarantee to Poland in March 1939,[41] just as it was to be a cause of the United States' Pearl Harbor disaster in 1941. It was becoming apparent by 1939 that Germany could not be understood through purely departmental analysis. Britain in the inter-war years had developed some integrated military planning around the Chiefs of Staffs Committee, and when this formed the basis for grand strategy in the Second World War it needed similarly integrated intelligence inputs.

From this emerged the wartime idea of machinery through which military, naval, air, political and economic analysis could be integrated into what can now be called '*national assessment*', or seeing the enemy as a whole. This approach contrasted sharply with German, Italian and

---

[41] For intelligence and the Polish guarantee see D. C. Watt, *How War Came: the Immediate Origins of the Second World War 1938–1939* (London: Heinemann, 1989), chapter 10.

Japanese intelligence. Private intelligence services had proliferated under Hitler, and in an official British estimate in 1945 of 'Why the Germans lost the War' one of the reasons given was the fragmented state of German intelligence, with no means of collating and appreciating it below the level of head of state.[42] Japanese wartime intelligence was equally inefficient and unsystematic.

After 1945 the Cold War gave special relevance to this lesson in both Britain and the United States. The communist threat seemed to span political, military, economic and subversive attacks, and needed equally comprehensive intelligence assessment. The intentions and capabilities of the intensely secretive Soviet and Chinese regimes had to be studied by putting together evidence from all sources and all sectors. The same procedures seemed applicable to lesser threats, and eventually to any overseas situations or foreign countries which brought together political, economic and military factors. Intelligence acquired this holistic dimension on a scale not foreseen in 1939 or even in 1945.

The English-speaking countries met these needs by creating new machinery. The British Joint Intelligence Committee (JIC) was effective from 1939 onwards as a means of bringing departmental knowledge and opinions together into a supra-departmental focus. As a body for assessment by committee it became a crucial part of Second World War apparatus, acquired great prestige, and has continued to be the basis of all subsequent British arrangements.[43] The United States created CIA as a national assessment agency, and the post of Director of Central Intelligence (DCI) as the President's intelligence adviser. These arrangements will be discussed in chapter 15. What needs to be noted here is that they added a new element to Anglo-Saxon intelligence structures. Analysis retained strong departmental connections, but with this extra 'national' layer added to it. On the whole this has remained characteristic of the English-speaking models; other countries have sought to imitate them but usually without noticeable success.

The manageable community

The introduction of national collection and national assessment both implied that intelligence was more than a set of independent

---

[42] E. E. Thomas, 'The Evolution of the JIC System Up to and During the Second World War' in C. Andrew and J. Noakes (eds.), *Intelligence and International Relations 1900–45* (Exeter: Exeter University Press, 1987), p. 233.

[43] Note that since the Gulf War the US community has started to create JICs as Joint Intelligence *Centers*, for inter-service intelligence support within the military community (see chapter 15). JIC here is used throughout to denote the British organization.

organizations. References to an 'intelligence community' remain an English-speaking speciality, and the phrase was not coined even there until well into the Cold War. But it sums up a gradual and often partial Western recognition that intelligence forms a national *system*; in some degree a national entity to be managed as a national resource.

This again was a British innovation, for which the ancient idea of Secret Service and the existence of the Secret Service Vote perhaps provided some sketchy foundation. Britain treated secret intelligence as a unity in the reviews of 1907–9 and 1919–21 that produced the pre-1914 Secret Service Bureau and the subsequent creation of the Security Service and SIS. A notional Secret Service Committee remained in being after 1921 but met only in 1931, and the idea of managing modern intelligence as an entity then disappeared for some years.[44]

The transition to an active sense of community came about in 1939. The JIC's national assessment role entailed some interdepartmental machinery. But even before it acquired this role the committee began to tackle the management and organizational problems produced by the prospect of war. Its terms of reference in 1939 included responsibility for 'the consideration of any further measures which might be thought necessary in order to improve the efficient working of the intelligence organisation of the country as a whole'. The British Official History points to this as a landmark; 'it was a concept that had been evolving for twenty years, but evolving slowly, haphazardly and only in response to events in the absence of any coordinating authority.'[45]

Throughout the war the JIC retained this role as the national committee of management as well as the national assessment committee. Its management was by no means complete. As part of the Chiefs of Staff structure it had no *locus standi* in the endless arguments between the two secret civilian agencies. More surprising with hindsight, it was no part in the structure that evolved for the management of Sigint, nominally part of the head of SIS's empire.[46] Nevertheless the wartime JIC's role of evolving and overseeing worldwide inter-service arrangements was the basis of the concept of intelligence as a manageable community.

Thus the current JIC's responsibilities include: 'to give direction to, and to keep under review, the organisation and working of British

---

[44] F. H. Hinsley and C. A. G. Simkins, *British Intelligence in the Second World War. Vol. IV: Security and Counter-Intelligence* (London: HMSO, 1990), p. 7.

[45] Hinsley, *British Intelligence in the Second World War*, vol. I, p. 43.

[46] This reflected what the official historian refers to as 'the "historic" aloofness of the SIS from the Whitehall committee system'. (Hinsley, *British Intelligence in the Second World War* vol. I p. 92.) For JIC attempts to intervene in Sigint matters see Hinsley vol. I p. 271 and vol. II pp. 21–4.

intelligence activity as a whole at home and overseas in order to ensure efficiency, economy and prompt adaptation to changing requirements.'[47] Commonwealth countries followed a similar post-war pattern. In the United States the DCI was originally established with a fairly loose 'coordination' role, but this was subsequently strengthened and widened to include budgetary responsibilities and supporting central staff.[48] As with national assessment, other Western countries have less well-developed national management. But there is usually some recognition of intelligence as a national resource, with some national management machinery and a national budget, however nominal in some cases. The 1939 JIC remit for managing intelligence was a decisive step. Along with departmentally-subordinate foreign intelligence, security intelligence on internal threats, national collection agencies and arrangements for national assessments, community management completed the modern system.

Intelligence and other organized knowledge

This development of intelligence did not evolve entirely under its own momentum; it was part of much wider developments in governments' use of information. In Britain between 1815 and 1870, 'the change from a haphazard to a scientific administration in town and country was as essential to the mechanism of a complicated industrial society as the provision of new methods of transport'.[49] Like military command, proactive government came to depend increasingly on the 'scientific' collection and analysis of information by experts. 'The social philosophy of Benthamism demanded a unified administrative state, run by professional experts, and based on the principles of investigation, legislation, inspection and report.'[50] Foreign and security intelligence was itself part of this wider growth of the 'Knowledgeable State'.[51] It may indeed have inspired parts of it; military intelligence was subsequently a

[47] *Central Intelligence Machinery* (London: HMSO, 1993), p. 23. This is substantially unchanged from the immediate post-war formulation. The JIC charter dated 27 February 1948 included the duty 'to keep under review the organization of intelligence as a whole and in particular the relations of its component parts so as to ensure efficiency, economy and a rapid adaptation to changing requirements'. (JIC (48) 21, India Office Library, reference L/WS/1/1051.)

[48] For the 1980s see Presidential Executive Order 12333 (1981) paragraph 1.4 for the make-up of the community and 1.5 for the DCI.

[49] E. L. Woodward, *The Age of Reform 1815–1870* (Oxford: Oxford University Press, 1938), p. 426.

[50] Dandeker, *Surveillance, Power and Modernity*, p. 121.

[51] M. Pearson, *The Knowledgeable State* (London: Hutchinson, 1982).

model for some law enforcement intelligence.[52] In two World Wars the growth of intelligence on the enemy was matched almost exactly by British government's development of professional statistical services to provide the mass of information it needed on its own resources.

Furthermore the development of intelligence reflected the growing role of organized information everywhere, not just in government. While military intelligence departments were evolving, information also began to be used systematically for the scientific management of business; 'starting somewhere about the eighteen eighties, there had been a steady evolution of thought and practice bearing on business management in Great Britain'.[53] In this last half of our own century intelligence developed as part of the information society. The massive present-day electronic transfers of intelligence data between technical collection outstations and headquarters, and between intelligence allies, are exact micro-scale replicas of the world's wider electronic picture of 'vast amounts of data criss-crossing the globe daily . . . Telecommunications networks are the freeways of post-industrial society.'[54] Intelligence's growing status in government illustrates the situation of developed countries in which 'the progressive bureaucratisation of life in the late twentieth century has resulted in orders of magnitude increases in the information stock. Making successful use of this stock is today the key to successful social functioning.'[55] The growth of intelligence is part of the wider, electronically-based information explosion.

Structure and characteristics

This then was the evolution of the modern Anglo-Saxon community. Of the elements in the current US structure (depicted in figure 1) the departmental units can be seen in the DIA and Army, Navy, Air Force and Marine intelligence organizations, in the State Department's Bureau of Intelligence and Research (INR), and in the intelligence units of the Department of Energy,[56] Treasury and (for some purposes) the Department of Commerce. (With the increasing importance of intelligence on narcotics the Drug Enforcement Administration (DEA) is also now

---

[52] For this influence in the United States see F. J. Donner, *The Age of Surveillance* (New York: Random House, 1981), pp. 47–8.

[53] L. Urwick, 'The Development of Scientific Management in Great Britain', *British Management Review* vol. 3 no. 4 (1938), p. 79.

[54] Quotations from B. Cronin and E. Davenport, *Post-Professionalism: Transforming the Information Heartland* (London: Taylor Graham, 1988), pp. 36–7.

[55] Cronin and Davenport, *Post-Professionalism: Transforming the Information Heartland*, p. 64.

[56] With a special importance on nuclear intelligence matters.

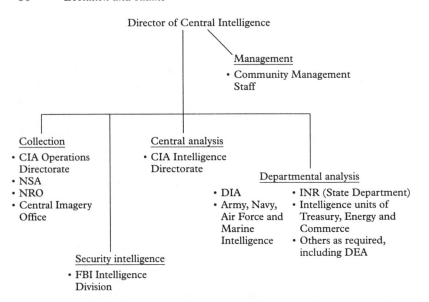

Figure 1 United States intelligence structure

frequently involved.) The security intelligence agency is the FBI's Intelligence Division. The national collection agencies are NSA for Sigint and the NRO and Central Imagery Office for imagery; CIA's Directorate of Operations is in effect the national Humint agency.[57] CIA, in its Directorate of Intelligence, is a central, non-departmental analysis agency. CIA's Director is also DCI.[58] As the community manager he is assisted by the Community Management Staff.

The British system has similar elements in the JIC community (figure 2). The DIS (working on defence intelligence) is its largest analytic body, but is still a departmental one, part of the Ministry of Defence, and is not a national agency. The Foreign and Commonwealth Office (FCO) and Treasury are the other permanent departmental members; others such as the Home Office attend as necessary. (These are operational Ministries without the clearly defined intelligence units possessed by their US equivalents, but they bring their departmental views to JIC deliberations. The FCO has its Research and Analysis Department but,

---

[57] Though the US armed forces also conduct quite extensive Humint operations.
[58] CIA also includes an important third element, the Directorate of Science and Technology. It has responsibilities for the planning and execution of covert technical operations of various kinds, and for some technical analysis. It also controls the Foreign Broadcast Information Service, the counterpart of the BBC Monitoring Service.

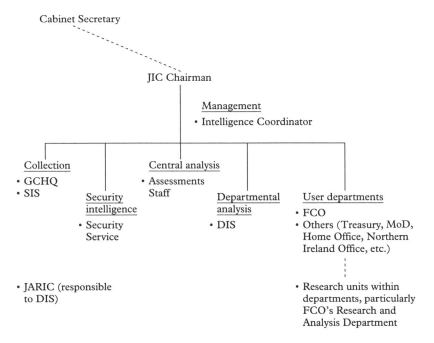

Figure 2 British intelligence structure

unlike its US counterpart, this is not an intelligence community member in its own right.) The Security Service is the security intelligence body. The collectors are the SIS and GCHQ. (JARIC is the national imagery analysis centre, but is a military service unit subordinate to the DIS and not a JIC member.) For the national assessment role there is no central analysis agency like the CIA's Intelligence Directorate, but the JIC as a committee is served by the Cabinet Office Assessments Staff. The managerial role is vested in the JIC itself and in the Intelligence Coordinator who sits as a member. Despite the differences between the British and US systems, the elements described in this chapter can be seen in both, arranged in accordance with the accidents of national intelligence evolution, as in the way that CIA combines the functions of Humint and central analysis. The same applies to other Western systems. In varying combinations the same entities tend to recur.

But the communities are by no means homogeneous. The agencies have their own character. In particular, security intelligence with its focus on internal threats is significantly different from the rest; the differences will be discussed later. Additionally the communities have some fuzzy boundaries. The permanent intelligence organizations are supplemented by part-time or temporary elements and those with only one foot in the intelligence camp. Thus operational naval vessels and aircraft can be deployed as temporary intelligence collectors, and sometimes combine intelligence with non-intelligence missions. As has just been explained, British FCO officials and others from policy departments play major parts in the JIC assessment process, without in any sense belonging to an intelligence organization. Defence attachés collect intelligence but have non-intelligence, diplomatic status.

There are also intelligence activities that take place below the level of central departments and national agencies just described, and are not usually included in thinking about the central community. In this sense there is an additional military intelligence 'community' stretching down from the top service level to the operational and tactical levels of command. Subordinate commanders need some intelligence resources under their own control, yet these cannot be ignored as part of the total intelligence picture. They also need some integration between levels; computers in the military intelligence hierarchy now need to be able to exchange data with those at the next command level up or down. The British Chief of Defence Intelligence is charged with 'the coordination of intelligence for British defence' at any level.[59] The DIA Director has a similar responsibility in the United States for intelligence in the regional commands. Armed services' intelligence makes up the main 'vertical' community of this kind; but the British Security Service, on a smaller scale, has its own network of liaison with the Metropolitan Police Special Branch and the regional police Special Branches.[60] Though in some ways these support local Chief Police Officers' responsibilities for public order, they are also part of national security intelligence resources under Security Service's guidance.

The significance of these 'downward' extensions of central intelligence, as of the fuzzy boundaries discussed in the earlier paragraphs, is

---

[59] *Central Intelligence Machinery*, p. 22.
[60] Personnel strengths of the Special Branches in the 52 British police forces are quoted as 520 Metropolitan (London); 1,400 England (outside London); 100+ Scotland; 280 Northern Ireland (*Statewatch* vol. 4 no. 6, p. 19, quoting Home Office and Scottish Office, *Guidelines on Special Branch Work in Great Britain*, July 1994). Duties include armed personal protection and port, airport and other immigration and naturalization work, as well as intelligence activities assisting the Security Service – the RUC (SB) plays a leading and not supporting role on terrorist activities within the Province. For Special Branch functions see House of Commons Home Affairs Committee 1984–5 *Fourth Report* (H.C. 71) 17 April 1985. Other figures quoted for Special Branch strengths in 1984 were 446 in the Metropolitan Police and 870 in other English and Welsh police forces (P. Gill, *Policing Politics: Security Intelligence and the Liberal Democratic State* (London: Cass, 1994), p. 228).

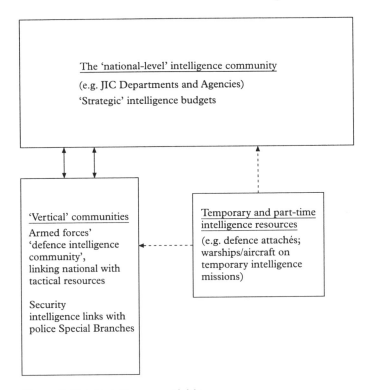

Figure 3 Total intelligence activities

that the complete national intelligence capability depicted in figure 3 is rather more diffuse and extensive than appears from the central institutions normally listed as the 'intelligence community'. Bureaucratic lines have to be drawn somewhere; and national intelligence budgets have to be built around the big, unambiguously 'intelligence' institutions. But demarcation lines are never perfect, and sometimes the vital action falls outside them. The key to British action against IRA terrorism has always been the intelligence effectiveness of the Royal Ulster Constabulary Special Branch (RUC (SB)), yet it has never been part of formal national intelligence overviews and budgeting; the same applies to the Metropolitan Police Special Branch, also heavily involved in anti-terrorist action. Intelligence has to be defined in terms of its organizations; but the blurring between some intelligence and non-intelligence bodies has to be recognized by those seeking to understand it – and by those who supervise it.

Nevertheless it is reasonably clear what the government intelligence system is and what it is for. First, it is separated from decision-taking; its basic role is providing information and not giving advice on what should be done about it. This distinguishes it from diplomacy – an institution for making and executing policy as well as getting information – and from decision-takers' own gathering and use of information. It is an information specialist; not 'intelligence' as sometimes used to describe the study *and use* of information.[61] Second, most of its targets are foreign. Security intelligence can have some purely domestic targets as well as overseas ones, but even the domestic ones are 'foreign' in the sense of being outsiders, with an 'otherness' that separates them from the state or society in some special way. Intelligence is about 'them', not 'us'; it is not self-knowledge. In this it is unlike governments' other information specialists on internal affairs, such as statistical services. Third is its special emphasis on forecasting; on foreign targets it is government's prophet. Fourth, it is a regular part of decision-taking and seeks to persuade its recipients of the authenticity and relevance of what it provides; it is more than just a passive reference system. Boundaries can be considered in more detail in chapter 7, but these are the main operational characteristics. They are combined with a professional ethic similar to that of other organized knowledge and research, with corporate assumptions about truth-seeking and persuasion. Like other professions, intelligence may fall well below its own standards in practice. But without some ethic of this kind it lacks justification for its separate institutional identity.

The incorporation of these features in permanent, specialized organizations make modern intelligence far removed from the relatively unorganized pre-Victorian period. Intelligence has gradually developed as one of government's regular sources of information and judgment, in a way that in the last fifty years has sometimes reversed its former relationship with diplomacy. Traditionally diplomats and Foreign Ministries have seen themselves as the experts on weighing up foreign states and their policies and intentions, using 'secret intelligence' as an input on the margins; now diplomatic reports are sometimes seen as just one source of material for *intelligence* evaluation. In previous times diplomats were expected to predict overseas *coups*; now Western surprise at overseas events is quoted as evidence of *intelligence* failure. Sir Reginald

---

[61] See quotation from Cronin and Davenport in my 'Introduction' note 4. Wilensky (see note 3 in the Introduction) also gave an account of intelligence's qualities as clear, understandable, reliable, valid, adequate and 'wide-ranging, because the major policy alternatives promising a high probability of attaining organizational goals are posed or new goals suggested'. (H. L. Wilensky, *Organizational Intelligence* (New York/London: Basic Books, 1967), preface p. viii.)

Hibbert, a retired British diplomat, once described the way in which the JIC has disturbed the previous authority of the FCO and Treasury in overseas matters thus:

There is now an invisible force exercising a certain pull on these great bodies, in much the same way as stars and planets invisible to the naked eye or even through telescopes can be deduced by astronomers to be influencing the courses of heavenly bodies, bending them from the trajectories that might be expected on the basis of visible data. The invisible force is exerted by the joint intelligence and assessment machinery in the Cabinet Office.[62]

The same might be said even more forcibly of the influence of the CIA in Washington *vis-à-vis* State Department. The last 125 years have seen intelligence develop into this position: at the very least, as one of governments' regular windows on the world.

Summary

Modern intelligence developed through 'foreign armies' components of the military staffs which were formed from the mid-nineteenth century onwards. Another origin was the growth of 'special policing' in roughly the same period. Later came the twentieth-century expansion of intelligence collection and the development of specialized agencies for it. Anglo-Saxon countries then developed means of assessing foreign countries as a whole, and of intelligence community management.

This evolution of intelligence has been part of much wider trends in the use of information, in government and outside it. As in all other arrangements for handling information, intelligence communities have some blurred edges. But they are reasonably coherent institutions for producing information and forecasts on foreign targets and internal security matters, linked to decision-taking but with some separation from it.

---

[62] R. Hibbert, 'Intelligence and Policy', *Intelligence and National Security* vol. 5 no. 1 (January 1990), p. 117.

3 Resources, stages and subjects

The previous chapter sketched modern intelligence's evolution. This one provides an introductory map of the system, with some impressions of its size, stages, categories and resource allocations.

Overall resources

Budgetary conventions are complicated by the intelligence extensions just touched upon. Formal distinctions are made between so-called 'strategic intelligence' – institutionally the national and central departments and agencies described in the last chapter – and the so-called 'tactical' resources under the control of military commands, or the Victorians' 'intelligence in the field'.[1] The United States intelligence budget has separate divisions for 'strategic' and 'tactical' resources, but most other countries include only the former.[2] But the order of magnitude of intelligence is clear enough. In 1976 the US superpower had just over 100,000 people in the defence-funded component of its 'strategic' community, excluding those funded outside defence, notably CIA. When everything else was added, including support staff and the

---

[1] Not to be confused with the normal military distinction between the strategic, operational and tactical levels of command. 'Tactical intelligence resources' is an intelligence term of art for everything below the national, 'strategic' level of control. The 'theatre resources' under General Schwarzkopf in the Gulf War were 'tactical' in this sense, though serving both the operational and tactical levels of command. In the same way some of the 'strategically' controlled resources such as satellites provided him with operational or tactical information.

[2] For the US distinction between the National Foreign Intelligence Program (NFIP) and Tactical Intelligence and Related Activities (TIARA) see D. Elkins, 'The Critical Role of the Resource Manager in the US Intelligence Community', *Defense Intelligence Journal* vol. 1 no. 2 (fall 1992), pp. 205–21. The NFIP budget is bigger than TIARA. It includes the General Defense Intelligence Program (GDIP) or 'that part of NFIP that finances intelligence elements in support of the fighting forces' (W. Jajko, *The Future of Defense Intelligence* (Washington D.C.: Consortium for the Study of Intelligence, 1993), p. 15). TIARA is recently said to have been superseded by the Joint Military Intelligence Program (JMIP) (*OSS Notices* vol. 3 issue 7, p. 11).

services' tactical efforts, the overall personnel total may have been in the region of 200,000.[3] The Soviet KGB and GRU combined were then much bigger overall, though perhaps not much bigger than their US opposite numbers if the KGB's vast non-intelligence activities were excluded. Unofficial figures subsequently put the cost of US intelligence at about $28 billion in 1994 – rather more than 10 per cent of the defence bill, and far more than the cost of the State Department.[4] The new Russian intelligence institutions have shrunk compared with their Soviet predecessors, but their resources and the possession of intelligence satellites may still just give Russia the status of a superpower, though a lagging one.[5]

For second-class intelligence powers like Britain and the continental NATO countries, the effort is smaller, proportionately as well as absolutely. Among these powers the West European average for 'strategic' intelligence at the end of the Cold War may have been somewhere in the range of 3–5 per cent of defence expenditure. (The much higher US proportion represents the great costs of intelligence satellites and their launchers, and also the inclusion of 'tactical' intelligence within the budget.) The three British civilian agencies GCHQ, SIS and Security Service were officially said in 1994 to cost £900 million annually with 10,500 employees.[6] If the published figures for the DIS,

---

[3] US Senate, *Select Committee to Study Governmental Operations with Respect to Intelligence Activities (The Church Committee) Final Report* (Washington D.C.: US GPO, April 1976), book I, p. 340. The 'national' defence-costed effort was put down as 100,000 people. Non-defence 'national' figures (particularly for CIA) were not given. Pages 330–1 state that the costs of 'tactical' intelligence activities of the armed services plus indirect support costs of intelligence and intelligence-related activities equalled those of the 'national' programme as a whole.

[4] J. H. Hedley, *Checklist for the Future of Intelligence* (Georgetown: Institute for the Study of Diplomacy, 1995), p. 1. The defence budget for 1994 was $240.5 billion; for the Department of State $4.03 billion. The $28 billion for the intelligence budget is assumed to include both the national NFIP programme and tactical TIARA (though this is never made explicit). The TIARA budget is said to be around $12 billion. (*Washington Post*, 17 March 1995, p. A6.)

[5] For the continued (but reduced) Russian satellite programme in the early 1990s see P. Clark, 'Soviet Space Programs' in D. Ball and H. Wilson (eds.), *Australia and Space* (Canberra: Australian National University, 1992). Up to the end of 1995 the reductions in Russian intelligence budgets since the end of the Cold War had been proportionately less than those of the armed forces. (I am indebted to C. N. Donnelly for this opinion.)

[6] *Treasury Supply Estimate* class XIX, March 1994, quoted expenditure of £974.5 million for 1993–4 and £881.5 million for 1994–5, with 6,076 people at GCHQ and 4,440 in SIS and the Security Service (*Supply Estimate*, and *Departmental Expenditure Report* CM 2481). Figures given in the Treasury Supply Estimates of March 1995 for 1995–6 were £793 million; overall staff totals were 10,108. Planned expenditure for the two succeeding years was £783 million and £780 million. The sharp decline in expenditure over 1993–4 and 1995–6 reflects the completion of big building projects costing £332 million, as well as some overall reductions. (*Supply Estimate* and *Departmental Expenditure Report* CM 2820, 1995.)

imagery interpretation at JARIC and other strategic defence intelligence elements are added to these, the total cost for that year comes out at about a billion pounds[7] – though the basis for including and excluding military personnel in the published figures is not clear, and the cost may have been rather greater.[8] Cold War costs have not been published; but the overall British intelligence strength at the end of it was probably significantly in excess of 15,000, though considerably less now.

Intelligence is cheap compared with armed force or policing; governments can afford to buy a lot of it for the cost of a frigate, or for the police manpower deployed on anti-terrorist protection. The British government is said to be spending almost as much on private consultancy fees for the Civil Service as a whole as it spends on intelligence.[9] But the total is still quite substantial. Intelligence has come to need quite large organizations. Like the United States, Britain spends more on intelligence than on diplomacy, though less than on overseas aid.[10]

---

[7] The British DIS is only loosely part of the intelligence budget, being essentially a Ministry of Defence agency; hence its exclusion from the published intelligence figures in the note above. Total 1994 costs attributed to military intelligence in the defence budget (including military survey, but presumably excluding tactical items) were £190 million (or £164 million net of appropriations in aid), of which about a third was the cost of the DIS. (*Treasury Supply Estimate* class I, March 1994; and MoD *Statement on Defence Estimates* CM 2550, April 1994, p. 41.) No MoD totals are identified in the comparable 1995 statements.

[8] An important obscurity is whether the MoD figures for 'intelligence' at note 7 above include the uniformed component of the national Sigint effort, under GCHQ control. It was officially revealed in 1993 that this component numbered about 3,000 (in addition to the GCHQ civilian strength of about 6,000). A note in the *Supply Estimate* for 1994–5 implies that the intelligence costs at note 6 above include this military contribution to Sigint, though the numbers of employees probably do not. The 1995 *Statement on Defence* (CM 2800, p. 114) referred to 'assistance to GCHQ and other agencies in obtaining intelligence' as 'Military task 1.11' but did not provide figures for this effort. (I am indebted to Michael Smith for data quoted at the 'intelligence' press conference held at the FCO on 24 November 1993.)

[9] A report by the Treasury and Civil Service Select Committee quoted about £500 million annually on consultancies (*Daily Telegraph*, 27 April 1994). Subsequently the figure for 1993–4 was recalculated as £865 million (Association of First Division Civil Servants, *FDA News*, April 1995, p. 5).

[10] Foreign and Commonwealth figures for 1994–5 were £688 million on overseas representation and the FCO itself, accounting for a total of 6,648 staff. The total of overseas aid was £1,913 million. The grand total for 'the Diplomatic Wing' (including international subscriptions, military assistance, the British Council and other FCO-funded organizations) was £1,138 million, or not far from the total cost of intelligence. The BBC Monitoring Service providing valuable 'open' information accounted for £18 million, making it a remarkably cost-effective information source. (*Treasury Supply Estimate* class II, March 1994.)

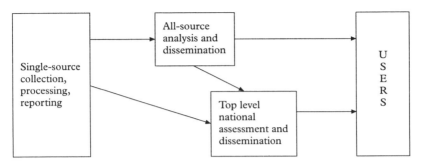

Figure 4 Intelligence process in outline

Process and stages

The previous chapter sketched the way intelligence evolved towards divisions between 'single-source' and 'all-source' agencies. Intelligence is a sequential, inter-agency process. The first stage is collection, with 'single-source' output, usually in the form of written reports, from each of the collection sources. The second stage is 'all-source analysis', which draws on all available information to produce 'finished intelligence'. Following these first two stages is the distribution ('dissemination') of intelligence's reports to the non-intelligence world of decision and policy – referred to by intelligence practitioners as their recipients, customers or consumers; for convenience here they will all be called 'users'. There can also be – but does not have to be – an intermediate stage between analysis and dissemination to users, when departments and agencies combine to produce special, interdepartmental, 'national' assessments for the top level of government. These divisions into stages are by no means clear-cut but they provide the system's basic framework shown in figure 4. They can be outlined here before being described in more detail later.

Collection

Most intelligence investment is in collection; over 90 per cent of US resources were devoted to it in the 1970s.[11] In sheer quantity the single-source reports from collectors to all-source agencies inside the intelligence system are much more voluminous than the all-source reports going to the users outside it, in the same way as reporters and news agencies produce much more raw news than newspapers

---

[11] Church Committee *Final Report*, book I, p. 344.

subsequently carry. It has been said that 'only 10 per cent of the intelligence product ever moves outside the walls of the intelligence establishment'.[12] In the Cold War the ratio of single-source reports monitoring current Soviet military activities to the volume of finished intelligence was even higher, perhaps at least a hundred to one.

Thus intelligence corresponds to an analogy drawn elsewhere between information processing and the oil industry.[13] Finding oil in the field is expensive, as is bringing a trial drill on stream. The production process entails blending and progressively refining different kinds of crude oil, with decreasing volume and added value at each stage. The final products come from central facilities and are then widely marketed and distributed. Intelligence has a similar emphasis on front-end costs and progressive refinement as data flows through the system. This applies particularly to the technical sources, Sigint and imagery, which often involve expensive equipment and 24-hour operations, plus the big, additional launch costs for US satellites; the US figures in the 1970s showed that 87 per cent of collection costs were then for technical operations, compared with 13 per cent for Humint.[14] Unofficial US figures in 1994 showed NSA as costing $4 billion for Sigint, the NRO $7 billion for satellites (presumably including some costs of Sigint ones, as well as for imagery), the Central Imagery Office $1 billion, and tactical military systems (mainly collection) $12 billion.[15] All collection, including Humint, mixes established production lines with a constant search for new sources and the need to replace those that fail; as with exploring for oil there are elements of unpredictability and luck. All this contributes to the 90 per cent of costs attributed to collection.

Another important reason for this balance is that the activity of the modern technical collection agencies extends well beyond the actual gathering of data to include its initial processing, exploitation and interpretation; their output is not 'raw material' in any real sense of the

[12] L. K. Johnson, 'Decision Costs in the Intelligence Cycle' in A. C. Maurer, M. D. Tunstall and J. M. Keagle (eds.), *Intelligence: Policy and Process* (Boulder and London: Westview, 1985), p. 193, quoting A. S. Brammer, *The Impact of Intelligence on the Policy Review and Decision Process – Part I: Findings* (Washington D.C.: Central Intelligence Agency, 1980), p. 19.

[13] M. F. Meltzer, *Information: the Ultimate Resource* (New York: Arlington Press, 1981), quoted by B. Cronin and E. Davenport, *Post-Professionalism: Transforming the Information Heartland* (London: Taylor Graham, 1988), p. 93.

[14] Church Committee *Final Report*, book I, p. 344. A senior American quoted a ratio of 1:7 between Humint and technical collection in 1984 (quoted in L. K. Johnson, *America's Secret Power: the CIA in a Democratic Society* (Oxford: Oxford University Press, 1989), p. 85 and endnote).

[15] *Washington Post*, 17 March 1995, p. A6.

term.[16] Selection and summarizing of the original material is usually needed, but often the material itself can only be unlocked through special techniques and skills, as when Sigint agencies break ciphers. Similarly photo-interpretation, though classified under 'collection', is a separate activity from acquiring the photographs. Other less esoteric techniques such as transcribing recordings and translating documents and other texts are equally manpower-intensive parts of 'collection processing'.

Hence the output of single-source collection incorporates substantial analysis and interpretation. This is part of intelligence production, but also feeds back in the reverse direction into collection steerage. Radio interception is guided by this supporting analysis on what signals to follow, how to identify them, and what data to record for further processing; similarly the results of photo-interpretation determine what additional imagery coverage is needed. Humint agencies for their part analyse the product of their sources to test them for signs of unreliability or deception. The Second World War experience confirmed that these processes need to be performed as part of the collection organization, closely linked with collection itself. It is as if some oil refining has to be done close to the well-head.

Thus the modern collection agency incorporates powerful processing and exploitation, with their resource consequentials; photographs need more people to interpret them than to operate their collection systems. The huge headquarters of US Sigint's NSA illustrates the scale of cryptanalysis and other single-source processing. Taking all sources together, there may now be as many people on first-stage processing and interpretation as on collection proper – though modern automation blurs the distinction between them.[17] One consequence of this processing and interpretation effort is that some substantial lines of single-source reports – particularly ephemeral ones supporting diplomatic negotiations or adding to diplomatic appraisals – continue to go direct to some users, in parallel with or by-passing the second, all-source stage. The effect is to modify the flow diagram, as shown in figure 5.

A further result of collection agencies' status as first-stage analysis centres is that each receives copies of most lines of the others' output.

---

[16] For a description of interpretation as applied to Second World War textual Sigint see W. Millward, 'Life In and Out of Hut 3' in F. H. Hinsley and A. Stripp, *Codebreakers: The Inside Story of Bletchley Park* (Oxford: Oxford University Press, 1993), pp. 17–29.

[17] Note that the Church Committee divided the 'collection' 91 per cent of the intelligence budget into 72 per cent collection and 19 per cent 'processing raw technical data' (Church Committee *Final Report*, book I, p. 344). In the subsequent twenty years the amount of collection processing has increased greatly, at the expense of pure collection.

Single-source agencies analyse their own material, but use the product of others for steering collection and analytic background; in practice it pays for single-source evidence to be collected, selected and processed in the light of all available knowledge, and not insulated from it so that it remains untainted by other sources. For the same reason collectors normally receive copies of all-source reports produced for non-intelligence users. One practical consequence is usually to multiply information flows several times over. A complete flow diagram would therefore show most kinds of intelligence reports flowing everywhere, apart from specially sensitive lines given a more restricted distribution. Flows from foreign allies add to the totals. The amount of data flowing inside the modern intelligence system can hardly be exaggerated.

All-source analysis and finished intelligence

Thus modern collection merges intellectually into the all-source stage; analysis and interpretation permeate both. Intelligence is evidence-driven, but most of the evidence emerges from processing of some kind; it does not have separable elements of 'facts' and 'interpretation'. A give-and-take between the two takes place at all stages, in the same way as historical research has been described as 'a continuous process of interaction between the historian and his facts'.[18]

In this the relationship between the big battalions of technical collection and the relatively small all-source agencies is important. The CIA's Intelligence Directorate is said to have some 1,500 analysts;[19] the British DIS now has a strength of perhaps 700–800, though by no means all of these are analysts; both are relatively small compared with the equivalent investments in technical collection. Single-source interpretations carry considerable authority, enhanced by their need to withhold details of their more secret sources and methods. Computer processing tends to massage raw data beyond recovery; modern technical collection is accused of creating a kind of 'virtual reality'.[20] Yet all-source analysts have to have some capacity for questioning these interpretations and getting at the original evidence. A healthy system needs overlaps and

---

[18] E. H. Carr, *What is History?* (London: Pelican, 1964), p. 30.

[19] Hedley, *Checklist for the Future of Intelligence*, p. 21.

[20] P. Kemp, 'The Fall and Rise of France's Spymasters', *Intelligence and National Security* vol. 9 no. 1 (January 1994). See also J. Der Derian, *Antidiplomacy: Spies, Terror, Speed, and War* (Oxford: Blackwell, 1992), p. 33 for intelligence and cyberspace, and p. 175 for the view that deeply secret technical sources 'resist corrective feedback'.

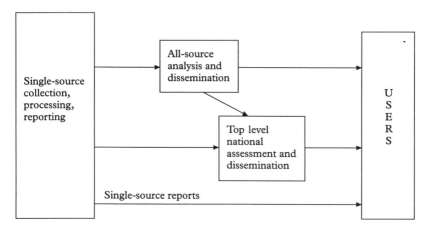

Figure 5 Fuller intelligence process

exchanges between the two stages, in a constant two-way process of arguing about conclusions.

Nevertheless there are advantages in having some institutional separation between the two, putting them in different organizations or at least in separate compartments if they come under the same management. Single-source producers quite legitimately analyse, and report their conclusions; and for this they use other sources and all-source reports as background. The crucial difference that must never be forgotten is between single-source and all-source *responsibilities*. Those engaged in collection and collection processing are experts on intelligence techniques (and enthusiasts for them); but their all-source colleagues are the experts on intelligence *subjects*. They have the final responsibility for evaluating all evidence on them. The essence of their work is therefore that they not only weigh different intelligence sources against each other but also draw on any available non-intelligence sources; they must not give special weight to secret evidence simply because it is secret. Policy-makers get some single-source intelligence reports direct, but if the subjects call for authoritative intelligence judgments they should call on the all-source experts; hence their importance. One picture of intelligence is therefore of extensive collection flowing to many recipients through the much smaller all-source stage (figure 6). The results of good collection can be lost if it is not properly interpreted on a multi-source basis. If there is any single guide to making sense of an intelligence system it is to be clear whether the output from any point is intended to be single-source or all-source.

Community assessment

The additional all-source process – national assessment, as in the British JIC assessments or the US National Intelligence Estimates (NIEs) – provides a meeting of minds through interdepartmental machinery. But this is an expensive process that can only be a selective service to top leaders on important issues; departmental representatives cannot be gathered together for everything. Most finished intelligence is produced by the individual all-source agencies and does not go through this interdepartmental stage; it is quite mistaken to suggest, for example, that all British intelligence finds its way to users via the JIC. Similarly most US product is by the CIA or the service agencies and not integrated into NIEs. Nevertheless the JIC/NIE processes remain the formal basis of important, top level conclusions. In the same way some local interdepartmental machinery of this kind may be needed overseas or locally; Britain had local JICs when extensive forces were based overseas, and similar machinery was set up in Belfast during the terrorist campaign.

Dissemination and user liaison

Disseminating intelligence product makes up another stage, although closely related to intelligence production. Its aim is the delivery of useful, user-friendly product at the right time, especially when timeliness is of the essence for decision-taking. Effective intelligence depends on having adequate communications with the recipients, not breaking down or being swamped in crises; communications are key parts of the system. This can mean having dedicated intelligence and intelligence-user networks, as in the way Ultra was signalled to commanders overseas in the Second World War through special communications units with secure ciphers.[21] Even of the Gulf War it was concluded by the Congressional investigation that 'the inability to reliably disseminate intelligence, particularly imagery, within the theater was one of the major intelligence failures in operations Desert Shield/Desert Storm'.[22] All

[21] For the move to dedicated communications see F. H. Hinsley with E. E. Thomas, C. F. G. Ransom and R. C. Knight, *British Intelligence in the Second World War* vol. I (London: HMSO, 1979), appendix 13.

[22] Report of the Oversight and Investigations Subcommittee, Committee on Armed Services, House of Representatives, *Intelligence Successes and Failures in Operations Desert Shield/Storm* (Washington D.C.: US GPO, 1993), p. 2. The Subcommittee also concluded (p. 28) that 'Intelligence distribution overall was very poor, particularly when it came to serving air fighting units. Both the hardware and the people failed.' It found (p. 4) that US communications 'were so stressed . . . that US forces seriously considered leasing time on Soviet communications satellites'.

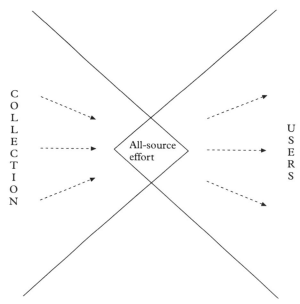

Figure 6 All-source stage as a funnel

intelligence is produced against time pressures; for timely intelligence there is the pace of events, and even for more considered production there is the need to meet the timetables of bureaucratic decision. Dissemination tends to be intelligence's Achilles' heel. Electronically there is never enough communications capacity.

But the service also entails an awareness of user needs through contact with them. Most liaison takes place between single-source collectors and their all-source consumers, but ultimately the key contacts are with the non-intelligence users. Intelligence's value depends entirely on them; it is only useful if they take it seriously. Close relationships between intelligence and users play a major part in determining intelligence's credibility and educating them on how to use it properly.

Hence intelligence everywhere needs to treat its recipients as if they were 'the customers' and 'the market' for a commercial firm. Good organizations put a lot of effort into looking after customers inside the intelligence world and real users outside it. There are intelligence equivalents of commercial 'distribution', 'sales' and 'consumer research' functions. Eliciting customer needs is important, and the archetypal intelligence producer is close to them, physically and mentally.[23] Salesmanship is part of the game; intelligence is not an impersonal delivery process.

The variety of intelligence recipients also needs to be emphasized. Single-source distribution within the intelligence system itself has extensive ramifications. Even among the ultimate non-intelligence users many levels are served; some top level readers receive intelligence direct, but most of it is delivered to lower levels of their departments, and is directly used there or drawn on as background for their policy recommendations. Diplomats abroad make tactical use of intelligence in executing foreign policy or forming their local assessments. Then there are all the military commands and other users below the national capital level. Police and military forces fighting terrorism have equivalent tactical needs, distinct from those seeking political solutions. Some commercial firms may need some intelligence to execute government contracts. Users are as varied as intelligence and government.

Diversity also applies to users' own attitudes to intelligence. Using intelligence properly is itself an art, but there is little training in how to be an intelligence user. Previous experience counts; exposure to Room 40's naval codebreaking in 1914–15 made Winston Churchill enthusiastic for Sigint twenty-five years later. Intelligence's mystique and formidable security restrictions usually help it to get users' attention, but make it more difficult for them to understand it. Except in defence, it is a less regular part of users' normal working lives than information in diplomatic telegrams or government statistics.

In short, intelligence defies description as a limited list of products serving a limited community of users. Its total distribution is too voluminous and varied for any single bird's eye view of all it provides. The senior officials and ministers who set annual intelligence budgets are driven by impressions of its overall value rather than by any comprehensive audit. Intelligence is as complex and untidy as other information flows.

However another approach to mapping and understanding it is to divide it into various separate categories. Divisions of this kind are often used for management purposes; for example the British formal

---

23 Many commentators have suggested that CIA's problems with its Washington customers owe a great deal to distance from them – the forty minute drive and need to find parking space on arrival. As long ago as in 1921, on a proposal to move the British cipher-breakers to a more distant part of London, Lord Curzon as Foreign Secretary wrote forcibly about the need for them to be in 'constant communication' with the Foreign Office's departments. (K. Jeffrey, 'The Government Code and Cypher School: a Memorandum by Lord Curzon', *Intelligence and National Security* vol. 1 no. 3 (September 1986), p. 455.)

'requirements and tasking' system distinguishes between those subjects on which 'secret intelligence is actively to be sought' and those on which 'intelligence should be reported on an opportunity basis'.[24] Such categorizing of intelligence can take various forms. One is simply in the broad distinction between foreign and security intelligence already mentioned in chapter 2's account of the modern system's origins; a second is to distinguish between its geographic targets; a third is in accordance with the subjects on which it produces. In practice these distinctions overlap; requirements and priorities for example tend to be set out in a mixture of country and subject targets. But each of these systems of categorization provides its distinctive picture of intelligence and the allocation of its resources. We can outline these pictures here.

Categories

Foreign and security intelligence

Most intelligence is foreign intelligence on overseas entities. Security intelligence's rather different nature is reflected in the British Security Service Act of 1989 which described the service's main role as:

The protection of national security and, in particular, its protection against threats from espionage, terrorism and sabotage, from the activities of agents of foreign powers and from actions intended to overthrow or undermine parliamentary democracy by political, industrial or violent means.[25]

The essence of these threats is that they operate internally rather than externally.

In practice foreign and security intelligence targets overlap. External threats have internal components and vice versa; espionage is foreign but is an internal threat, while few terrorist organizations are without overseas connections. The cross-border nature of the IRA target and its overseas sources of arms and explosives makes it a typical mixture of foreign and domestic elements. Counter-terrorism also extends security intelligence to the protection of armed forces, ships, aircraft and nationals abroad. Internal threats are not necessarily from the state's own citizens. Much terrorism is avowedly international; and large-scale international migration now merges the home and overseas components of 'security' even more than before. Similarly national exports, as in British firms' contacts with the Iraqi arms industry, have both foreign

---

[24] *Central Intelligence Machinery* (London: HMSO, 1993), p. 13.
[25] Security Service Act 1989 1(2).

and domestic dimensions. Foreign intelligence is often collected on home territory, and security intelligence overseas.

Hence there are no rigid distinctions. Nevertheless security intelligence has some distinctive features. It has some affinities with police forces. The theme of *detecting* specific activities drives it in a way that does not apply to the same extent to foreign intelligence agencies; unlike them it is not basically an intelligence *disseminating* agency (although it has to be on some subjects; terrorist targets cut across this and other distinctions). Its minority status in most Western communities reflects the standing of internal threats. Though the overlapping of foreign and security intelligence must be emphasized, some rough idea of the proportions of the two comes from comparing the British Security Service's personnel strength of just over 2,000 with the foreign intelligence total of SIS's 2,000, and GCHQ's 6,000 and the unspecified military intelligence numbers.[26] For those countries with greater threats to their regimes, security intelligence looms larger. Thus the KGB's tradition was essentially as an internal security organization, with powerful overseas-looking extensions for monitoring and counteracting the worldwide manifestations of the counter-revolutionary threat; the external and internal threats were seen as a unity.

Geographic targets

One foreign target classification is simply by country or geographic area. The Soviet Union and the Warsaw Pact were the biggest Western target in the Cold War; the Middle East has always been another, smaller focus for coverage; China has a similar interest, especially for the United States; specific threats such as Argentine claims over the Falklands point to other identifiable targets of this kind. The Church Committee's figures of US allocations in 1975 showed 65 per cent of expenditure to be then directed at the Soviet Union and 'US commitments to NATO' (presumably coverage of other Warsaw Pact countries); 25 per cent on Asia, most of it against China; 7 per cent on the Arab–Israeli confrontation in the Middle East; 2 per cent on Latin America; 1 per cent on the rest of the world.[27] Britain's allocation was broadly similar, with less on China and more on the Middle East.

Even then these figures probably did not properly reflect worldwide and multinational issues, or non-state targets and international trade without a clear geographic identity. Coverage of Soviet activity was in

---

[26] *Treasury Supply Estimate* class XIX, March 1994.
[27] Church Committee *Final Report*, book I, p. 348.

practice never restricted to targets on the geographical Soviet landmass or Soviet forces; coverage of the Middle East and elsewhere was partly to monitor Soviet influence there. Geographic breakdowns are now likely to be even more misleading, since there is even more emphasis than twenty years previously on general categories like nuclear proliferation and the surveillance of international arms trade. Targets are now 'less countries than topics'.[28] Nevertheless geographic targets provide one rough map of intelligence effort, in rather the same way as a geographical basis was used in a recent official attempt to chart and prioritize the British FCO's needs for in-house research.[29] A key question for present intelligence can be put in geographic terms: how much of the Cold War effort is still needed on the former Soviet target?

Subjects

In categorization by subjects intelligence has normally appeared with 'political', 'military' and 'economic' labels. Thus the Church Committee classified the US effort of the 1970s as 54 per cent 'military', 15 per cent 'scientific and technical' (in practice, at that time, mainly related to Soviet military power), 3 per cent 'political', and 3 per cent 'economic', though there was also an unascribed 25 per cent 'general' category.[30] British allocations were not dissimilar.

This categorization by subject outputs has its own weaknesses. Some collection systems cover multiple targets; satellites are tasked with multiple targets at any one time and can be shifted on to others. Other systems are giant vacuum-cleaners, sweeping up everything and then selecting 'wanted' material of varying kinds. The subject terminology is vague. The 'political intelligence' label covers both the internal politics of foreign states and their international relationships. Economic intelligence likewise covers both foreign economies and international trade and finance. Activities like the clandestine action of one foreign state against another fall outside the normal categories. Subjects overlap and duplicate each other.

Nevertheless something can be said about rather arbitrary classes. To take foreign intelligence first: by far the biggest segment of it everywhere

---

[28] Johnson, *America's Secret Power*, p. 80.

[29] Foreign and Commonwealth Scrutiny, *The Need to Know: Research and Analysis Department and Library and Records Department* (FCO Report, 1993), appendix K. For each geographical area this applies twelve different criteria for assessing the need for in-house research, each on a scale of 0–3. The same method can be applied to the need for intelligence. But there is no provision for functional, multi-area subjects.

[30] Church Committee *Final Report*, book I, p. 347.

has been defence intelligence, in the broad sense of everything pertaining to foreign military power and activities, not just 'military intelligence' in its original sense. No doubt the 70 per cent or so in the 1970s has been revised downwards, but defence subjects probably remain the biggest intelligence target, centring on armed forces and their importance in some areas as internal political actors. The subjects extend to defence industries, arms exports and international attempts to control nuclear and other proliferation. There is also the mass of detail needed in case one's forces have to fight; this still includes some topography, like the 'beach intelligence' that turned out to be so central to planning the re-taking of the Falklands.[31]

Defence intelligence also extends to foreign military activities and foreign wars; following the progress of the Iran–Iraq war was a long-standing intelligence commitment in the 1980s. By extension it also includes armed insurrection overseas with and without foreign support, and mixed situations of politics, violence, externally-inspired subversion, the overt use of armed force and the dissolution of states through ethnic conflicts. Intelligence on such situations may often be subsidiary to public news and diplomatic reporting; but Bosnia, Somalia, Cambodia and Chechnya indicate the need for additional information on confused military situations. Surveillance of foreign conflicts of one kind and another has become a routine defence intelligence commitment, with thirty or so civil and international wars in progress at the time of writing.

Defence subjects also provide special opportunities for intelligence collection. Armed forces have their wide variety of communications, radars and other electronic equipment with emissions capable of being intercepted by foreign Sigint, and their panoply of military equipment capable of being observed by satellite imagery. Users' needs for intelligence and collectors' opportunities for meeting them probably combine to make defence in all these aspects still the biggest subject.

Other foreign intelligence subjects are smaller. 'Internal' political intelligence (on the politics of other states) is relatively inexpensive to collect, as indicated in the US figures for the 1970s; most political information comes from open sources and embassy reporting. The other side of that coin is 'external' political intelligence, on other states' foreign policies and general thinking. This merges in turn into what might be called 'diplomatic support' on specific issues. Hibbert (quoted in chapter 2) has suggested that covert intelligence as a whole adds about 10 per cent to the total sum of diplomatic reporting. He rates its value as

---

[31] Discussed in a personal account, E. Southby-Tailyour, *Reasons in Writing* (London: Cooper, 1993).

mainly confirmatory and tactical, giving 'immediacy, practicality and focus to general conclusions that had already been reached'. Intelligence is an aid to the normal business of foreign policy: coping with the daily pressures to decide on the line to take on particular issues, and how to do it. Immediate support for negotiation is particularly valuable when available; peeping at others' hands has always been part of diplomacy, though it sits uneasily with modern ideas of diplomatic respectability.[32] As put by well-informed writers, in US intelligence 'the entire range of covert intelligence collection – including electronic surveillance, agent insertion, and the theft of documents – is deployed against foreign negotiators (some allies excepted, if they return the favor)'.[33] Tactical diplomatic support of these kinds applies whether the subjects are 'political', 'economic' or any of the other manifold categories of international affairs.

The related economic intelligence has no doubt increased from the 3 per cent ascribed to it in the 1975 US figures. But 'internal' economic intelligence on foreign economies has always been relatively inexpensive in collection terms; though great effort was put into assessing Soviet GNP during the Cold War, the data was mainly drawn from published sources. Covert collection applies to particular issues rather than the macro-level. Rather the same applies to international trade and financial flows. Most of the basic data is available from open international statistics. 'Diplomatic support' applies to trade and other economic negotiations as to other matters: intelligence collection may be able to provide important tactical information, but does not make intelligence the subject's national authority.

Nevertheless economic intelligence has been much discussed as one of the current growth areas. The recent US paper just quoted on negotiating intelligence said that economic targets now account for 40 per cent of the total collection effort.[34] The figure points to the problems of defining by subjects. Some of the 'economic' effort discussed there is also diplomatic support. Other parts of it include efforts on ' "bad actors" in the international market-place guilty of past violations of sanctions, money laundering, sale of fissionable materials

---

[32] 'Diplomatic support' remains to some extent an undiscovered part of intelligence history. Thus the official history of intelligence in the Second World War does not include intelligence's support for diplomacy with allies and neutrals; while the official history of wartime foreign policy (Sir E. L. Woodward, *British Foreign Policy in the Second World War* (5 vols.) (London: HMSO, 1970–6)) makes no reference to intelligence.

[33] L. K. Johnson and A. Fletcher, 'CIA and the Collection of Economic Intelligence', *World Intelligence Review* vol. 13 no. 5 (1994), p. 3.

[34] Johnson and Fletcher, 'CIA and the Collection of Economic Intelligence', p. 1.

and weapons parts, or aiding and abetting terrorist organizations', and on tracing profits and laundering operations of narcotics dealers;[35] many of these could be described under other categories. But, definitions apart, economic intelligence can be assumed to be a growth area, particularly on the borderlines with defence and other subjects.

There is also counterintelligence. This is habitually used with a variety of meanings; thus there is usually an established counterintelligence division within the national Humint agency (for example in CIA), targeted on foreign espionage organizations. Some American writers use the term differently, to describe all defensive measures. But counter-intelligence is used here with a wider meaning of 'intelligence on foreign intelligence': getting information on *all* foreign intelligence threats – not just espionage ones – by *any* means (Sigint and other sources, as well as agents and defectors). Thus it has recently been officially confirmed that it was Sigint's breaking of enciphered intelligence messages that provided the essential leads into high-level Soviet espionage in Britain and the United States in the late 1940s. Similarly, Soviet espionage later in the Cold War penetrated Western Sigint. Counterintelligence is used here to convey the multi-disciplinary effort to penetrate the many different disciplines of the adversary.

In resource terms counterintelligence in this wide sense has always been small in the West, but its penetration of the KGB and GRU was a key activity in the Cold War, while penetration of Western intelligence was always the highest Soviet priority. Counterintelligence was 'a battle between professionals, complex and subtle; but the stakes are high, because if you have an entirely reliable agent in a senior position you have an asset whose benefits will stretch far beyond a battle between the two Services'.[36] Presumably the need is now reduced but not eliminated.

Among the foreign intelligence categories are non-state targets. Some fall into the economic category: quasi-state enterprises and private firms, including the multinationals who are sometimes also political actors. International terrorist movements and their overseas contacts, merging into state support, have become major non-state targets over the last twenty-five years, in foreign as well as security intelligence. Narcotics and major international crime are others. Technical means of collection now have increasing scope for searching for small individual targets of this kind, and the proportion of non-state ones is probably increasing. But

---

[35] Johnson and Fletcher, 'CIA and the Collection of Economic Intelligence', pp. 3–4.
[36] J. B. Lockhart, 'Intelligence: a British View' in K. G. Robertson (ed.), *British and American Approaches to Intelligence* (London: Macmillan, 1987), pp. 41–2.

they are so varied that they span most of the subject categories just discussed.

Then there are the resources on security intelligence subjects.[37] Counterespionage is close to counterintelligence. Counterintelligence can be seen as attacking foreign espionage services as if from the inside, typically by recruiting agents within them; while counterespionage is detecting specific foreign espionage attacks and neutralizing them. Typically this is through surveillance of foreign intelligence officers and investigating leads, but it can also be by breaking cipher traffic intended for agents or referring to them.[38] There is presumably still some counter-espionage, directed partly against Russia's continuation of Cold War Soviet efforts.[39] Other internal threats of subversion and sabotage and their connotations of covert foreign influence or domestic unconsti-tutionality are now barely significant.[40] By far the greatest current security intelligence target is now its coverage of terrorism, shared with the foreign intelligence agencies. This constituted three-quarters of the British Security Service's work in 1994 with a special concentration on Irish terrorism.[41]

Hypothetical subject allocation

Intelligence effort cannot be neatly categorized. Both geographic and subject labels obscure the wider intelligence role of understanding foreign countries or areas 'in the round' or all aspects of particular issues and situations, sometimes local, sometimes worldwide. Thus intelligence coverage throughout the 1970s and 1980s of the details of civil war, foreign invasion and governmental collapse in the Lebanon might be called political or defence intelligence, but it was essentially an effort to understand the situation as a whole. Referring to diplomatic work, a British ambassador said recently that 'I hate it when I have to fill in the form once a year, where I have to say how much political work,

---

[37] For a discussion of these security intelligence subjects – the security intelligence 'mandate' – see L. Lustgarten and I. Leigh, *In from the Cold: National Security and Parliamentary Democracy* (Oxford: Clarendon Press, 1994), chapter 14.

[38] As for example in the recent official American confirmation that the Rosenbergs, executed in 1953, were first detected as atomic spies through the breaking of Soviet messages (*The Times*, 13 July 1995).

[39] In Britain countering espionage took up less than a quarter of the Security Service's resources in 1994 (S. Rimington, Richard Dimbleby Lecture: *Security and Democracy* (London: BBC Educational Developments, 1994), p. 4).

[40] Countering subversion took up less than 5 per cent of the Security Service's resources in 1994 (Rimington, *Security and Democracy*, p. 6).

[41] Rimington, *Security and Democracy*, p. 7.

how much information work, how much economic work, how much commercial work I do, because this [job] has been a sort of wonderful mixture of all four.'[42] Intelligence has this same kaleidoscopic quality, in which the separate subjects merge and re-form into constantly changing patterns.

Nevertheless a *hypothetical* Western breakdown of resources in the first half of the 1990s between some of the subjects given here may convey something of what intelligence is 'about'. It is no more than an illustrative guesstimate; and it deals in resource inputs, not the volume or value of outputs. It might run roughly as follows:

- Normal defence intelligence including international arms trade and nuclear proliferation. 35%
- Defence intelligence surveillance of foreign conflicts and insurgency. 15%
- Intelligence on foreign states' internal politics, general foreign policies, internal economies and international economic policies. 10%
- Tactical support to diplomacy and other international negotiations of all kinds, including economic. 10%
- Intelligence on terrorism (spanning foreign and security intelligence). 20%
- Counterintelligence, counterespionage and residual security intelligence subjects; other miscellaneous subjects like narcotics and international crime. 10%

Chapter 19 speculates further on current needs.

Associated activities

For completeness the other intelligence-associated activities can be mentioned here. The most important of these is intelligence's assistance in preserving its own side's secrets as well as gathering those of others. Counterintelligence and counterespionage have already been mentioned, but intelligence's support for information defences goes further. The traditional official British formula of the 'intelligence and security agencies' reflects something of this dual offensive–defensive role. Defensive information security is discussed further in chapter 10.

There are other less deeply embedded roles. Intelligence's international connections can be used for back-channel diplomacy; as when Jim Callaghan, the British Prime Minister, asked the head of SIS to see

---

[42] Quotation from Sir Brian Fall, Ambassador to Russia and some of the new Republics in the former Soviet Union, in R. D. Edwards, *True Brits: Inside the Foreign Office* (London: BBC Books, 1994), p. 203.

that the Argentine government was aware of his covert deployment of naval forces to protect the Falklands in 1977.[43] Intelligence also works closely with deception. Military deception is an operational activity; strictly speaking it is not intelligence. But intelligence should be the expert on the foreign intelligence organizations to be deceived, and if it controls a double agent it provides the deception channel. Intelligence is also deeply connected with Electronic Warfare – the war of jamming, counter-jamming and spoofing, using the electromagnetic spectrum as a new dimension of warfare – though technically it is a separate military discipline.[44]

However the best known of intelligence's allied activities is 'covert action', or clandestine activities deniable by governments. Historically the British idea of Secret Service always included covert action alongside secret intelligence. At the 'soft' end of the covert action spectrum are 'agents of influence', covert political finance and media operations of all kinds, forgery and black propaganda; towards the 'hard' end are covert support for opposition groups, Resistance forces, insurgents and terrorists, and the active conduct of sabotage and other paramilitary operations. All governments need to do some things in peacetime that fall outside diplomatic and other official channels. Humint agencies with their secret skills and contacts tend to be the natural organizers, as in the successful Western operation with Pakistani military intelligence to supply military assistance to the Mujaheddin resistance to the Soviet occupation of Afghanistan.[45]

On the other hand covert action usually involves only a small part of the Humint agencies, not intelligence as a whole. It does not *have* to be done by intelligence. In the Second World War British covert action was under the separate Special Operations Executive, and covert propaganda under the Political Warfare Executive. In the mid-1980s the US Administration deliberately kept the Iran-Contra affair out of CIA to evade Congressional oversight. Some paramilitary operations such as the attempt to rescue the US embassy hostages from Iran come under straightforward military control.

Whether covert action is an inherent part of intelligence can be left as a matter of semantics. US writers have argued that collection, analysis, 'counterintelligence' (including defensive information protection, in a different sense from 'intelligence on foreign intelligence' as used here),

---

[43] For this episode (still not fully explained) see A. Danchev (ed.), *International Perspectives on the Falklands Conflict* (London: Macmillan, 1992), pp. 138–9; J. Callaghan, *Time and Chance* (London: Collins, 1987), p. 375.

[44] See chapter 7.

[45] See M. Yousaf and M. Adkin, *The Bear Trap* (London: Leo Cooper, 1992).

and covert action are intelligence's 'four major interrelated elements'.[46] All organizations pick up varied activities. But despite CIA's lurid reputation for covert action, only 3 per cent of its staff were connected with it in 1987, and it accounted then for only 5 per cent of the CIA budget; the total is now less.[47] This book concentrates on the essence of Western intelligence: providing information and forecasts on which others take action, not taking action itself – unlike the Soviet equivalent, in which covert action was intrinsic.

Summary

The Western intelligence system is two things. It is partly the collection of information by special *means*; and partly the subsequent study of particular *subjects*, using all available information from all sources. The two activities form a sequential process. In practice the link between them is not always complete; some single-source output by-passes the subsequent all-source stage and goes direct to users. The significance of this direct service varies between users and subjects. But the essence of the modern system is that it embraces the two related activities of single-source collection and all-source analysis.

Intelligence for doing these things is a sizeable though not massive activity, definable (with some fuzzy edges) by national intelligence budgets. Collection – including processing and single-source analysis – is by far the biggest element; and within it Sigint and imagery are bigger than Humint.

In terms of subjects (and organization) there is a distinction between foreign and security intelligence, though the two overlap. Geographically the most striking feature of Western intelligence in the Cold War was the predominance of the Soviet target; presumably there is now a more even geographic spread, though the growth of non-state and multi-area targets complicates these descriptions. In terms of subjects the principal current

[46] R. Godson (ed.), 'Introduction', *Intelligence Requirements for the 1990s* (Lexington, Mass.: Lexington Books, 1989), p. 4. For papers on covert action see R. Godson (ed.), *Intelligence Requirements for the 1980s: Covert Action* (Washington D.C.: National Strategy Information Center, 1981). For further discussion of counterintelligence and information security see chapter 10. There is considerable discussion of the definition of counterintelligence and its relationship with security in articles in R. Godson (ed.), *Intelligence Requirements for the 1980s: Counterintelligence* (Washington D.C.: National Strategy Information Center, 1980), and the counterintelligence section of Godson, *Intelligence Requirements for the 1990s*, pp. 127–63. Most writers accept some distinction between the two, as does Godson in his introductions to the two volumes.

[47] R. M. Gates, 'The CIA and Foreign Policy', *Foreign Affairs* vol. 66 no. 2 (winter 1987), p. 216. Said by 1995 to absorb only 2 per cent of CIA resources (Hedley, *Checklist for the Future of Intelligence*, p. 5).

features are probably the continued size of defence-related intelligence; the importance of national and international terrorist threats; and the role of intelligence in direct support of diplomacy.

This chapter has introduced the system and its variety. The different components can now be looked at in more detail.

Part II

Components and boundaries

4   Collection sources

Human intelligence (Humint)

Humint is intelligence obtained from people. The figures quoted in the last chapter showed that it is a relatively inexpensive part of collection; but it remains an important producer as well as the oldest. Collecting it resembles the journalist's skill in cultivating sources and persuading them to talk. Diplomacy has its confidential sources compatible with diplomatic status and practice, and one role of Humint agencies is simply to get information from people diplomats cannot meet.

In exercising this skill Humint has a pyramid of sources, with relatively non-sensitive, bread-and-butter ones at its base and increasingly sensitive ones towards the apex. The pyramid is illustrated in figure 7. At the base is organized information-gathering from travellers, experts and casual informants who have information to give about foreign targets – like the eighteenth-century British merchant captains whose debriefings on what they had seen in French and Spanish ports were mentioned in chapter 1. This straightforward Humint similarly gathers information from refugees and emigrants. Arguably the increased openness of the world reduces the need for collection of this kind; but not completely. Not everything can be seen from satellites, and certainly not things kept indoors.

Peacetime Humint of this kind is unspectacular but necessary, with the occasional high quality windfall. In the 1950s refugees brought valuable information about the Soviet missile programme. In the last few years defections from Iraq have brought important information on Saddam Hussein's nuclear programme.[1]

There is also a separate category of 'military Humint'. Forces in internal security operations and UN peacekeeping collect useful information from talking to the local population. Wartime deserters volunteer information on order of battle and morale, and prisoners-of-war talk

---

[1] For example, *The Times*, 23 August 1995.

despite prior warnings not to reveal more than name, rank and number; POW interrogation is a major wartime source. But these battlefield-related Humint sources are better regarded as part of military 'battlefield intelligence' (discussed below) than as parts of the peacetime Humint pyramid.

On the whole the unspectacular human sources contribute pieces of the intelligence jigsaw, rather than highlights. Exploiting them in the Cold War was an unglamorous job which fell mainly to military organizations by historical accident; the professional Humint organizations tended to concentrate on higher-level sources. Yet some capacity for peacetime interviewing at this basic level needs to be part of any self-sufficient national system, for example to get intelligence on Iraq or other secretive regimes.

Passively finding out what people know merges into more proactive collection. Casual contacts can be asked to seek out specific information. Even to maintain a contingency plan to evacuate one's nationals across a foreign beach in the event of civil war, someone has to find out beforehand if vehicles will sink into the sand, and the local guide-books are unlikely to help. It should be recalled that in the main British seaborne landings in Malaya in 1945 only 4,500 out of a planned 9,000 vehicles got across the beaches, largely through bad beach intelligence – and this was in an unopposed landing a month after the Japanese surrender.[2]

Ad hoc contacts of these kinds move towards the upper half of the Humint pyramid as they become standing relationships, for example with insiders in the international arms trade. Then there is the deliberate recruitment of new sources inside particular targets, but even these have different degrees of clandestinity. Some are 'unconscious' sources, thinking that they are providing information for journalistic or commercial use. Others are themselves at the shady end of the commercial information business, like those involved in Soviet programmes to acquire Western high technology. Others again use genuine business positions to supply information to their own governments, as in the way British businessmen in the Matrix-Churchill case provided details of Iraq's defence production. Patriotic espionage of this kind is practised by oppressed minorities and occupied populations. Examples were the intelligence work of the Resistance in Hitler's occupied Europe, their predecessors in occupied France in the First World War reporting on the passage of German troop trains, or the successful Soviet partisan networks of the Second World War.

---

[2] S. Woodburn Kirby with M. R. Roberts, G. T. Wards and N. L. Desoer, *The War Against Japan, Vol. V: The Surrender of Japan* (London: HMSO, 1969), p. 270.

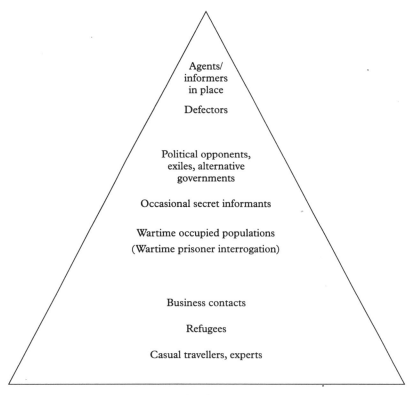

Figure 7 Humint's pyramid of source sensitivity, quantity and value

Higher still in the pyramid are the archetypal spies. The Cold War had its Soviet 'illegals', or trained intelligence officers operating permanently in the West under assumed identities to recruit and run agents. There were also the high-level defectors encouraged and helped in 'coming over' for the information they could provide or as a reward for previous services. At the very top are the agents in place, consciously spying against their own countries, and informers who provide information from within terrorist or other clandestine organizations.

The motives for deep espionage of these kinds are as varied as human nature. Communism after 1917 introduced ideological espionage, or reintroduced it with an intensity not seen since the Reformation, and the Cold War reinforced it on both sides. Towards the Cold War's end the USSR was the main loser, as disillusion with the regime widened; those like Gordievsky spied for the West through a desire to undermine the Soviet system. The Arab-Israeli conflict has produced similar effects, with nationalism, race, and religion playing the role of Cold War ideology. Most of the Americans caught spying against their country in the last twenty years have been motivated by money. Somewhere between money and ideology there are other motives: seeking foreign political support for a change of regime, or reinsuring against such a change; personal frustration or inadequacy; the thrill of 'beating the system'; the flattery of being made to feel someone; sexual attraction. The Cold War also had its blackmail and entrapment, with the spy irrevocably committed after taking the first step. Similar factors presumably apply to terrorists who act as informers. Yet in some parts of the world selling information to foreign governments may be part of the accepted mores.

Since the late nineteenth century Western societies have seen espionage against themselves as the most serious kind of treachery, though the association with treachery as 'adhering to the king's enemies' goes back further.[3] It is seen as a special betrayal of trust, arousing the sort of visceral fears reflected in Rebecca West's comment on William Joyce (executed in 1946 for treason, though not for espionage): 'He sinned that sin which travesties legitimate hatred because it is felt for kindred, as incest is the travesty of legitimate love.'[4] Sometimes the spy appears as an emotional casualty, as summed up in the British Security Commission's description of Geoffrey Prime – sentenced in 1982 to thirty-five years imprisonment for espionage from within the British Sigint organization – as 'an unhappy and unfulfilled man, a sexual and social misfit whose failures left him with a sense of inferiority and insecurity'.[5]

Whatever the motives, most modern spies seem unusual or unlucky people, but such generalizations are not very profitable. A retired US Humint officer concluded that potential spies are as plentiful as potential alcoholics, with the same variety of causes.[6] Whatever the reasons, the twentieth-century Humint agencies gave espionage a new intensity and a new character; like other intelligence collection it has become organized, professionalized, with its own expertise or 'tradecraft'. The world has

---

[3] 'Even prior to the 1351 [Treason] Act, betraying secrets to the king's enemies had been regarded as treason'; in an eighteenth-century case there was a judicial pronouncement that 'The sending or collecting of intelligence for the purpose of sending it to an enemy . . . or the hiring of a person for that purpose is an overt act [of adhering to the enemy].' (L. Lustgarten and I. Leigh, *In from the Cold: National Security and Parliamentary Democracy* (Oxford: Clarendon Press, 1994), p. 200.)

[4] R. West, *The Meaning of Treason* (London: Penguin, 1965), p. 13.

[5] *Report of the Security Commission*, Cmnd 8876 (London: HMSO, May 1983), paragraph 6.2.

[6] M. Copeland, *The Real Spy World* (London: Weidenfeld and Nicolson, 1974), p. 147.

disappeared of Edwardian officers doing some gentlemanly spying on furlough; as in the way one of the British officers imprisoned by the Germans in 1910 for spying on the Frisian coast is said to have measured depths of water off the beaches while sea-bathing at Sylt and Amrum.[7] The most valuable modern Humint asset is the long-serving agent in place, undramatically copying documents, and drawing a regular supplementary income as part of an apparently normal life. He or she may be an ideologue or patriot, or have begun as one; or may have been moved by the accidents and mixed motives that create other criminals.

Even at the top of its pyramid Humint has its distinct limitations compared with the technical sources. The identification and recruitment of potential agents takes a long time. Communications with their controllers are the most vulnerable point and have to be limited; their reporting is therefore slow, and usually excludes 'real time' intelligence. Agents' observations and recollections are subject to the usual human frailties; they are liable to go off the rails and their reliability cannot be counted on. The controller can never be completely sure that they are not fabricating or distorting reports or, worse, acting as double agents, providing deceptive material and penetrating the intelligence service they claim to be working for. Humint has a reputation with its users for unreliable information, and its agencies are always torn between source protection and revealing enough to establish its credibility.

Despite these limitations it still has special advantages. The most dangerous spies throughout the Cold War were West German secretaries supplying the East German intelligence service with secret documents; the most dangerous of an agent's weapons is uncontrolled access to a Xerox copier. Documents have a comprehensiveness greater even than satellite photographs or deciphered telegrams, and a highly placed agent can provide additional oral explanations and background. Humint agencies can try to recruit agents in secretive states where intelligence otherwise has no access. In the same way informers provide almost the only means of penetrating non-state terrorism; and security intelligence has always needed informers on subversive movements and other internal threats.[8]

Espionage can also help other collection activities. Human sources are sometimes needed to plant bugging devices. Cipher-breaking has often been assisted by obtaining copies of codes and cipher material through

---

[7] According to a note made by Erskine Childers on the trial, quoted in A. Boyle, *The Riddle of Erskine Childers* (London: Hutchinson, 1977), p. 162.
[8] For a discussion of various categories of informant see P. Gill, *Policing Politics: Security Intelligence and the Liberal Democratic State* (London: Cass, 1994), pp. 154–61.

human sources. Acquiring agents with this kind of cryptographic access was always one of the KGB's highest priorities; the Walker family compromised US naval ciphers over many years of the Cold War.[9]

Hence the Humint agencies tend to be a flexible all-purpose resource, in peace and war, with a 'can do' spirit that suits them for tackling secret overseas jobs that no one else can undertake. They are not limited to cultivating human sources. They may be the only people able to acquire foreign equipment or computer software, as in the Soviet targeting of Western technology or the West's Cold War acquisition of Soviet military equipment for examination. CIA's Humint role expanded early in the Cold War into its Directorate of Science and Technology and its important work in pioneering new forms of collection, from the U-2 programme and early imagery satellites to the attempts to recover a sunken Soviet submarine or the warheads of Soviet missiles test-fired into the Pacific.[10] In the Second World War the Polish agent networks even took on the unglamorous job of providing weather reports.[11] There are the roles already mentioned in alternative diplomacy and covert action.

When all these roles are added to the other parts of its pyramid it is not surprising that the Humint agencies have been a twentieth-century growth area, though on a smaller scale than those established purely for technical collection. Soviet and Warsaw Pact espionage gave the Soviet Union good windows onto most aspects of Western policy, although it is still not clear how effectively the information was used. Though the main Western response was in technical collection, it also had its major Humint successes. Israeli Humint has been a key element in its battle against terrorism, and the same applies to others' terrorist coverage. Even Canada, which does not conduct espionage overseas, uses informers for internal security purposes, and has a relatively overt organization for interviewing immigrants and travellers with useful knowledge.

Signals intelligence (Sigint)

Sigint has become the most prolific twentieth-century source. Some of it has continued to depend on physical access to communications, as in governments' ability to get access to foreign diplomatic telegrams from

[9] For an account see P. Earley, *Family of Spies: Inside the John Walker Spy Ring* (London: Bantam, 1989).

[10] J. T. Richelson, *The US Intelligence Community* (Cambridge, Mass.: Ballinger, 1985), pp. 189–90.

[11] M. R. D. Foot, *Resistance* (London: Granada, 1978), p. 27. For a discussion of agent reporting and technical sources see pp. 22–8.

the second half of the nineteenth century onwards. Some physical line-tapping of telegraph lines was practised during the American Civil War. An extension of tapping in the trench warfare of the First World War was intercepting the 'earth return' parts of the enemy's telephone circuits at distances of up to 300 yards.[12] In the 1950s the British and Americans tapped Soviet communications through the use of the Berlin 'tunnel' and a similar operation in Vienna.[13] Much later in the Cold War there were reports of US tapping of underwater cables off the Soviet coast.[14]

But the real impetus for modern Sigint came early in this century from the introduction of radio for naval, army and (later) air communications. Radio is electromagnetic radiation in 'free space'. Just how widely it radiates depends on its technical characteristics, but intrinsically it is a non-private means of communication. The First World War demonstrated how armies' and navies' use of radio provided their opponents with commensurate intelligence opportunities, joining the old craft of cryptanalysis with a new one of radio interception, aided initially on the Allied side by the luck of capturing German naval codebooks. Radio interception was the basis of the war's big Sigint successes. The German victory at Tannenberg owed a lot to the interception of Russian orders sent in plain language; and cipher-breaking was a major element in the British naval strategy of distant blockade of the German Fleet from Scapa Flow and Cromarty.

Sigint's importance increased even further in the Second World War with the much greater use of radio. It also saw the introduction of electronic 'non-communications' emissions, particularly radars and radio beacons. The Battle of the Atlantic was at times a cryptanalysts' war; cipher-breaking (by both sides, sometimes at the same time) was a major factor in determining whether U-boats found Allied convoys or were evaded by them. Professor Hinsley has argued that the Allied cryptanalytic successes shortened the war against Germany by three or four years.[15] Another historian concluded that 'in the Pacific as on the German fronts the end came years earlier, and many thousands of lives

[12] M. T. Thurbon, 'The Origins of Electronic Warfare', *RUSI Journal* vol. 122 no. 3 (September 1977), p. 57.

[13] For an account from the Soviet side see G. Blake, *No Other Choice* (London: Cape, 1990), pp. 20–5, 180–2.

[14] Described in R. Woodward, *Veil: the Secret Wars of the CIA 1981–1987* (London: Headline paperback, 1988), chapter 23, pp. 555–76.

[15] F. H. Hinsley, 'British Intelligence in the Second World War' in C. Andrew and J. Noakes (eds.), *Intelligence and International Relations 1900–45* (Exeter: University of Exeter Press, 1987), p. 218.

were saved, because of their [the cryptanalysts'] ability to read the enemy's signals.'[16]

After 1945 the Cold War combined with the technology of the electronic age to increase Sigint's importance still further. The Eastern and Western Blocs conducted continuous monitoring of each other's forces. The West's Sigint bases around the Soviet periphery were part of the Cold War's political geography; Sigint sites were similar components of the Soviet military presence in Eastern Europe and their bases in the Third World.[17] Close-range interception from ships and aircraft became part of the Cold War pattern. Sigint along with imagery led the super-powers to develop intelligence satellites.

An academic study of the Soviet effort in 1989 illustrates the potential scale and diversity of modern Sigint. It claimed that 'the Soviet Union maintains by far the largest Sigint establishment in the world.' This was said to be five times the size of the US establishment, with 'more than 500' ground stations at home and abroad. To these were added 'Sigint operations in diplomatic establishments in some 62 countries', 'some 63 dedicated Sigint ships' plus the use of others when opportune, 20 specifically designed or modified aircraft types and drones, several types of Sigint satellites, and 'various sorts of trucks and other vehicles for [clandestine] Sigint purposes'.[18] Some of this activity may have been as duplicative as much other Soviet intelligence. Nevertheless the description shows something of the modern scope, and corrects the impression that Soviet intelligence remained heavily Humint-oriented. Neither side has revealed its Cold War successes and failures, but it is clear that Western Sigint joined with satellite imagery in redressing the East–West imbalance in transparency with which the Cold War began.

Sigint's growth was not limited to this Cold War context, and few nations are now without a Sigint organization of some kind. Everywhere the multiplication of communications and other electronics has created equivalent opportunities for interception of all kinds, covering individuals, groups and business institutions as well as states. There has been an ever-increasing proliferation of military emissions of all kinds, and hence in their interception. Sigint supports and is bound up with

[16] R. Lewin, *The American Magic: Codes, Ciphers and the Defeat of Japan* (London: Penguin, 1983), p. 17.
[17] For Western intelligence bases see R. E. Harkavy, *Bases Abroad: The Global Foreign Military Presence* (Oxford: Stockholm International Peace Research Institute (SIPRI)/Oxford University Press, 1989), chapter 6, pp. 149–230.
[18] D. Ball, *Soviet Signals Intelligence (Sigint)* (Canberra: Strategic and Defence Studies Centre, Australian National University, 1989), p. 136.

Electronic Warfare, which has become a branch of military technology everywhere, with its equipment a significant item in international trade in military equipment.

More than any other part of the intelligence system, Sigint has been part of the computer and communications revolution; most of its stages are now linked to computers and electronic communications. Yet it is still quite manpower intensive, with a need for individual flair and craft co-existing with the skills needed for operating information production lines and computer-intensive research complexes. It provides the paradigm of the modern high-technology intelligence organization and its mixture of technology and human skills.

Sigint techniques

Sigint is conventionally sub-divided into communications intelligence (Comint), based on the interception of communications, and electronic intelligence (Elint) on non-communications emissions. At the heart of Comint is cipher-breaking, the contest between the cryptanalysts on one side and those who design ciphers and use them on the other. The inherent advantages of the defence are matched by its scope for human frailty and the greater intellectual challenge presented by the offence; states are always confident about the security of their own ciphers and find it hard to exclude laziness in their use. The only safe generalization over the centuries is that more ciphers have been broken than was ever thought likely in advance. Nowadays the cryptanalytic battle is a contest of applied computer power as well as the specialist skills of defence and attack.

The two World Wars showed the value of the relatively rich information concealed under high-grade ciphers. They also showed the cumulative value of the less revealing messages sent in lower-grade ciphers or in plain language. They also showed that even when cipher-breaking produces plain language it still has to be translated and interpreted. Diplomatic telegrams are drafted to minimize ambiguity and their meaning usually needs little exegesis after translation. On the other hand, armed forces' and other messages are in specialized language which needs interpretation, and the intelligence interest is often less in what is being conveyed to the legitimate recipient than in what can be inferred. Uninteresting military administrative messages are the classic leads for reconstituting order-of-battle. Intercepted conversations on any subject are even more allusive and full of half-stated meanings. The intercepted material of all kinds is often only a random sample of the complete exchanges. For reasons of these kinds most of it needs a significant element of interpretation; good intelligence is never handed out on a plate.

Nevertheless message texts and translated conversations are a window, however opaque, on to the minds of their originators and recipients. Comint based on them has a special depth, 'hardness' and credibility. Sometimes, as in the Second World War, it also has immediacy, the ability to read messages almost as quickly as the legitimate recipients. These are characteristics of this material at its best.

There are also various *non-textual* techniques and outputs. One is 'traffic analysis', based on reconstructing the layout of communications networks and identifying their stations. Identification is usually by understanding their systems of secret radio identification callsigns and other external transmission features, without necessarily being able to break any messages. The reconstruction of network structure shows organization and order-of-battle, as when the analysis of German Air Force radio callsign allocations resolved major British debates in late 1940 and early 1941 about German aircraft strengths, by showing that the fighting establishment of a Staffel was nine and not twelve aircraft as had previously been believed.[19] The behaviour of these networks on the air – for example the passing of unusually heavy or light volumes of traffic – provides pointers to activities and intentions. Radio discipline attempts to restrict all these external features but operational necessity and human frailty show through, here as elsewhere. A Soviet military textbook of 1977 listed typical operators' errors as follows:

Operating the radios at high power, tuning the emitting antenna for transmissions [sic], prolonged tuning of the transmitter, excessive service talk, unnecessarily repeated calls, failure to switch off radio transmitter high voltage after completion of calls, failure to change callsigns simultaneously on all radios, and the presence of individual 'signatures' and 'recognition signs' of particular radio operators.[20]

Another non-textual contribution is the location of Comint and Elint targets when transmitting, by cross-bearings from groups of direction-finding (DF) stations. Traffic analysis and DF work closely together; if a radio network can be identified by one and located by the other, units and formations can be placed on a map. Naval warfare has been profoundly influenced by the ability to locate ships if they transmit, and

[19] F. H. Hinsley with E. E. Thomas, C. F. G. Ransom and R. C. Knight, *British Intelligence in the Second World War* vol. I, pp. 299–302.
[20] D. A. Ivanov, V. P. Savel'yev and P. V. Shemanskij, *Fundamentals of Command and Control* (Moscow, 1977, US Air Force translation), p. 269.

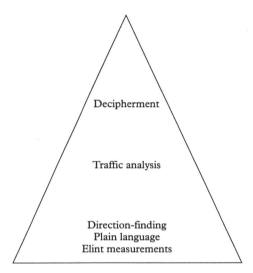

Figure 8 Sigint's pyramid of source sensitivity, quantity and value

the consequent dilemmas about whether to break radio silence to convey reports and instructions while at sea.

A further contribution is the measurement of signal parameters, particularly of Elint emissions. Deductions can then be made from these measurements about the equipment emitting the signals, for example the characteristics of a target radar system. Electronic Warfare depends largely on the ability to use these measurements to distinguish hostile from friendly emissions and take appropriate action.[21]

These non-textual techniques can establish targets' locations, order-of-battle and movement. Even when messages are not being deciphered, traffic analysis of the target's C³I system and its patterns of behaviour provides indications of his intentions and states of mind, in rather the same way as a neurologist develops insights about a silent patient by studying EEG traces from the brain. Textual and non-textual Sigint can be fused together, each adding to the other; though the textual sources can provide a depth of knowledge not available from the other.

Thus Sigint has its own hierarchy of sources, illustrated in figure 8. The breaking of high-grade ciphers such as the German Enigma ranks at the top, rather like a high-grade Humint agent. Below that there are

---

[21] For the general theme of electronic intelligence and its use in countermeasures see T. Devereux, *Messenger Gods of Battle. Radio, Radar, Sonar: the Story of Electronics in War* (London: Brassey's, 1991).

techniques of intermediate value; and at the bottom there are bread-and-butter operations like the routine monitoring of foreign radars and the scanning of plain language. The diversity and interaction of its techniques and its potential for immediacy give it its position as the biggest modern intelligence investment. But all Sigint derived from radio depends on the target going on the air; the enemy denies intelligence from his radar if he accepts the penalty of switching it off. And for every offensive Sigint technique there are counters to block it. Sigint is one of the purest contests between intelligence attack and security defence.

Imagery

Observation is an integral part of military and naval operations. Men have always watched for signs of the enemy on land or the departure of his ships from port, climbing hills or ships' masts to gain height. Balloons were first used in the wars of the 1790s, and again in the American Civil War, the Siege of Paris in 1870, and the Boer War.[22] Similarly some record of observations has always been needed, and sketching became part of military professionalism. Photography came to complement it in the nineteenth century, and was used experimentally in balloons from the American Civil War onwards.[23] But modern imagery is derived from the conjunction of cameras with the use of aeroplanes for reconnaissance early in the First World War. Aerial photography became a major element of intelligence in that war of trenches, artillery bombardments and the deployment of divisions and munitions for the next Big Push.

The range of aircraft in the Second World War added strategic coverage over the enemy's homeland. Though it has received less attention than the cipher-breaking successes, the Western Allies' imagery from reconnaissance aircraft in the second half of the war was an important part of their intelligence superiority. It was built around central machinery for priorities and planning, and a specialist inter-service and inter-Allied organization for photographic interpretation. By the end of the war the Allied Central Interpretation Unit had a daily intake of 25,000 negatives, and totals of 5 million negatives and 40,000 detailed interpretation reports in its library, all in those pre-computer

---

[22] P. Mead, *The Eye in the Sky: History of Air Observation and Reconnaissance for the Army 1785–1945* (London: HMSO, 1983), chapters 3, 4.

[23] S. S. Beitler, 'Imagery Intelligence' in G. W. Hopple and B. W. Watson (eds.), *The Military Intelligence Community* (Boulder: Westview, 1986), p. 76; quoting G. B. Infield, *Unarmed and Unafraid* (New York: Macmillan, 1970), pp. 19, 31 for use in the Civil War.

days indexed and retrievable by hand methods.[24] Airborne reconnaissance and imagery interpretation emerged from the two wars as distinctive skills, comparable with those of Sigint operators and analysts or Humint agent-runners and interrogators.

Since 1945 imagery has expanded to become as important as Sigint in its contribution to defence intelligence, although it is less important elsewhere. As with the other sources, part of peacetime imagery consists of routine collection, in this case mainly from aircraft. Typical ingredients are shots of ships and aircraft in international waters and airspace, along with snapshots taken by military attachés, military missions and travellers, all taken with varying degrees of openness and clandestinity. 'Border' photography by high-flying aircraft, seeing into a target's territory without penetrating into his airspace, was a Cold War routine, sometimes combined with Sigint collection. Imagery from aircraft supplemented by drones is now the main means of wartime battlefield surveillance, targeting and bomb damage assessment, and recently has been of special importance in the surveillance of Iraq and Bosnia.

There is also some imagery interpretation based on non-intelligence collection. Media photography and foreign television broadcasts have the potential to provide material for specialist imagery examination, in the same way as foreign newspapers and sound broadcasts are studied. Improvements in the resolution of commercially-available satellite imagery has added another dimension to these public sources, though governments may still seek to exercise control over this commercially available *glasnost*.[25]

But the main impact of peacetime imagery since 1945 has been in the special applications devised for the Cold War. The first of these was clandestine overflying of target territory. Some flights of this kind over Germany were undertaken by both the British and the French in the 1930s, before the time of radar detection. In the first ten years of the Cold War military aircraft were used for occasional clandestine flights over the Soviet Union. The USA then used the specially developed, high-flying U-2 aircraft for these missions from 1956 until one was shot down in May 1960 in well-publicized circumstances. These overflights then ceased, though the U-2s continued to be used elsewhere, including Taiwanese flights over China. The most spectacular U-2 success was the

---

[24] *History of JARIC*, p. 7. (Privately published; available in Intelligence Corps Museum, Ashford, Kent.)

[25] For the suppression of commercial satellite material after the invasion of Kuwait see *Trust and Verify* (Bulletin of the Verification Technology Information Centre (VERTIC), London), no. 13 (August/September 1990).

928 photographs taken in six minutes on 14 October 1962 which revealed the presence of Soviet missiles in Cuba.[26]

Specialist high-flying aircraft of this kind have been a US speciality. Other nations mount their clandestine overflights where the stakes are high enough, but the political constraints on peacetime violations of international law are usually compelling. Hence the importance of the second special means of imagery collection: the US and Russian photographic satellites which appeared in low earth orbit (roughly 200–1000 km in height) from the early 1960s onwards, thereby filling a major Cold War gap. Large swathes of the adversary's territory could be seen regularly and reliably, instead of being pictured through the more limited results of occasional U-2 operations. It is difficult to exaggerate the practical and psychological effects of this transparency. As President Johnson said in 1967, 'Before we had the photography our guesses were way off. We were doing things we didn't need to do. Because of the satellites I know how many missiles the enemy has.'[27] In the 1960s the assessment of current Soviet capabilities in large, observable objects became accurate and confident for the first time.

This satellite imagery gradually achieved tacit acceptance, though the US programmes were kept highly secret to avoid provoking the USSR.[28] Soviet claims that it was a form of espionage were abandoned after they acquired their own systems, and the Outer Space Treaty of 1967 confirmed that the heights used by satellites were above national airspace.[29] As will be discussed in chapter 9, their use acquired some protection through the superpowers' arms control agreements of the 1970s and their tacit agreement not to proceed with operational anti-satellite (ASAT) systems.[30]

Satellite characteristics

Apart from their freedom from peacetime political limitations on aircraft flights over foreign territory, satellites have obvious technical advantages

---

[26] Beitler, 'Imagery Intelligence', p. 78.   [27] Beitler, 'Imagery Intelligence', p. 79.

[28] G. M. Steinberg, *Satellite Reconnaissance: the Role of Informal Bargaining* (Westport: Praeger, 1983), pp. 47–59; J. L. Gaddis, *The Long Peace: Inquiries into the History of the Cold War* (Oxford: Oxford University Press, 1987), pp. 201–2. For a convenient history and description of American intelligence satellites see J. Richelson, 'US Space Reconnaissance after the Cold War' in D. Ball and H. Wilson (eds.), *Australia and Space* (Canberra: Australian National University, 1992).

[29] The first of the Soviet Cosmos series was launched in March 1962. For the reversal of the Soviet position in August 1963 during the negotiations which led eventually to the 1967 Outer Space Treaty, see Steinberg, *Satellite Reconnaissance*, pp. 62–4; also Gaddis, *The Long Peace*, pp. 203–5.

[30] Gaddis, *The Long Peace*, pp. 209–12; Steinberg, *Satellite Reconnaissance*, chapters 4–6.

to offset their great cost. Aircraft need to return to base, and have the risks of survivability in war. Satellites' height, speed and endurance give them the advantages of a super-aircraft. Their orbital geometry can be optimized in conjunction with the earth's rotation for many different purposes, including high or low resolution images, frequent passes over the same areas, or worldwide coverage. Successive passes can provide any desired combinations of vertical and oblique shots. Whatever the permutations adopted, the common factor is far wider areas of coverage than from an aircraft mission.[31]

The emergence of satellites has been accompanied by technical advances in photography itself. One is the dramatic improvement of resolution; whatever the truth of stories about car number plates being discernible in satellite imagery, satellite photographs can now record quite fine detail. Other advances have reduced the limitations imposed in the first twenty-five years of the satellite programmes by darkness and cloud cover, particularly over areas like Central and Eastern Europe in winter. Infra-red photography now has an ability to penetrate haze and darkness, recording contrasts in reflected heat rather than in reflected light. In daylight, specialized colour film can detect 'cut' vegetation used for camouflage. Potentially the most important advance has been 'radar imagery', in which active radar systems provide pictures for subsequent analysis, independent of normal visibility. Radar echoes of ships at sea or military hardware on land are recorded and analysed rather like pictures in the visible light spectrum, marking the beginning of true all-weather coverage.

Technical improvements have also transformed timeliness. Intelligence from the early satellites was delayed since photographic film had to be ejected periodically and returned to earth, or retained in the satellites until they were de-orbited at the end of their missions. Digitized pictures can now be beamed to ground stations, directly or via satellite-to-satellite relay, almost at the time they are taken, in effect as a form of television relay. Moreover improvements in communications enable pictures to be relayed direct to operational commanders. Whatever criticisms were made in the post-mortems, the Gulf War of early 1991 demonstrated all the power of US imagery, with platforms ranging from satellites to aircraft and battlefield drones, images across the whole spectrum of passive and active photography, and a distribution and analysis system which linked all levels from the national leadership to fighting units; 'imagery was the intel of choice in

---

[31] For a short explanation of the choices of imagery orbit see B. Jasani, *Exploiting Space for Conventional Defence and Security* (London: RUSI, 1990), appendix A.

this war.'[32] Satellite like any other imagery also has a special credibility with decision-takers; photographs were used in early August 1990 to convince Saudi Arabian rulers on the Iraqi threat after the Kuwait invasion, just as U-2 photography was used to brief European leaders at the beginning of the Cuba crisis in 1962.

Imagery's value

Despite all this power, satellites' output has the intrinsic limitations of any imagery. Photo-interpretation is still largely a human skill based around 'five S's': size, shape, shadow, shade and surrounding objects.[33] Human flair remains as important as in any other intelligence skill, even though it is now greatly assisted by computer programmes for image enhancement and measurement and preliminary target recognition. It is less instantaneous than some kinds of Sigint exploitation; hence the complaints after the Gulf War about delays in battle damage assessment during the bombing campaign.[34]

Another limitation is that imagery obviously can only see what is there to be seen, not what is concealed or does not yet exist. It cannot see what is in a hangar or in the designer's mind, though it may be able to detect clues. In the Cold War it was a marvellous tool for detecting large unconcealed objects like Soviet ICBM silos, but could not forecast future programmes; it did not prevent the US error in the 1960s in underestimating the rate of the Soviet missile build-up. Where military equipment gets smaller and more concealable and technical interest shifts to the internal details of 'smart' weapons, the relative value of external observation declines. It is of only marginal value in low-intensity operations like those of the IRA on the Northern Ireland border or terrorists in South Lebanon.

A third limiting factor is that imagery consists (literally) of snapshots or series of them. Continuous surveillance may be possible in some circumstances, for example from battlefield drones equipped with television relays, but most imagery interpretation is built around individual aircraft sorties or satellite passes. 'Stationary' satellites in geostationary orbits are too high to take photographs; imagery needs 'low'

---

[32] Report of the Oversight and Investigations Subcommittee, Committee on Armed Services, House of Representatives, *Intelligence Successes and Failures in Operations Desert Shield/Storm* (Washington D.C.: US GPO, 1993), p. 15.

[33] Beitler, 'Imagery Intelligence', p. 83.

[34] Sir Peter de la Billière, *Storm Command: a Personal Account of the Gulf War* (London: HarperCollins, 1993), p. 278.

satellites in orbits. Monitoring of change in a particular target therefore depends on the revisit rate. For satellites in photographic orbits there is a trade-off between covering large areas and revisiting the same ones, but the best practicable revisit rate in daylight for a single satellite is said to be about once a day.[35]

In war, or other situations in which aircraft can be used over the target territory, satellite and conventional imagery are complementary. High-flying drones (at heights up to about twenty-five km) may eventually be able to provide extended peacetime coverage of areas visible from international airspace and loiter to survey them, unlike a satellite on its fixed passes. But the power of satellite imagery lies not only in the scope of its observation but also in its unique ability to survey foreign territory unchallenged in peacetime. Against this has to be set its cost, which has made it up to now an effective US–Soviet (now US–Russian) monopoly, though China may have had some limited capability, and France acquired it in 1995; an Israeli satellite launched in the same year may also have had an intelligence role.[36] It is characteristic of intelligence's big league. Britain has hung on to it through the American relationship and the material it provides.

Finally there are also some resemblances between the satellites' significance for imagery and for Sigint collection. Imagery's cameras have to be able to see their targets; similarly the reception of some (not all) radio and other electronic emissions depends on having an (approximately) straight 'line of sight' path from the transmitter to the interception site, not shielded by the curvature of the earth. Height enlarges imagery's areas of coverage, and in the same way helps these kinds of Sigint collection. The specialist U-2 aircraft built for imagery were also equipped with receivers for Comint and Elint emissions within the USSR that could not be intercepted by normal operations on its borders.[37] Specialist Sigint satellites were developed by the USA and USSR along with the imagery ones: satellites gave both imagery and Sigint the ability to 'see' targets – literally for imagery, metaphorically for Sigint – to which there was no other access. Imagery required low orbits; while for Sigint a much wider range of heights has been needed, ranging from relatively low orbits not far from the heights used for imagery to high,

---

[35] Jasani, *Exploiting Space for Conventional Defence and Security*, appendix A, p. 45.

[36] The French Helios intelligence satellite was launched in July 1995 (*The Times*, 8 July 1995). An Israeli vehicle (OFEK 3) was launched in April of the same year; it was to pass over Syria, Iraq and Iran every 90 minutes (*The Guardian*, 6 April 1995).

[37] A. Price, *The History of US Electronic Warfare Vol. II: The Renaissance Years* (Alexandra, Va.: The Association of Old Crows, 1989), pp. 158–60.

geo-stationary ones similar to those used for communications and TV relay.[38]

Satellites for both imagery and Sigint represented a quantum jump in intelligence capability, probably the biggest since the introduction of radio interception in the First World War. In the Cold War the revolution they produced was somewhat greater in imagery than in Sigint. Imagery of the USSR after the U-2 shoot-down needed satellites; on the other hand a proportion of Sigint's Comint tasks were interceptable at longer ranges and indeed unsuitable for satellites, though satellite interception became by far the most powerful source on the radar-like Elint targets. Powers without satellites could still retain some status in Sigint, but in imagery the US's satellite monopoly produced a special Western dependence on it.

In aggregate the overall effects of satellites represent something like the Dreadnought revolution in Edwardian navies, and raise big questions of intelligence strategy for those without them. Should nations seek a stake in satellite collection; and, if so, through dependence, cooperative alliances, regional or international endeavours, areas of national niche-manship, or self-sufficiency? For those contemplating having their own satellites, where do the priorities lie between imagery and the various kinds of electronic collection? Only a superpower can have all these systems. Whatever other efforts are mounted nationally or in collaboration, satellites for the foreseeable future will emphasize the United States' unique intelligence status and others' reliance on it.

Other smaller sources

Other smaller technical sources bear on military targets. Nucint is the specialized world of nuclear intelligence, in which satellites are deployed to detect above-ground nuclear explosions, seismology records underground ones, air sampling monitors radioactive material in the atmosphere, and gamma rays reveal the presence of nuclear material at close range. Radint comes from conventional long-range radars, including those developed for space tracking, plus special over-the-horizon (OTHR) varieties; it was developed mainly as a by-product of those radars' Cold War role of providing operational early warning on missile and aircraft attacks. Acoustint is underwater sonic collection.

---

[38] 'High' satellites are also used for the infra-red detection of missile launches, as for Scud launches during the Gulf War. Though often classified among intelligence assets, they are really operational warning systems, like Early Warning radar (though on different principles). For the distinction between these and 'intelligence' sources see discussion in chapter 7.

Like Radint, this is a product of operational sensors, but it developed in the Cold War into large-scale Western and Soviet systems for underwater location and fingerprinting, with large fixed arrays, special shipborne listening operations, and the constant tracking of submerged submarines. Though the techniques and results are very different, it is an underwater equivalent of Sigint. Some acoustic intelligence also exists above water, as part of a growing area of 'remote sensing' of military forces by unattended devices that detect sound, vibration and smell. The defensive counterpart of Radint, Acoustint and these other detection techniques is the development of military equipment's 'signature reduction' and 'stealth'. Various other 'Int' acronyms have been coined by the USA to cover other specialized sources.[39]

There are other, non-technical ones. One is the old art of opening letters, in various guises. In both World Wars censorship organizations served intelligence as well as preventive information control. Mail censorship was closely related to telegram censorship and the Sigint it produced, for example on the German economy.[40] Periodic accusations were made in the Cold War about the covert opening of diplomatic bags. There were other unconventional Cold War operations such as cable-tapping.

Apart from these smaller regular sources and other opportunistic ones, there are two other bigger sources, less covert in nature. One is security intelligence's surveillance and observation of people, cars, buildings and so on; in effect, normal police surveillance at a more sophisticated level and applied to intelligence targets. Typical examples are the visual surveillance of diplomatic premises, the tailing of foreign intelligence officers and suspect agents, and similar observation in counter-terrorist situations and counter-insurgency campaigns. Visual surveillance complements security intelligence's phone-tapping, mail-opening, informers and other sources.

The second is the range of military intelligence's battlefield-type sources, mainly from wartime contact with the enemy but with some

---

[39] These include Masint ('scientific and technical information obtained by quantitative and qualitative analysis': a generic term covering most technical collection other than Sigint and imagery); Photint or 'classified and interpreted photographic material'; Rint or 'unintentional electromagnetic energy'; Fisint (foreign instrumentation signals intelligence, a category of Sigint); and Telint (telemetry interception and analysis, part of Fisint) (F. Reese Brown, 'Behind the Drums and Bugles', *International Journal of Intelligence and Counterintelligence* vol. 6 no. 3 (fall 1993), p. 394).

[40] For Second World War details see Hinsley, *British Intelligence in the Second World War* vol. I, p. 224, for economic intelligence; for counterespionage see F. H. Hinsley and C. A. G. Simkins, *British Intelligence in the Second World War. Vol. IV: Security and Counter-Intelligence* (London: HMSO, 1990), pp. 185–6.

peacetime applications. The main sources are POW interrogation and the study of captured equipment and captured documents. POW interrogation at both the 'quick' tactical and 'deep' strategic levels is a major wartime source, but had its peacetime parallels in post-Second World War military responsibilities for the interrogation of refugees and escapees overseas. Similarly the examination of captured foreign equipment is a wartime routine with unexpected applications; collecting serial numbers from equipment on Middle East battlefields in the Second World War was surprisingly useful for working out enemy production rates. Its Cold War parallels were in the covert acquisition of foreign technology and equipment.[41] The wartime collection of foreign documents on the battlefields also had its Cold War equivalent, in the acquisition of targets' military handbooks and documents.[42] Military intelligence also uses specialized surveillance and observation, as demonstrated in the work of special forces in the Falklands and Gulf campaigns and in Northern Ireland. In the Cold War there was some routine visual observation of foreign forces, for example around Berlin.

Some of this military collection merges into intelligence 'collection' in a different sense: gathering wartime information which is available but still needs some specialist intelligence arrangements to acquire and organize it. An important part of wartime air intelligence is the routine debriefing of aircrews after their missions; indeed organizing an effective flow of front line information from contact with the enemy is one of military intelligence's basic responsibilities. Even modern battlefield intelligence sometimes exploits purely open sources, sometimes unexpected ones; in planning its offensive in the Gulf War, Centcom (US Central Command) needed information on the trafficability of sands in the wastelands of Southern Iraq for tank attacks, and found some of it in archaeologists' diaries written early this century.[43]

This organized collection of easily available material can be a function of specialized civilian as well as military units. Foreign newspapers and books need to be acquired and translated in peace and war; the Victorian

---

[41] For US 'material exploitation and recovery operations' see Richelson, *The US Intelligence Community*, pp. 187–90.

[42] For the value of captured documents (and the interaction of military battlefield sources, tactical Sigint, and imagery) see Sir David Hunt's masterly review (of H.-O. Behrent, *Rommel's Intelligence in the Desert Campaign*) in *Intelligence and National Security* vol. 2 no. 2 (April 1987): 'Documents captured in action are of very great value. They are authentic, and often immediate. Those which contain distribution lists help enormously in establishing the enemy's order of battle. A captured code-list is a boom to the Sigint sections. Prisoners are the bread and butter of order of battle intelligence' (p. 381).

[43] House of Representatives, *Intelligence Successes and Failures in Operations Desert Shield/Storm*, p. 12.

intelligence departments' earliest 'collection' was the provision of funds for this purpose.[44] An indication of the scale of press collection in the Second World War is given by the size of the British enemy press reading unit in Stockholm, with a staff rising to sixty.[45] In the United States the peacetime monitoring of foreign public broadcasts operates under CIA; the British BBC Monitoring Service which does the same work is not under intelligence control but does have official funding. Sources of these kinds require some specialized collection, even though they are overt rather than covert.

Summary

Intelligence collection is gathering information without targets' cooperation or knowledge. Usually it is by special, covert means designed to penetrate targets' organized secrecy. But it includes some less covert means, particularly for wartime battlefield collection. The complete picture of intelligence collection is:

• Sigint, imagery (dominated in peacetime by satellite sources) and Humint.
• Smaller technical sources such as Nucint, Radint and Acoustint.
• Surveillance for internal security purposes.
• Wartime battlefield-type sources (POWs, captured material and documents, specialized observation), with some peacetime applications.
• Specialized arrangements for acquiring non-intelligence information and material, including information from operational contact with the enemy in war (though these are often a responsibility of all-source and not collection agencies).

Sigint, imagery and Humint are the main sources, account for the main part of intelligence expenditure and give collection its principal characteristics. These can be outlined in the next chapter.

---

[44] See for example B. Parritt, *The Intelligencers* (Ashford, Kent: Intelligence Corps Association, 2nd edition 1983), p. 97, for an 1870 War Office recommendation that 'A sum of money, say £250, should be inserted in the Estimates each year for the purchase of foreign newspapers, books, etc.'

[45] C. G. McKay, *From Information to Intrigue: Studies in Secret Service Based on the Swedish Experience 1939–45* (London: Cass, 1993), pp. 101–6. For the conclusion that some three-fifths of the economic intelligence obtained on Germany and German-occupied Europe in the Second World War came from press and similar sources see F. H. Hinsley with E. E. Thomas, C. F. G. Ransom and R. G. Knight, *British Intelligence in the Second World War*, vol. II (London: HMSO, 1979–89), p. 130 (note)

5   Collection characteristics

Observations and messages

In the collection just described there are some regular associations between sources and subjects. Imagery's output is mainly defence intelligence, including arms production and details of road and rail communications and the rest of the military infrastructure. Sigint produces something on almost everything, though during the Cold War its main output in bulk was on day-to-day Soviet military activities. Humint agencies produce less military material and more on political and economic matters, plus special contributions on other states' clandestine activities and on terrorism. The smaller technical sources are all defence-related, as are those associated with the battlefield. Peacetime surveillance and observation are characteristic of security intelligence.

These associations illustrate a distinction between two basic kinds of collection. One produces evidence in the form of observations and measurements of *things*. The other produces access to human thought-processes, or *meaning*. The distinction resembles the difference between the evidence used in archaeology and conventional historiography. Archaeology deals in artefacts and physical traces, while historians base themselves on documents and other human recollections. Both kinds of evidence contribute to historical truth, but with answers to different kinds of question. Inferences from archaeological observation and measurement are not the same as from documents or oral records.[1]

Thus imagery produces the kind of evidence used by archaeologists (who indeed now use aerial photography); while Humint and Sigint have the ability to produce texts not unlike those used by historians. The first

---

[1] The analogy with archaeology and historiography was developed from R. G. Collingwood, *An Autobiography* (London: Oxford University Press, 1939) and subsequent writing about historiography. I am grateful to Jamie Bell for drawing my attention to discussion on this theme in J. Chadwick, 'The Use of Mycenaean Documents as Historical Evidence' in *Colloquium Mycenaeum: Actes du Sixième Colloque International sur les Textes Mycéniens et Egéens à Chaumont sur Neuchâtel, 7–13 Septembre 1975* (University of Neuchâtel, 1975).

kind of collection and data can be called 'observational' intelligence. Much of it deals with hardware like military equipment; but it also observes people *en masse* as army units, or individuals as objects under surveillance. Sometimes in topographical intelligence it includes natural features, but most of it is concerned with human artefacts.

Observation leads to measurement and description, which occur not only in imagery and surveillance but also in other sources. Thus part of Sigint – not all of it – consists of measuring aspects of radio signals, for example to establish the technical characteristics of radars or to locate transmitters by DF. The same applies to Nucint, Radint, Acoustint and most of the other smaller categories. Collection of all these kinds is observation and measurement, as if from 'outside' the targets.

Intelligence on thought and meaning, on the other hand, comes from contact with targets' minds, however remotely. This comes from access to communication in some kind of understandable language, or sometimes numerical form, conveying information, thoughts and intentions.[2] There is no convenient word to describe collection with this kind of 'inside' access, but essentially it is based on targets' 'messages' of one kind or another, conveyed by the originators in spoken or written communications. Access to them is usually associated with Sigint, but is not confined to it. Humint sources provide copies of documents and report on conversations. War also provides opportunities for capturing documents, as in the *Automedon* case in 1940 in which the Germans were able to hand captured British Cabinet papers to the Japanese; their revelation of British weakness in South-East Asia is thought to have encouraged Japan to plan for war.[3] Collection outputs of all these kinds can be called 'message-like' intelligence.[4]

---

[2] Professor Susan Strange distinguishes between *modes* of communication ('by signs; by literate modes, using language and words; and by the numerate mode using numbers'); *means* of communication ('including speech, both face-to-face and at a distance as by telephone, and writing both by hand and by various kinds of machine beginning with printing presses and going on to typewriters and computers'); and *channels* of communication when this is not face-to-face ('whether by pony express or mail coach, by telegraphy cables, by radio transmission, or by geo-orbital satellite') (S. Strange, 'Finance, Information and Power', *Review of International Studies* vol. 16 no. 3 (July 1990)).

[3] For a short summary see A. Gordon, 'The Admiralty and Imperial Overstretch' in G. Till (ed.), *Seapower: Theory and Practice* (London: Cass, 1994), pp. 76–8. The influence on Japanese policy is discussed in L. Allen, *Singapore 1941–1942* (London: Cass, 1993 edition), pp. 3–4.

[4] A similar distinction between 'physical intelligence' and 'verbal intelligence' has been developed independently by David Kahn, for example in his 'Toward a Theory of Intelligence', *Military History Quarterly* vol. 7 no. 2 (winter 1995), pp. 92–7.

Observational and message-like mixtures

This distinction between observational and message-like material and collection needs qualification in several ways. First, although some sources uniquely provide one kind of evidence or the other, others provide mixtures of both. Imagery and surveillance produce observational evidence *par excellence*. The same applies to most of the smaller technical sources; underwater intelligence is 'observing' vessels from the noise they make,[5] and Nucint is about sets of measurements. But Humint can provide both kinds of evidence. Thus some espionage is clandestine observation, as in the French Resistance's observation of coastal defences before the 1944 invasion or the V-1 and V-2 sites being built in the same year; while other espionage obtains message-like evidence in the form of documents or agents' reports of overheard conversations. Documents found on the battlefield are another kind of message-like intelligence. POWs may reveal what they have *seen*, but also what they *know*, and like other human sources they may provide a mixture of the two.

Sigint in particular combines the two kinds of intelligence. The deciphered messages of the Second World War were prime examples of message-like intelligence, as are intercepted conversations. But locations from DF and deductions from signal parameters are observational intelligence. Traffic analysis is a mixture of both kinds. It is based mainly on observations about signal networks and analysis of their structures and behaviour; but it also uses the 'messages' conveying stations' identities provided by their encoded identification callsigns, if it is able to decode them.

Adaptability for inferences

A second qualification is that the primary difference between the two categories does not limit the secondary inferences that can be drawn from them. The enemy's intentions about an impending attack can be inferred from imagery's observations of his physical preparations for it. Similarly the nature of physical objects and activities can be inferred from oblique documentary references. Professor R. V. Jones recalls that part of the original evidence that German rocket development was located at Peenemünde was the ranking of the research establishment there near the top of the list of addressees for a routine instruction about petrol

---

[5] There are some underwater communications, but intercepting them is not a significant feature of underwater intelligence.

coupons.[6] Intelligence analysis spends its time making inferences and putting different sources together.

Nevertheless the distinction between observational and message-like material is a fruitful way of understanding why particular kinds of collection are more direct and less inferential on some subjects than others. Evidence of any kind involves some interpretation; nevertheless sources have characteristic ground on which they are 'harder' than others. The observational sources are relatively 'hard' on physical entities such as military hardware, but need more inference in discerning the target's intentions or otherwise reading its mind. The leap from observational sources' answers to 'what?' and 'when?' questions to solving 'how?' and 'why?' ones can be quite a long one. Message-like sources need interpretation but are nevertheless stronger than the observational ones on non-physical subjects such as organization, reasons, policies, plans, and intentions; all the intangibles that can only be expressed in language.

Thus the comment has been made about the archaeologist that, despite the inferences that he can draw on trade, industry and centres of government, he suffers from one major drawback if there are no written records: 'his people are dumb . . . The archaeologist then is in much the same position as the interpreter of aerial photographs: his information is hard fact, but its interpretation is often difficult and conjectural.'[7] Rather like expert archaeological excavation, US satellite imagery in the Cold War produced great transparency upon Soviet military hardware, but was relatively unilluminating about underlying Soviet motivations. These needed regular access to high-level message-like sources and a sustained effort to interpret them.[8] Access to what targets think and say has its special place in understanding the present and forecasting the future.

This explains some of the source–subject connections. Defence intelligence needs details about foreign military hardware, and benefits greatly from imagery on them. A photograph of a piece of equipment

---

[6] R. V. Jones, *Most Secret War: British Scientific Intelligence 1939–1945* (London: Hamish Hamilton, 1978), p. 348.

[7] Chadwick, 'The Use of Mycenaean Documents as Historical Evidence', p. 24. He draws parallels between archaeology and imagery; the interpretation of Homer's account of the Trojan war and uncorroborated agent reports; and the work of epigraphists on Mycenaean Linear B tablets and intelligence officers with decrypted military texts.

[8] Apart from questions of covert message-like sources, it has been argued that insufficient attention was paid to 'open' Soviet military literature in the Cold War; see M. E. Herman, 'Reflections on the Use of Soviet Military Literature', *RUSI Journal* vol. 133 no. 2 (summer 1988).

tends to be better evidence than references to it in communications. (Actually a purloined handbook might be even better, though in war there would always be a fear that it was not up to date, or 'planted' in order to deceive.) Diplomatic intelligence on the other hand is about other countries' perceptions and policies, all expressed as 'messages' of one kind or another. Moreover, varieties of evidence have varying credibility on different subjects. For the consumer, photographs are persuasive evidence about objects; documents or deciphered texts about intentions. Both classes of evidence need specialized interpretation, and even with it will not dispel uncertainty; but both have greater credibility when they seem to be direct than when they need more complex inferential chains.

Special message-like power

A third qualification is that the dichotomy between observational and message-like sources is not complete, since in the right circumstances the second can provide the best of both worlds. A target's C³I system contains not only its thinking, orders, policy and plans, but also the information flows on which these are based – flows which in the modern world are increasingly dense and explicit. Breaking into the opponent's military C³I gives access not only to his thinking but also to his locations, inventories and the other information *he* needs to transmit. Thus the most consistently useful items of British Sigint in the Second World War were the deciphered daily strength and logistic returns of German units; reports on enemy tank strengths and fuel stocks formed the basis of successful British Desert War generalship.[9] This applies even more to modern organizations with their computer-generated status reports. Good C³I access through documents and messages provides short cuts to the totals that would otherwise have to be worked out by counting from individual observations; as in the way the *Automedon* material provided the Japanese for the first time with an authoritative account of British dispositions in Singapore and Malaya.

This does not invalidate the complementarity of different sources. Message-like ones bring their own disadvantages; it is easier for the target to safeguard documents than to conceal physical objects, and the richness of his C³I content gives him a special incentive for protecting it. Armed forces in peacetime encipher communications even when they do not seek to conceal their activities from satellite observation. Message-

---

[9] R. Bennett, *Ultra and Mediterranean Strategy* (London: Hamish Hamilton, 1989), p. 46.

like sources also lend themselves to deceptions like forged documents, and the risk makes intelligence distrust them unless there is confirmatory observational evidence. (One of Sigint's strengths is that because it provides both kinds of evidence there is an analytical interplay between them.) Moreover the potential of 'messages' from the target's C³I applies only where the target is communicatively inclined. The instructions of secretive dictatorships carry little information or explanation. The risk of yielding message-like intelligence to enemies is precisely why clandestine organizations cut down on communication and contact.

So intelligence works in practice with what is can get, and has to be cautious about relying completely on any single source; as in the classic Second World War case in which excellent high-grade Sigint of the planned Axis attack on the First Army led to the American defeat at Kasserine, because Rommel changed his mind after his initial orders were issued and deciphered by the Allies.[10] Putting different sources together is part of most intelligence advances; the early conclusions about the German rocket programme in the Second World War came from fusing the diverse sources of reports from a Danish engineer, a 'bugged' conversation in a POW camp, an aerial photograph, other agent reports and some Sigint clues.[11] It is usually unwise to allocate particular targets to just one means of collection.

Nevertheless there are horses for courses. In particular, where high-class message-like material is available from Sigint or well-placed Humint, it can provide a high degree of insight, as well as good pointers to the future. The reports of Western agents like Penkovsky and Gordievsky cast more light on Soviet thinking than the voluminous mass of Western intelligence observations. One test of an intelligence system's contact with a target's mind is how much it needs to use language skills; one symptom of the Cold War was that quite large areas of Western all-source analysis could get by without feeling they needed to read Russian. Observational intelligence has its own equivalent skills: the professional experience of the photographic interpreter, the pattern-recognition abilities of the Sigint traffic analyst, and so on. But they do not penetrate targets so directly. Messages (in their widest sense) have a special value as a source, but precisely for this reason are more protected by secrecy. The mixture of observational and message-like attacks makes up one of collection's most pervasive characteristics.

[10] F. H. Hinsley with E. E. Thomas, C. F. G. Ransom and R. C. Knight, *British Intelligence in the Second World War* vol. II (London: HMSO, 1981), pp. 585–95.

[11] Jones, *Most Secret War*, pp. 332–48.

Fragility and secrecy

Modern collection is the descendant of ancient 'secret intelligence': something more covert than normal 'intelligence' or information. As Lord Dacre has put it

Secret intelligence is the continuation of open intelligence by other means. So long as governments conceal a part of their activities, other governments, if they wish to base their policy on full and correct information, must seek to penetrate the veil . . . [The end] is to complement the results of what, for convenience, may be called 'public' intelligence: that is, intelligence derived from the rational study of public or at least available sources.[12]

Intelligence collection seeks to penetrate what is denied to normal information gathering.

Secret intelligence of this sort has always been given special protection. Agents have always had their identities concealed. Cipher-breaking in its early years was regarded as a black art, part of the occult; and even in more rational centuries its product was handled with special care. Modern 'covert intelligence' inherits this long history of concealment.

There are three reasons for its modern secrecy. One is when intelligence is useful because the target does not know that it has been collected; secrecy is the basis of its value, or gives it added value. Thus advance knowledge of the enemy's plans may open up the possibility of a surprise ambush – but only if he does not know that you know, irrespective of *how* you know. The same applies where intelligence's value is in countering the enemy's surprise, as when intelligence enables a terrorist attack to be itself ambushed. In all these situations the secret is the fact that one knows, not how one knows.

But these are comparatively rare in peacetime. Usually there is no penalty, and even some advantage, in being known to know something; British diplomacy benefits from the general impression of being well informed. Even where items of intelligence need protection on account of their content, the need is usually a short-term one.

Thus most intelligence secrecy springs not from content but from the methods used to collect it. Hence a second reason for covert status in peacetime may be doubts over collection's legality and propriety. Foreign espionage usually violates its target's domestic law, as may bugging and computer hacking. Espionage has an undefined legal status in international law; Geoffrey Best's comment on its position in the laws of war,

---

[12] H. Trevor-Roper, *The Philby Affair – Espionage, Treason, and Secret Services* (London: Kimber, 1968), p. 66.

that 'the spy remains in his curious legal limbo; whether his work is honourable or dishonourable, none can tell', applies even more to peace.[13] But intelligence's use of diplomatic premises is dubious in international law; and so also may be intelligence attacks upon them.[14] There are also some questions about the legality of intercepting international commercial communications.[15] Intelligence operations are violations of international law if they intrude upon national territory, airspace and territorial waters in peacetime. Legal considerations apart, knowledge that they are conducting some kinds of collection is liable to affect governments' domestic or international images; domestic and foreign criticism may fuel each other.[16] Revelations can affect relations with particular governments; hence the secrecy originally given to US satellite imagery on President Kennedy's instructions, to avoid putting the Soviet Union in a position in which it might feel it had to protest.[17]

However the main reason for secrecy is the third one: collection's vulnerability to countermeasures, and the consequent need for source protection. States have the apparatus of governmental secrecy at their disposal to defeat foreign collection; terrorist groups have their own punishments for informers. Intelligence depends on how well or badly its targets apply defensive measures. If its successes are detected counter-

---

[13] G. Best, *War and Law Since 1945* (Oxford: Oxford University Press, 1994), p. 291.

[14] The Vienna Convention of 1961 quotes diplomacy's function of information gathering 'by all legal means' (Article 3) and provides for the 'inviolability' of diplomatic premises and communications. The premises themselves 'must not be used in any manner incompatible with the function of the mission as laid down in the present Convention or by other rules of general application' (Article 41). It has been pointed out that the Convention's list of diplomatic functions is not exclusive, and is prefaced by '*inter alia*'; but this is a fairly weak legalistic defence. For brief discussion see G. V. McClanahan, *Diplomatic Immunity: Principles, Practices, Problems* (London: Hurst, 1989), p. 162. Note that the 1963 Consular Convention lists collection 'by all lawful means' without this qualification.

[15] The International Telecommunications Convention of 1973 included the provision, taken from earlier ITU agreements, that 'Members agree to take all possible measures, compatible with the system of telecommunication used, with a view to ensuring the secrecy of international correspondence.' (Article 22.1.) There is however an escape clause (22.2) for the use of information for law enforcement and treaty observance. Armed forces' radio communications are of course excluded from these ITU provisions.

[16] Domestic criticism tends to concentrate on security intelligence and its effects on individual liberty, but may also take the view that states' international information-gathering should conform to liberal standards; thus all espionage 'is (apart from certain extreme cases) positively immoral'. (L. Lustgarten and I. Leigh, *In from the Cold: National Security and Parliamentary Democracy* (Oxford: Clarendon Press, 1994), p. 225.)

[17] J. L. Gaddis, 'The Evolution of a Reconnaissance Satellite Regime' in A. L. George and others (eds.), *US-Soviet Security Cooperation* (Oxford: Oxford University Press, 1988), p. 357.

measures can be taken. Spies can be eliminated; ciphers changed or more carefully used; improvements made to camouflage.

Hence collection's fragility. Most of intelligence's special secrecy is related to protecting 'sources and methods' (in the US terminology derived from the DCI's mandate in the 1947 National Security Act), rather than the value of the intelligence content. For the most part what is being protected at any particular time is the *future* supply of intelligence, not the information a particular source has already provided.

The fragility varies. Textual Sigint from cipher-breaking is specially vulnerable to countermeasures, and revelations of success in one place are liable to have results over much wider areas. Had the Germans realized that the Enigma cipher was being broken it could have been used more securely; and since it was being used by all the German services the revelation of success in one place could have had far more widespread results. Agents are even more immediately vulnerable; though sound tradecraft by their controllers should prevent the detection of one agent from revealing leads to others. Imagery can be defeated by camouflage and restricting appearances in the open; the USSR embarked on an extensive programme of this kind in response to US satellite surveillance. Nevertheless imagery is rather less vulnerable than these other sources; military forces cannot stay permanently under cover in barracks.

This lesser fragility of imagery applies even more to the smaller defence intelligence sources. The revelation of a successful POW interrogation will not cause POWs to dry up as a source. It might lead the wartime opponent to marginal improvements in his counter-interrogation training, but there are limitations on its effectiveness; the Gulf War showed how captured Western aircrew could be 'broken' by interrogation under torture, despite thorough anti-interrogation training.[18]

Moreover we saw in the previous chapter that each covert source has its own pyramid of fragility. In the Cold War Humint from interviewing refugees was far less fragile than reports from agents in place. Sigint has its relatively non-fragile elements; in particular Elint is less sensitive than Comint, since radar emissions cannot be enciphered in the same way as communications. Bread-and-butter imagery warrants far less secrecy than clandestine photography or the product of satellites.

In practice almost all intelligence collection merits (and gets) some protection, but special additional secrecy is given to the main sources. The actual degree of this protection usually reflects some combination of

---

[18] For a first-hand account of Iraqi methods against British aircrew, see J. Peters and J. Nichol, *Tornado Down* (London: Signet, 1993), chapters 14–20.

fragility and future value; on both grounds message-like sources tend to get higher protection than observational ones. Great protection is given to the identities of agents, but there is a recognition that they are liable to be lost in the end. In Sigint the legacy of the Second World War was to give textual Comint an exceptional degree of protection and to apply special procedures to many other lines of Comint output. Much the same secrecy has been applied to US satellite imagery, though with rather less cause. It is now being treated with rather less sensitivity, as has recently been demonstrated in the wholesale declassification of this imagery up to 1972.[19]

Secrecy and intelligence's value

Security procedures vary between sources but there are similar general effects. Collection agencies are high-security organizations with exceptional degrees of physical security protection, personnel vetting and the compartmentation of information on the 'need-to-know' principle (that information should only go to those who positively *have* to have it, not to those to whom it *might* be useful). Their output is subject to stringent controls over who can see it and whether its reports can be retained. Collection details are often omitted or disguised to prevent the identification of precise sources, and the content may be generalized for the same reason. There may be restrictions on taking action on particular kinds of intelligence; one of the Second World War rules for protecting the Ultra source was to prohibit any action based on this material without the 'cover' provided by other collection such as air reconnaissance.

Secrecy of these kinds has to be applied as a set of automatic procedures. There is no means of knowing in advance how alert targets are to foreign intelligence, and what will or will not lead them to take countermeasures against it. The logical result for intelligence collection is simply to reveal as little as possible. The US journalist Bob Woodward illustrates the rationale in a graphic reconstruction of a dialogue with an official over proposed *Washington Post* disclosures about the tapping of underwater cables off the Soviet coast:

But the Soviets know, Bradlee [the *Post*'s editor] said. Ah, he [the official] asked, but precisely who? Which Soviets . . . ? There might have been an internal Soviet cover-up. Look at it from the Soviet view: a quiet compromise some four or five years ago in some sea; . . . end of the matter. But look at the alternative if you publish: a general alarm would go off in the Soviet military or the KGB requiring

---

[19] CIA, *Center for the Study of Intelligence Newsletter* no. 3 (spring 1995), p. 2.

a full investigative response – the motherland had been the victim of espionage, specific place and time. A search would begin for more espionage . . . the Soviets would get up on their toes. Precisely where the United States government did not want them. This might lead to the compromise of other US operations, totally unrelated . . . He lectured gently. A story in the *Post* could put the issue on the desk of the new Soviet leader, Gorbachev . . . Publication, he said, 'would send the issue of US espionage right up his rosy red rectum . . . They [the KGB] probably did not tell him [of the existence of the tap] – they conceal fuck-ups in the Soviet system like ours . . . '[20]

And again:

Why should we not print what the Soviets already know? It has to do with the atmospherics of intelligence operations, the official said. Any reporting of the nuts and bolts of how information is obtained raises consciousness all around the world. The best intelligence coups occur because someone on the other side makes a mistake, overlooks something, fails to check. The biggest leaks may be staring them in the face. To push their noses into the issues of intelligence might uncork counterintelligence forces we want bottled up.[21]

Security policy has to take these imponderables into account. Targets are not predictable, rational actors over taking security precautions. Intelligence can hardly be blamed for taking extreme views about the need for secrecy over what it is doing.

But secrecy has major effects. Compromises have to be made over revealing intelligence sources to recipients, who always want to judge the material presented to them partly by knowing its provenance. (The British disguising of Enigma decrypts as agent reports in the early part of the Second World War was not a success; users did not attach sufficient weight to them.)[22] Similar compromises exist over allowing users to take action on intelligence items; intelligence agencies weigh the immediate gains against the risks of losing the source for the future. Intelligence's practical value to users is also reduced by the detailed regulations about its handling, storage and incorporation into non-intelligence papers; the typical policy-making user often cannot keep sensitive intelligence in his normal working files, or is nervous about referring explicitly to it in his policy submissions. Within the intelligence system itself secrecy shapes the organizational culture at all stages; handling secret material determines procedures and sets attitudes even where analysis is based largely on open data. International exchanges add further layers of secrecy. In all

---

[20] B. Woodward, *Veil: the Secret Wars of the CIA 1981–87* (London: Headline, 1988), pp. 562–3.

[21] Woodward, *Veil*, p. 566.

[22] F. H. Hinsley with E. E. Thomas, C. F. G. Ransom and R. C. Knight, *British Intelligence in the Second World War* vol. I, pp. 138, 145.

these ways perfect source protection conflicts with perfect intelligence handling and use.

In practice, peacetime secrecy is often overdone; special codewords and limited distributions become departments' badges and means of protecting and extending their territory. It becomes assumed that higher categories of secrecy equate with better intelligence quality, and new ones proliferate. Secrecy's mystique is a source of influence for intelligence as a whole. Admiral Stansfield Turner's attempt as DCI to simplify US classification procedures was seen as an attack on the US intelligence bureaucracy, and as such was successfully obstructed.[23]

Yet the instinct for source preservation is a sound one. No one else will look after the future if the collection practitioners do not. There is an astonishing propensity to leak information revealing intelligence sources and methods without realizing the consequences. Leakiness applies everywhere, not just among the openness of Washington. The British community remembers with horror the public revelation by a Labour ex-Minister in the House of Commons, on the day after the Falklands were invaded, that 'we have been reading its [Argentina's] telegrams for many years'.[24] No one on the Western side can have an easy conscience about the way in which circulating the information obtained from him led eventually to the execution of Penkovsky.[25] The Second World War's technical cipher-breaking would have been vitiated without the attention to the special channels and restrictions set up to use the material without compromising its source. Intelligence lives all the time with the need to balance intelligence's circulation and use against the risks.

Collection agencies

Structure and relationships

This source protection reinforces the authority of the big collection agencies. The growth in the speed and capacity of electronic communications has greatly increased their ability to have data passed in bulk from the field to the headquarters for processing, and retransmitted nationally and internationally. But the technical agencies still have to be seen not

---

[23] S. Turner, *Secrecy and Democracy: the CIA in Transition* (New York: Harper and Row, 1986), pp. 253–7, 277.

[24] E. Rowlands, *Hansard*, 3 April 1982, col. 650.

[25] GRU Colonel, recruited by SIS 1961, detected 1962, executed 1963. For brief account see C. Andrew and O. Gordievsky, *KGB: the Inside Story of its Foreign Operations from Lenin to Gorbachev* (London: Hodder and Stoughton, 1990), pp. 389–94.

as monolithic institutions but as federations, reconciling central organization against varied and competing armed services' interests. Sigint and imagery embody the Second World War lessons that some centralized 'strategic' control is essential, but that it also has to accommodate devolved 'tactical' activities dedicated to supporting single services and local service commanders. The results are mixed civilian and military structures with quite elaborate delegations to military commanders, especially in the United States. Imagery is less civilianized than Sigint, but the problems of reconciling mixed interests and multiple levels are no smaller.[26]

Hence there are 'field' stations in Sigint and their equivalents in 'first phase' imagery interpretation, all sending some output from local exploitation direct to users at various command levels. No tidy division is possible between strategic and tactical services; in the Gulf War US reconnaissance satellites under 'national' control provided a wide range of genuinely tactical as well as strategic intelligence. US generals complain that they do not have satellites under their own control, and argue that they need intelligence assets that respond directly to them.[27] The civilian practitioners argue for the efficiency and flexibility of centralized direction. The debate is similar to those about whether air support in the land battle – or air transport, or artillery – should be parcelled out locally or kept under some central control. There are no simple solutions.

On the whole the big sources have strong and separate institutional identities, reinforced by separate security procedures. Yet some collection is not divided neatly between separate agencies. Counterespionage agencies' search for hidden messages in intercepted mail merges into the activities of the decipherers. In the US community CIA does not have a monopoly of Humint collection but shares it with the armed forces; dispositions at the end of the Second World War meant that throughout the Cold War US and British interviewing of refugees tended to remain

---

[26] For the organizational problems of providing a project and control structure for US imagery, see W. E. Burrows, *Deep Black: the Secrets of Space Espionage* (London: Bantam, 1988), pp. 205–13.

[27] Thus General Schwarzkopf argued after the Gulf War that 'we just don't have an immediately responsive intelligence capability that will give the theater commander near real time information that he personally needs to make a decision . . . the intelligence community should be asked to come up with a system that will . . . be capable of delivering a real time product to a theater commander when he requests that.' (Report of the Oversight and Investigations Subcommittee, Committee on Armed Services, House of Representatives, *Intelligence Successes and Failures in Operations Desert Shield/ Storm* (Washington D.C.: US GPO, 1993), p. 30.)

under military intelligence control.[28] Humint organizations also participate in some close access technical operations and telephone tapping, sharing the general field with Sigint and security intelligence agencies.[29] There are joint operations in which separate disciplines need to collaborate. Close access technical collection of electronic emissions includes telephone-tapping, cable access and interception, bugging and other forms of eavesdropping and the exploitation of unintended radiations. Long-distance computer hacking has recently been added as a possible technique. In many ways these esoteric activities form separate sub-categories of collection, often with multi-agency involvement. Even when activities are separate there is often synergy between them. As mentioned earlier, espionage can acquire information that helps with cipher-breaking; while Sigint can for example provide terrorist leads for Humint coverage or security intelligence surveillance.

The organizational picture is therefore of general 'agency competences'. Huminters are experts on people and clandestinity overseas; Siginters on decipherment and electronic emissions; imagery practitioners on reconnaissance and interpreting pictures; security intelligence on matters with domestic connotations and possible outcomes in legal processes. But collection constantly develops across organizational boundaries. Inter-agency rivalries and turf fights coexist with cooperation. One of the community's challenges is coping with the problems and opportunities presented by this inter-agency dimension of collection.

Role in the complete system

The general picture is of the big, technical collection agencies' power; they have evolved almost as intelligence centres in their own right, and since the Second World War the system's centre of gravity has shifted towards them. The division between single-source and all-source responsibilities was described earlier; but so also were the services of 'unassessed' single-source material direct to non-intelligence users, short-cutting the all-source stage. These are not occasional aberrations but are an integral part of modern arrangements. One question is whether the single-source agencies have got out of control.

Military practice and doctrine are quite clear. Military intelligence

---

[28] For the involvement of the US services in Humint, see J. T. Richelson, *The US Intelligence Community* (Cambridge, Mass.: Ballinger, 1985), pp. 182–5. For Humint overlaps and coordination see W. Jajko, *The Future of Defense Intelligence* (Washington D.C.: Consortium for the Study of Intelligence, 1993).

[29] For CIA technical operations see Richelson, *The US Intelligence Community*, p. 186.

goes to military commanders via their all-source staff. Unprocessed single-source data is officially 'information', and becomes intelligence only through 'the conversion of information into intelligence through collation, evaluation, analysis, integration and interpretation'.[30] (However no one in practice actually makes this semantic distinction; everything intelligence collects and produces is 'intelligence'.) Intelligence histories are therefore full of cautionary tales about single-source dangers. Intelligence in the Soviet and Nazi systems is a warning of the distortion that came from feeding selected, unassessed titbits to dictators. British naval intelligence had to learn the hard way in the First World War that Sigint had to be integrated into proper intelligence appreciations if its value was not to be wasted.[31] The daily service of selected Enigma decrypts demanded by Winston Churchill in the Second World War could be dangerously misleading, lacking as they did any professional staff appreciations of their contexts and significance. Reading Rommel's signals to Germany encouraged Churchill in his repeated pressure for Middle East offensives, not realizing from the texts that Rommel was prone to exaggerate his shortages to bolster his own cases for additional supplies and reinforcements.[32]

In the same vein the British Official History of the Second World War mentions the more general drawbacks of this direct service, 'not least for the Chiefs of Staff, the Directors of Intelligence and the Permanent Under-Secretary at the Foreign Office, who found that the Prime Minister was liable to spring on them undigested snippets of information of which they had not heard'; and points out that 'it was no substitute for an efficient and regular procedure for coordinating intelligence and channelling it to the central authorities in such a way that what was truly important caught their attention'.[33] More recently, Admiral Turner has been critical of NSA's services of Sigint direct to high-level US policy-makers. 'Scooping the rest of the Community is the game; the NSA plays it well and the overall intelligence effort suffers.'[34] The case against direct single-source services seems well made.

---

[30] North Atlantic Treaty Organization, *Intelligence Doctrine* (NATO Military Agency for Standardization, August 1984), paragraphs 302–3 and Annex A-6 Glossary.

[31] P. Beesly, *Room 40: British Naval Intelligence 1914–18* (London: Hamish Hamilton, 1982), chapter 11, pp. 169–83.

[32] Hinsley, *British Intelligence in the Second World War* vol. II, p. 456. For German quartermasters' tendency to exaggerate their shortages and needs, see Bennett, *Ultra and Mediterranean Strategy*, p. 151.

[33] Hinsley, *British Intelligence in the Second World War* vol. I, p. 296.

[34] Turner, *Secrecy and Democracy*, pp. 275–6; see also pp. 235–6. For Z. Brzezinski's appetite as National Security Adviser for single-source Sigint reports see Woodward, *Veil*, p. 8. For another description of US services of 'raw' Sigint see B. D. Berkowitz and

But a lot depends on what goes to whom. It is sensible for military material to go via military all-source staffs; and the same principle applies to reports on terrorism. But this does not apply to other single-source intelligence, particularly for support to diplomacy. Some of this stands on its own feet. Diplomats want to know how their conversations have been reported (or misreported) by their interlocutors; political leaders want insights into their personal chemistry with their foreign opposite numbers. Hibbert had single-source reports in mind when he spoke of covert intelligence as follows:

> It confirms in an authentic way . . . assessments which have already been reached on the 80 per cent or so of information gained from non-secret sources . . . Its great value is often that it gives immediacy, practicality and focus to general conclusions which have already been reached . . . It gives you the negotiating ploy at the next meeting or the initiative which is to be launched next month. Its value is usually tactical; strategy depends more on the picture put together from the broader, non-secret general intelligence material.[35]

For working diplomats it fills out the picture, often on quite ephemeral matters, but does not need full intelligence treatment. At very senior levels it is sometimes part of specially secret top level negotiation or policy execution, kept to very small circles; whatever the merits of US policy in the Iran-Contra affair, its execution was based partly on support from single-source Sigint reports.[36]

There is also the sheer scale of events and the information bearing on them. The idea that all-source intelligence should assess everything is a dream. Assessing information is decision-takers' day-to-day business; most foreign policy-making happens on the wing; there are no strong all-source staffs to make inputs on everything. Senior officials and their staffs read some single-source intelligence in the same way as they read diplomatic telegrams or media items – as part of the massive, ephemeral information background. Even military intelligence doctrine allows for some direct flows to operational staffs in war.[37]

A. E. Goodman, *Strategic Intelligence for American National Security* (Princeton: Princeton University Press, 1989), p. 35. For a cautiously realistic view see A. S. Hulnick, 'The Intelligence Producer – Policy Consumer Linkage: a Theoretical Approach', *Intelligence and National Security* vol. 1 no. 2 (May 1986), p. 229.

[35] R. Hibbert, 'Intelligence and Policy', *Intelligence and National Security* vol. 5 no. 1 (January 1990), pp. 112–13.

[36] C. Powell with J. E. Persico, *Soldier's Way: an Autobiography* (London: Hutchinson, 1995), pp. 307–8.

[37] NATO *Intelligence Doctrine*, paragraph 401(d) and Glossary. There is also an image in current US intelligence literature of military 'stovepipes', whereby technical collection finds its way directly to the top level without going through the intermediate level of all-source assessment on the way.

Even where big decisions are called for – and even on wartime military matters – single-source services still have their uses. The closer leaders can get to the facts the greater their confidence and conviction. Christopher Andrew has described how Churchill's direct contact with the Ultra material added to the incisiveness of his wartime leadership.[38] Van Crevald has argued in his history of military command that commanders need to supplement their staff systems with some form of 'directed telescope' that can enable them to focus selectively on raw, 'unstaffed' reality.[39]

Thus intelligence, like any other information service, does not lend itself to tidy solutions; information always seems messy. Nevertheless single-source services make leaders and their staffs their own intelligence assessors. When many individual reports circulate separately there is the danger that no one pulls them all together. The single-source agencies' expertise is on their own material; yet most of the big advances in understanding difficult targets come from putting different kinds of information together. When intelligence influences governments' views on major matters it should be all-source and authoritative.

Summary

Collection and the processing/interpretation associated with it are by far the biggest part of modern intelligence. Most collection produces 'observational' intelligence; but there are also the (often richer) seams of 'message-like' evidence of what targets are reporting, thinking and saying. The main Western collection investments are now in the big technical sources: Sigint and (US) satellite imagery. But at its most successful Humint still has a special ability to penetrate secretive states and terrorist organizations.

Source fragility is one of collection's main features, particularly for the 'message-like' material. Balances have to be struck everywhere between complete protection and optimum use. But secrecy's effects run throughout the complete intelligence system and are its most distinctive feature.

Collection's organization is based on separate, single-source agencies for the main sources; they are almost intelligence centres in their own right. Some of their product stands on its own feet and goes direct to

---

[38] C. Andrew, 'Churchill and Intelligence' in M. I. Handel (ed.), *Leaders and Intelligence* (London: Cass, 1989).

[39] M. Van Crevald, *Command in War* (Cambridge, Mass.: Harvard University Press, 1985), p. 75 on.

policy-makers, not through further analysis by all-source intelligence staffs; this applies particularly to the direct support of diplomacy. But when it has a bearing on big decisions single-source material needs to pass through the all-source stage. This can now be discussed.

6   All-source analysis and assessment

Analysis

All-source work is a continuation of single-source processing, as defined in the official British description of the DIS as being to 'analyse information from a wide variety of sources, both overt and covert'.[1] NATO doctrine divides it into a sequence as follows:

- *collation*, or the routine office work of recording incoming information
- *evaluation*, of the reliability of the source and credibility of the information
- *analysis*: identifying significant facts, comparing them with existing facts, and drawing conclusions
- *integration*, of all the analysed information into a pattern or picture
- *interpretation*, or 'deciding what it means in terms of what is likely to happen in the future'.[2]

But it is not really a neat progression of this kind. As in the rest of the intelligence process, each stage is recycled back into the others. *Analysis* is used here to cover it, though 'evaluation' and 'interpretation' catch some of the flavour rather better, and 'assessment' is also used in a sense to be discussed here. The tangible output is finished intelligence, but there are others: oral briefings; the body of stored knowledge for future intelligence use (as 'data bases' and analysts' memories); and feedback to steer collection.

Unlike collection, there is nothing esoteric about all-source analysis itself. Immediate reporting is rather like good-quality daily journalism or radio news services, and the other extreme – long-term intelligence production – resembles the general run of research. All-source foreign intelligence practitioners are much the same as analysts anywhere:

---

[1] *Central Intelligence Machinery* (London: HMSO, 1993), pp. 21–2.
[2] North Atlantic Treaty Organisation, *Intelligence Doctrine* (NATO Military Agency for Standardization, August 1984), Annex F.

specialists in subjects, working at speeds varying with the job, with the aim (normally) of product for distribution. Security intelligence is slightly different; those who seek to detect espionage and terrorism are rather more like detectives than the journalists or researchers who produce accounts of situations and subjects. But the techniques of analysis are similar everywhere.

However some points give the all-source stage its flavour. These can be discussed here.

Material

The all-source integration of the different intelligence sources was described in chapter 3. Sigint, imagery, Humint and the other sources may each provide its own distinctive viewpoint; all-source analysis evaluates them critically against each other and produces a composite picture. What needs to be emphasized is that the material for all-source analysis extends to the many non-intelligence sources, including 'open' material that is publicly available as well as the information acquired by governments by non-intelligence means. Most of this non-intelligence material – such as diplomatic telegrams, news agency reports and the mass of other media coverage, and operational reports from contact with the enemy in wartime – can flow directly into the all-source stage. Some of it, such as the monitoring of foreign radio broadcasts and acquisition of foreign journals, may involve the special collection arrangements under intelligence aegis mentioned at the end of chapter 4. But however this non-intelligence material is acquired its exploitation is an all-source responsibility.

Its importance varies enormously. Clearly there is no open source evidence on espionage. Terrorism is also largely clandestine, though its press announcements and political propaganda have to be studied in detail. In wartime there is relatively little purely open information – though German newspapers in the Second World War were quite revealing, despite Nazi censorship – but information gained through operational contact with the enemy is an important all-source input. In peacetime the balance between intelligence and non-intelligence sources is more even. Military forces have to provide extensive public information about themselves, while still preserving operational and technical secrets. Foreign political intentions may be deducible almost entirely from media coverage and diplomatic reporting, with intelligence collection providing a small, extra dimension. Whatever the size of the non-intelligence input, assessing it jointly with intelligence collection is a special all-source responsibility.

This is now particularly important in an increasingly open world with a rapidly increasing volume of open source intelligence, including commercial data bases as well as the media. (Internet, though not necessarily of much use to intelligence, has recently caught the public imagination as an epitome of this new world of international computer access to data of all kinds.) Linked with this need to exploit publicly available information is the harnessing of 'grey' intelligence, defined as 'information which is not published or widely diffused but to which access can be gained, provided that one knows it exists and has adequate channels of communication'.[3] Intelligence's complete flow diagram is therefore as shown in figure 9.

Data organization

Linked with this need to acquire inputs of all types are the problems of organizing analysis. Intelligence is full of institutional barriers and need-to-know security restrictions, both inside the all-source stage and between it and the collectors. The all-source analyst must be close to his collectors, both to steer their collection and single-source analysis and to discuss interpretations with them. Part of his job is to know the pitfalls of the various sources, and when their collectors are carried away by professional enthusiasm for them. Ideally he would be able to draw on their records for his own analysis, but this is usually impossible on security grounds.

Irrespective of access to collectors, the all-source analyst needs his own information infrastructure, providing him with ready access to both covert and open source material. One of the best tests of any intelligence organization's long-term quality is the state of its indexes. This is true of single-source interpretation – accounts of Bletchley Park in the Second World War reiterate the importance of the indexes there[4] – but applies even more to all-source work. Modern information technology, properly applied, now promises really substantial advances in its analytic quality. But whatever the methods used an institution is not a proper analysis agency unless it has a reliable institutional memory.

[3] S. Dedijer and N. Jéquier, 'Information, Knowledge and Intelligence' in their *Intelligence for Economic Development: an Inquiry into the Role of the Knowledge Industry* (Deddington, Oxon.: Berg, 1987), pp. 18–19, quoted by J. Sigurdson and P. Nelson, 'Intelligence Gathering and Japan: the Elusive Role of Grey Intelligence', *International Journal of Intelligence and Counterintelligence* vol. 5 no. 1 (1991), p. 21.

[4] For example, 'the most significant of the back rooms was the Index', W. Millward, 'Life In and Out of Hut 3' in F. H. Hinsley and A. Stripp, *Codebreakers: the Inside Story of Bletchley Park* (Oxford: Oxford University Press, 1993), pp. 24–5. For remarks in similar terms in other Bletchley Park reminiscences see pp. 35, 49, 68–70.

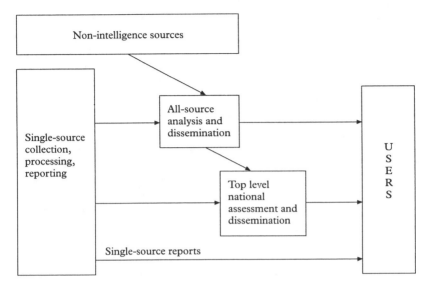

Figure 9 Complete intelligence process

Objectives

All-source intelligence exists to provide the best possible, authoritative accounts and judgments on the subjects with which it deals, with a special preoccupation with uncertainty and forecasting. Most of the evidence is 'soft' rather than 'hard', usually subject to the targets' secrecy and deception, or the risk of it. The questions posed to it range over both present and future – and occasionally over the past, for example in assessing whether the attempted assassination of the Pope in the early 1980s had been a Soviet plot – but in important reports the forecast tends to be the bottom line.

This should not give intelligence a responsibility for complete futurology. When he was CIA's Deputy Director for Intelligence, Robert Gates divided decision-makers' needs into secrets and mysteries. 'Secrets are things that are potentially knowable', while in mysteries 'there are no clear-cut answers, often because the other leaders themselves do not know what they are going to do or have not worked out their problems'.[5]

---

[5] Remarks by R. Gates on 'Analysis' in R. Godson (ed.), *Intelligence Requirements for the 1990s* (Lexington, Mass.: Lexington Books, 1989), p. 115. The same analogy is used in B. Berkowitz and A. Goodman, *Strategic Intelligence for American National Security* (Princeton: Princeton University Press, 1989), chapter 4.

There is a distinction between aspects of the future for which there are some foreign plans and intentions, knowable in principle, and the 'soft' future not envisaged by anyone. The perfect penetration of Saddam Hussein's entourage would have provided evidence that he was considering the Kuwait invasion; the difficulty of doing this does not obscure the fact that these intentions existed and were there for intelligence to reconstruct if it had enough evidence and understanding. Similarly during the Cold War military technical staffs on both sides were trying to draft specifications for tanks twenty years ahead, *inter alia* by deciding how their opposite numbers were answering the same question; this was knowable, however difficult. On the other hand the form that the First World War would take was not planned or envisaged by governments in advance, and was not knowable in that sense; failure to forecast its length and destructiveness may have been a failure, but not of intelligence in the modern sense.[6]

But this line between forecasting and guesswork is a thin, often nonexistent one. A secretary of the British JIC complained just after the Second World War that the Committee's time was being wasted with unanswerable questions; but in mysteries governments still turn to someone for answers. Intelligence cannot always avoid the role of government's seer. Its educated guesses may be better than policymakers' own or are at least a second opinion.

This all adds to the quota of uncertainty. All-source analysis has to calibrate it; most finished intelligence should embody probability estimates as well as information and forecasts. Conveying probabilities is one of intelligence's art forms, usually through stylized verbal codes (such as 'likely, 'probable' and 'possible'). Stock phrases like 'It is not impossible that such-and-such will happen' give it the reputation of sitting on the fence. Yet intelligence's duty is to convey the range of uncertainty as accurately as possible.

Another all-source objective is persuasion. Its aim is to convince its readership about what it says, often without being unable to declare its sources and reasoning in full. Persuasion is partly through the written word, partly by personal briefings and contacts; Britain goes in for written reports, while in the United States 'the policy culture is very

---

[6] But compare with Professor May's verdict that 'pre-1914 intelligence bureaus got little things right but big things wrong'. He argues that 'intelligence bureaus – and governments – failed to ask or at least reflect on large questions, such as, for example, how new technology might change the character of war'. (E. R. May, 'Conclusions' in his *Knowing One's Enemies: Intelligence Assessment before the Two World Wars* (Princeton: Princeton University Press, 1986), pp. 504–5.) Intelligence in 1914 was more like a military thinking and planning staff than it is today.

much an oral one and, given how fast policy deliberations move, written products often arrive too late or out of focus'.[7] But in both communities what the Americans call 'wordsmithing' – giving great attention to precise formulations – ranks high in the intelligence culture.

Output

The varied subject-matter is matched by the variety of all-source output. There is no general categorization of report types, but they fall broadly into the three general classes dubbed by Kent as 'current-reportorial', 'basic-descriptive' and 'speculative-evaluative'.[8] Current-reportorial intelligence describes what has happened recently and is happening now. Basic-descriptive output is centred on relatively fixed facts of a situation; for example military and economic strengths. Speculative-evaluative reports deal more with the future, and with assessing what intelligence actually means to the users. These categories can be given some modern amplification.

First, most reporting falls into Kent's current-reportorial category, dealing with current (i.e. very recent) events and short-range forecasting. Intelligence is in this respect a quality newspaper, in which the latest 'news' predominates in bulk. It produces its evaluations of important overseas situations, individually or in regular series. The CIA Daily Brief to the President, the comparable US Defense and State Department products, and the JIC's weekly 'Red Book' are the intelligence equivalents of daily and weekly broadsheets' foreign news summaries and articles. This predominance of current reporting also applies to single-source output, as in the Cold War's mass of reports on current military activities. Presumably some 'warning' surveillance of this kind continues to be needed elsewhere, as in monitoring Iraqi military moves, or Argentine activities which might indicate a renewed threat to the Falklands. Similarly there is a need for short-term reporting of overseas conflicts. Immediate reporting looms even larger if the state's own forces are engaged in active UN or similar operations.

Second there is longer-term output. Most of it falls into Kent's basic-descriptive category, like military order of battle; part of the Cold War NATO routine was the annual alliance reassessment of Warsaw Pact military strength, as the nominal basis for political decisions on NATO

---

[7] G. F. Treverton, 'Estimating Beyond the Cold War', *Defense Intelligence Journal* vol. 3 no. 2 (fall 1994), p. 10.

[8] S. Kent, *Strategic Intelligence for American World Policy* (Hamden, Conn.: Archon Books, 1965 edition), p. 8.

capabilities. Long-term reporting of this kind extends to other considered accounts, as in projections of targets' political and economic prospects and regular multi-dimensional 'outlooks for country X'. Reporting of this kind is geared to users' general preoccupations or standing requirements rather than specific policy decisions. Thus the JIC periodically assessed the fundamentals of Soviet policy in the Cold War in papers of a general kind, not tied to specific governmental decisions. Other similar reports appear when a situation has changed or a new one arisen; but still to provide policy background.

Third is the least voluminous but most important category of reports: those both current and long-term which fit Kent's speculative-evaluative category. Their essence is that they are geared to use by particular users, often for their forecasting content; metaphorically they are applied rather than pure science. Military intelligence in the field gives its commander its daily input to the 'estimate of the situation' for his daily decisions. At higher levels governments request specific studies in connection with forthcoming decisions. Examples might be the 'threat assessments' underlying decisions on garrisons of troops overseas or the type and scale of major items of military procurement.

Other reports in this third category are not specifically commissioned by users, but are produced on intelligence's initiative on developments that explicitly or implicitly point to a need for decisions – for example, warning of imminent military attack or other direct threats to national interests or security. The US assessments on Soviet missiles in Cuba, and on likely Soviet responses to various possible US courses of action, were prime examples of finished intelligence directly geared to decision-taking.[9] Other intelligence has an obvious policy relevance even if not linked with specific threats, if for example it reports changes in a situation in which the government is already involved.

Reports of this kind are the closest form of intelligence to the policy process. They are still on the intelligence side of the dividing line, although the line is sometimes difficult to discern. All intelligence is produced to be of use, of some kind at some time; but this third category is aimed most directly as being immediately useful. Typical US formulations about intelligence's support of top policy have product of this kind in mind, as when Allen Dulles, the US DCI, called it 'a most vital function of the entire work of intelligence – how to deal with the mass of information about future developments so as to make it useful to

---

[9] For references and examples see R. L. Garthoff, *Reflections on the Cuban Missile Crisis* (Washington D.C.: Brookings, 1989).

our policymakers and planners as they examine the critical problems of today and tomorrow', or Senator Church described it as forming 'the building blocks of national security policy'.[10]

'Short-term' and 'long-term' serve to distinguish the first two of Kent's categories. Terminology for his speculative-evaluative reports is more confusing. US writing uses 'estimates' (for 'estimate of the situation'), but applies it also to many routine productions. Military intelligence everywhere tends to use estimates for compendiums on foreign military strength. The British term 'assessment' conveys the speculative-evaluative flavour, but it too is applied indiscriminately. (In high-level reportage, 'we assess' has become a slightly portentous synonym for 'we think' or 'we conclude'.) 'Opportunity analysis' has been coined more recently in the United States to indicate a particularly close link with decisions, but perhaps has connotations with policy opportunities rather than threats.[11] 'Assessment' is used in this book as a matter of convenience to denote all non-routine, potentially policy-significant reporting of this kind, aimed at the top level. (There is some point to this distinction from analysis, since there is quite an important distinction between the art of making and writing assessments and doing the basic research on which knowledge of the subject depends.) But the diversity of intelligence product and the absence of clear-cut categories must be emphasized.

There is an equal diversity about the scale of distribution. Assessments close to policy decisions may be restricted to top governmental eyes, while other more general reports (for example the Cold War descriptions and forecasts of Soviet capabilities) cascade from top to lower levels, with addressees running into hundreds. At the lowest level there are all the necessary mass-distribution items, like the routine but necessary 'form at a glance' guides to all foreign forces. In the absence of these guides the British Royal Marines complained that, when hurriedly embarking in the Falklands Task Force, they had to get their information about Argentine forces from Plymouth Public Library.

No national system has a complete inventory of intelligence output and readership, although particularly secret categories develop their own

---

[10] A. W. Dulles, *The Craft of Intelligence* (New York: Harper and Row, 1963), pp. 156–7, 161; quoted in H. P. Ford, *Estimative Intelligence: the Purposes and Problems of National Intelligence Estimating* (Lanham, Md.: University Press of The United States with Defense Intelligence College, 1993), p. 33. Senator Church's remarks to the US Senate on 11 November 1975 are also quoted in *Estimative Intelligence*, p. 32.

[11] As in J. Davis's monograph *The Challenge of Opportunity Analysis*, published by CIA's Center for the Study of Intelligence, July 1992.

special designations and access lists. The lower the level the more the scale of dissemination increases; routine military productions may have thousands of copies. Even for higher grade and higher level material it is hard to keep regular lines of production to small numbers; the need-to-know restrictions on distribution always fight against demands to be kept in the picture. International distribution is a further multiplier. Despite all its secrecy, intelligence is a large-scale publishing business.

Organization

The evolution of all-source organizations was sketched in chapter 2, but the picture of the organizations mentioned there needs some qualification.

In the first place the organizational division between collection and all-source analysis is by no means complete. It is bridged in the West's best known intelligence institution, the CIA, which contains both, though collection and analysis operate there almost as if they were separate organizations, and CIA's size makes it *sui generis*. Conventional, non-satellite imagery in most countries has tended to remain a service-run activity, even if a joint-service one meeting all national needs as in Britain; the idea of independent imagery collection and interpretation agencies is really a phenomenon of US satellite collection. The other smaller defence collection sources are also run by the defence intelligence agencies; for example large areas of underwater collection in the Cold War remained under naval control, while the all-source technical intelligence staffs were the natural people to oversee the detection of nuclear tests and radioactivity from nuclear warheads. Service involvement in some Humint collection has already been mentioned; one of the interesting suggestions in the 1992 Congressional Boren–McCurdy proposals for intelligence reorganization was to give CIA control over all types of Humint, including operations run by the US services. In summary, the so-called analysis agencies also run significant amounts of collection, even if not the principal sources.

Secondly, divisions between collection and all-source entities apply in any case only on 'foreign intelligence' subjects, not to security intelligence ones. As has already been mentioned, security intelligence organizations tend to collect much of their own material for their own purposes (shaped by their function of detection rather than assessment and dissemination). These agencies normally run their own surveillance, human sources, mail interceptions and telephone taps, and in some countries they conduct their own Sigint interception of foreign radio communications with agents.[12] Generally they take some inputs from other agencies, and conversely collect foreign intelligence for them on home territory. If Humint agencies are the experts on clandestine operations overseas, security services have special roles on home territory.[13] But on the whole they are rather more self-contained than most other parts of the system.

All-source responsibilities

Hence all-source organizations have the anomalies to be expected in anything that has evolved and not been planned *ab initio*.[14] But their essence is in the special responsibility for authoritative intelligence judgments. A key element is empathy or the ability to see things through the targets' eyes: the intelligence equivalent of the historian's ability to discern 'an inner rationale', or 'some underlying pattern of thought or intention'.[15] According to E. H. Carr, the historian's craft involves 'the capacity to rise above the limited vision of his own situation in society and in history'.[16] Intelligence needs this same ability to get outside its own preconceptions, in short- as well as long-term analysis.

It may seem that this can be taken for granted in any serious analysis, yet understanding the target cannot easily be pursued with the single-mindedness of an academic researcher. As was brought out in chapter 3, intelligence has to persuade its users, and it is useless if it fails to do so. It has to be close to them, regard them as its 'customers', anticipate their needs and build up its own credibility. The importance and effects of the intelligence–user relationship recur in many parts of this book. It dominates recent US thinking about intelligence, in which great concern is shown that the gaps between it and policy-makers are too wide. Before

---

[12] For Sigint monitoring by the French security intelligence service see J. T. Richelson, *Foreign Intelligence Organizations* (Cambridge, Mass.: Ballinger, 1988), p. 173. For the relationship of the British Radio Security Service, controlled by the Security Service, and the central Sigint organization in the Second World War, see F. H. Hinsley and C. A. G. Simkins, *British Intelligence in the Second World War. Vol. IV: Security and Counter-Intelligence* (London: HMSO, 1990), pp. 72–3, 131–7, 181–3.

[13] For the role of the British Security Service in carrying out some 'foreign intelligence' operations on British soil on behalf of other agencies see L. Lustgarten and I. Leigh, *In from the Cold: National Security and Parliamentary Democracy* (Oxford: Clarendon Press, 1994), p. 495, ascribed to an official interview.

[14] With the possible exception of the German BND, created by General Gehlen and his US supporters after 1945 as a completely new start, and profiting from the lessons of intelligence under Hitler.

[15] For the analogous historiographical theory see P. Gardiner (ed.), 'Introduction', *The Philosophy of History* (Oxford: Oxford University Press, 1974). The quotations are from pp. 5 and 7.

[16] E. H. Carr, *What is History?* (London: Penguin edition, 1964), p. 123.

he became DCI, Gates illustrated the new mood of striving for a closer relationship when he spoke of wanting his analysts to be 'down in the trenches with the policy-makers'.[17] The US 'opportunity analysis' mentioned earlier in this chapter predicates this increased contact, and practical recommendations for achieving it have been summarized in an authoritative article published by CIA on 'Bridging the Intelligence–Policy Divide'.[18] There is a consensus that a closer intelligence–policy relationship is among the most important aims for the American community.

Thus intelligence has to achieve empathy with its users as well as its targets; but there is some conflict between the two requirements. At one level this conflict is simply in time management: cultivating users is time-consuming, at the expense of analysis. Moreover concentrating on producing currently useful output may lead to neglecting surveillance for unlikely threats, or long-term effort to get inside targets' minds. There are also the effects of user relationships on analytic conclusions. Intelligence is part of the government system it supports, and the closer it is to it the more its output may be consciously or unconsciously slanted to make it more acceptable. At a deeper level still there are the inherent problems of intelligence's own assumptions. By getting closer to its users intelligence will tend to share more of their mind-sets and mis-perceptions.

A mixture is therefore needed of intimacy and distance; intelligence needs to be a part of government's brain, but with a permeable membrane separating it from the decision-taking centre. Aspects of this relationship will arise in later chapters. What should be noted here is how its condition and effects vary between different national systems, and even within them; there is no single intelligence–user problem, but many different ones. CIA may have had great difficulty in getting its views of the USSR heeded by the hawkish first Reagan Administration, and may now be rightly concerned over its access to the present top policy-makers; but for defence intelligence the danger has usually been of being too close to military vested interests (see chapter 14). On the whole the current emphasis on the need for closer intelligence–user contacts must be seen as a US phenomenon rather than a British one. It springs in most respects from the particular size, complexity and geographical spread of the Washington intelligence and policy communities. By contrast the same anxiety is not found over intelligence's relevance and impact in

---

[17] Godson, *Intelligence Requirements for the 1990s*, p. 111.
[18] J. A. Barry, J. Davis, D. D. Gries and J. Sullivan, 'Bridging the Intelligence–Policy Divide', CIA *Studies in Intelligence* vol. 37 no. 6 (1994).

the much smaller 'Whitehall village', in which top level British assessment is located and operates; if the system there runs risks, they are that intelligence and policy can be too close rather than too distant. Good user relationships are important everywhere for intelligence to be effective, but the problems of reconciling them with independent judgment vary from place to place.

What does not vary, however, is the weight of assessment responsibility. The spectacular Western examples of warning failures to be discussed in chapter 13 turned, not on intelligence's lack of credibility or contact with users, but on deficient all-source analysis and failure to recognize warning signals amid many other distractions. Something of the special burdens of all-source responsibility at the top level – for authoritative judgment, warning and drawing attention to intelligence casting doubt on accepted policies – was conveyed in testimony by Admiral Inman when he gave evidence to the US Senate Committee's hearings on the appointment of Gates as DCI. Speaking of his time as deputy DCI and the difficulty of assimilating all the implications of incoming evidence at the top, Inman recalled 'a day in the life of the DDCI' as follows:

You begin with a schedule at the start of the morning and a foot of message traffic that are about a foot high [*sic*]. And you have appointments all day long and meetings that you are moving to consecutively without breaks. But there are breaks when people break in to tell you something that's going on that they think you need to know. Or the phone rings, either to challenge some issue, too much time over bureaucratic fights over turf, but over also substantive matters.

And you finish that full day and there may well be an evening function to attend, and you still have that stack of material you are trying to get through.

Well, the worry you have when you go home is when people burst in to tell you those things in the middle, was there something you missed in the process?[19]

Or as put by an Israeli officer:

[The journalist] can entirely ignore his own mistakes. They'll be forgotten by the time tomorrow's headlines appear. Not so with the intelligence analyst. If he proves to be wrong on a cardinal issue, he will doubtless hang for it, quite literally in some regimes. In Israel, thank God, he will only be fired.[20]

The all-source effort is small by comparison with collection. Nevertheless a valuable Western principle has evolved – by accident, not conscious design – that those collecting and processing information

---

[19] Senate Select Committee on Intelligence, *Hearings on Nomination of Robert M. Gates to be DCI* vol. I (Washington D.C.: US GPO, 1992), p. 933.
[20] S. Gazit, 'Intelligence Estimates and the Decisionmaker' (paper given at the US Army War College, 17–18 May 1988; quoted in Ford, *Estimative Intelligence*, p. 35).

should not normally have final responsibility for evaluating it. In the Cold War this was one of the fundamental differences between the West and the Soviet system, where the covert collection of the KGB was presented direct to the leadership without in-built checks and balances.

This Western separation brings with it the problem of getting the right balance of resources between the technical miracles of collection and the less dramatic all-source activity of putting things together. The collection agencies are much more than just purveyors of data; they shape it with their own interpretations. They attract resources more readily than the all-source stage, which is sometimes dismissed as rather mechanical 'collation'. Yet without effective all-source work the effects of collection successes are lost. The modern growth of open source, non-intelligence information alongside the intelligence sources makes this work all the more crucial. Britain has tended to underinvest in it compared with collection; the same may also be true of the United States.

Summary

All-source analysis fuses the output of the various different kinds of intelligence collection, and at the same time draws on all available information from non-intelligence sources. It is government's expert on its particular subjects. Its quality depends on institutional memory, and needs modern information technology for its data-handling, storage and retrieval. Its output ranges from the intelligence equivalents of daily and weekly newspapers to bulky reports of long-term interest. Amid this wide variety its bearing on policy is most direct in 'assessments', linked with particular decisions or calling for them. These give special emphasis to the all-source responsibilities for forecasting and calibrating degrees of uncertainty.

In practice all-source organizations also tend to have some collection responsibilities; in particular, security intelligence is not divided between separate single-source and all-source agencies. Nevertheless some support for Western ideas of intelligence objectivity comes from the fact that the principal collectors do not normally have final responsibility for evaluating their product.

In weighing the different kinds of material available to it, the all-source stage's task is to see its targets through their own eyes. It has to combine this with close relations with its users, while keeping its intellectual independence. Without an effective all-source effort the much bigger investment on covert collection can be wasted. The right balance is needed between the two.

7   Boundaries

We have described intelligence's processes and institutions, and the functional divisions between them. It is concerned with information (and forecasts), and not action; and has a predominant (though not exclusive) orientation towards overseas affairs. But even on these it is not government's only authority for information and forecasting. We noted in chapter 2 that some intelligence activities are conducted on the fringes of the formally-defined intelligence communities; and chapter 6 referred to non-intelligence sources. Intelligence thus sits alongside diplomatic reporting, economic advisers, networks of international statistics on trade, health and similar matters, and private government-to-government exchanges. Military forces get some information about the enemy from various kinds of battlefield observation and contact, under operational and not intelligence control. Internal security merges into law enforcement intelligence. Among these many activities some organizations are designated as 'intelligence' and some are not. The question to be considered here is how far it can be identified with distinctive activities and product.

Official statements

Official statements relate to intelligence's *raison d'être*. The British intelligence and security services are now based on statutes which refer to general purposes of 'national security', with particular reference to defence, foreign policy and internal security threats, national 'economic well-being' and support for the prevention or detection of serious crime.[1] The JIC is officially charged with responsibilities 'to monitor and give early warning of the development of direct or indirect foreign threats to

---

[1] Security Service Act 1989 and Intelligence Services Act 1994. For discussion of the concept of 'national security' see L. Lustgarten and I. Leigh, *In from the Cold: National Security and Parliamentary Democracy* (Oxford: Clarendon Press, 1994), chapter 1; and P. Gill, *Policing Politics: Security Intelligence and the Liberal Democratic State* (London: Cass, 1994), chapter 3.

British interests, whether political, military or economic' and 'to assess events and situations relating to external affairs, defence, terrorism, major international criminal activity, scientific, technical and international economic matters'.[2] The US DCI and CIA were originally established 'to correlate and evaluate intelligence relating to the national security'.[3] By 1981 US intelligence was charged with providing 'the necessary information on which to base decisions concerning the conduct and development of foreign, defense and economic policy and the protection of the United States' national interests from foreign security threats'.[4]

But these are very general statements. The Cold War which influenced their formation emphasized national security issues. The current agenda of foreign affairs now gives more prominence to economic and other non-security subjects like environmental and international health matters, and poses the question whether intelligence should expand in the same way. First it is convenient to consider varied views on the breadth of intelligence's subject-matter.

Broad, middle and narrow views

We have already seen how the military idea of regular intelligence inputs to decision-taking came to be applied to top government in the Second World War. This wartime experience gave rise to a slightly triumphalist US literature; intelligence using the methods of scholarship had helped to win the war, and could help to keep the peace. Later writers, reacting to the domestic post-Watergate attacks in the 1970s, argued in a similar vein that intelligence was an indispensable part of the United States' superpower equipment. It was seen to be the key to sensible overseas policies; rather as others argued at the same time that social research was the key to enlightened domestic governance.

These thoughts owed much to Kent in the book quoted in the last chapter.[5] As a Yale academic turned intelligence professional he wrote a liberal plea for intelligence as applied scholarship. US security needed objective knowledge, and intelligence existed to provide it, with a special objectivity free from the distortions of executive responsibility. Intelligence was the pursuit of *all* information, not covert information for its

---

[2] *Central Intelligence Machinery* (London: HMSO, 1993), p. 23.
[3] National Security Act 1947, Sec. 102(d)(3).
[4] Executive Order 12333, 4 December 1981, paragraph 1.1.
[5] S. Kent, *Strategic Intelligence for American World Policy* (Hamden, Conn.: Archon Books, 1965 edition).

own sake; scholarship could solve most problems from open sources and proper analysis was the key.

This was the traditional military doctrine of 'proper' intelligence, that

Intelligence in a military context is the product of our knowledge and understanding of the terrain, weather, activities, capabilities and intentions of an actual or potential enemy . . . It is the aim and function of an intelligence organization, at any level, in peace and war, to provide the knowledge required by those who formulate policy and make plans and decisions.[6]

But Kent applied it on a wider front, and set the terms of later discussion about intelligence's breadth. As its title suggests, his book was actually about intelligence and national security, but the philosophy and tone were the basis for a rather broader view.[7] To give an example of the fashion that emerged with the reviews of US intelligence in the 1970s:

The task of the intelligence officer is to tell the policy-maker what has happened throughout the world in the recent past, what is happening currently (and why), and what the future is likely to hold.[8]

Or from the 1980s:

In an age that has experienced both a communications revolution and an information explosion, the idea that knowledge is power should not be hard to understand or justify. We believe that to be successful in its foreign policy, a nation – whether democratic, autocratic, or totalitarian – needs accurate political, economic, and military intelligence regarding its rivals, its competitors, its enemies, and – yes – even its friends.[9]

Or in the 1990s:

What should the new priorities be? Are there topics of sufficient import to the nation's well-being to replace the Soviets as the focus of US intelligence? There are, and for the simple reason that we live in an information age. Increasingly, having the best information is the key to success in almost any line of endeavour

---

[6] North Atlantic Treaty Organisation, *Intelligence Doctrine* (NATO Military Agency for Standardisation, August 1984), paragraph 104.

[7] For confirmation that Kent saw the information needed for domestic governmental operations as 'intelligence', see the charts between pages 210 and 211 in *Strategic Intelligence for American World Policy*. The book starts off (page 3) by saying that 'Intelligence means knowledge. If it cannot be stretched to mean all knowledge, at least it means an amazing bulk and assortment of knowledge.' It is not clear where he drew the line between the work of the existing intelligence community and other kinds of 'intelligence'.

[8] Paper by W. J. Barnds, 'Intelligence Functions', published in *Commission on the Organization of Government for the Conduct of Foreign Policy* (the Murphy Commission), *Report of the Commission* (volume 7) (Washington D.C.: US GPO, June 1975), appendix U, p. 13.

[9] A. C. Maurer, M. D. Tunstall and H. M. Keagle (eds.), 'General Introduction' to *Intelligence: Policy and Process* (Boulder and London: Westview, 1985), p. 6.

... Information always has been power, but today there is more opportunity to obtain good information, and the United States has more capability to do that than any other nation.[10]

Hence there is a view of intelligence which Abram Shulsky has likened to seeing it as 'a universal social science that seeks to understand, and ultimately to predict, all sorts of political, economic, social and military matters'.[11]

Distinguished US practitioners have tended to go along with this line. Ray Cline has echoed Kent's breadth.[12] Two former DCIs have done the same, and have envisaged intelligence as potentially providing an international information service available to all governments.[13] There is little comparable British writing, though a former Director General of Intelligence wrote in similar vein that intelligence officers had to be 'capable of objective study in relation to national interests conceived in the broadest terms', and that the highest intelligence skills included 'a facility for surveying the totality of international affairs'.[14]

The outcome is the belief that intelligence should be wide-ranging, a lens through which the totality of foreign affairs can be viewed, and the conviction that it should be *scholarly*, mainly using open rather than covert sources. As *The Times* put it in 1991:

The world is still dangerous. There are still things on the other side of the hill that we should like to know. But in increasingly open societies there are better ways of finding them out than by spying: reading the scientific journals, buying the better newspapers, even watching television or listening to the radio. They are more accurate and reliable than the useless profession has ever been. With less risk of being killed.[15]

Intelligence on this liberal view resembles a version of university 'area studies' faculties – the analogy is appropriate since these apparently

---

[10] S. Turner, 'Intelligence for a New World Order', *Foreign Affairs* vol. 70 no. 4 (fall 1991), pp. 150–1.

[11] A. N. Shulsky, *Silent Warfare: Understanding the World of Intelligence* (Washington D.C.: Brassey's, 1991), p. 161.

[12] R. S. Cline, *Secrets, Spies and Scholars: Blueprint of the Essential CIA* (Washington D.C.: Acropolis Books, 1976), pp. 261–72.

[13] See S. Turner, *Secrecy and Democracy: the CIA in Transition* (New York: Harper and Row, 1986), pp. 280–5; W. E. Colby, 'Comprehensive Intelligence for Advancement' in S. Dedijer and N. Jéquier (eds.), *Intelligence for Economic Development: an Inquiry into the Role of the Knowledge Industry* (Deddington, Oxon.: Berg, 1987); W. E. Colby, 'Reorganizing Western Intelligence', in C. P. Runde and G. Voss (eds.), *Intelligence and the New World Order: Former Cold War Adversaries Look Towards the 21st Century* (Buxtehude: International Freedom Foundation, 1992), pp. 126–7.

[14] Major-General Sir Kenneth Strong, *Intelligence at the Top: Recollections of an Intelligence Officer* (London: Cassel, 1968), pp. 243, 245.

[15] *The Times*, leader, 11 December 1991.

developed out of US academics' experience in Second World War intelligence.[16] It would astonish those brought up with the quite different Soviet view of intelligence as essentially a matter of secret sources.

Yet official statements in practice have not been quite so wide, with a national security connection dating from CIA's creation by the National Security Act and subordination to the National Security Council. Roy Godson, a leading academic in the subject, has also seen intelligence as 'an integral part of national security policy'.[17] Other writers have made a similar identification.[18] Kent himself recognized in the preface to his 1965 edition that the growth of technical collection had somehow changed his mainly open source picture, though he concluded that 'the eternal verities remain'.[19] National security cannot be accurately defined and there are debates whether economic and environmental 'security' are part of it or different from it.[20] But for intelligence the term conveys something more limited than a universal lens. Intelligence on this 'middle' view is a national security system of some kind, hard as it is to define what this means.

There also have been some narrower formulations, with suggestions that intelligence has a more sharply defined territory. In a paper prepared for the US Murphy Commission in the 1970s it was urged that

intelligence organisations have steadily tended to reach further and further out from their primary tasks; and that there is a unique expertise pertaining to the use of intelligence materials . . . when intelligence analysts produce reports and studies bearing a rich lode of material unique to intelligence then they can most legitimately claim a right to be heard by policy people . . . the exact degree of intelligence content required to establish this legitimacy is not easy to state but it

---

[16] R. Winks, *Cloak and Gown: Scholars in America's Secret War* (London: Collins, 1987), pp. 114–15. See also the review by B. F. Smith (*Intelligence and National Security* vol. 6 no. 2 (April 1991), pp. 498–9) of B. M. Katz, *Foreign Intelligence. Research and Analysis in the Office of Strategic Services* (Cambridge, Mass.: Harvard University Press, 1989): 'Katz makes a strong case for the view that the R and A [Research and Analysis Department] experience exerted a profound influence on aspects of American postwar academic life, especially its role in advancing interdisciplinary approaches to economics, and a strong synthesizing trend among US intellectual historians.'

[17] R. Godson (ed.), *Intelligence Requirements for the 1980s: Intelligence and Policy* (Lexington, Mass.: Lexington Books, 1986), p. 3.

[18] For an example, drawing on definitions developed by Godson, intelligence collection was defined as 'The acquisition of specified information . . . that relates to any other government, political group, military force, or individual, and that is important in relation to our national security.' (R. deGraffenreid, 'Intelligence and the Oval Office' in Godson, *Intelligence Requirements for the 1980s*, p. 11.)

[19] Kent, *Strategic Intelligence for US World Policy*, preface, pp. xiv–xv.

[20] See B. Buzan, *People, States and Fear: the National Security Problem in International Relations* (Brighton: Wheatsheaf Books, 1983), especially chapters 5 and 9.

becomes evident when the policy officer realises that he is reading material pertinent to his concerns which has not been available to him in his own daily traffic.[21]

In the United States Jack Davis has usefully suggested that governments turn to intelligence when it has 'comparative advantage' over other information and advice.[22] In a more forcible statement a British academic, Ken Robertson, has argued that

A satisfactory definition of intelligence ought to make reference to the following: threats, states, secrecy, collection, analysis, and purpose. The most important of these is threat, since without threats there would be no need for intelligence services . . . A threat is not simply an unknown factor which may affect one's interests but is something capable of causing serious harm or injury . . . [Intelligence's] unique element is secrecy – the secret collection of someone else's secrets.[23]

The present author argued in 1989 that intelligence is grounded in the contests between it and its targets' defensive security: 'Intelligence uses all types of information but is geared essentially to penetrating those areas in which concealment and deception are endemic.'[24] As Shulsky subsequently put it, 'Fundamentally, intelligence seeks access to information some other party is trying to deny.'[25] Intelligence on these views is bound up with other parties' secrets. But on the whole rather broader views have held the floor.

Intelligence in practice

There is no doubt that breadth is a characteristic of US intelligence. Gates wrote in 1987 that

The range of issues [studied] is breath-taking – from strategic weapons to food supplies, epidemiology to space, water and climate to Third World political instability, mineral and energy resources to internal finances, Soviet laser weapons to remote tribal demographics, chemical and biological weapons proliferation to commodity supplies . . . [26]

---

[21] R. J. Smith, 'Intelligence Support for Foreign Policy in the Future' in Murphy Commission, *Report*, Appendix U, volume 7, pp. 78–9.

[22] 'Comparative advantage' is illustrated as existing through such factors as 'research, special sources, extensive data bases, advanced methodologies'. (J. Davis, *The Challenge of Opportunity Analysis*, published by CIA's Center for Study of Intelligence, July 1992.)

[23] K. G. Robertson, 'Intelligence, Terrorism and Civil Liberties', *Conflict Quarterly* (University of New Brunswick) vol. 7 no. 2 (spring 1987), p. 46.

[24] M. E. Herman, paper 'British and US Concepts of Intelligence: Barriers or Aids to Cooperation?' (BISA/ISA conference, London, March 1989), p. 28.

[25] Shulsky, *Silent Warfare*, p. 175.

[26] R. M. Gates, 'The CIA and Foreign Policy', *Foreign Affairs* vol. 66 no. 2 (1987–8), p. 218.

The Intelligence Directorate of CIA indeed *is* much like an expanded set of university 'area studies' faculties. Turner commented astringently that

The analytic branch of the CIA is given to tweedy, pipe-smoking intellectuals who work much as if they were doing research back in the universities whence many of them came. It probably has more Ph.Ds than any other area of government and more than many colleges. Their expertise ranges from anthropology to zoology. Yet, for all that, they can be wrong.[27]

This CIA Directorate studies foreign countries in the round, mainly from open sources, produces distinguished area experts and publishes numerous unclassified publications. Most other intelligence communities have similarly broadened their output at least to the extent of economic studies. Yet intelligence considered as a whole is far removed from a university campus. The secrecy of covert collection has widespread effects, permeating the whole system. The allocation of resources emphasizes defence intelligence and subjects such as terrorism that have substantial covert contents.

Thus intelligence presents apparently contradictory pictures. To reach a balanced view about its characteristics the essential thing, here as elsewhere, is to differentiate between the collection and all-source parts of the system. The distinctive features of the two are different, and need to be considered separately.

Intelligence collection and other information gathering

Peacetime characteristics

Information on most foreign targets comes from both intelligence and non-intelligence sources. There is nothing special about intelligence's content; tactical information on diplomatic negotiations can be obtained through diplomatic contacts as well as by intelligence means. The central feature of intelligence collection is collecting information without its targets' consent or cooperation, and often without its knowledge. States give their consent to the existence of diplomats and diplomatic reporting, but not to intelligence sources.

Moreover the methods of intelligence collection are on the whole distinctive. Cipher-breaking and imagery interpretation have scarcely any non-intelligence equivalents. As for Humint the difference between it and diplomatic methods is fairly clear. For diplomacy the Vienna Convention of 1961 specified its information gathering as ascertaining

---

[27] Turner, *Secrecy and Democracy*, p. 113.

conditions in the host country *by all lawful means*; although not defined and tested the term has associations with diplomatic practice and local domestic law.[28] Diplomatic cover is of course used by intelligence collectors, and diplomats' more confidential sources can overlap with Humint's less secret ones. But there are reasonably clear dividing lines between acceptable diplomatic methods and those of secret intelligence. Diplomats' sources are in principle avowable and not bought; intelligence's are unavowable, vulnerable to countermeasures, and protected by secrecy.

The main area of overlap between the two is in the defence attaché system, which evolved in the nineteenth century largely to supply the military intelligence departments that were developing at the same time. Defence attachés belong to both the diplomatic and intelligence worlds, as indeed is recognized in the special procedures for their accreditation.[29] Their intelligence connections vary. In the Cold War they were licensed intelligence observers pushing their luck against the risk of being declared *persona non grata* by the host country; but they kept their diplomatic status. The Soviet and Western Military Missions in Germany after 1945 similarly mixed intelligence collection with quasi-diplomatic status. On the other hand the new military inspection teams established by the international arms control agreements of the 1980s and 1990s are careful to avoid intelligence associations. There are also the relatively non-sensitive intelligence sources discussed in chapter 4 such as the interviewing of refugees. But on foreign targets, in peacetime, most intelligence is based on distinctive collection methods, known to exist but without much international legitimacy, of a covert character protected by secrecy.

This equation of intelligence collection with distinctive methods does not apply in security intelligence. Though this makes some use of Sigint and other special intelligence techniques, most of its collection is the same as used in normal policing. Law enforcement also employs informers, surveillance and telephone-tapping as part of its armoury. Standards may be different but the methods are broadly the same. Security intelligence collection is distinguished by its purpose and targets – the protection of internal security arrangements, the detection of espionage, terrorism and the related threats – rather than by its methods.

---

[28] Vienna Convention 1961, Article 3 part 1.

[29] Like ambassadors (but not other members of diplomatic missions), the appointment of service attachés may be subject to the specific consent of the receiving country (Vienna Convention, Article 7, discussed in M. Hardy, *Modern Diplomatic Law* (Manchester: Manchester University Press, 1968), p. 28).

Nevertheless, with this exception, the generalization about special intelligence methods fits peacetime. Intelligence collection is directed at targets that need special means to penetrate them. Peacetime collection broadly fits Robertson's description of intelligence's special quality – the secret collection of others' secrets.

Intelligence and military operations

In war the distinction between intelligence and non-intelligence methods of collection becomes less clear-cut. Intelligence then includes a greater proportion than in peacetime of the less specially secret 'military battle-field' intelligence elements already described. At the same time fighting forces themselves obtain information about the enemy and use it directly. Observation has always been part of war, as has operational reconnaissance. These activities have been transformed in this century by radar, and by its incorporation into target acquisition for weapons systems. Infra-red detectors, acoustic sensors and low light television now supplement other kinds of observation. Electronic Warfare – typically involving receivers aboard aircraft which give immediate warning when a hostile missile radar has locked on, and the on-board jammers which then counter the radar – is another ever-growing field in which information is acquired and acted upon without intelligence involvement.

'Combat information' of this kind (to adapt NATO terminology, to distinguish it here from intelligence) is intrinsic to military operations. Moreover it was of peacetime importance in the Cold War, when intelligence collection was complemented by permanently operating warning systems, such as satellite and radar surveillance for detecting missile launches and early warning radar for aircraft approaches. In the same way the ships and maritime aircraft of East and West tracked each other unceasingly, using and producing above-water and underwater operational observations in the process.

In practice demarcation lines are drawn in what would otherwise be a continuum. These are illustrated in figure 10. Such divisions between military 'Int' and 'Ops' have always been controversial. The 1904 edition of the British Regulations for Intelligence Duties in the Field thought it necessary to distinguish carefully between 'intelligence reconnaissance' organized by intelligence staff and 'reconnaissances in force' controlled like normal operations.[30] In the First World War there were bitter cap-badge battles between the British Artillery and Intelligence Corps

---

[30] *Regulations for Intelligence Duties in the Field* (London: War Office, 1904), pp. 1–2.

over who should run 'Artillery Intelligence' for artillery targeting: the artillery won, and was careful to name those posted into the job as 'reconnaissance officers' and not 'intelligence officers'.[31] Since 1945 the proliferation of the 'electronic battlefield' has produced long-running and unresolvable doctrinal battles about boundaries between Sigint and Electronic Warfare. Intelligence's own inbuilt distinctions noted earlier between its 'strategic' and 'tactical' resources add to the complications. Thus in the Gulf War, the Coalition was supported by 'strategic' intelligence assets like US satellites controlled 'nationally', 'tactical' intelligence controlled by local intelligence staffs in the theatre, and 'combat information' reconnaissance under 'operations' staff, as for example in the use of airborne radar surveillance. The picture is further confused because collection could be shifted from one subordination to another, as in the way British tactical intelligence collection units were put under operational artillery control.[32] But the essential point is that not all battlefield information is intelligence-driven; some of it is acquired as an integral part of combat.

It must be emphasized that part of intelligence's wartime job is ensuring that this combat information can get quickly into intelligence channels for intelligence staffs, just as all-source analysis needs to exploit diplomatic reporting and open source material in the same way in peacetime. The improvement in British intelligence in the Desert War after mid-1942 included eliminating the delays over getting British units' 'enemy reports' from the operational chain into intelligence channels.[33] Similarly there is no doubt about the need to have operational units functioning under temporary intelligence control for specific purposes. But the fact remains of the battlefield boundaries between intelligence and non-intelligence control.

In some ways these are merely bureaucratic turf fights; yet in others they affect the intelligence system and its budgets. The important institutional point is that wartime intelligence collection is not the same as the totality of wartime information. Information was important in both the Battles of Britain and the Atlantic; but what is chiefly remembered about it in the first is the immediate *combat information* produced by British radars, and the rather different *intelligence* from cipher-breaking in

---

[31] B. G. S. Bidwell and D. Graham, *Fire-Power* (London: George Allen and Unwin, 1982), p. 104.

[32] Major General R. Smith, 'The Gulf War: the Land Battle', *RUSI Journal* vol. 137 no. 1 (February 1992), p. 2.

[33] F. H. Hinsley with E. E. Thomas, C. F. G. Ransom and R. C. Knight, *British Intelligence in the Second World War* vol. II (London: HMSO, 1979–89), p. 410.

INTELLIGENCE		COMBAT INFORMATION
'National' intelligence resources	'Tactical' intelligence resources	Non-intelligence sensors/activities (Operational recce, combat observation, radar, Electronic Warfare, etc.)
Central 'strategic' control	'Local', sub-strategic control	Operational control
• Produces for use at all levels, according to needs and sources	• Used at operational and tactical commands	• Immediate use in combat or for operational warning • Use not dependent on intelligence staff • Data made available to intelligence staff for incorporation into intelligence analysis

Figure 10 Relationship between strategic intelligence, tactical intelligence and combat information

the second.[34] The biggest development in information-gathering in the war was probably radar, not intelligence.

Some rationales for the distinction are discernible. Using the distinction between observational and message-like intelligence drawn in chapter 5 provides some guide. Observational data can be either intelligence or combat information, but the latter tends to be of the simple, factual 'What Where When?' kind; message-like evidence on the other hand tends to be intelligence, especially if it provides rich information on the present or intentions for the future. Secrecy is another. Sources needing special protection are part of intelligence, though the converse does not apply: non-fragile sources such as POW interrogation and captured documents and equipment are also

---

[34] For radar in the Battle of Britain as information see P. B. Stares, *Command Performance: the Neglected Dimension of European Security* (Washington D.C.: Brookings, 1991), pp. 32–8. For intelligence in the same battle see F. H. Hinsley, *British Intelligence in the Second World War* vol. I (London: HMSO, 1977), pp. 176–82. His verdict (p. 182) is that intelligence knowledge of German Air Force organization and order of battle was of increasing help as background; and that tactical Sigint 'made an important contribution to the effectiveness of Fighter Command during the crucial weeks of August and the first half of September [1940]'. But the use of radar was decisive.

intelligence, not combat information. Distance is a criterion; long-range sources tend to come under intelligence and not under operational control near the front line. Perhaps the most important criterion historically has been the degree of human intervention versus *immediacy* and *automaticity*. Observations like radar plots capable of near instantaneous use are combat information; intelligence implies some greater degree of human analysis between collection and use. Even the lowest level imagery is intelligence since film has to be developed and pictures interpreted. In the same way Electronic Warfare is distinguished from Sigint by providing information directly and immediately for 'threat detection, warning, avoidance, target acquisition and homing', and undertaking jamming, deception and other means as *direct* parts of the battle 'to prevent or reduce an enemy's effective use of radiated electromagnetic energy'.[35] This is a fine distinction, since EW is closely bound up with Sigint; it draws on the store of detailed Sigint information about enemy emissions and sometimes contributes to it. Nevertheless it is an operational and not an intelligence activity; boundaries between the two have to be drawn somewhere.

These are still unclear distinctions, particularly since the technology for combat information is now as complex as for intelligence collection. The 'distance from the front' distinction between the two is blurred where immediately usable operational information can be generated from satellites. The most confusing modern factor of all is the impact of computers in eliminating the human analysis formerly associated with intelligence. Now that surveillance satellites can be programmed to flash target identifications and locations in 'real time' direct to ships or tactical battlefield commanders without human intervention, the traditional intelligence-operations distinctions are obscured. Perhaps the most abiding intelligence trademark is its collection's vulnerability to countermeasures and hence secrecy for source protection.

Armed forces can be left to work out these boundaries. Their significance here is that the rationales for armed forces' intelligence collection have to take account of what distinguishes it from non-intelligence combat information. In practical terms the modern 'information war' embraces effort on collecting and denying combat information as well as intelligence. Battlefield combat information collection, for example in new generations of battlefield drones, is intelligence's complement, or sometimes its rival for funding. The electronic 'information war' does not necessarily mean *carte blanche* for Sigint.

---

[35] NATO, *Intelligence Doctrine*, definitions p. A-4.

All-source boundaries

Where assessment really counts

Here the issue is not where information came from but the subjects for analysis; on what do governments look to all-source assessment for authoritative inputs? Here some moves have been made to implement the 'broad' model of all-source intelligence as a universal subject lens for this purpose. CIA has consistently widened its study of foreign problems. The British Assessments Staff in the early 1970s was seen by some observers as a counterpart of the Central Policy Review Staff established after the 1970 election.[36] Attempts to find a higher profile for economic intelligence go back at least twenty-five years; Britain established a special economic JIC in the late 1960s, working almost entirely on non-intelligence evidence. In the United States Cline proposed some twenty years ago that a 'Central Institute for Foreign Affairs Research' should be established to manage all overseas analysis and research in government as a unity.[37] US agencies have had strengthened intelligence responsibilities for narcotics intelligence, and an inter-agency task force on this subject was established at CIA in the late 1980s.

The end of the Cold War led to renewed calls for broader subject-matter. Carver urged in 1990 that US intelligence had to focus on Western Europe; and also that 'the place of economics at the intelligence table must now be moved well above the salt', so that it could monitor worldwide technological developments which might affect US security or economic interests.[38] Turner came out even more strongly in favour of economic intelligence a year later: 'as we increase emphasis on securing economic intelligence, we will have to spy on the more developed countries – our allies and friends [Japan and the European Union] with whom we compete economically – to whom we turn first for military assistance in a crisis.'[39] The arguments for broadening have not been limited to economic and technological subjects; a member of the Senate Intelligence Committee staff commented in 1992 that 'The Treasury Department, the Commerce Department, the Environmental Protection Agency, the Drug Enforcement Agency, and the Centers For Disease

---

[36] W. Wallace, *The Foreign Policy Process in Britain* (London: Allen and Unwin, 1976), pp. 78–91, 127.

[37] Cline, *Secrets, Spies and Scholars*, p. 265.

[38] G. A. Carver, 'Intelligence in the Age of Glasnost', *Foreign Affairs* vol. 69 no. 3 (summer 1990), p. 166.

[39] Turner, 'Intelligence for a New World Order', p. 154.

Control may all become increasingly important recipients of intelligence information.'[40]

This may all be true for the production of usable items of single-source intelligence to supplement other information on foreign negotiating positions, whatever the subjects. The puzzle is that no comparable breadth of all-source analysis and output is yet reflected in the subjects on which intelligence *assessment* bears most strongly on policy. Its greatest influence as an authority is still in the difficult-to-define national security field. Warnings and threats have a central place; the shock of the Falklands invasion led the British JIC to amend its terms of reference to bring out this special responsibility. Governments look primarily to intelligence assessment for the world of 'hard power'.

Policy decisions do not depend on it to anything like the same extent on other subjects. In international trade and finance the assessments that really count are still those of Treasuries, Central Bankers, Economic Advisers, Government Statistical Services and all the other official and private experts. National economic strategies and national positions on issues like US–West European economic relations are not determined by intelligence estimates. The same applies to shorter-term issues; intelligence is still not the authority for forecasting short-term currency movements, stock market crashes or movements in foreign opinion. Collection may contribute covert intelligence on all these issues; but all-source assessment is not central to decision-taking on them. Governments' big international economic and financial decisions are not taken on the basis of formal British JIC assessments or US NIEs.

Assessment also commands more authority on potential opponents, neutrals or areas of disturbance than in cooperation or negotiation with friends. Yet states deal for most of the time with cooperating countries, and the logic of 'broad' intelligence is that it should study friends as much as enemies. Kent faced up to the issue and was clear that 'if one should want to know, intelligence should be able to estimate the chances of nationalization of a particular British industry in the next six months and the effect such a move would have on Britain's balance of payments.'[41] Covert intelligence may indeed collect snippets of information on friends and allies; but all-source intelligence is rarely the authority on them. British policy towards the United States has not been based on JIC findings. No doubt CIA includes Britain in its West European papers,

[40] J. Sims in A. N. Shulsky and J. Sims, *What is Intelligence?* (papers for Working Group on Intelligence Reform, 29 April 1992); published by the Consortium for the Study of Intelligence, Washington, p. 13.

[41] Kent, *Strategic Intelligence for American World Policy*, p. 60.

but there is no evidence that US policy towards Britain has been significantly based on them; there are too many other experts.[42] The same probably applies to British decisions on European Union matters.[43] Even in military matters the assessment of friends and allies is usually made by leaders and their policy staffs, not the intelligence machine. British and US military leaders do not use intelligence to evaluate each other's military plans and policies; instead they have usually talked to each other. The British JIC was not generally blamed because the government was taken by surprise by the US invasion of Grenada. There is no logical reason why it should not be listed as a significant intelligence failure; but the fact is that US invasions are not listed as a warning target.

Thus all-source intelligence has not acquired the breadth of impact that some writers have advocated; its influence remains skewed towards particular issues. The special British economic JIC did not survive for more than a decade. Failures in British international economic policy are blamed on government statistics, but not on intelligence. Economic decisions, however much entwined with political considerations, still tend to be taken in a different frame of reference from national security ones, and with a smaller input from intelligence assessment.

Explanations

Parts of this situation reflect the existence of the other continuously operating foreign assessment machine: the diplomatic system. A general in battle is in constant consultation with his chief intelligence officer and relies on him for knowledge about the enemy. But Foreign Ministers form and conduct day-to-day policy with their (non-intelligence) Foreign Office officials and ambassadors abroad, all of whom are professional assessors of foreign affairs, as reflected in a British description from overseas:

Our task [from Colombo] is to ensure that our desk in Foreign Office's South Asia Department fully understands all the background to what is happening here politically and economically . . . The Foreign Office is the custodian of information about countries throughout the world, and we have to keep them aware of what is going on. They have to brief Ministers, maybe very

---

[42] For a CIA assessment of British prospects in its 'Review of the World Situation' in 1949, see P. Hennessy, *Never Again: Britain 1945–1951* (London: Vintage edition, 1993), p. 383.
[43] For a recent British description of its policy-making structure for European Union matters, see B. G. Bender, 'Whitehall, Central Government and 1992', *Public Policy and Administration* vol. 6 no. 1 (spring 1991), pp. 15–20.

quickly, sometimes without the time to consult us. They have to answer questions in the House. They must be prepared when the next crisis in the world arises.[44]

The special contribution of the FCO comes from its amassed and living knowledge of overseas countries. Among this knowledge diplomats tend to think of 'intelligence' as the covert, single-source reports that add something to their picture; but that putting the picture together for day-by-day policy-making remains their job, not intelligence's. An authoritative insider, speaking on Mrs Thatcher's decision in April 1985 to allow British bases to be used for the US bombing of Libya, referred to advice about likely Arab reactions prepared by the FCO, not the intelligence community.[45] All-source assessment comes into such pictures when it can supply something that others cannot. Otherwise diplomats may make up their own minds; they do not *automatically* seek intelligence assessment, in the way that any sensible general would.

The same applies even more to those in Treasuries and economic departments who are engaged in day-to-day international economic and trade matters. They have their own overseas contacts, often with intimate professional exchanges of information. Like Foreign Offices, they have their own policy and planning staffs, supported by statisticians, economists, and departmental research units.

In these circumstances all-source intelligence assessment is seen to supply two things. One is information and forecasts on subjects where the intelligence machinery is felt to have an expertise that others lack; military power is the first area to which Foreign Offices and economic departments look outside themselves for expert advice. The same applies to the many mixtures of military and other subjects, or the study of foreign wars in detail; indeed to anything where there are significant elements of defence expertise, secrecy and intelligence collection.

The other is the value of the national intelligence machinery as a means of ironing out potential interdepartmental difficulties, with authoritative assessment free from policy recommendations. British Ministers and senior officials respect an interdepartmental intelligence conclusion more than a departmental opinion linked with its own suggested action and vested interests. In the United States intelligence

---

[44] S. Jenkins and A. Sloman, *With Respect, Ambassador* (London: BBC, 1985), pp. 49–50.
[45] Statement by Sir Charles Powell, BBC Television, *Newsnight*, 2 July 1992. His point was that the advice (presumably against permitting American UK-based aircraft to be used) was wrong. Lord Howe gives a slightly different version of his position as Foreign Secretary (G. Howe, *Conflict of Loyalty* (London: Macmillan, 1994), pp. 504–6).

assessment has a special role in promoting some coherence in foreign policy between State Department and the White House. There is no other instrument quite like the JIC or NIE procedure for interdepartmental consensus-building; and even when there is no NIE a CIA assessment is seen to be free of policy involvement. Arguably the British system legitimizes a consensus around FCO views (and occasionally MoD ones, depending on the subject). But the system only works in this way through tacit assumptions about what subjects lend themselves to this intelligence treatment.

The national security connection

This account suggests that there is a risk of confusion between the subjects that all-source intelligence needs to study and the issues on which its assessments make their impact. There is no dispute that analysis has to range widely, not only over sources but also in subjects. Economics, demographics, 'soft' cultural factors and other non-security subjects are all part of understanding foreign countries properly. This holistic approach is needed for a proper understanding even of military power and other apparently circumscribed issues.

But this does not necessarily mean that intelligence has its competitive advantage (to revert to Davis's phrase) over the whole field of its holistic analysis. Kent first advocated its broad role immediately after the Second World War when governments had fewer sources of objective analysis and policy evaluation than they have today, and it is not surprising that it was then seen as an all-purpose lodestar. Now 'policy analysis' claims to be as objective and wide-ranging an institution as Kent's intelligence.[46]

There is still the question whether intelligence should now expand its function to turn Kent's doctrine into reality. On security intelligence this can be disposed of fairly easily. It overlaps with normal law enforcement; as in the way already noted in which British police Special Branches support the Security Service on the one hand, and local Chief Constables on the other.[47] But despite current speculation it is unlikely that security intelligence will become the criminal intelligence *authority* for parts of 'normal' crime. Intelligence *collection* may help law enforcement where it has unique technical assets and access, as has happened for some time

---

[46] For the development of policy analysis by British 'think tanks', see S. James, 'The Idea Brokers: the Impact of Think Tanks on British Government', *Public Administration* vol. 71 no. 4 (winter 1993).

[47] See chapter 2.

over narcotics; thus British intelligence has served the National Drugs Intelligence Unit with some kinds of covert collection in the past. But this is not to be taken as expanding intelligence's all-source remit. The drugs research effort remains part of law enforcement, not of an expanded intelligence community.

On foreign intelligence the answer about expansion is probably geared to the distinctive intelligence specialization in 'them' and not 'us', and its avoidance of direct policy recommendation. Intelligence's historical expertise is in understanding adversarial relationships and difficult targets; in 'closed' situations where information is concealed or manipulated, and where there are high risks of misperception. Its highest skill is using difficult evidence to see such situations through the elusive 'enemy eyes'. It is not an expert on its own side and its policies.

Yet on relatively open subjects it may be better to start from policy analysis than from intelligence assessment of 'them', divorced from policy recommendation. In the British system the JIC has existed in close relationships with the FCO's Policy Planning Staff, but there have always been different aims and methods. Intelligence concentrates on understanding and forecasting foreign situations with difficult information, often in forms that can be exchanged with close allies; the Planning Staff's reviews of situations may appear similar at first sight but are in fact the background to its own-side policy recommendations. Issues on Britain and the European Union are perhaps better illuminated by a planning paper than an intelligence assessment; so too is the United States' relationship with Europe. Considering policy issues may even produce better forecasts; thus members of the British Central Policy Review Staff have claimed that it was considering British fuel policy in the early 1970s that led them, and not the intelligence machine, to forecast the OPEC hike in oil prices that subsequently occurred with the Yom Kippur war.[48]

The relationship between foreign and domestic political issues heightens the difficulties of expanding intelligence. Most of the new non-security subjects of foreign policy are bound up with domestic politics in ways that do not apply to the same extent to the older ones. The British Foreign Secretary suggested in 1988 that 'There is no longer any such thing as a purely domestic policy . . . Open economies are interdependent, and have to be outward-looking'; the corollary is that there is no such thing as purely 'foreign' economic policy, and the same applies to

---

[48] T. Blackstone and W. Plowden, *Inside the Think Tank: Advising the Cabinet 1971–83* (London: Heinemann, 1988), pp. 76–7.

immigration, transport, environmental and similar issues.[49] It has been noted in the United States, in discussing the expansion of intelligence, that 'in many cases, we cannot distinguish clearly between foreign and domestic information'.[50] Arguably such issues are best approached by policy analysis of 'What we should do', not through policy-free intelligence assessment. It has been suggested in Britain that additional machinery is needed for a more strategic view of foreign policy; but an interdepartmental policy analysis element, based on an expanded Policy and Planning Staff, might be a better bet than developing a much broader range of JIC assessments.[51]

On this view 'intelligence is somehow rooted in concealment . . . Its techniques derive their special character from dealing with this deliberately created obscurity.'[52] This certainly does not mean a concentration on covert *sources*; assessment must be all-source, and holistic in its background. But it tends to mean concentration on *subjects* on which there are usually some covert contributions. Handling national security matters and their element of secrecy has framed intelligence's place in decision processes. Its skills were formed in the Cold War in which it could be said that 'there are no experts on the Soviet Union; there are only varying degrees of ignorance'.[53] It might be unwise to dilute this specialization. This is not to deny that the world is changing, that 'we appear to be moving from a world of geopolitics to one of geo-economics'.[54] But it is an argument against assuming that the intelligence community machinery that evolved for the first set of problems is the most suitable way of assuring well-informed governments on the second.

In any case, it is unrealistic to expect that the whole breadth of foreign affairs (and related domestic ones) could be served by a single intelligence assessment machine, particularly in the complexity of Washington. A secret of successful intelligence assessment is to keep the machinery small. Senator Boren, speaking about US intelligence reorganization, set out the admirable aspiration of making the CIA Intelligence Directorate into a world class think tank; but it may be mistaken to think that it

---

[49] Sir Geoffrey Howe, speech to Foreign Press Centre, Tokyo, January 1988, quoted by C. Tugendhat and W. Wallace, *Options for British Foreign Policy* (London: RIIA/ Routledge, 1988), p. 41.

[50] Shulsky (paper) in Shulsky and Sims, *What is Intelligence?*, p. 26.

[51] For the case for more strategy, see P. Hennessy, *The Intellectual Consequences of the Peace* (Strathclyde: Strathclyde Papers on Government and Politics, 1990), pp. 24–31.

[52] Quotations from Herman, *British and US Concepts of Intelligence*, pp. 24, 28.

[53] Quoted by D. Wedgwood Benn, *From Glasnost to Freedom of Speech* (London: RIIA/ Pinter, 1992), p. 10; the original is attributed to Paul Winterton.

[54] J. E. Spence, 'Entering the Future Backwards: Some Reflections on the Current International Scene', *Review of International Studies* vol. 20 no. 1 (January 1994), p. 7.

could ever have an unrivalled position as *the* think tank.[55] A US comment on intelligence's place has argued that the structure of information processing

should depend on the particular type of information involved, on who has the greatest chance and incentive to collect it, on what the legal ramifications of centralizing or dispersing it would be, and so forth. And as for a single center for information gathering and analysis, a center on which the government would place primary reliance in determining the whole range of its national security policies (including international economic, environmental, and health issues, to say nothing of international terrorism and drug trafficking), we should recognize that for the utopia it is.[56]

In all countries there are other expert bodies; and there may be some subjects on which it is unproductive to separate intelligence assessment from policy-making.

Summary

Intelligence collection is directed against targets that do not consent to it and usually take measures to frustrate it. In peacetime, on foreign targets, most of this collection is therefore by special means which distinguish intelligence from governments' non-intelligence ways of acquiring information. However this does not apply to security intelligence within national territory; its main methods used there are substantially the same as those used for law enforcement.

In war the distinction between intelligence and non-intelligence methods is less clear-cut. Intelligence's special, covert methods remain unique to it, but there is more battlefield intelligence collection by less covert means. Moreover the techniques of battlefield intelligence merge into those of military 'combat information' (including Electronic Warfare), collected as an integral part of combat, and under operational and not intelligence control. The military distinctions between these last two kinds of collection embody elements of bureaucratic accident and convenience, but there is some rationale. Battlefield intelligence is somewhat less immediate and more penetrating, complex and fragile (and hence secret) than combat information. However satellites and computers are now obscuring some of these distinctions.

All-source intelligence by contrast is not distinctive in its methods. Its character comes from its separation from policy recommendation and its general foreign policy orientation (plus the domestic aspects of internal

---

[55] Quoted by Shulsky in Shulsky and Sims, *What is Intelligence?*, p. 24.
[56] Shulsky in Shulsky and Sims, *What is Intelligence?*, p. 30.

security). Within this general framework its subjects and areas of foreign study have to be broad. But its output is more sought by governments on enemies than on allies, and on situations with elements of secrecy than on those where all information is in the public domain. All-source intelligence must not be biased towards material from covert sources. But it tends to be more authoritative on issues on which these contribute substantially, rather than on completely 'open' subjects.

Future governments can of course use all-source analysis in any way they want. But up to now its contribution has been greatest on subjects with some 'national security' content or implications. It is probably right that this should remain the norm.

Part III

Effects

8   Intelligence and national action

The previous group of chapters described the intelligence system and its boundaries. This group covers its effects; what it does for governments. The present chapter deals with its most important purpose: affecting decisions. Chapter 9 discusses its contribution to arms control and other measures of international security. Chapters 10–12 describe its other effects, as a defence of national secrecy; a set of international threats; and the promoter of its own set of international relationships.

Rational action and the intelligence dimension

Intelligence is produced to influence government action, however remotely. Before the modern system developed Clausewitz was inclined to discount it in warfare; important things could never be known with sufficient reliability at sufficient speed. 'Many intelligence reports in war are contradictory; even more are false, and most are uncertain . . . In short, most intelligence is false.'[1] The commander's intuition and will-power were better foundations for generalship.

This was before the growth of organized, permanent collection and analysis, and by the second half of the century there were more positive views about intelligence. A British book in 1895 agreed with Clausewitz that 'It is beyond the nature of things to avoid getting meagre, inexact or false information', but contradicted him by adding ' . . . for all that he [the commander] must strive to acquire as much positive intelligence as he can, as it is on this alone that he can base his most important resolutions.'[2] The view became firmer with twentieth-century experience, above all the importance of intelligence in the Second World War.

From this came the modern belief in intelligence as an indispensable

---

[1] Carl von Clausewitz, *On War* (Princeton: Princeton University Press, 1976) (ed. and trans. by M. Howard and P. Paret), p. 117. For discussion of Clausewitz's view see D. Kahn, 'Clausewitz and Intelligence' in M. Handel (ed.), *Clausewitz and Modern Strategy* (London: Cass, 1986), pp. 117–26.

[2] Col. G. A. Furse, *Information in War* (London: Clowes, 1895), p. 12.

component of decision-taking. In his book Kent portrayed it as the essence of rational government. 'Our policy leaders find themselves in need of a great deal of knowledge of foreign countries. They need knowledge which is complete, which is accurate, which is delivered on time, and which is capable of serving as a basis for action.'[3] This needed applied scholarship: 'Research is the only process which we of the liberal tradition are willing to admit is capable of giving us the truth, or a closer approximation to the truth, than we now enjoy.'[4] Intelligence-based action was the antithesis of leadership by ideology. 'I do not wish to be the one who rejects all hunches and intuitions as uniformly perilous, for there are hunches based on knowledge and understanding which are the stuff of highest truth. What I do wish to reject is intuition based upon nothing and which takes off from the wish.' Intelligence represented rationality, and the statesman who rejected it 'should recognize that he is turning his back on the two instruments by which western man has, since Aristotle, steadily enlarged his horizon of knowledge – the instruments of reason and scientific method'.[5]

Intelligence also received similar though more muted approval in military orthodoxy; at about the same time as Kent wrote his book, the British Chiefs of Staff listed 'Maintaining our Intelligence Organisations at a high standard of efficiency' among the 'Fundamentals' of post-Second World War defence.[6] Writers on military matters have propounded intelligence as the force multiplier and optimizer. According to Michael Handel,

Good intelligence will act as a force multiplier by facilitating a more focused and economical use of force. On the other hand, when all other things are equal, poor intelligence acts as a force divider by wasting and eroding strength. In the long run, therefore, the side with better intelligence will not only use its power more profitably but will also more effectively conserve it.[7]

R. V. Jones has written similarly that

The ultimate object of intelligence is to enable action to be optimized. The individual or body which has to decide on action needs information about its opponent as an ingredient likely to be vital in determining its decision; and this

---

[3] S. Kent, *Strategic Intelligence for American World Policy* (Hamden, Conn.: Archon Books, 1965 edition), p. 5.

[4] Kent, *Strategic Intelligence for American World Policy*, pp. 155–6.

[5] Kent, *Strategic Intelligence for American World Policy*, pp. 203, 206.

[6] Chiefs of Staff Report on Future Defence Policy, 22 May 1947, reproduced in M. Dockrill, *British Defence Since 1945* (Oxford: Blackwell, 1989), p. 135.

[7] M. Handel, 'Intelligence and Military Operations', *Intelligence and National Security* (Special Issue: 'Intelligence and Military Operations') vol. 5 no. 2 (April 1990), p. 69.

information may suggest that action should be taken on a larger or smaller scale than that which otherwise would be taken, or even that a different course of action would be better.[8]

The intelligence dimension has still not been integrated into writing on the nature of war; reading the enemy's mind is still neglected in the literature on generalship. Official texts still tend to place intelligence in the second rather than first rank of military attributes.[9] Nevertheless there is no dissent from the general idea that it is one of the keys to successful military action.

Gathering and using intelligence is also part of what is now expected of modern government's adherence to rational procedures in other matters. Intelligence failure is a regular subject for media investigation, as are governments' failures to act on what they get, as in the British Matrix-Churchill case. A participant in the Washington intelligence-policy process wrote in 1976 that

> In recent years the institutionalization of intelligence in Washington has become so irreversible, the processes themselves so pervasive, the products so indispensable, the penalties for spurning them so disagreeable and most of the intelligence officers so durable that the policy-maker must suffer intelligence gladly.[10]

The official statement of the United States Security Strategy in 1990 saw intelligence as 'the "alarm bell" to give us early warning of new developments and new dangers even as requirements grow in number and complexity'.[11]

Other governments also publicize the links between intelligence and national security. The British government made vivid pronouncements about the importance of Sigint to defend the 1984 ban on national trade unions at GCHQ. GCHQ was 'one of the security and intelligence agencies on which our national security, and to a degree that of our allies, depends'.[12] It played 'a unique and vital role in the security of the

---

[8] R. V. Jones, 'Intelligence and Command' in M. I. Handel (ed.), *Leaders and Intelligence* (London: Cass, 1989), p. 288.

[9] Thus there is no reference to intelligence in the current British army's 'Principles of War' in *Design for Military Operations – The British Military Doctrine* (Army code 71451, 1989), Annex A. Its 'Information Requirements' (p. 46) emphasize the dangers of having too much information rather than too little.

[10] T. L. Hughes, *The Fate of Facts in the World of Men – Foreign Policy and Intelligence-Making* (New York: The Foreign Policy Association Headline Series no. 233, December 1976), p. 22.

[11] *National Security Strategy of the United States* (The White House: March 1990), p. 29.

[12] Sir Geoffrey Howe (Secretary of State for Foreign Affairs) in the GCHQ debate, 27 February 1984, *Hansard*, col. 25.

United Kingdom'.[13] The ban was imposed only because of 'the critical importance and special nature of the work'.[14] Despite the political controversy about the ban, the agency's importance was not contested by the government's opponents.[15]

This might suggest that there is little more to be said. Every government has an intelligence system to make it better informed than it would be without it. Wise governments note intelligence's indications of risks, rather as private organizations pay for and use the risk assessments available on a commercial basis. What intelligence produces may well be incomplete, inaccurate or positively misleading in particular cases; but decision-takers that use it regularly are likely to have a better track-record than those that manage without it, just as government statistics for all their faults give leaders something better than guessing. Intelligence's role is to collect the information and build up the special knowledge needed to understand 'them' and not 'us'. The mere fact of incorporating intelligence's inputs into a regular decision-making process entails some government commitment to rationality and concern for reality. Except by those who believe like Marxists that events are shaped by great historical forces and not the quality of individual decisions, it may seem that intelligence's effect can almost be taken as read.

But not quite. Even if intelligence is useful, those setting its budgets have to decide *how* useful it is; how much does it really matter? This entails some understanding of the intelligence–decision couplings, and whether they give special support to particular actions. This chapter considers these two aspects of intelligence's value.

Decisions as black boxes

Set-piece decision-taking might be expected to have an easily observable intelligence-decision linkage; thus military doctrine emphasizes methodical decision-taking, with specified intelligence inputs (as EEIs or Essential Elements of Information) and clear decision outputs.[16] Yet in

---

[13] Lord Trefgarne in the Lords' debate on the same subject, 8 February 1984, *Hansard*, col. 1254.

[14] Lord Trefgarne, from the same speech, *Hansard*, col. 1259.

[15] For the present author's views on the issue see M. E. Herman, 'GCHQ De-Unionisation 1984', *Public Policy and Administration* vol. 8 no. 2 (summer 1993), commenting on H. Lanning and R. Norton-Taylor, *A Conflict of Loyalties: GCHQ 1984–1991* (Cheltenham, Glos.: New Clarion Press, 1991). Lanning and Norton-Taylor are strongly opposed to the union ban at GCHQ but do not dispute the importance of the work.

[16] EEIs (Essential Elements of Information) are defined as 'critical information requirements at a theatre's various levels of command'. They are 'identified in operational

practice it is not clear what causes what. The intelligence input may well be 'soft' rather than 'hard' data, embodying uncertainty, alternatives and speculation. Intelligence forecasts may themselves alter the situations on which they forecast. As well as clear-cut government decisions there are also all kinds of less structured ones and reflex reactions, as well as decisions not to do anything. There are also the constraints on action. Even if intelligence points to what should be done it may be impossible to do it; the best warnings of attack may lead to no action if there is nothing that can be done.

Even when there are identifiable intelligence inputs and decision outputs, the decision thought-process tends to be a mystery, like a black box with no external indication of its internal circuitry. Decision-takers cope with complex information and analysis through short-cuts, 'satisficing' and 'bounded rationality'.[17] Decisions are 'framed' by extraneous factors besides formal information inputs.[18] 'Information is only one of the many resources which policy-makers use to reach a decision.'[19] Besides information and forecasts, decisions involve judgment, political sense, leadership and determination in pursuing objectives. 'In a sense, rational or analytical decision-taking stands as an ideal to which decision systems aspire. The conditions in which foreign policy operates, however, make this goal impossible.'[20]

Thus foreign policy is not a simple translation of objectives into decisions in the light of information. It

involves complex processes in which values, attitudes, and images mediate perceptions of reality provided by various sources of information . . . The components of any definition of a situation will vary with conditions in the system,

doctrine in peacetime and regularly refined'. (*Design for Military Operations – The British Military Doctrine*, p. 46.)

[17] See for example H. A. Simon, *Administrative Behaviour* (New York: Macmillan, 1959). In this and subsequent work Simon 'showed that the assumptions that economic rationality made about human capacities, knowledge and information-processing procedures were quite unreasonable. The consequence was his model of "bounded rationality" . . . [that] argued (what was later proved) that individuals limit the alternatives considered, value their information-processing costs more highly than assumed, and settle for a process of "satisficing," that is, they assure themselves that the consequences of their decisions will be "good enough" for their purposes and proceed accordingly.' (R. E. Lane, *The Market Experience* (Cambridge: Cambridge University Press, 1991), p. 47.)

[18] For references and discussion see Lane, *The Market Experience*, chapters 3 and 6, especially pp. 52 and 100.

[19] R. Davidson and P. White (eds.), 'Introduction' in *Information and Government* (Edinburgh: Edinburgh University Press, 1988), p. 5.

[20] M. Clarke, 'The Foreign Policy System: a Framework for Analysis' in M. Clarke and B. White, *Understanding Foreign Policy: the Foreign Policy Systems Approach* (Aldershot, Hants: Elgar, 1989), p. 53.

internal political structure, degree of urgency in a situation, and political roles of policy makers.[21]

In short there are no clear wiring diagrams for the connections between intelligence items and specific action. Intelligence may be ignored, as when the British command ignored the intelligence on German deployments just before the Arnhem assault.[22] Governments can cut intelligence communities out of sensitive decisions altogether, as seems to have happened over the Israeli invasion of the Lebanon in 1982.[23] The British JIC process was similarly insulated from the planning for the 1956 Suez operation.[24] If intelligence is used, users consciously and unconsciously *select* from what is presented to them. Some users like Kissinger value secret single-source material but are uninterested in all-source assessment, preferring to be their own assessors.[25] Even diligent users who pay attention to everything interpret intelligence's careful expressions of uncertainty and alternatives in the light of their own prejudices. 'Interested policy-makers quickly learn that intelligence can be used the way a drunk uses a lamp post – for support rather than illumination.'[26] Intelligence's ideal is to transfer its own analyses, forecasts and estimates of probabilities to the user's consciousness *in toto*. But it is doing well if it ever gets near it. The decision-taking black box works through selectivity.

The effect of intelligence therefore depends on its institutional reputation and the personal chemistry between practitioners and users. Studies of Allied military leaders in the Second World War suggest that their initial experience of it determined their subsequent attitudes.[27] In one historian's view, the collective record of Allied leaders in the Second World War left a lot to be desired, for a variety of reasons: lack of knowledge and training; wariness after unfortunate earlier experiences; the determination of authoritarian personalities to impose their own will.[28]

Thus intelligence is at the mercy of users' unpredictable attitudes

---

[21] K. J. Holsti, *International Politics: a Framework for Analysis* (Englewood Cliffs, N.J.: Prentice-Hall, 1983 edition), p. 355.

[22] B. Urquhart, *A Life in Peace and War* (London: Weidenfeld and Nicolson, 1987), pp. 72–6.

[23] S. Gazit, 'Intelligence Estimates and the Policy-Maker' in M. Handel (ed.), *Leaders and Intelligence* (London: Cass, 1989), pp. 282–7.

[24] *The Naval Review* vol. 79 no. 4 (October 1991), pp. 356–61 (private accounts).

[25] For criticism of this propensity of Kissinger's, see R. S. Cline, 'Policy Without Intelligence', *Foreign Policy* no. 17 (winter 1974–5).

[26] Hughes, *The Fate of Facts in a World of Men*, p. 24.

[27] Handel, *Leaders and Intelligence*.

[28] H. C. Deutsch, 'Commanding Generals and the Use of Intelligence' in Handel, *Leaders and Intelligence*, pp. 194–260.

towards it; but it tries to make its own luck with them through persuasion, personal relations and marketing. One purpose of some routine intelligence output is to get users accustomed to it and build up credibility for the future. But it can never regard users' minds as blank sheets on which it can write whatever it chooses. Its presentation of its product always has to have an eye to its users' preconceptions. Even so, users' absorption is selective.

Education and conditioning

The coupling between specific intelligence and identifiable decisions is however only one way in which intelligence affects action. Intelligence-driven decisions tend to come from the cumulative effect of successions of reports, not from individual items.[29] Studies of information bring out the time-lags in information's effects; it is not consumed once and for all like a material product, but has recurrent and unpredictable 'waves of usefulness',[30] or it may never be used at all. Information is inherently wasteful: 'virtually every flow of knowledge may have its admixture of waste, some of the effort of producing it proving either abortive or superfluous.'[31] No one knows in advance what will turn out to be useful or how it will be used. There is the observation that government information as a whole works not instrumentally but indirectly, affecting action by seepage and 'enlightenment', providing an intellectual setting for actions rather than their precise raw material.[32]

In all these respects intelligence is the same as other information. Chapter 6 set out the spectrum between intelligence reports intended as users' background, like weekly summaries, and the assessments geared to specific use. Most intelligence is produced as background current-reportorial reports and short-term forecasts meeting intuitive criteria of 'relevance' and 'significance'. Those in CIA who produce the *President's Daily Brief* and the *National Intelligence Daily* do not expect them to lead regularly to immediate action, any more than newspapers expect to change the world with every issue. Of all the contents of daily and weekly high-level intelligence summaries only a minute proportion feed directly into decisions. The same applies to the even more voluminous single-

---

[29] See for example the account of the accumulation of evidence on German missile development in R. V. Jones, *Most Secret War: British Scientific Intelligence 1939–1945* (London: Hamish Hamilton, 1978), chapters 38 and 44.

[30] F. Machlup, *Knowledge and Knowledge Production* (Princeton: Princeton University Press, 1980), p. 174 note.

[31] Machlup, *Knowledge and Knowledge Production*, p. 177.

[32] Davidson and White (eds.), 'Introduction', *Information and Government*, p. 2.

source services direct to users. There are also the intelligence efforts devoted to surveillance for warning against unlikely events; the voluminous near real-time flows of reports against Soviet military activities during the Cold War were almost completely useless (in the sense that they led to no action), but fully justified as warning trip-wires.

Consequently the role of most intelligence is not driving decisions in any short term, specific way, but contributing to decision-takers' general enlightenment; intelligence producers are in the business of educating their masters. Education provides knowledge that may influence unforeseeable future decisions; a background item today turns out to be useful tomorrow or next year. Intelligence has the same unpredictable effects as information in newspapers. Enlightenment works at the level of 'the policies which precede policy . . . [which] lie in the area of predispositions and felt associations which exist in men and hover in institutions'.[33] Negatively, it reduces the proportion of users' action based on misconceptions; knowledge drives out error.

Arranging this mental furniture merges into influencing decision-takers' style and psychology. One of the effects of Western Allies' high-grade intelligence in the second half of the Second World War was simply to reduce uncertainty in decision-taking and support methodical strategies of systematically seeking overwhelming local superiority and planned risk-reduction, without constant worries about being surprised and the need to insure against it.

These factors complicate the intelligence-decision coupling. Intelligence producers cannot peer too far into all the varieties and unpredictabilities of use. In large part they have the techniques of educators. Their best normal test of value is simply whether users say that what they have been given has interested them; hard evidence from them of actual use is a bonus. This 'soft' criterion complicates critical attempts to evaluate intelligence investments as value for money.

Tackling this problem of evaluation is a basis for chapter 16. But some generalizations can be attempted now on the kinds of decisions intelligence supports in war and peace.

War

Optimization and transformation

Wartime intelligence is now well documented, but historians still have the problems of reconstructing actual effects. Some leaders acknowledge

---

[33] Hughes, *The Fate of Facts in a World of Men*, p. 13.

intelligence debts more than others; Montgomery never acknowledged his to Ultra.[34] Yet war provides the best laboratory for intelligence. Victory is a clear objective; intelligence has an unambiguous role of understanding the enemy; it has a higher priority than in peace and attracts more talent. Language for evaluating it is available in the arithmetic of war: casualties, material losses, territory and time. Thus the British official historian of the Second World War has quantified the effect in terms of time, and has argued that British and US cipher-breaking shortened the war in Europe by three or four years.[35]

Generalizations about wartime effects are still not easy. Obviously intelligence alone does not make for victory without force to use it. Better Allied intelligence in the early years of the Second World War would not have avoided defeats by more effective German forces, though it might have reduced the scale of disaster. Whether intelligence is good or bad has to be judged by two standards. One is its accuracy in an absolute way compared with reality, and the other is its quality compared with the opponent's; it is possible for both sides to have good or bad intelligence about the other.[36] The effects may not be the same at the strategic, operational and tactical levels of command; and at a tactical level the combat information discussed in the last chapter (like the effects of radars in air warfare) gets mixed up with intelligence proper. Intelligence effects also operate via the commanders' personalities and psychology; Sigint in the Pacific War 'led aggressive risk-takers to become even more audacious but it led cautious ones to become not more prudent but rather more calculated'.[37] In any case intelligence is only part of overall 'command performance'.[38] The Germans in

---

[34] Deutsch, 'Commanding Generals and the Use of Intelligence', pp. 211–15.

[35] F. H. Hinsley, 'British Intelligence in the Second World War' in C. Andrew and J. Noakes (eds.), *Intelligence and International Relations 1900–45* (Exeter: University of Exeter Press, 1987), p. 218.

[36] For this point, and illuminating discussion of intelligence and command, see J. Ferris and M. I. Handel, 'Clausewitz, Intelligence, Uncertainty and the Art of Command', *Intelligence and National Security* vol. 10 no. 1 (January 1995), pp. 40–1. But note also the 'intelligence-security contest' and 'counterintelligence contest' to be discussed in chapter 10. In it offensive intelligence superiority tends to produce better information security for its own side than the enemy's, and intelligence inferiority the reverse. Good intelligence has defensive applications which degrade the enemy's collection.

[37] Ferris and Handel, 'Clausewitz, Intelligence, Uncertainty and the Art of Command', p. 40.

[38] B. G. Blair, *Strategic Command and Control: Redefining the Nuclear Threat* (Washington D.C.: Brookings Institution, 1985), pp. 1–13, and P. B. Stares, *Command Performance: the Neglected Dimension of European Security* (Washington D.C.: Brookings Institution, 1991), chapters 1–3. 'Command performance' is Stares' term (as is 'command fluency' in what follows).

capturing Crete in 1941 showed superior 'command fluency', but their intelligence within it was inferior.[39]

But with all these qualifications two complementary intelligence dimensions can be suggested. The main one has already been indicated: the optimization of resources, in ways that lend themselves to quantification, or at least to analogies in quantified terms. Commanders' descriptions of the added value produced by good intelligence tend to be as the equivalent of so many extra troops, aircraft or warships. They are partly rhetorical but nevertheless provide some indication of scale. War is partly a matter of 'the concentration of superior forces at the decisive time and place', coupled with the corollary of 'economy of effort', or not wasting resources.[40]. On the effect on command:

With accurate information, uncertainty about the surrounding environment can be reduced and decisions affecting the readiness, movement, and application of military force can be taken with clearer understanding of the likely costs and benefits. If processed and delivered promptly, information can also provide more time for these decisions to be taken and, moreover, implemented with successful results. Overall it permits a clearer assessment of a situation, generates policy choices to achieve a specific outcome, and allows those choices to be weighed for their relative payoff.[41]

Or, briefly, 'information can help military organizations to handle their resources efficiently'.[42]

Thus the basic arithmetic of Second World War strategy in Europe was manpower and numbers of divisions. Germany underestimated total Soviet resources, overestimated those of Britain and the USA (through Allied deception) and got its military planning wrong. It believed that the Western Allies had twice as many divisions as they actually had, and allocated between one- and two-thirds of its scarce resources in France and Southern Europe to guard against non-existent dangers.[43] The Allies

---

[39] A. Beevor, *Crete* (London: Murray, 1991), part two. The Sigint evidence of the German plan of attack was passed to the Allied commander, but apparently with orders prohibiting him from acting on it; these are discussed in detail in R. Bennett, *Behind the Battle: Intelligence in the War with Germany* (London: Sinclair-Stevenson, 1994), pp. 281–4. Nevertheless it was command failure that lost the battle. It was said after the war that 'a hundred extra wireless sets would have saved Crete'. (Quoted by Stares, *Command Performance*, p. 57.)

[40] *Design for Military Operations – The British Military Doctrine* Annex A (Principles of War), p. 68.

[41] Stares, *Command Performance*, p. 19.

[42] J. Ferris, 'Ralph Bennett and the Study of Ultra', *Intelligence and National Security* vol. 6 no. 2 (April 1991), p. 480.

[43] For German calculations of Soviet manpower see B. Wegner, 'The Tottering Giant: German Perceptions of Soviet Military and Economic Strength for "Operation Blau" (1942)' in C. Andrew and J. Noakes (eds.), *Intelligence and International Relations*

got the calculations right. The measured style of their offensives and the German failures against them illustrate intelligence as the arithmetical optimizer. If 'the effective distribution of superior resources was in large part the key to the Allies' success in the Second World War',[44] then good intelligence was an important contributory factor.

Obviously there are various degrees of this optimization. Yet occasionally it seems to move to another dimension, in which intelligence moves from optimization towards *transformation* effects. Intelligence not only optimizes but also determines the nature of operations and campaigns as well as the outcomes; the war is in some real sense an intelligence war. This transformation has not been explored and there is no ready-made typology for it, but three examples can be suggested.

One is where the style of combat in land warfare with a low force-to-space ratio emphasizes movement and surprise, transcending material power. Luttwak describes a dialectic between two styles of strategy: attrition based on the direct deployment of strength, and 'relational manoeuvre' for 'the application of some selective superiority against presumed weaknesses, physical or psychological, technical or organizational'.[45] The blitzkrieg effect of the second is 'above all *the unbalancing of command decisions* [italics in original]'.[46] Its deep penetration battle is 'an information race'.[47] The military aim in war of movement is often expressed as 'getting inside the enemy's decision-cycle' so that he is always overtaken.

Hence battle incorporating this information race can turn particularly on intelligence, for both the attacker and defender. The success of the German blitzkrieg in France in 1940 was based on mobile forces and a superior C^3I system, which included accurate intelligence assessments of French vulnerability in the Ardennes and better battlefield intelligence as the campaign progressed.[48] By contrast Britain was not geared to exploit sufficiently quickly the Sigint that was then becoming available. Sufficient intelligence – in speed of delivery as well as quality – may be a necessary condition for effective fluid warfare of this kind.

---

[44] *1900–45*, pp. 293–311. For conclusions on the campaign in the West see Ferris, 'Ralph Bennett and the Study of Ultra', p. 477.

[44] J. Gooch (ed.), *Decisive Campaigns of the Second World War* (London: Cass, 1990), p. 3.

[45] E. N. Luttwak, *Strategy: the Logic of War and Peace* (Cambridge, Mass.: Belknap, Harvard, 1987), p. 94. For related ideas of momentum in war and its psychological leverage, see R. Simkin, *Race to the Swift* (London: Brassey, 1985).

[46] Luttwak, *Strategy*, p. 108.

[47] Luttwak, *Strategy*, p. 106.

[48] Stares, *Command Performance*, pp. 25–6. But note that in this and other examples of the 'information race' intelligence and combat information (see previous chapter) are both involved.

Another example of transforming effects may be maritime warfare, if intelligence is able to provide advance warning of enemy movement, rather than just current positions. As far back as the Armada intelligence has guided the strategic mobilization and deployment of British fleets. In the early months of the First World War the Grand Fleet was forced by the German submarine threat to withdraw to its Scottish bases, and the successful German bombardment of East Coast ports in late 1914 could have led to a consistent German strategy of bombardment, attacks on British coastal trade and interference with cross-Channel support for the forces in France. To be able to counter such operations the Grand Fleet had to be able to weigh anchor at its northern bases at the same time as the German fleet left its North Sea ports. After the end of 1914 British codebreaking was able to provide its fleet with the warning needed. The resulting Battle of the Dogger Bank in early 1915 dissuaded the Germans from further operations of this kind.[49] Intelligence was the basis of a successful reactive use of British sea power.

Intelligence can also determine the ways in which sea power can be used offensively. In the Second World War the British use of maritime power to interdict Axis seaborne supplies to North Africa turned on deciphered messages giving advance information of convoy movements.[50] In a rather different way decipherment by both sides influenced the Battle of the Atlantic's style as a battle with long-distance shore-based control on both sides, turning on concentrating U-boat wolf-pack attacks on the one hand and re-routing convoys on the other. In these maritime examples, in one way and another, intelligence not merely increased effectiveness but influenced the character of operations.

A third kind of operations transformed or at least heavily influenced by intelligence is long-range bombardment, including strategic air attack. Bombardment needs targets and some assessment of vulnerabilities and effects. Its modern ranges are such as to need intelligence for them, not just the visual observation and other combat information that sufficed as 'artillery intelligence' in the First World War. Hence intelligence is a major determinant of bombardment's form. The strategic air offensive against Germany in the Second World War depended on targeting and bomb damage assessments from airborne photographic reconnaissance. Sigint on the German forces' oil shortages eventually produced the successful concentration on oil targets in the war's final

---

[49] P. Beesly, *Room 40: British Naval Intelligence 1914–18* (London: Hamish Hamilton, 1982), pp. 308–9.

[50] F. H. Hinsley with E. E. Thomas, C. F. G. Ransom and R. C. Knight, *British Intelligence in the Second World War* vol. II (London: HMSO, 1981), pp. 319–24.

year.[51] US satellite and conventional imagery had similar effects on the air offensive in the Gulf War. The strategy of any long distance bombardment is driven at least partly by the state of target intelligence.

Attacks and defence

Whether intelligence is optimizing or transforming, there is still the question whether it favours attack or defence. Attackers use surprise, and David Kahn has argued that intelligence is the classical counter to it.[52] Intelligence is 'essential to victory only in defense . . . [It] is a defining characteristic of defense; it is only an accompanying characteristic of offense.'[53] After its initial disasters, the USA's exploitation of the Japanese naval cipher helped it in effective strategic defence in the Pacific in 1942, including the Battle of Midway.[54] Precise intelligence on German plans of attack helped the British to save Egypt at Alam Halfa in 1942; 'Montgomery won his first battle by believing the intelligence with which he was furnished.'[55] Intelligence superiority by the intended victim leaves the surpriser open to ambush. It enabled the British to inflict heavy losses on Rommel's last spoiling attack in the North African campaign, at Medenine; 'surprise had been indispensable for the success of the [German] plan, and Rommel had indeed attacked in the belief that the Eighth Army was unready.'[56] It facilitated defence and counter-stroke on a bigger scale in the Battle of Kursk and its aftermath.[57] High quality intelligence made a major contribution to the British defence of Malaysia in the operations against Indonesian 'confrontation' in 1963–6, 'a satisfactory and successful campaign, skilfully and economically conducted.'[58] At the end of his study of German intelligence in the

---

[51] F. H. Hinsley with E. E. Thomas, C. A. G. Simkins and C. F. G. Ransom, *British Intelligence in the Second World War* vol. III part 2 (London: HMSO, 1988), chapter 54. The Bletchley view was that this 'may have been the outstanding service rendered by Special Intelligence to the strategic air war in Europe' (p. 497).

[52] As argued in G. J. A. O'Toole, 'Kahn's Law: a Universal Principle of Intelligence', *Journal of Intelligence and Counterintelligence* vol. 4 no. 1 (spring 1990).

[53] D. Kahn, *Hitler's Spies* (London: Arrow paperback edition, 1980), p. 510, quoted in O'Toole, 'Kahn's Law: a Universal Principle of Intelligence', p. 39.

[54] R. Lewin, *The American Magic: Codes, Ciphers and the Defeat of Japan* (London: Penguin, 1983), chapters 4–7.

[55] Sir Edgar Williams (Montgomery's Chief Intelligence Officer), quoted in R. Bennett, *Behind the Battle: Intelligence in the War with Germany 1939–45* (London: Sinclair-Stevenson, 1994), p. 100.

[56] Hinsley, *British Intelligence in the Second World War* vol. II, p. 596.

[57] See D. M. Glantz, 'Soviet Operational Intelligence in the Kursk Operation', *Intelligence and National Security* vol. 5 no. 1 (January 1990).

[58] For references to this cross-border intelligence see Lord Carver, *Seven Ages of the British Army* (London: Grafton, 1984), pp. 310–13.

Second World War, Kahn has suggested that over the centuries Britain has tended to have effective intelligence in conflicts with continental European states because

this balance-of-power policy, which is a reactive, or defensive, technique, requires intelligence to succeed . . . each nation's attitude toward intelligence may be seen as an expression of its geography and its internal dynamics. Britain was a sea power, essentially defensive . . . she needed intelligence. Germany was a continental power . . . Her armies, attacking, did not require intelligence. And so she failed to develop it.[59]

This is a thought-provoking theory. Yet in practice intelligence superiority can also favour the offence. The Germans' reading of British naval ciphers during the invasion of Norway in 1940 favoured the aggressor. The Japanese triumph in planning Pearl Harbor depended partly on good local target intelligence on the US anchorage and its defences. In early 1944 Sigint on Japanese deployments led Admiral Nimitz to aim the US attack on the Marshall Islands at Kwajalein, in the centre of the group, instead of the perimeter islands as had been expected.[60] More generally, Sigint in the Pacific 'allowed the United States to defeat Japan far more speedily and at lower cost' in its recapture of island bases.[61] Similarly intelligence superiority was the foundation of the Allies' successful strategic deception over the Normandy invasion in 1944. Even apart from the effects of deception, intelligence on the enemy's defensive positions can do something to counteract the defender's inherent advantages, as in the way the Normandy success owed much to the detailed intelligence put together on beaches and defensive positions. In general terms, good intelligence's ability to help the aggressor to achieve local superiority should be as important as its potential for warning the defender against surprise. Further study of the theory may indeed show that intelligence's warning value to the defender can be equalled by its ability to tell the attacker whether he is about to achieve surprise or not, thereby giving him the option of avoiding what would otherwise be a 'surprise failure'.

Strength and weakness

Rather the same ambiguity emerges from the relationship between intelligence and material strength. In facilitating the effective use of force intelligence might seem to be of relatively greater value to the weak than

---

[59] Kahn, *Hitler's Spies*, p. 513.   [60] Lewin, *The American Magic*, p. 195.
[61] Ferris and Handel, 'Clausewitz, Intelligence, Uncertainty and the Art of Command', p. 35.

the strong. Ferris argues persuasively that the German 'fire brigade' strategy after autumn 1942 of deploying élite forces to defeat Allied attacks or force expensive battles of attrition depended on advance warning:

There is a direct correlation between the success of German intelligence and operations throughout the last three years of the war. Whenever Germany did correctly assess the intentions of its foes, whether around Monte Cassino in the spring of 1944 or directly to the east of Berlin in February 1945, its forces had their maximum effect; indeed they demonstrated the feasibility of German defensive strategy . . . Indeed had the German Army possessed the Allies' intelligence, it might well have forced a stalemate in Europe.[62]

But the evidence about intelligence's special importance to the weak seems as unproven as its affinity with defence. Examples of successful campaigns by weaker sides guided by effective intelligence are quite hard to come by. From the Second World War the predominant impression is that the Allies' intelligence superiority coincided with their superior material resources from 1942 onwards.

This suggests some other possible conclusions. One is that, besides optimizing the use of military power, wartime intelligence can itself be partly a reflection of it. Allied Second World War intelligence superiority was itself nourished in some ways by the military superiority which it supported. Thus its imagery depended on air superiority. It was the battlefield victors, not the vanquished, who benefited most from POW interrogation and captured documents. Those with effective command of the sea were consistently more successful at capturing the crucial cryptographic material for parts of naval cipher-breaking.

Another is that the development of effective wartime intelligence takes time, but gets a particular impetus from defeat in the early years of war;[63] military men need a sharp shock to overcome their lack of intelligence interest and competence. The Allies' disasters in the early stages of the Second World War were more potent intelligence teachers than success was to the Axis. On the German side even the considerable naval crypt-analytic successes in the first half of the war were never absorbed into a properly integrated intelligence system.[64] For Britain on the other hand Alam Halfa in 1942 'saw operations welcome intelligence into full partnership for the first time . . . Hitherto " . . . information about the enemy was frequently treated as interesting rather than valuable. We had

[62] Ferris, 'Ralph Bennett and the Study of Ultra', p. 481.
[63] I owe this suggestion to John Prestwich, ex-Bletchley.
[64] Bennett, *Behind the Battle*, p. 174.

had good intelligence before; henceforth we were going to use it." '[65] In the same way the vast Japanese successes of 1941–2 perhaps blinded them to their intelligence inefficiency.

Peace

Knowledge is part of peacetime state power or influence; it is 'a resource which some societies may be able to exploit more successfully than others . . . Those who know more, and can manipulate what others know, have more power . . . Knowledge and ideology structures, it can be argued, are vital frameworks of foreign policy, not merely peripheral additions to it.'[66] Intelligence is part of this decision-takers' contact with reality. But in peacetime the effects are more diffuse than in war; and success and failure are themselves often debatable. A writer inclined to be critical of the effects of intelligence on high policy concluded with the careful judgment that

Intelligence may not be able to find the truth; even less may it be able to persuade others that it has found it. But keeping the players honest, not permitting disreputable arguments to thrive, pointing out where positions are internally contradictory or rest on tortured readings of the evidence would not be a minor feat. While it would not save the country from all folly, it would provide more assistance than we get from most instruments of policy.[67]

Perhaps one principal effect is simply to encourage decision-takers towards a style based on evidence and analysis, rather than intuition and conviction. This is part – not an unimportant part – of rational leadership.

However it is even harder than in war to generalize on where it most matters. Intelligence's peacetime successes tend to remain secret, but some peacetime conclusions can be offered. First, parts of nominal peace are simply less violent versions of war, and intelligence there has extensions of its wartime power for the application of force. Thus it is central to counter-terrorism and negates terrorism's characteristics of invisibility and surprise. Defeating terrorism usually depends on intelligence success and not the force available; sometimes, as in the Northern Ireland campaign, military force has intelligence-gathering as a principal

---

[65] Bennett, *Behind the Battle*, p. 100, quoting Sir Edgar Williams.
[66] C. Farrands, 'The Context of Foreign Policy Systems: Environment and Structure' in Clark and White, *Understanding Foreign Policy*, pp. 95–6.
[67] R. Jervis, 'Strategic Intelligence and Effective Policy' in A. S. Farson, D. Stafford and W. K. Wark (eds.), *Security and Intelligence in a Changing World: New Perspectives for the 1990s* (London: Cass, 1991), pp. 179–80.

aim. The most sustained and effective use of tactical intelligence in peacetime since the Second World War has probably been in the Israeli campaigns against Arab terrorism; the ability to take counter-action has helped to set the terms of its relationships with the Arab world. On the analogy with war, intelligence on terrorism is a transforming element.

Second, apart from intelligence's influence on particular decisions, there is the cumulative influence on national standing of having well-informed policies. This has been particularly relevant to Britain as a nation of declining economic power wishing nevertheless to maintain world status. The Foreign Secretary claimed in 1992 that 'In recent years Britain has punched above her weight in the world. We intend to keep it that way.'[68] Intelligence has been one element in this position. Good intelligence has helped Britain to play bad hands with some finesse.

Third, effects on the actual conduct of diplomacy have some parallels with wartime use. Tactical intelligence support adds to certainty and confidence in foreign policy execution; as already quoted from Hibbert, it gives immediacy, practicality and focus to existing general con-clusions.[69] It has been claimed that after Britain ceased to intercept and decipher foreign diplomatic dispatches in 1844 'British diplomacy necessarily suffered, and the loss of foreign interceptions in 1844 helps to explain the contrast between previous success and subsequent failures, illustrated for example by Palmerston's career.'[70] Christopher Andrew has argued that French diplomacy was less effective in the years immediately before 1914 than hitherto, since the German diplomatic ciphers had been made unreadable after a French indiscretion.[71] Decrypted telegrams which provided most of the Turkish delegation's correspondence contributed to British negotiating tactics at the Lausanne conference in 1922–3.[72] The literature about intelligence focuses on how it affects policy. But in practice the main effects are more tactical, at least for diplomatic intelligence sent to Foreign Offices and their posts. As Ferris has put it, 'in practice, intelligence rarely affects the

---

[68] Douglas Hurd, 'Making the World a Safer Place; Our Priorities' (*Daily Telegraph*, 1 January 1992), quoted by W. Wallace, 'British Foreign Policy after the Cold War', *International Affairs* vol. 68 no. 3 (July 1992), p. 438.

[69] Chapter 5, note 35.

[70] K. Ellis, *The Post Office in the Eighteenth Century* (Oxford: Oxford University Press, 1958), p. 141.

[71] C. Andrew, 'Codebreakers and Foreign Offices' in C. Andrew and D. Dilks, *The Missing Dimension* (London: HarperCollins, 1995), pp. 37–8.

[72] K. Jeffrey and A. Sharp, 'Lord Curzon and Secret Intelligence' in Andrew and Noakes, *Intelligence and International Relations 1900–45*.

determination of policy – although it does happen. Frequently however it does affect its execution of policy.'[73]

Fourth, there is intelligence's role as defence against peacetime surprise. The diplomatic equivalent of military surprise is not part of most foreign affairs. 'Unlike military men, diplomats and run-of-the-mill political leaders do not like to surprise each other.'[74] But there is some deliberate surprise in peacetime, pre-empting normal reactions; examples include Hitler's re-militarization of the Rheinland in 1936, the 1939 Nazi–Soviet Pact, the US–Chinese rapprochement of 1971, Sadat's expulsion of Soviet advisers in 1972, and his peace initiative with Israel in 1977. Intelligence may fail in this warning role, as in the British failure to detect the making of the Nazi–Soviet Pact.[75] But it is some counterweight to surprise tactics.

These points suggest that intelligence's general peacetime effect is to optimize national positions, not transform them. Yet there is a serendipity factor. The greatest single coup produced by an item of diplomatic intelligence was the British use of the deciphered Zimmerman telegram as a lever in securing the United States' entry to the First World War. This emerged unpredictably from what had previously been an unspectacular line of German diplomatic traffic. Arguably the firm intelligence on Libyan support for terrorism in April 1986, leading to the US air attack aimed at the Libyan leadership, was a similar case of a relatively small (but authentic) piece of intelligence having a big result. Most use of intelligence consists of undramatically optimizing national influence; but sometimes – often unpredictably – it is crucial, transforming peacetime action in the way it sometimes transforms war. Perhaps in some ways it is like medicine; doctors in general practice are said to spend most of their time on things that affect patients' quality of life, but occasionally their role is life-saving. Intelligence has something of the same variation.

---

[73] J. Ferris, 'The Historiography of American Intelligence', *Diplomatic History* vol. 19 no. 1 (winter 1995), p. 97.

[74] M. Handel, *The Diplomacy of Surprise: Hitler, Nixon, Sadat* (Cambridge, Mass.: Harvard University Center for International Affairs, 1981), p. ix.

[75] For a summary of British intelligence on the Soviet–German negotiations see D. C. Watt, *How War Came: the Immediate Origins of the Second World War 1938–1939* (London: Heinemann, 1989), pp. 372–4. For a fuller treatment of this British intelligence failure see the same author's article, 'An Intelligence Surprise: the Failure of the Foreign Office to Anticipate the Nazi–Soviet Pact', *Intelligence and National Security* vol. 4 no. 3 (July 1989), pp. 512–34. For Soviet use of information from an agent in the Foreign Office's communications section, see Watt's 'Francis Herbert King: a Soviet Source in the Foreign Office', *Intelligence and National Security* vol. 3 no. 4 (October 1988).

Summary

Intelligence's justification is that it influences action in useful ways. But these uses are very varied: some reports are used immediately, while others are useful in the distant future; many more reports influence decisions through their cumulative effects; others still have long-term educational or psychological value. Warning surveillance is a precaution against what may never happen.[76] Much intelligence is never used at all. In all these ways it is like other information.

Nevertheless the effect is to optimize national strength and international influence, on varying scales. In war it assists the effective use of force. Sometimes in war (and counter-terrorism) it goes further and transforms the ways in which action takes place. In peace its effects are often in diplomatic execution rather than the making of foreign policy. In both war and peace intelligence's consistent impacts are its cumulative, relatively unsurprising contributions to effectiveness and influence. Overlaying any regular patterns there is serendipity or luck.

These are central points for assessing intelligence's importance. However there are the other effects listed at the beginning of this chapter. These can be considered in what follows.

---

[76] Warning surveillance is sometimes spoken of as *insurance*. Lawrence Freedman has pointed out in a different context that insurance policies do not stop accidents happening or equip one to cope with them; instead they give compensation. Warning is a precaution against surprise rather than *post facto* compensation. (L. Freedman, 'The Use and Abuse of Threats', *Brassey's Defence Yearbook* (London: Brassey's, 1995), pp. 4–5.)

9   International action

The last chapter discussed intelligence's effects on national action related to national interests. It also plays some part in arrangements geared to promoting international security, through unilateral and multilateral action and international treaties. This part can now be examined. International security is considered here only in its most limited sense, of avoiding wars or limiting them.

Security through states acting *on* or *for* others

Intelligence is drawn on for any kind of national action, including intervention in others' conflicts or mediation between them with international security motives. The United States' ability to intervene or mediate as a world guardian draws on its superpower intelligence, and depends significantly upon it. Good diplomatic intelligence probably helped Kissinger to pave the way for Arab–Israeli agreements after the Yom Kippur war, and President Carter to bring about the Camp David settlement. The same applies to other states acting as guarantors or brokers, like Britain in seeking a Cyprus settlement.

National intelligence itself can also be offered as part of mediations and guarantees. As part of the Yom Kippur war's ceasefire Kissinger offered to provide both sides with imagery from U-2 overflights of the disengagement area, as some safeguard against surprise attack.[1] After the Sinai II Agreement in September 1975 this material was provided from U-2 sorties flown every seven to ten days at 70,000 feet, routinely or at Egyptian or Israeli request, over the neutral Buffer Zone and the Limited Force Zones.[2]

---

[1] H. Kissinger, *Years of Upheaval* (London: Weidenfeld and Nicolson, with Michael Joseph, 1982), p. 828. Similar proposals were also made as part of the Israeli–Syrian settlement, p. 1254.

[2] V. Kunzendorf, *Verification of Conventional Arms Control* (*Adelphi Papers* 245) (London: IISS/Brassey's, 1989), p. 18. For details of the agreements, see A. James, *Peacekeeping in International Politics* (London: Macmillan, 1990), pp. 114–15.

The US package also included various technical observation devices deployed in conjunction with the UN force, but the U-2 agreement was a significant use of intelligence activities and their results to guarantee information from agreed operations which would otherwise have been regarded as covert violations of national airspace. Subsequently US imagery is said to have been provided in support of the Egyptian–Israeli Peace Treaty of 1979. The Multinational Force and observers then established for verification received the analysed results (not the original photographs) as a basis for discussion with both parties.[3] Intelligence briefings to both parties are said to have been part of US intervention in 1990 to prevent India–Pakistan relations drifting towards war over Kashmir.[4] It will be surprising if US satellite imagery does not also figure among the carrots and sticks in any future Middle East settlement, for example to replace the Israeli surveillance capacities that will be lost by withdrawal from the Golan Heights.

This use of national intelligence to support international security also applies to action by groups of nations. Common action needs shared information, in peace as well as war. Intelligence is part of international cooperation against terrorism and in sanctions as applied over the conflict in the former Yugoslavia. The same applies to arrangements such as those of the Missile Technology Control Regime, the Nuclear Suppliers Group and the Australia Group to coordinate national export limitations on various kinds of weapons proliferation. National intelligence tips off collaborating nations, or is used to keep them up to the mark; international arrangements between intelligence professionals underpin political collaboration of this sort or pave the way for it.

Conflict resolution by the United Nations

The need for common information applies equally when action is through international institutions. The Korean and Gulf Wars provided obvious examples of 'alliance intelligence', mainly from US sources, in UN-sponsored war. There is no insuperable problem over intelligence-sharing in operations of this kind against a common enemy. But the need for intelligence also exists in peacekeeping situations where the UN stance is neutral, and in comparable non-UN operations such as those of the Multinational Force sent to the Lebanon in 1982 and NATO forces

---

[3] H. Hanning (ed.), *Peacekeeping and Technology: Concepts for the Future* (New York: Report of International Peace Academy no. 17: report of a 1983 Task Force), p. 18.
[4] Statement by Robert Gates, BBC radio programme *Open Secrets*, 21 March 1995.

around and over the former Yugoslavia. We can concentrate here on such operations under the UN umbrella.

Well-established and relatively passive UN peacekeeping gets by without needing much intelligence. However there are its more active operations of recent years, where neutral peacekeeping verges upon more active 'peace-making' and preventive operations without antagonists' consent. These need more intelligence product, for successful on-the-spot and diplomatic mediation, decisions for the effective use of forces, planning and protection of humanitarian assistance, and UN contingents' own self-defence. Operations in Somalia and the former Yugoslavia have illustrated these UN needs for intelligence on threats, disputants and the local situations generally. The UN prefers to talk of 'military information' rather than 'intelligence',[5] but in reality its forces need it very much as they would need intelligence in purely national operations, but with the added problems of an alliance setting and the UN's official neutrality. A British unit commander in Bosnia commented that 'that strategy [for delivering humanitarian aid] and its specific mission was based on the possession of information'.[6] A more senior officer from the British Central Staff commented that 'intelligence is a vital element of any operation and the UN needs to develop a system for obtaining information without compromising its neutrality'.[7] Some measures have been taken for intelligence within the UN, but more of it is needed. How to provide it is discussed in chapter 20.

Conflict reduction between potential contestants

Arms control verification

National intelligence also supports arms control and confidence building arrangements *between* states. Covert collection backs up treaty inspection and other confidence-building arrangements. Surprisingly it also became the subject of some treaty legitimation itself.

The origins of this role were in the East–West strategic nuclear arms control negotiations of the late 1960s. Intelligence estimates provided the arms control baseline: 'it was in large but unrecognised measure American confidence in the quality of its intelligence on Soviet forces during the late 1960s and early 1970s that allowed strategic arms

---

[5] Article by C. Bellamy, *Independent*, 31 January 1994.
[6] Col. A. D. A. Duncan, 'Operating in Bosnia', *RUSI Journal* vol. 139 no. 3 (June 1994), p. 12.
[7] Rear Admiral J. J. R. Tod, 'UN Perspectives of Current Security Arrangements', *RUSI Journal* vol. 139 no. 1 (February 1994), p. 35.

limitation negotiations to begin at all.'[8] Intelligence was even more important for its collection capabilities. As long as on-site inspection of compliance with arms control was unacceptable to the Soviet Union, intelligence's ability to verify at long-distance became a crucial issue, not only for US proposals but also for Congressional approval.

Hence US collection capabilities determined the forms of arms control. SALT I was cast in terms of launchers (missile sites and missile tubes in submarines), not missile production, because launchers were what imagery satellites could see. The limitations on throw-weights and MIRV'd warheads in SALT II were possible because US interception and analysis of radio telemetry from Soviet missiles yielded data on such characteristics.[9] The US–Soviet Standing Consultative Committee was created as a mechanism for handling intelligence-based complaints about treaty breaches. What emerged has been described by John Gaddis as a 'reconnaissance satellite regime' between the Cold War superpowers.[10]

This received some treaty recognition. The existence of intelligence satellites had been accepted from 1963 onwards, but only tacitly; and there were US fears that they might be disarmed in some way – for instance through the operational deployment of experimental ASAT programmes for knocking them out in space, or extensive camouflage to conceal missiles from satellite imagery. The result was the agreement incorporated as Article XII of the 1972 ABM Treaty and Article V of the SALT I Agreement, repeated as Article XV of SALT II, that

1. For the purpose of providing assurance of compliance with the provisos of this Interim Agreement [Treaty], each Party shall use national technical means of verification at its disposal in a manner consistent with generally recognised principles of international law.
2. Each Party undertakes not to interfere with the national technical means of verification of the other Party operating in accordance with paragraph one of this article.
3. Each party undertakes not to use deliberate concealment measures which impede verification by national technical means of compliance with the provisions of this Interim Agreement [Treaty]. This obligation shall not require changes in current construction, assembly, conversion, or overhaul practices.

---

[8] W. H. Kincade, 'Challenges to Verification: Old and New' in I. Bellamy and C. D. Blackmore, *The Verification of Arms Control Agreements* (London: Cass, 1983), p. 26.
[9] Telemetry from missiles was like the radio-telemetry now used by Grand Prix engineers to monitor engine performance and other systems in their cars while racing. Telemetry analysis in intelligence was like intercepting these transmissions and trying to reconstruct a racing car from them with no other information about it.
[10] J. L. Gaddis, *The Long Peace* (New York: Oxford University Press, 1987), pp. 195–214.

These 'national technical means' (NTMs) have often been identified with satellite collection, but are not limited in this way; missile telemetry for example was collected by ground-based US sites in Iran as well as by satellites, and by Soviet vessels in the Atlantic.[11] This was the first international recognition of intelligence collection, and the first undertaking not to interfere with it and to limit concealment from it.

The position was changed in the later US–Soviet arms control of the 1980s and subsequently, when on-site inspection became acceptable to the USSR and assumed a major role in verification. But this non-intelligence activity still benefited from synergy with NTMs, as for example in their ability to trigger the limited numbers of on-site 'challenge inspections' permitted by treaty.[12] The NTM provisions were repeated in the INF and START treaties, along with agreements for some specific displays of equipment to imagery satellites.[13]

All this was breaking new ground. The most surprising feature was an explicit agreement as part of SALT II that the NTM provisions covered the interception and analysis of radio-telemetry and limited its encipherment. Both parties' imagery satellites were by then an open secret, and in any case the practical scope for hiding ICBM silo construction from them was limited.[14] Telemetry interception and analysis on the other hand were part of the closely guarded Sigint world. The SALT II negotiations in the 1970s turned increasingly on parameters verifiable from telemetry, and there were US fears that it would be cut off by the

---

[11] An official US definition of NTMs is as 'assets which are under national control for monitoring compliance with the provisions of an agreement. NTMs *include* photographic reconnaissance satellites, aircraft-based systems (such as radar and optical systems), as well as sea- and ground-based systems (such as radar and antennas for collecting telemetry)' (emphasis added). (*Verifying Arms Control Agreements: the Soviet View* (Washington D.C.: US GPO 1987), p. 84, quoted by Kunzendorf, *Verification of Conventional Arms Control*, p. 74.)

[12] For this synergy see M. E. Herman, 'Intelligence and Arms Control Verification' in J. B. Poole (ed.), *Verification Report 1991* (London: VERTIC, 1991), pp. 187–96; and Kunzendorf, *Verification of Conventional Arms Control*, pp. 52–9.

[13] Thus Article XII of the INF Treaty provided for each side to be able to request six open displays per year of road-mobile ground-launched missiles at operating bases; not later than six hours after receiving a request, roofs of all launcher structures were to be slid open, and missiles and launchers moved into the open for a period of twelve hours. (J. K. Leggett and P. M. Lewis, 'Verifying a START Agreement: Impact of INF Precedents', *Survival* vol. 30 no. 5, September/October 1988, p. 413.) The START I agreement included similar provisions for monitoring mobile ICBMs; see A. S. Krass, 'Update: Verification and START: a Progress Report' in J. B. Poole and R. Guthrie, *Verification Report 1992* (London: VERTIC, 1992), p. 57.

[14] Though it was thought necessary to agree as a 'Third Common Understanding' attached to Article XV of the SALT II Treaty that 'no shelters which impede verification by national technical means . . . shall be used over ICBM silo launchers'.

growing Soviet encipherment of its information channels.[15] From 1977 onwards the US demanded assurances that further telemetry encipherment was covered by the ban on 'concealment measures which impede verification by national technical means', and after two years the Soviet Union accepted as part of SALT II that neither party would 'engage in the deliberate denial of telemetric information, such as through the use of telemetry encryption, whenever such denial impedes verification of compliance with the provisions of the Treaty'.[16] The effect was to halt the spread of this encipherment. Later the START agreement of 1991 banned this encipherment completely, and took other measures to ensure that telemetry data was available to the other party.[17]

This regime was still a strange one. It had no definition of NTMs, or of the 'recognized principles of international law' to be applied in using them.[18] Their legitimization applied only to verifying the arms control treaties, not to their other, simultaneous intelligence collection. It was an unequal agreement. Given America's openness, the USSR was much less dependent than the USA on verification by NTMs. It probably got something out of its satellite imagery and its telemetry interception off Florida, but the dependence upon NTMs was mainly American, and it was the US who sought their protection and was the main gainer from having them safeguarded in the agreement.[19]

[15] For an account of the US attitude and subsequent negotiations, see S. Talbot, *Endgame: the Inside Story of SALT II* (London: Harper and Row, 1979), pp. 194–202, 221, 237–60.

[16] 'Second Common Understanding' attached to Article XV. For an account of these negotiations, see R. P. Labrie, *SALT Handbook* (Washington D.C.: American Enterprise Institute for Public Policy Research, 1979), pp. 410–12.

[17] The treaty required the broadcasting of all telemetric information and banned any practice – including encryption, encapsulation and jamming – that denied access to it by NTMs. It also required the provision of full telemetry tapes and certain information that helped in their interpretation. This was 'a new and highly significant commitment to transparency in military affairs'. (Details and quotation from A. S. Krass, 'Update: Verification and START: a Progress Report' in Poole and Guthrie, *Verification Report 1992*, p. 59.)

[18] Though there is an echo in a UN resolution on the principles of arms control verification; 'any verification system should correspond to the generally recognized principles and norms of the UN Charter and other fundamental sources of international law.' (Final Document UN First Special Session on Disarmament, 1978 (UN Document A/S – 10/2), quoted by B. R. Tuzmukhamedov, 'Verification of Disarmament' in A. Carty and G. Danilenko, *Perestroika and International Law* (Edinburgh: Edinburgh University Press, 1990), p. 49.)

[19] It was argued at the time by some Americans that the guarantee of unenciphered telemetry might be used by the USSR to deceive the United States about Soviet ICBM accuracies by producing suitably doctored readings. (See for example W. R. Harris, 'Counterintelligence Jurisdiction and the Double-Cross System by National Technical Means' in R. Godson (ed.), *Intelligence Requirements for the 1980s: Counter-Intelligence* (Washington D.C.: National Strategy Information Center, 1980), pp. 71–3.) There is no indication that this fear of Soviet technological duplicity was justified in practice.

Nevertheless the agreements were still remarkable. Adversaries were prepared to refer to intelligence sources of great importance and sensitivity. The US insistence on how much depended on telemetry analysis was an unusual revelation of sources and methods. There were no precedents for recognizing each other's collection – and, most important of all, undertaking not to take defensive countermeasures against it. There was no precedent for adversaries agreeing to send radio transmissions *en clair*. Despite the tightly limited context, the US–Soviet agreement about NTMs, in the middle of the Cold War in which intelligence played an important part, was a remarkable event.

NTMs also acquired some multilateral status. References to them were incorporated in the CFE agreement, in which signatories accepted the principles of non-interference and cooperative measures with them.[20] In CSCE's Stockholm Document signed by thirty-five nations in 1986 they were recognized as having a role in monitoring compliance with agreed international confidence and security building measures (CSBMs).[21] By 1989 it was thought that 'the principle of using NTM (without interference) is, thus, well established and recognized by all participants in the new negotiations on conventional arms control.'[22] But with the end of the Cold War this multilateral status has disappeared from view. It remains to be seen whether legitimized collection by NTMs has a future, or was a historical curiosity of the Cold War.

Intelligence and non-intelligence transparency

The cases of legitimized NTMs are special ones, in which intelligence received a measure of the target's consent and cooperation. But intelligence collection as a whole must be clearly distinguished from the arms control inspection and transparency by CSBMs on which many international security agreements are now based. These treaty-based agreements for cooperative information collection have led to the creation of national inspection agencies, deliberately without visible 'intelligence' connections for the same reasons as have led the UN to adopt the euphemism of 'military information'.[23] Treaty inspection has

---

[20] Signatories agreed not to interfere with national or multinational technical verification or impede it by concealment; and to consider cooperative measures to enhance national or multi-national verification (VERTIC, *Trust and Verify* no. 4, October 1989).

[21] Kunzendorf, *Verification of Conventional Arms Control*, p. 52.

[22] Kunzendorf, *Verification of Conventional Arms Control*, p. 52.

[23] For an account of the British inspection unit, see R. L. Giles, 'Implementing Arms Control: a Survey of the Work of JACIG' in Poole and Guthrie, *Verification Report 1992*, pp. 159–62. (JACIG is the 'Joint Arms Control Implementation Group'.)

developed as a new kind of legalized, quasi-diplomatic information gathering, or an extension of the older role of defence attachés. Inspection teams no doubt report what they have seen to their national intelligence organizations, just as defence attachés do; but inspectors, like attachés, are on the legitimate side of the wavy line between 'unrecognized' intelligence and 'recognized' non-intelligence collection. However, intelligence and international inspection have a synergy. CSBMs have some specific treaty limitations; for example Sigint sensors are barred from the aircraft flights of inspection authorized by the Open Skies agreement of 1992, and the technical definition of their photography is restricted to the standard of telling a tank from a lorry.[24] Covert intelligence collection provides additional reassurance (and deterrence) against cheating and deception to circumvent agreed international transparency. The evader or deceiver has the task of defeating the undeclared and unpredictable intelligence collection of its potential victim (and its supporters), as well as treaty inspection.[25] Furthermore it was pointed out many years ago that evasion and deception have two components: not only the concealment and deception measures, but also the organization needed to plan and implement them. Intelligence carries with it the threat of detecting the second component as well as the first.[26] It gives some greater force to arms control treaties, and to transparency arrangements such as the UN's Register of Conventional Arms, than if national good faith were verifiable only by whatever inspection was agreed and sanctioned.

Summary

National intelligence has some applications for international security. The American superpower draws on its intelligence when intervening or mediating in others' disputes, and has provided services of intelligence (particularly imagery) as part of conflict resolution. Groups of nations

---

[24] US Senate Select Committee on Intelligence, Report 103-44, *Intelligence and Security Implications of the Treaty on Open Skies* (Washington D.C.: US GPO 69-010, 1993), pp. 8–11.

[25] There was of course an extreme US Cold War view that all their intelligence collection was under a kind of Soviet control, which demonstrated Soviet military prowess when it was in Soviet interests to do so; 'they have not made things impossible which they could have made impossible; they were willing to leave them difficult.' (A. Katz, 'Verification and SALT: a Different Line of Insight' in L. Pfaltzgraff Jr, U. Ra'anan and W. Milberg, *Intelligence Policy and National Security* (London: Macmillan, 1981), p. 144.)

[26] L. C. Bohn, 'Non-Physical Inspection Techniques' in D. G. Brennan (ed.), *Arms Control and Disarmament* (London: Cape, 1961), p. 348.

involved in collective action to combat terrorism and limit arms transfers exchange intelligence as part of this cooperation. The need for intelligence applies even more to UN peacekeeping and other operations.

Intelligence has also played a major part in verifying arms control agreements. One unpredictable result was some mutual US–Soviet recognition in the 1970s of National Technical Means of intelligence collection, and agreements to limit each side's security measures, including telemetry encipherment. Later agreements have emphasized on-site inspection as the primary means of verification. But intelligence sources support this non-intelligence observation and act in synergy with it. In this and other ways intelligence can be used to contribute to international security as well as serve purely national ends.

10 Intelligence and security

The last two chapters discussed how intelligence influences the main world of action. This one deals with its effects on another, specialized area: governments' own secrecy and information control. They want accurate information and good forecasts about other states; but they also want to control what these others are able to find out about them, so they erect information defences. Counterespionage and counterintelligence have already been noted in this defensive role. This chapter describes more fully how offensive intelligence is connected with defensive information protection.

The terminology is confusing. The protection of information is *information security*, usually shortened in this context to 'security'. It should not be confused with 'security' as *national security* and its subdivisions into external and internal security; or with *security intelligence* (already discussed) on threats to internal security. Information security supports national security but is not limited to this area of government activity (see figure 11).

Governments want 'security' (information security) over a wide range of matters. Thus the country's internal security includes information security measures to frustrate foreign espionage, and external security includes similar measures to protect military and diplomatic communications against foreign interception and exploitation. But some things outside any reasonable definition of the national security area also need information security protection, for example sensitive economic and financial information or even confidential information about individuals.

In practice some kinds of information security overlap with physical protection against other threats; control of access to government premises, for example, is protection against terrorism as well as espionage.[1]

---

[1] The NATO definition of security links information and non-information security. It is 'the condition achieved when designated information, *material, personnel, activities and installations* are protected against espionage, *sabotage, subversion and terrorism* . . . ' Allied Intelligence Publication No. 1 – *Intelligence Doctrine* (Brussels: NATO, 1984), p. A-7 (emphasis added).

But the security considered here is essentially the safeguarding of information. Information security in this sense has a national community of officials and service officers engaged in policy-making, standards-setting and oversight for it. Intelligence participates in this activity and supports it.

This does not mean that security of this kind is an integral part of intelligence. Reference has already been made to the US view that it is, in rather the same way as covert action is included.[2] Officially security tends to be regarded as a separate but related activity. In NATO doctrine

Intelligence and security are closely related activities, in that one of the aims of security is to prevent the acquisition of intelligence by the enemy, and it is one of the aims of intelligence to penetrate enemy security. Therefore the planning of effective intelligence acquisition requires a knowledge of security measures, particularly those of a potential enemy. Likewise the planning of effective security requires a knowledge of intelligence acquisition methods; again, particularly those of an enemy or potential enemy.[3]

The information security apparatus is best seen as a special kind of intelligence user, but with intimate intelligence involvement in it.[4] This chapter describes first its elements and then the various ways in which intelligence supports it.

Security techniques and organization

Information security has three components: 'protective security' intended to defeat or blunt intelligence collection; the detection and neutralization of intelligence threats; and deception. The first puts up

---

[2] For covert action see chapter 3. For US handling of the definition of 'security' see A. N. Shulsky, *Silent Warfare: Understanding the World of Intelligence* (Washington D.C.: Brassey's, 1991), pp. 99–129, also note 2, p. 202; 'For our (theoretical) purposes . . . security should be considered as part of counterintelligence since it serves the same function.' Also articles in R. Godson (ed.), *Intelligence Requirements for the 1980s: Counterintelligence* (Washington D.C.: National Strategy Information Center), and the counterintelligence section of R. Godson (ed.), *Intelligence Requirements for the 1990s* (Lexington, Mass.: Lexington Books, 1989), pp. 127–63. Most writers accept some distinction between counterintelligence and passive security, as does Godson in his introductions to the two volumes.

[3] NATO, *Intelligence Doctrine* (1984), chapter 1 paragraph 107.

[4] While much has been written about intelligence and deception, the literature on defensive security and its effects is relatively small. An official history is F. H. Hinsley and C. A. G. Simkins, *British Intelligence in the Second World War. Vol. IV: Security and Counter-intelligence* (London: HMSO, 1990), but the emphasis is on counterespionage and the use of agents as deception. For the best discussion of the security–intelligence interaction at the military operational level, see J. Ferris, 'The British Army, Signals and Security in the Desert Campaign, 1940–42', *Intelligence and National Security* vol. 5 no. 2 (April 1990), pp. 255–91.

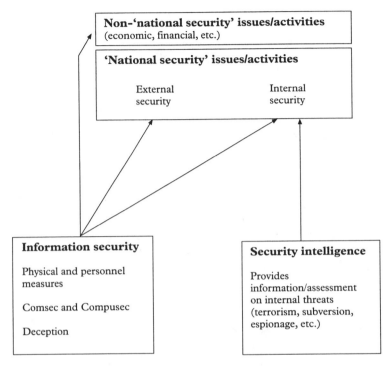

Figure 11 Various meanings of 'security'

passive, defensive screens; the second is active defence by eliminating the opponent's offensive intelligence threat; the third defeats hostile intelligence by deceiving or confusing it. Their forms and relationships are set out in figure 12.

Protective security

Most security consists of defensive protective measures which are mirror-images of offensive intelligence techniques. Thus the counters to Humint collection include personnel, physical and document security, typically personnel vetting, control of travel and contacts with foreigners, restriction of physical access to premises, and rules for the classification, custody and transmission of documents; all underpinned by the general concept of the need-to-know, or restraint in distributing information.

In the same way, Communications Security ('Comsec') provides countermeasures to Comint, the communications aspects of Sigint. Comsec is defined by NATO as

The protection resulting from all measures designed to deny to unauthorized persons information of value which might be derived from the interception and study of telecommunications, or to mislead unauthorized persons in their interpretation of the results of such a study. Communications security includes transmission security, crypto-security and the physical security of communications, security materials and information.[5]

'Emcon' (emission control) is an armed forces term for the limitation of electronic emissions of all kinds. The more recent development of computer security ('Compusec') deals with the security of computer information against computer hacking or the interception of unintended radiations. Despite the complex acronyms, the principles of electronic security are simple: limit intended transmissions to the minimum; eliminate unintended radiations; make it difficult for the interceptor to find, identify and locate transmissions; limit what can be deduced from their external features; encipher or otherwise deny access to the information content; and deny unauthorized access to computers.

Similarly camouflage and concealment are the passive counter-measures to imagery. Noise reduction is the defence to acoustic intelligence. 'Signature reduction' is used as a generic term for measures of this kind to make military targets less visible to radars and other detection devices such as those that pick up thermal emissions. Prisoner-of-war interrogation has its counterpart in training to resist interrogation. Close-range eavesdropping and bugging have their parallel techniques of counter-eavesdroping and 'sweeping'. Leaks of information into open sources are countered by wartime censorship. Each form of offensive intelligence collection breeds a related defensive expertise.

Detection and neutralization

Apart from these passive measures, the defence sometimes has the possibility of eliminating or nullifying the opponent's intelligence collection by direct action if it is detected. Agents can be arrested; foreign intelligence officers under diplomatic cover can be expelled; bugs can be put out of action; close-range eavesdropping can occasionally be jammed. Some collection may lend itself to physical elimination even in peace, as in the North Koreans' capture of the US intelligence collection vessel 'Pueblo' in 1969.

War obviously increases the scope for physical action of this kind. Aerial reconnaissance is subject to enemy action, as is other close-range

---

[5] NATO, *Intelligence Doctrine* (1984), Annex A, p. A-2.

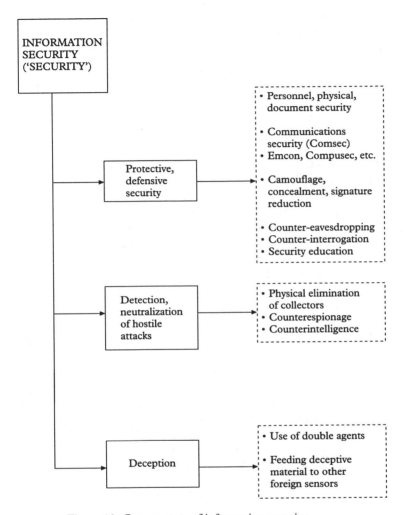

Figure 12 Components of information security

collection – as for instance when Rommel's successful tactical army Sigint unit in the Western desert was captured.[6] Intelligence centres and long-range collection sites might come under modern attack as part of the interdiction of command-and-control systems.

[6] Ferris, 'The British Army, Signals, and Security in the Desert Campaign, 1940–42', p. 286, referring *inter alia* to H.-O. Behrendt, *Rommel's Intelligence in the Desert Campaign* (London: Kimber, 1985).

However the scope for direct action in peacetime is uneven. Agents are particularly vulnerable, but the bulk of technical collection is long-range and passive, not vulnerable to physical action or jamming. Satellite collection in the Cold War was effectively protected by the informal US–USSR agreement not to proceed with the deployment of operational ASAT systems.[7]

Deception

Deception is defined by NATO as 'Those measures designed to mislead the enemy by manipulation, distortion or falsification of evidence to induce him to react in a manner prejudicial to his interests.'[8] It has acquired its own specialist literature, and only a brief outline need be given here.[9] It is an adjunct to security, presenting information to deceive or confuse, while security seeks to conceal by withholding. Deception works by making false evidence – false reports through agents, false documents, bogus radio traffic, deceptive displays – available for foreign intelligence collection. Successful deception is usually designed to fit in with and magnify its target's own preconceptions. Its ideal is to make the victim deceive himself, while minimizing the amount of genuine information that has to be given to build up source credibility.

Deception applies mainly in war. Its peacetime significance is exaggerated, since the literature about it tends to expand it to include the much more general run of governments' propaganda and news presentation. Deception is best thought of as part of an orchestrated *plan* to induce the victim to do something he would not otherwise do. In the right circumstances it can be a potent and positive adjunct to security and surprise, as the Second World War and the Gulf War showed. Its most pervasive effect in the Cold War was however that the deception *threat* caused all intelligence to be treated with caution, casting doubt on good as well as bad. Humint in particular tends to be devalued in this way, by users' fears that its reports may have been planted by the opponent.

---

[7] For details of ASAT tests and negotiations, see P. B. Stares, *Space and National Security* (Washington D.C.: The Brookings Institution, 1987), chapter 6.

[8] NATO, *Intelligence Doctrine* (1984), p. A-3.

[9] See for example D. C. Daniel and K. L. Herbig (eds.), *Strategic Military Deception* (New York: Pergamon, 1982); M. Handel (ed.), *Strategic and Operational Deception in the Second World War* (London: Cass, 1987); R. V. Jones, *Reflections on Intelligence* (London: Heinemann, 1989), pp. 107–45.

Security structures

Like intelligence, responsibility for secrecy became institutionalized. The Victorian military intelligence departments had nominal responsibility for the provision of ciphers and security in the field. Fears of German espionage led to the foundation of the British Secret Service Bureau in 1909. The two World Wars and the fear of communism were as powerful a stimulus to security as to intelligence. As with intelligence, it was slowly realized that security needed interdepartmental coordination of its measures, in a defensive security community that mirrored the way in which offensive intelligence operated across the boundaries of targets and techniques. Western experience in the Cold War was that little was achieved by having high quality ciphers if Soviet intelligence was able to recruit cipher clerks who could provide copies of them. Since complementary intelligence attacks have a synergy between them, the defence needs a similar capacity to integrate security measures across organizational boundaries. Not the least of the British achievements in the Second World War was the establishment of the Security Executive and an interdepartmental security structure alongside, and linked with, the Joint Intelligence Committee and the control of strategic deception.[10] In recent years the USA has developed its own comparable concept of Opsec, or all-source operational security embracing the full range of defensive measures.[11]

Thus governments need organized security policies and actions, and intelligence makes its special inputs to them. Security authorities are its specialized customers. Additionally, part of national information security is intelligence's own protection; in this respect intelligence is also in a sense one of its own users. The intelligence inputs to national

---

[10] The key elements were the Security Executive, the Bridges Panel and the Inter-Services Security Board (Hinsley and Simkins, *British Intelligence in the Second World War. Vol. IV*, pp. 52–3, 73–4, 247–8 (note), 247–9). For the control of deception see M. Howard, *British Intelligence in the Second World War. Vol. V: Strategic Deception* (London: HMSO, 1990), pp. 3–30, especially p. 27. For cipher security see F. H. Hinsley with E. E. Thomas, C. F. G. Ransom and R. C. Knight, *British Intelligence in the Second World War* vol. II (London: HMSO, 1981), appendix 1, 'British Cypher Security during the War', pp. 631–4.

[11] For the case for establishing an information security structure in the United States, see US Senate Select Committee on Intelligence: Report 99-522, *Meeting the Espionage Challenge: a Review of The United States Counterintelligence and Security Programs* (Washington D.C.: US GPO, 1986), pp. 59–65. For an excellent summary of Opsec and information security in general, see G. F. Jelen, 'The Defensive Disciplines of Intelligence', *International Journal of Intelligence and Counterintelligence* vol. 5 no. 4 (winter 1991–2).

information security as a whole (including intelligence's own defensive needs) are shown in figure 13, and can now be described.

Intelligence contributions to security

Threat assessments for defensive security measures

Security, like other action, needs to be based on intelligence assessment. Hence the intelligence threats posed by other countries are assessed on evidence about their foreign intelligence organizations, gained by what was described in chapter 3 as counterintelligence or 'intelligence on foreign intelligence'. Foreign intelligence organizations are the most security-minded of all targets, and intelligence attacks on them are difficult. Imagery can provide some information on external facilities such as foreign interception stations, but not on their activities and successes. Sigint on foreign intelligence communications can sometimes provide important insights, as demonstrated by the British penetration of the German Abwehr ciphers in the Second World War.[12] In the world of bugging and eavesdropping, the discovery of the opponent's technical devices gives some idea of his capabilities. Usually however the main sources on intelligence threats are the infrequent human ones – defectors and intelligence officers recruited within foreign intelligence services. The picture of intelligence threats tends to be made up of scraps of evidence plus rare windfalls from these human sources.

Hence the intensive study of foreign intelligence is hard going, and sometimes raises questions about how much effort it is worth putting into it. In the Cold War counterespionage and counterintelligence against Soviet Humint were very important, but other coverage of Soviet intelligence was of doubtful priority; it was occasionally unclear for example how important it was to know precisely what Soviet satellites could photograph, and whose job it was to work it out. Threat assessments can be mirror-images of the offensive capabilities of one's own side; because the West was not initially skilled in close-range eavesdropping, it was some time before the extent of Soviet bugging of Western embassies in Moscow in the 1940s and 1950s was properly appreciated.[13] On other occasions assessment put forward a 'worst case' view of Soviet threats, in the good cause of making governments security-

---

[12] For details see Howard, *British Intelligence in the Second World War* vol. V, pp. x–xi and *passim.*

[13] For Soviet bugging in Moscow see C. Andrew and O. Gordievsky, *KGB: the Inside Story of its Foreign Operations from Lenin to Gorbachev* (London: Hodder and Stoughton, 1990), pp. 374–7.

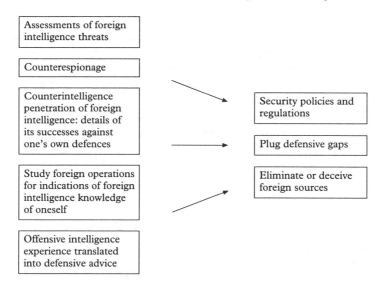

Figure 13 Intelligence support for information security

conscious; some exaggeration of this kind may have crept into US perceptions of the threat from the Soviet drive to acquire Western technology.[14] But despite the difficulties of making realistic intelligence threat assessments, sensible security policies must start with them

This applies not just to general foreign capabilities but also to specific details. Western security in the Cold War over the testing of new electronic emissions depended for example on precise evaluations of how far they could be intercepted by the ubiquitous Soviet 'Sigint trawlers' hovering off NATO coasts. Similarly if there is personnel security vetting for risks of ideological espionage, someone has to define what the ideological threats are and who might exploit them.

Counterespionage

Counterespionage has already been described. Its detection and neutralization of foreign espionage is the biggest effort devoted to direct

---

[14] See US Senate Select Committee on Intelligence: Report 99-522, *Meeting the Espionage Challenge*, provoked by the espionage detections which caused 1985 to be dubbed 'the year of the spy'. Its conclusion was that 'Taken together, the damage to national security from espionage, technology theft and electronic surveillance amounts to a staggering loss of sensitive information to hostile intelligence services' (p. 16). Against this conclusion, and the subsequent evidence of the Ames case, must be set the view of former KGB officers that their Humint collection had largely run out of steam by the 1980s.

action against foreign intelligence threats. As part of security intelligence it is in some ways distinct from the main intelligence community. It is pre-eminently detection-oriented, as compared with other intelligence's search for wider understanding. From one viewpoint counterespionage can be seen as a discrete contribution to information security.

However this is an incomplete picture. In the first place, counter-espionage deals with only one kind of hostile intelligence threat – human sources, and not foreign Sigint or imagery. Even more important is the close link with its own national counterintelligence organizations, already indicated in chapter 3. Counterespionage detects and eliminates individual cases of hostile espionage, which may provide trails back into the intelligence organizations controlling them; while counter-intelligence's penetration of intelligence adversaries from inside can provide counterespionage with leads. Thus despite its institutional separation counterespionage is closely linked with counterintelligence's efforts to penetrate opponents' intelligence, negate its successes, and even exploit them.

Penetrating foreign intelligence

In the wide sense used in this book – 'intelligence on foreign intelligence' – counterintelligence does not only provide the evidence for threat assessments. When successful it also produces specific evidence of current foreign penetrations of one's own side. Leads for counter-espionage have just been mentioned, but on penetrations by other foreign sources – for example Sigint – counterintelligence information about them can be used to strengthen the security defences involved and stop the adversary's exploitation of weaknesses. The effectiveness of Soviet security in the early stages of the Cold War was partly because its defensive countermeasures were based on good inside information from its agents within the West; the longest-lasting damage done by the ideo-logical spies like Philby was to blow the Western technical sources that existed in the early Cold War period.[15] Soviet espionage continued to obtain such results against technical collection; thus the details it obtained in the 1970s of US satellite intelligence programmes provided the basis for Soviet defensive security programmes to reduce the effects of satellite surveillance.[16] Similar Soviet counterintelligence penetration

---

[15] For references to the compromise of Western successes against Soviet ciphers in the early Cold War period, see J. L. Gaddis, 'Intelligence, Espionage and Cold War Origins', *Diplomatic History* vol. 13 no. 2 (spring 1989), pp. 198 (note), 205.

[16] J. T. Richelson, *The US Intelligence Community* (Cambridge, Mass.: Ballinger, 1985), p. 120.

was shown in the cases that broke in the 1980s of the British analyst Prime and the American Pelton, both of them Soviet agents who passed details to their controllers of UK–US Sigint successes against Soviet communications.

In these ways intelligence adversaries are engaged in a 'counterintelligence contest', seeking to penetrate and capture each other, and to avoid being penetrated and captured themselves. This will be discussed in more detail later in this chapter.

Operational inferences

Apart from penetrating it, inferences about hostile intelligence's successes can also be made from surveillance of the enemy non-intelligence activities which it informs. Complete support for security entails scrutinizing incoming intelligence about enemy forces and their communications for any evidence that what they do reflects intelligence-derived knowledge about one's own side. One of the features of British Second World War Sigint analysis was the scrutiny of all decrypted German messages for evidence of any reading of Allied codes and ciphers.[17]

But looking at foreign activity in this way needs an effort organized particularly for that purpose. Despite accumulating evidence of superior Allied intelligence, the Germans in the Second World War consistently refused to accept that the Enigma could be broken cryptanalytically.[18] The British were equally complacent about their vulnerable naval ciphers for the first part of the war.[19] The USA appears to have been taken completely by surprise by the revelations that the KGB had broken its naval ciphers throughout the 1970s and the first half of the 1980s with material supplied by the Walker family.[20]

Poachers and gamekeepers: advice and standards

In the ways just described security is supported by collection and analysis on foreign intelligence. But this is only half of intelligence's contribution to it. The other half is where intelligence acts as part of the

---

[17] Hinsley, *British Intelligence in the Second World War* vol. II, p. 643.
[18] For the German navy's examination of the evidence of cipher insecurity, see T. Mulligan, 'The German Navy Evaluates Its Cryptographic Security', *Military Affairs* 49 (1985), pp. 75–9.
[19] Hinsley, *British Intelligence in the Second World War* vol. II, appendix 1, pp. 634–40.
[20] For a summary of the Walker case see P. Earley, *Family of Spies* (New York: Bantam, 1989).

security apparatus itself, putting its own offensive expertise to defensive use in the role of poacher turned gamekeeper. It sets defensive standards and supplies specialized security material. In addition to its intelligence concern for internal threats, the British Security Service has special responsibilities for defensive security standards against Humint attacks, including standards for the vetting of individuals and the protection of documents. These responsibilities are so wide-ranging that it is a defensive 'security' as well as an 'intelligence' organization.

Other agencies also have their defensive roles. Cipher-breakers have long been recognized as the best people to devise their own state's ciphers; as early as the eighteenth century the British cryptanalysts were being asked to construct them.[21] In recent years it has become accepted good practice for Comsec (and latterly Compusec) to be a responsibility of the national Sigint organization.[22] The same principles apply elsewhere. Those devising defences against eavesdropping need technical advice from eavesdropping practitioners; camouflage techniques should draw on the photo-interpreters' tricks of the trade; and so on. Some lines of technical research can be sponsored for both offensive and defensive purposes; offensive and defensive professionals have this close relationship.

This function of helping with standards and techniques probably represents the most consistent intelligence contribution to security. Whatever the difficulties of assessing the precise state of intelligence threats, intelligence has its own offensive expertise to offer. The quality of this offensive intelligence experience helps to determine the quality of the defence.

Security responsibilities and intelligence contests

Those then are intelligence's contribution to defensive security. Its relationship with it is closer than with a normal user. Those responsible for security are the operational arms of government, but intelligence agencies make the inputs described here. One effect is to give parts of the intelligence community important advisory and executive responsibilities within their national information security communities.

---

[21] D. B. Horn, *The British Diplomatic Service* (Oxford: Oxford University Press, 1961), p. 234.

[22] For details of the US NSA's responsibilities in these fields, see articles by K. D. Bryan and J. T. Devine, *Journal of Electronic Defense* (Alexandria, Va.: The Association of Old Crows) vol. 10 no. 6 (June 1987) and vol. 11 no. 2 (February 1988). The association of the British Sigint organization with cipher security after the First World War is described in Hinsley, *British Intelligence in the Second World War* vol. II, appendix 1, pp. 631–4.

Another effect of security requirements (including those of intelligence itself) is to commit part of intelligence to the counterintelligence contest with its opponents. The nature of this particular contest needs to be carefully defined. All intelligence collection is part of a contest with opposing security systems. Mention was made in chapter 4 of the perpetual contest between those devising ciphers and those trying to break them, and all other collection entails similar contests. Campaigns against opposing security defences involve devoting considerable effort to building up a 'technical base' of knowledge on security defences and techniques for breaking through them. From this offensive collection comes the defensive value just described, of enabling intelligence to provide technical advice and backing to its own side's defences.

Thus offensive superiority over enemy defences is translated into defensive pay-offs. In the Battle of the Atlantic it was the offensive break-back into the German naval Enigma in 1943 that produced the conclusive evidence, from the scrutiny of operational messages to U-Boats, that the Germans were reading an important British naval cipher, and hastened its replacement by a more secure system.[23] Superiority has progressive effects; victories in intelligence produce increasingly good security, and vice versa. Western successes in the combined offensive–defensive intelligence contest in the Second World War are summed up in the fact that 'leaving aside the decryption of tactical codes and cyphers . . . the Allies were reading from early 1943 some 4,000 German signals a day and a large, if somewhat smaller volume of Italian and Japanese traffic, whereas to Germany, Italy and Japan virtually all the Allied cyphers had by then become invulnerable.'[24] These figures illustrate the way in which one small offensive break-through in this reciprocal intelligence–security contest leads progressively to others, and at the same time feeds back into defensive superiority. There is an analogy with Liddell Hart's military theory of 'expanding torrents' for battlefield attacks – the theory which was later drawn on for blitzkrieg.[25] A small breach in defences enables mobile forces to sweep through, 'turning' enemy defences from the rear and causing the breach to expand like a river breaking its banks. In rather the same way, victory in the intelligence and security contest goes to whoever seizes the technical initiative, makes the first offensive breach and exploits it to the full.

[23] Hinsley, *British Intelligence in the Second World War* vol. II, p. 637.

[24] F. H. Hinsley, 'British Intelligence in the Second World War', *Cryptologia* vol. 14 no. 1 (January 1990), p. 2.

[25] For the theory see B. Liddell Hart, *The Liddell Hart Memoirs* vol. I (London: Cassell, 1965), pp. 44 on.

But the counterintelligence contest can be separated from this main intelligence–security engagement. It is intelligence's specialized attempts to penetrate foreign intelligence and at the same time to inhibit it from attacking one's own side. Counterintelligence therefore takes the form of a set of sub-contests, subordinate to the main intelligence-security contest, which fit inside it and inside each other like Russian dolls. One level is counterintelligence's targeting of the opponent's intelligence; having an agent inside the adversary's intelligence system reveals the identity of his spies and enables them to be neutralized. Inside the contest at this level is another one, in which penetration is directed against the opponent's own counterintelligence apparatus; the object is to see if this has penetrated one's own offensive intelligence effort. Logically this series of counterintelligence compartments within compartments could continue as an infinite regression. If arranged in order of descending size as in figure 14, their essence is seeking evidence of the opponent's penetration at the level next above. Success at these levels carries with it the possibility of not merely eliminating the intelligence threat but also of capturing it; achieving a position in which the opposing system is under one's own control without the adversary's realizing it. Such is the counterintelligence wilderness of mirrors.

Of course counterintelligence is never as complete as this suggests, but some further examples can be given of its successes. At the first level just described, the British agent network controlled from Holland was rolled up completely by the Germans at the outbreak of the Second World War, through British underestimates of the risks of penetration.[26] In the Cold War Philby provided details of Western agents to the KGB, and Western agents like Gordievsky provided the same in reverse. Some Western intelligence networks established in the USSR were detected at an early stage and operated subsequently under Soviet control.[27] Another example of the way in which agents within intelligence could cause close-range technical intelligence collection to be neutralized was when Blake gave his Soviet controllers the details of the UK–US tapping of the Soviet cables in Berlin.[28]

Access to the opposing intelligence organization at this level also provides the possibility of detailed control of deception. The British success in deception over the location and timing of the Normandy invasion in the Second World War, through apprehending and 'turning'

[26] C. Andrew, *Secret Service: the Making of the British Intelligence Community* (London: Sceptre edition, 1986), pp. 609–16.

[27] For examples see Andrew, *Secret Service*, p. 687, and Gaddis, 'Intelligence, Espionage and Cold War Origins', pp. 199, 206.

[28] G. Blake, *No Other Choice* (London: Cape, 1990), pp. 20–5, 180–2.

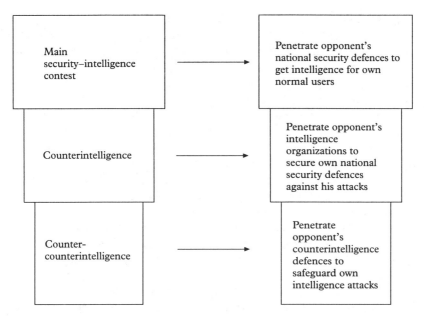

Figure 14 Levels of intelligence contests

Abwehr agents and reading Abwehr ciphers, was the classic example of having a segment of hostile intelligence under one's own control and being able to fine-tune the deception process.[29]

Similarly the Cold War also saw penetrations at the second level of counterintelligence: getting access to the opponent's own counter-intelligence organization. Philby as a Soviet agent was head of SIS counterintelligence and he claims that in that position he was able not only to warn his Soviet controllers that one of their intelligence officers had asked for British asylum in Turkey, but also to defer British reaction to the request until the KGB had had time to eliminate the potential defector.[30] In 1983 there was a near mirror-image of this access; the KGB had an offer from within British counterespionage in the form of the disaffected Security Service officer Michael Bettaney, but Gordievsky as a British agent within the KGB station in London was able to tip off the British authorities and Bettaney was arrested.[31] It has recently been suggested that Gordievsky himself was later betrayed by the CIA

---

[29] For the Double Cross system see Howard, *British Intelligence in the Second World War* vol. V, pp. 3–13 and *passim*. For Abwehr ciphers see note 12 above.

[30] K. Philby, *My Silent War* (London: MacGibbon and Kee, 1968), pp. 125–34.

[31] Andrew and Gordievsky, *KGB*, p. 501.

employee Ames, recruited by the KGB within CIA's counterintelligence branch.[32] Apart from counterintelligence results at these different levels, members of foreign intelligence organizations can also be a source of valuable non-intelligence information. Penkovsky, Gordievsky and the other Western agents within Soviet intelligence provided information over wide areas of Soviet activity, not just on its intelligence.

Hence counterintelligence has diverse ramifications. Its primary purpose is to protect national defensive information security by getting inside foreign intelligence organizations that threaten it; but its secondary role is defending its own offensive intelligence operations by penetrating opposing counterintelligence. The big dividends from successes in these areas account for intelligence's apparently incestuous preoccupation with its opposite numbers in the Cold War.

In this an analogy can be drawn between intelligence and some aspects of air power. Intelligence's objectives are to provide information and forecasts to its users, and at the same time to assist their information security. But to win the main intelligence–security contest it needs counterintelligence to counter the opponent's intelligence offensive and safeguard its own. An operational ideal is to defeat the opposing intelligence system *en route* to winning the main intelligence–security contest. In a similar way the defeat of the enemy's air force is a precondition of command of the air and the full use of air power. Soldiers look to air power to 'keep the enemy's aircraft off their backs'; while airmen seek to neutralize enemy air forces as a precondition of using their offensive power to the full. Counterintelligence is rather like 'counter-air' operations: attacking enemy airfields to inhibit his use of air power and maximize the opportunities for one's own. Counterintelligence victory has parallels with command of the air.[33]

Support for security in the 1990s

In practice even in the Cold War intelligence support for security needed only a modest proportion of intelligence resources, even when the Soviet intelligence threat seemed large and paramount. Defensive security

---

[32] Aldrich Ames, a long-term CIA employee then working in the Counterintelligence Center, was arrested in February 1994 and subsequently sentenced to life imprisonment for espionage for the KGB and its successor since 1985. For an introduction to the extensive literature about him see A. S. Hulnick, 'The Ames Case: How Could It Happen?', *International Journal of Intelligence and Counterintelligence* vol. 8 no. 2 (summer 1995).

[33] For the concepts of air power used in this analogy, see Air Vice Marshal R. A. Mason, *Air Power: a Centennial Appraisal* (London: Brassey's, 1994), particularly p. 37.

advice did not need big investments of manpower. Counterespionage was a sizeable but not overwhelming part of security intelligence. Counterintelligence was a specialized, minority occupation, looming larger in the genre of le Carré spy novels than in day-to-day business; practitioners could spend a lifetime in intelligence without coming into contact with it.

In the 1990s it is not even clear what the modern intelligence threats are, and what information really needs to be protected. But security cannot be abandoned completely. Espionage has not been eliminated; neither has technical collection. Armed forces have to keep some secrets in peacetime in case they ever have to fight, and they need adequate wartime security, even in small wars. Diplomatic services and other government departments need to retain confidential communications. The international media has no respect for national secrets. As long as covert intelligence itself continues it will need to keep its own secrets and defend itself against attacks. Even friendly states can be tempted to seek important information about their enemies by penetrating their allies' intelligence, as when the Israelis accepted the offer of espionage from the US intelligence officer Pollard who provided them with high-quality US intelligence on Middle East targets.[34] In addition, commercial security is now a topical subject. Intelligence supports the security of firms working on classified government contracts, and has some wider influence over protecting commercial secrets and privacy from foreign intrusion.

Hence offensive collection agencies continue to play a part in information security. The electronic revolution is turning Comsec, Compusec and similar electronic security activities into increasingly important adjuncts of Sigint. There are still extensive investments in the physical, documentary and personnel aspects of security, including personnel vetting. In all these passive defensive measures intelligence advises on threats and defensive methods. Some counterespionage effort is still needed. On the other hand a prolonged counterintelligence effort is hardly justified in the absence of a long-standing and threatening intelligence adversary; though Second World War and Cold War experience suggests that intelligence needs to retain some capability and doctrine.

This involvement in the defensive world has a bearing on the general size and quality of offensive collection. Intelligence power deals with controlling the information accessible by other states as well as acquiring intelligence about them. States wanting high defensive security standards require offensive collection capable of giving sophisticated advice.

[34] W. Blitzer, *Territory of Lies* (New York: Harper and Row, 1989).

National decisions on intelligence investments need to take this into account.

Summary

Intelligence supports its own state's information security by advising on and setting standards for defensive, protective security measures. It also supplies assessments of intelligence threats; engages in counter-espionage; and seeks evidence of hostile countries' intelligence successes through counterintelligence penetrations of their organizations and through scrutiny of these countries' operational actions. The counter-intelligence ('intelligence on foreign intelligence') element in these activities is part of a specialized 'counterintelligence contest' against adversaries. All these activities support intelligence's own information security, as well as that of its government and armed forces as a whole.

Threats to national information security are now far less clear than in the Cold War. But some defensive security will continue to be needed, as will intelligence support for it, particularly intelligence's ability to set national defensive standards in the light of offensive experience. This is a factor to be taken into account in national decisions on the sophisti-cation of collection needed.

11 Intelligence threats

The last three chapters described the various ways in which intelligence is used by those who receive it. This one discusses its indirect effects on its foreign and other targets.

International relations in peacetime consist partly of threats. 'Each state exists, in a sense, at the hub of a whole universe of threats . . . [They] vary enormously in range and intensity, pose risks which cannot be assessed accurately, and depend on probabilities which cannot be calculated.'[1] In war, threats and measures to counter them are basic parts of operations. In both peace and war intelligence collection can be one of the threats. One of its effects in the Cold War was that it added to the total of mutually perceived threats. Another effect is that threats of intelligence collection against them oblige military forces to take information security measures which reduce their operational effectiveness. A third effect is that threats of counterintelligence against intelligence organizations reduce their effectiveness in the same way.

Political effects of intrusive intelligence

It may be true that 'the greatest intelligence success of the Cold War, for both sides, was the development of the reconnaissance satellite, the effect of which was greatly to diminish the fear of surprise attack.'[2] But this was hardly how the East and West saw each other's intelligence at the time. Parts of it added to the mutual 'enemy image'. Here we consider these parts.

Much of the Cold War intelligence effort probably had little effect of this kind. Intelligence staffs were not threatening in themselves; nor were both sides' big efforts in relatively long-distance technical collection,

[1] B. Buzan, *People, States and Fear: the National Security Problem in International Relations* (Brighton: Wheatsheaf Books, 1983), pp. 88–9.
[2] J. L. Gaddis, 'Intelligence, Espionage, and Cold War History' in his *The United States and the End of the Cold War* (New York: Oxford University Press, 1992).

fairly remote from its targets. US bases around the Soviet periphery loomed larger as military threats than as threats from the intelligence activities located on them. Rather the same applied to the large Soviet Sigint station in Cuba; it was part of the general affront posed by the Castro regime and Soviet presence, but never emerged as a significant issue in US–Soviet relations comparable with the size of the 'Soviet Brigade' there.[3] Distance and anonymity gave some political insulation to technical collection of this kind. Satellite collection was eventually accepted as an uncontentious use of international airspace. Massive investments in 'distant' technical collection were part of the Cold War, but did not intensify it.

But some other collection had a special intrusiveness on those who were its targets. Espionage has always had this quality. The Cold War had its embassy-related collection involving diplomats, diplomatic cover and diplomatic premises. Technical collection also had its special category of 'close access' operations by ships and aircraft, with physical intrusion or near-intrusion into territorial waters or national airspace. These activities overlapped with each other and were all growth industries, with cumulative effects that made them into threats at a political level.

Espionage

The record of Cold War espionage needs no recapitulation here. It was seen by each side as a threat not just to national secrecy, but also to state and society, and the sheer scale and intensity heightened these effects. According to Gaddis, 'it is now a matter of record that during the 1920s and 1930s the Russians launched an ambitious effort to recruit agents, chiefly in Great Britain but also in the United States, who might rise over time to positions of influence or even authority in those countries. The sheer scope of this operation is extraordinary in retrospect.'[4] As he has put it in discussing the effects on the West, 'why did the Russians run such risks?'[5] The evidence of Soviet espionage during the Second World War from the Gouzenko case in Canada in 1945 and the spy cases of

---

[3] For the 'discovery' of the Soviet 'Brigade' in 1979, and its effects in derailing US ratification of SALT II, see R. L. Garthoff, *Détente and Confrontation: American–Soviet Relations from Nixon to Reagan* (Washington D.C.: Brookings, 1985), chapter 24. For more recent information on the facts of the case see D. D. Newsom, *The Soviet Brigade in Cuba: a Study in Political Diplomacy* (Bloomington, Ind.: Indiana University Press, 1987).

[4] Gaddis, 'Intelligence, Espionage, and Cold War History', pp. 89–90.

[5] Gaddis, 'Intelligence, Espionage, and Cold War History', p. 90.

the 1940s contributed to the West's disillusion with its wartime ally. Espionage can be included among Stalin's methods, of which Gaddis has concluded that 'seeking security by dubious means, he managed only to alarm and in consequence to provoke the West into rearming'.[6] Western attempts in the late 1940s and early 1950s to develop their espionage and resistance groups inside the Communist bloc and the USSR itself presumably had the reciprocal effects of fortifying Soviet threat perceptions.

These mutual effects continued throughout the Cold War. To some extent espionage and counterespionage were left to the professionals, but governments and public opinion on both sides were exposed to the long succession of spy cases which brought intrusive intelligence to their attention. It would be surprising if this were not a continual influence on the mutual 'enemy images' of irreconcilable hostility.

Intelligence collection and embassies

Cold War espionage was closely linked with the position of intelligence officers as agent-runners and recruiters, operating from embassies under diplomatic cover; and linked with this was the position of embassies and diplomats as intelligence targets. None of this was new, but the Cold War encouraged it on an unprecedented scale, and Soviet embassies acquired their increasingly top-heavy intelligence presence.[7] KGB entrapment and blackmail became hazards of diplomatic life behind the Iron Curtain, in addition to the penetration of premises by locally employed staff. Inducing defections and handling defectors became a new international phenomenon. The KGB overseas had its additional role of spying on its own embassies but still could not prevent a steady defection trickle.

The growth of embassy radio communications also gave increased cover for radio interception; sixty-two Soviet embassies were said to be interception sites late in the Cold War.[8] Embassies also became the objects of bugging and many other kinds of short-range technical attack,

---

[6] Gaddis, 'Intelligence, Espionage, and Cold War History', p. 100.

[7] The FBI considered in 1986 that at least 30 per cent of Soviet Bloc officials and representatives in the United States were professional intelligence officers. (US Senate Select Committee on Intelligence: Report 99-522, *Meeting the Espionage Challenge: a Review of The United States Counterintelligence and Security Programs* (Washington D.C.: US GPO, 1986), p. 21.) Of twenty civilian 'diplomats' at the Soviet Embassy in Copenhagen in 1966, fourteen were KGB or GRU (O. Gordievsky, *Next Stop Execution* (London: Macmillan, 1995), p. 152).

[8] For Soviet activities see D. Ball, *Soviet Signals Intelligence (Sigint)* (Papers on Strategy and Defence no. 47) (Canberra: Australian National University, 1989), pp. 38–70.

so that eventually conversations, typing and enciphering became secure only in specially constructed citadels. The new US embassy in Moscow had to be abandoned unused, hopelessly penetrated with microphones and bugs.[9] Gordievsky's autobiography gives a graphic account of the precautions taken in the Soviet Embassy in London against the threat of British bugging.[10] Embassies became the centres for an intelligence game with its own rules derived from diplomatic immunity, intensive surveillance to sort out intelligence officers from genuine diplomats, and the scope for restrictions and 'PNG' ('Persona Non Grata') expulsions, all tempered by the scope for reciprocal reprisals.

Thus the Cold War had its complement of espionage-related diplomatic incidents. Some of these had direct effects on political relationships: the expulsion of 105 Soviet intelligence officers from London in 1971, triggered off by a KGB defector, froze Anglo-Soviet relations for some years. There were similar large-scale expulsions from London, Washington and Paris in the 1980s, though without such obvious political effects; the large-scale reciprocal US and Soviet expulsions in 1985–6 did not seem to delay the revolution in the political relationship.[11] One effect was however to impair embassies' ability to carry out even genuine diplomacy.

The cumulative effects of these incidents on national threat images are entwined with those of espionage cases, but are rather harder to estimate. Professional diplomats took enemy intelligence coverage of them largely in their stride, and Western ones may occasionally have seen Soviet bugging as a means of communicating with the other side. Yet it is difficult to believe that intangible effects did not follow, at least from the scale of the Soviet effort. National perceptions were surely affected, in varying degrees on both sides, by embassies' resemblance to medieval castles – under a kind of intelligence siege, but with their intelligence sally-ports from which their inhabitants struck at the attackers.

'Close access' technical operations

There was also a large class of rather different 'close access' operations, mainly for Sigint, imagery and other technical collection. Common

---

[9] For a summary see R. Nelson and J. Koenen-Grant, 'A Case of Bureaucracy in Action', *International Journal of Intelligence and Counterintelligence* vol. 6 no. 3 (fall 1993).

[10] Gordievsky, *Next Stop Execution*, pp. 257–8.

[11] For the 1971 expulsions see C. Andrew and O. Gordievsky, *KGB: the Inside Story of its Foreign Operations from Lenin to Gorbachev* (London: Hodder and Stoughton, 1990), pp. 435–6. Figures for 1985–6 in R. Kessler, *Moscow Station: How the KGB Penetrated the American Embassy* (New York: Pocket Books, 1989), p. 193.

features in a variety of operations were close approaches to national territory, territorial waters and airspace, and occasional penetrations into them. Even without actual intrusion, close approaches could be seen as provocation.

Overflights of the Soviet Union had a special importance from the late 1940s up to the U-2 shoot-down in 1960. Before the launch of the first US satellites they were virtually the only Western way of observing Soviet military capabilities, but were also the most provocative Western activities. (As far as is known there were no comparable overflights of Western territory by the Soviet Union.)[12] The US Air Force mounted authorized and unauthorized operations in the first half of the 1950s, along with its not very successful programmes of 'overflights' by unmanned imagery and Elint balloons; about 44 were recovered out of 448 released.[13] British crews are now said to have also carried out some sorties using US aircraft, and there may also have been a long Royal Air Force flight in the first half of the 1950s by a photo-reconnaissance Canberra to the newly discovered missile test range at Kapustin Yar.[14] The eighteen US U-2 overflights in the 1956–60 period then provided the first systematic (if very incomplete) attempt to view Soviet missile capabilities.[15]

Close access also developed on a much bigger scale for other technical collection. The technical trend after 1945 towards the use of higher radio and radar frequencies put an increasing premium on close-range collection through the use of border sites, ships and aircraft; aircraft had a special value because of the height from which they could collect. Daily flights by all NATO and Warsaw Pact countries along the adversary's borders were part of the Cold War routine. Most of these were on the fringes of the target's airspace, but occasionally were within it; the over-flying U-2s carried technical collection besides imagery equipment, and other routine border flights sometimes penetrated Soviet airspace

12 There were recurrent reports of diversions of Soviet civil aircraft from authorized routes, but none of specialized photographic or Sigint overflights.

13 P. C. Unsinger, 'Whales in the Air' (Review), *International Journal of Intelligence and Counterintelligence* vol. 6 no. 3, p. 406.

14 S. Alsop, *The Center: People and Power in Political Washington* (London: Harper and Row, 1968), p. 216. For reminiscences by British participants in overflights of the USSR, see *Daily Telegraph*, 7 February 1995, previewing BBC *Newsnight* TV programme, 9 February 1994.

15 W. E. Burrows, *Deep Black: the Secrets of Space Espionage* (London: Bantam, 1988), pp. 53–81. Other details of US airborne collection are in J. T. Richelson, *The US Intelligence Community* (Cambridge, Mass.: Ballinger, 1985), pp. 115–17, 123–9, 304–5. A figure of eighteen U-2 overflights was quoted by a Soviet officer, BBC *Newsnight* programme, 9 February 1994. *Newsnight* also claimed that Strategic Air Command made unauthorized overflights in the first half of the 1950s.

through genuine navigational errors.[16] There were also tactics of deliberate provocation, with aircraft making feint approaches designed to stimulate air defences and enable Sigint stations to monitor reactions. An American has recalled of electronic collection missions that 'sometimes we would fly missions over the Black Sea . . . To tickle the Soviets a little and create more activity we would do a straight approach towards Sevastopol, turn and run out. Then we would listen to the racket.'[17] A former US Assistant Secretary for Defense has commented on these US operations between 1945 and 1964 that:

First, we could understand the subordination of [the] Soviet command systems. Next, we could understand their strategy and tactics. We learned quite a bit of what is going on, from the locations of their radars . . . We learned how they reacted, and how promptly they reacted, to actions. Also the radar Order of Battle information was very useful.[18]

Soviet airborne collection was conducted on generally similar lines, though with more of the routine flights dubbed 'milk-runs' and less provocation.[19]

At the same time as close access flights of these kinds there was other technical collection of varying degrees of secrecy. At sea, the penetration of territorial waters by submarines (as in the Soviet operations off the Swedish coast, and the extensive Western ones in Soviet Northern and Pacific waters) was complemented by technical collection and observation by surface warships, and by constant 'marking' of one side by the other. The USSR also developed a large force of specialist Sigint collection vessels deployed on semi-permanent patrols; by mid-1987 there were sixty-three of them in eleven classes.[20] The United States and some other Western nations had their equivalents on a much smaller scale. There were persistent reports of clandestine Soviet collection from commercial lorries in Western Europe.[21] Other reports were of US tapping of Soviet underwater cables and planting of bugs linked with satellites.

Some of these various close access operations were intended to be covert, though suspected and occasionally detected. Many more,

---

[16] A. Price, *The History of US Electronic Warfare. Vol. II: The Renaissance Years* (Alexandra, Va.: The Association of Old Crows, 1989), pp. 157–60.

[17] Price, *The History of US Electronic Warfare*, p. 87.

[18] Statement by Dr Gene Fubini, quoted in Price, *The History of US Electronic Warfare*, p. 312.

[19] Ball, *Soviet Signals Intelligence (Sigint)*, pp. 108–18

[20] Ball, *Soviet Signals Intelligence (Sigint)*, pp. 80–107. Richelson, *The US Intelligence Community*, pp. 127–9, lists the equivalent US platforms.

[21] Ball, *Soviet Signals Intelligence (Sigint)*, pp. 71–9.

particularly those by aircraft and surface ships, were only lightly concealed. In them a form of East–West confrontation was played out daily, in mounting intrusive collection and reacting to it.

For the participants and those supporting them it was an all-absorbing contest of resources, enterprise and technical ingenuity: partly routine, mixed with resolution, endurance and a spice of courage. Its heavy concentration around Soviet borders, particularly the Baltic, the German border, the Barents Sea and the Pacific coast, reflected the Cold War's geo-politics. Soviet air and sea operations extended to the areas of Western home bases, and had the worldwide dimension provided by the specialist seaborne collectors and aircraft bases overseas; but geography made this effort less concentrated than the West's, with less cumulative intrusion. Western collection, with air and sea operations added to its forward land bases, was on the Soviet periphery looking in, while Soviet collection looked out, on targets of varying directions and depths centred on the distant main adversary, the USA. If the Central Asian approaches to India were the venue for Kipling's nineteenth-century Great Game between Britain and Tsarist Russia, its post-1945 equivalent in close access technical collection was played out around the approaches to the Soviet Union.

The political significance of this technical collection went largely unobserved at the time, and has still not been assessed by Cold War historians. The West had its national mechanisms for authorizing operations, and some technical coordination between close allies; but there is no evidence of any assessment at the time of the overall political effects of all these different Western operations combined.[22] In any case these were not obvious; the close access war grew under its own momentum and became part of the Cold War scenery. Indeed much of it became military routine on both sides.

But only up to a point. There was always scope for mistakes, and there were periodic incidents. US aircraft were regularly shot down in the early years, mainly because navigational equipment did not then preclude accidental overflights of Soviet territory.[23] An American participant's

[22] For US control procedures (under the Joint Chiefs of Staff), see Richelson, *The US Intelligence Community*, pp. 305–6.

[23] Burrows, *Deep Black*. He claims (p. 59) that almost forty US aircraft were lost by the end of the 1940s; for subsequent incidents in 1952–3 see p. 67. The US Defense Department is said to have admitted that forty aircraft were shot down between 1950 and 1970 (*Daily Telegraph*, 7 February 1994). The figure of forty seems high unless it includes the results of navigational errors by some aircraft not on specifically intelligence missions. Burrows claims that at that stage some US missions were provided with fighter escorts. Price (see other notes) records twelve shoot-downs (two by China) of US aircraft on Elint missions up to 1959; his list excludes photographic reconnaissance missions.

account of one B-29 'Sitting Duck' mission in 1947 has elements of Irish humour about it:

We were supposed to make a little dip into Anadyr Bay, which is a big [Soviet] bay maybe 120 miles wide and 120 miles deep . . . we were supposed to make a little 'V' into it. All of a sudden I looked at the radar and I called Kelly. I said 'Kelly, we're over land!' . . . I said 'Flanagan (1st navigator), what the Hell are we doing?' Flanagan said 'Well, we've hit a reverse jet stream and we're trying to get out. It's carried us inland about 50 miles and we're making about 20 knots ground speed.'[24]

The US destroyer *Maddox* was engaged in Sigint collection in the Tonkin Gulf in August 1964 when it was attacked by North Vietnamese torpedo boats, with subsequent US retaliation that effectively started the air war over Vietnam.[25] A US submarine was involved in a collision with a Soviet one as recently as February 1992, 'within eyesight of Russian territory' according to a Russian spokesman.[26]

Airborne collection led to two particularly significant bits of Cold War history. The U-2 shoot-down in May 1960 caused the break-up of the Paris Summit Conference between East and West. The Soviet destruction over Kamchatka in September 1983 of the South Korean airliner on flight KAL 007, erroneously identified as a US aircraft penetrating Soviet airspace, produced a tragic loss of life and helped to bring Soviet–US relations to one of their lowest points. Over the incident 'each side . . . converted its ready suspicions and worst assumptions about the other into accusations that could not be proved or disproved, but that tended to be believed by its own side and bitterly resented by the other.'[27] US reactions contributed to the situation in which there were some Soviet fears of a pre-emptive US nuclear strike.

As with espionage and embassy operations, accusations of intrusive technical collection were useful propaganda sticks with which to beat the enemy. But Cold War imperatives of 'demonstrating resolve' sometimes reinforced the technical arguments for close access, and the general effect of intrusion and the inevitable incidents must have been to stoke threat

---

[24] Price, *The History of US Electronic Warfare*, p. 37.

[25] Price, *The History of US Electronic Warfare*, pp. 304–5, summarizes the incident and discusses the evidence that the second 'attack' on the US vessels which provoked the US retaliation was a phantom caused by freak radar conditions.

[26] For references to intrusive US submarine operations see Richelson, *The US Intelligence Community*, pp. 129–30, 304. For the 1992 collision see B. Surikov, 'Warsaw Pact Planned 14-Day Push to Atlantic', *Armed Forces Journal*, September 1992.

[27] Garthoff, *Détente and Confrontation*, p. 1016. For a summary of subsequent Russian revelations about the affair see 'Yeltsin Releases Documents', *Foreign Intelligence Literary Scene* vol. 11 no. 5 (1992), pp. 1–2.

perceptions. Airborne collection and other collection in Soviet backyards presumably appeared as a flexing of US muscle, touching on the regime's special sensitivity over secrecy and the defence of national territory; there were overtones of Strategic Air Command's power, particularly when this was virtually unchallenged in the 1950s. There were also the clear violations of Soviet sovereignty; Krushchev's outbursts after the U-2 incident followed the decade of Western overflights. Widespread Soviet maritime and airborne collection also played its own part in Western fears of worldwide Soviet ambitions, though perhaps not so dramatically. Close access collection surely had some part in Cold War psychoses on both sides.

Thus intrusive collection as a whole added positive threats to the Cold War climate. Espionage stimulated visceral feelings about the enemy within; close access technical collection violated or threatened national borders; operations from and against diplomatic missions had aspects of both. Possibly there was a rough overall symmetry; the USSR invested more heavily in espionage and in intelligence from and against embassies, while the West mounted more concentrated close access collection at sea and by air. But both sides did some of everything, with political effects. The Cold War showed that intrusive intelligence can be among the catalogue of peacetime threats. Implications for the post-Cold War world can be considered at the end of this book.

Operational effects

Apart from the peacetime political results of intrusive intelligence, there are the results of intelligence as an operational threat. Warning systems are 'threats' to surprise attack; at least they make potential aggressors think twice about whether they can achieve surprise, and the risks of not doing so. Examples are necessarily hard to come by; but one factor leading the Soviet Union to abandon its ideas of a strike on China in 1969 *may* have been the West's ability to detect preparations.[28]

More substantially, all collection, non-intrusive as well as intrusive, leads its targets to take security measures, with some penalties for those taking them. At a very general level security measures affect the societies taking them. Real and exaggerated threats from Western intelligence served to reinforce the totalitarianism of the Soviet system; and libertarians have claimed that even in the West the security measures of the Cold War induced elements of a wartime psychology. Certainly the

---

[28] See Garthoff, *Détente and Confrontation*, pp. 207–10.

practice of 'positive vetting' in official service sprang directly from the evidence of Soviet ideological espionage, but in some form now seems a permanent feature.

At a practical level information security costs money and affects efficiency. It has to take the form mainly of rules based on pessimistic assumptions about the extent of the intelligence threats. Initiative and short cuts on security matters have to be discouraged, since those concerned cannot know if they are giving opposing intelligence a breakthrough. Information flows are constrained by the need-to-know principle. Written and electronic communications are delayed by document security procedures, the need for encipherment and the dangers of open telephones.

Similar threat effects apply particularly to war and military concepts and operational style. There are ample wartime examples of the conflict between information security and the use of initiative; the British fighter pilots who sighted the German battleships during their transit of the English Channel in February 1942 but kept radio silence in accordance with regulations were just one example of the many caught between the two.[29] Besides assisting its own side directly, intelligence inhibits the enemy and limits his options, including the extent to which he can count on surprise and can afford to take risks to achieve it. Even in peacetime, security limited military training and delayed weapons development in the Cold War. Transparency to satellite surveillance introduced a new and still barely appreciated limiting factor into military calculations everywhere.

Similar constraints apply to clandestine opponents in peace. Terrorism has to be highly security-conscious; it is forced by the intelligence threat to it to adopt cell structures and maximum secrecy, with all the limitations these bring for the scope and flexibility of terrorist action. Government's ability to tap telephones may have provided fewer operational leads as IRA terrorist units became increasingly security-conscious; but it remains a serious brake upon the flexibility and control of their operations. Security also affects inter-state cooperation. Confidential exchanges depend on trusting others' ability to keep secrets, and security makes states think twice about international collaboration that involves sharing them. The known scale of the East German espionage threat within the Federal Republic during the Cold War was always a factor tipping the scales against bringing the FRG into the full

---

[29] F. H. Hinsley with E. E. Thomas, C. F. G. Ransom and R. C. Knight, *British Intelligence in the Second World War* vol. II (London: HMSO, 1981), pp. 185–7.

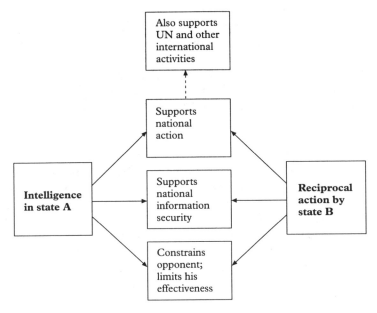

Figure 15   Effects of intelligence power

range of Anglo-Saxon collaboration.[30] Similarly the weakness of Free French ciphers in the Second World War was one reason why de Gaulle was not given advance notice of the Normandy invasion.[31]

All these are effects of a state's or an organization's own security measures. These defensive measures are reactions to the threat posed by opposing offensive intelligence; intelligence as perceived by its targets affects them at one remove. Like military power, intelligence power has some effect as a force in being. This can be added to its combined effects as shown in figure 15.

The threat effect applies particularly to military command and control and the associated communications. Security is often an argument against technical innovation; vulnerability to interception was one of the reasons used against developing radio for mechanized warfare in the

---

[30] See for example J. Eisenhammer, 'A Nation Still Gripped by the Long Arm of the Stasi', *The Independent*, 18 October 1990 – 'The extent to which East Berlin followed the most intimate goings-on in politics, security and business in West Germany can have few parallels in the history of interstate espionage.'

[31] F. H. Hinsley and C. A. G. Simkins, *British Intelligence in the Second World War. Vol. IV: Security and Counterintelligence* (London: HMSO, 1990), p. 255 (note).

British army in the 1930s.[32] Ferris has pointed out how the British army's effectiveness in mobile desert warfare in the first half of the Second World War was crippled by cumbersome cipher systems; command and control channels became choked and could not cope with the pace of operations unless messages were sent in clear, with the equally disastrous results of handing operational intentions to the enemy.[33] Even with modern technology there is still a perpetual tug-of-war between security on the one hand and communications effectiveness on the other. Some weaknesses in British army communications in the Desert Storm attack were a price paid for the rigid radio security observed to achieve operational surprise; according to the Commander of the British First Armoured Division, his Divisional-level radio nets became fragmented during the movement of the attack through being out of practice, 'a result of the long period of Radio Silence in support of the Deception Plan . . . I only became aware of how rusty we were when it was too late to do anything about it.'[34]

Hence one of the fundamental conditions of this century's warfare has been that radio communications and other electronic emissions are potential sources of information to the enemy. The fog of war and the modern versions of Clausewitz's 'friction' – the difficulty in getting anything done in war precisely as intended – come in substantial measure from trying to communicate with one's own side without thereby assisting the opposition. Ferris notes that

Only a traitor used radio, only a fool did not; this dilemma haunted all commanders of the Second World War . . . Without radio there was no certainty of command. With it there was no guarantee of secrecy. The rise of radio led to a new system of relationships (which might be called 'C³IS') between command, control, communications, signals intelligence and signals security.[35]

With the risk of radio interception, the struggle between security and efficiency in communication 'must end in a complex compromise. Their requirements must be balanced at the highest possible level of marginal efficiency, where no further gains can be made in either direction save through suffering greater losses in the other.'[36]

---

[32] B. G. S. Bidwell and D. Graham, *Fire-Power* (London: George Allen and Unwin, 1982), p. 172.

[33] J. Ferris, 'The British Army, Signals and Security in the Desert Campaign, 1940–42', *Intelligence and National Security* vol. 5 no. 2 (April 1990).

[34] Major General R. Smith, 'The Gulf War: the Land Battle', *RUSI Journal* vol. 137 no. 1 (February 1992), pp. 4–5.

[35] Ferris, 'The British Army, Signals and Security in the Desert Campaign, 1940–42', p. 256.

[36] Ferris, 'The British Army, Signals and Security in the Desert Campaign, 1940–42', p. 259.

Naval warfare in the North Sea in the First World War illustrated this dilemma between an 'information-rich' style of command to maximize information flows for one's own side, and a secure style designed to minimize enemy intelligence.[37] When at sea the German Fleet made more efficient use of radio than the British. Thus at Jutland it extricated itself through efficient radio commands, while the British side used flag signals that often could not be read, and minimal radio communication. Fear of German DF was a factor in the British parsimony over using radio; signals from the Admiralty to Jellicoe at sea in 1914–15 included regular exhortations to keep radio silence. The absence of a similar German recognition of the British interception threat contributed to the more extensive and more efficient German use of radio at sea. Yet over time this greater German use of radio worked in favour of the British, by providing greater amounts of traffic for their cryptanalysts to work on, and conversely the apparently ineffective British use of radio helped to limit the equivalent German Sigint penetrations. The two struck different balances between C[3] effectiveness and taking precautions against intelligence threats.

Moreover this difference applied not only to the C[3] systems as a whole but also to the 'I' element of C[3]I: the dissemination of intelligence as part of the information flow. The general British inhibitions about using radio applied even more strongly to transmitting Sigint results to the fleet at sea. These were passed in inadequate quantity to a very short list of recipients. This has been the subject of much criticism, particularly of the service during the Jutland battle. But one consequence was that, even when the Germans had some success in reading British codes, the extent of Room 40's successes never became apparent from the traffic decrypted on the German side. On the other hand the equivalent German results when available from their Sigint were disseminated by radio to their fleet with fewer inhibitions. Hence the British became aware of German codebreaking successes from their decrypts of German traffic, and were stimulated to improve their own codes. The Battle of the Atlantic example already quoted showed the same features of the reciprocal intelligence-security contest; the full German use of Sigint results in directing U-Boats confirmed British suspicions about their own ciphers.

These are old examples. The military electronics industry now

---

[37] Details in what follows are from P. Beesly, *Room 40: British Naval Intelligence 1914–18* (London: Hamish Hamilton, 1982). Admiralty exhortations to maintain radio silence at sea are quoted on p. 59.

produces defensive detection-resistant and secure communications systems, but the offensive technology keeps pace with them by producing increasingly sophisticated interception devices. Improved cipher security and sophisticated communications divert resources that could otherwise provide bigger and faster communications capacity. The same principles also apply to the threat of message-like intelligence obtained by human sources, or by Humint and Sigint combinations in bugging, or computer hacking and similar means. They apply not only to war but also to lesser conflicts.

Thus the conflict between operational effectiveness and security remains. Recognizing that one is an intelligence target constrains one's actions and command fluency, while (as Ferris points out) failing to recognize the threat leads to security failure. In war and similar situations intelligence as a perceived capability has these operational effects on its opponents.

The counterintelligence threat

These threat effects also apply within intelligence itself; indeed hostile intelligence imposes more constraints on the intelligence world than on the non-intelligence one, since intelligence depends so much on its own source protection. In war and Cold War the counterintelligence contest already discussed imposes its own defensive penalties on intelligence production and use. Agencies take special security precautions that are even more stringent than their users' restrictions on operational information. Intelligence is kept in separate compartments and not shared; institutional memory is limited by rules about destroying material after use; overseas liaisons are restricted by the risk that foreign partners may be penetrated; there are all the limitations on the use of intelligence by recipients. Security conflicts with efficiency in intelligence as elsewhere. The threat of Soviet technical eavesdropping slowed down the agencies' introduction of information technology even within Western territory, because of the cost of the extra precautions that were needed. The KGB's effectiveness must have been limited by the rule that its intelligence officers in embassies overseas could make only the briefest notes of their instructions from the Centre.[38] 'The sheer quantity and complexity of KGB regulations designed to protect the security of its records and communications are partly self-defeating. Residences are

---

[38] C. Andrew and O. Gordievsky, *Instructions from the Centre* (London: Hodder and Stoughton, 1991), p. 229.

required to fill in too many forms, to obey too many instructions and to follow too many bureaucratic procedures.'[39]

The counterintelligence conflict has other less tangible results. The threat of positive action against foreign intelligence puts it on the defensive; the KGB was always cautious over operations in the UK after the large-scale expulsions of Soviet intelligence officers from London in 1971. It takes a long time for an intelligence agency to recover from finding that it has had a highly placed traitor in its ranks. 'The suspicion or actual evidence that your own intelligence service has a traitor within the house is the most miserable event that can happen to your Service ... It destroys morale, upsets judgement, destroys personal relationships, and gravely threatens inter-allied confidence.'[40] After repeated defections to the West, the KGB in its later days may have had a progressive collapse of morale. One KGB officer recounted then that 'the fundamental rule is to survive, and to endure until the end of the posting without being expelled from the country.'[41] US and British Cold War intelligence was periodically distracted by fears about earlier Soviet penetration and deception, as in the British investigation into the possibility that a former Director-General of the Security Service had been the KGB's Fifth Man. At a more general level neither side in the Cold War could run the security risk of allowing its intelligence analysts to travel across the enemy's frontiers to see the foreign target at first hand; assessment on both sides was handicapped by the fear of having one of its analysts defect to the enemy, lend himself to blackmail into collaboration, or simply reveal secrets through loose talk.

Fears of deception through intelligence penetration also inhibit intelligence judgments, as in the school of thought in the 1960s that the West's agent sources had been vehicles of Soviet deception designed to lull Western fears of the Cold War threat. As Robin Winks pointed out in his account of James Jesus Angleton, the controversial head of counterintelligence in CIA until 1975, penetration – and the threat of it – constitutes a form of political action, putting a virus into the bloodstream of its intelligence target.[42] It produces the special counter-

---

[39] Andrew and Gordievsky, *Instructions from the Centre*, p. 233. The authors add, referring to Gordievsky's experience as a British agent within the system, that 'As a result, they tend to take short cuts, some of which made this volume [of KGB documents] possible.'

[40] J. B. Lockhart, 'Intelligence: a British View' in K. G. Robertson (ed.), *British and American Approaches to Intelligence* (London: Macmillan, 1987), p. 42.

[41] V. Kuzichkin, *Inside the KGB* (London: Deutsch, 1990), p. 106. For details of counter-surveillance precautions see also pp. 154–6 and 188–92; and Andrew and Gordievsky, *KGB*, p. 619.

[42] R. Winks, *Cloak and Gown: Scholars in America's Secret War* (London: Collins, 1987), pp. 422–4.

intelligence mentality: slightly paranoid, considering the possibility of manipulation and deception everywhere:

Angleton was the ideal man for this game. He could keep track of agents, doubled, tripled, turn and turn again . . . Angleton saw everything in relation to everything else. He saw questions in the round, immediately ticking off relationships, ramifications, subquestions which others did not think of. If a double agent were suspected, might one not learn about that duplicity by an examination of the precise time sequence and content of information . . . ? If there were a change in Israeli intelligence, how would this influence South Africa? If Communist China appeared to be breaking with the Soviet Union, might this not be merely a very long-range strategic deception?[43]

A British professional concluded that 'broadly speaking no highly intelligent, sensitive, counterintelligence expert should be involved in this fascinating specialization for more than about twelve years.'[44]

Thus in the counterintelligence contest the *threat* of one contestant's counterintelligence affects the other; it consumes his effort in searching for penetrations of his own intelligence and imposes security constraints that limit his effectiveness and value. Combined with manifested successes, the threat goes further. One aspect of naval power pitted against a superior foe has been described as 'the attrition of the enemy's will and means'.[45] The same is true of successful counterintelligence. As with the other threats, this effect is reciprocal between long-term intelligence antagonists.

Summary

Intelligence has some effects as a threat on those who are conscious of being its targets. Long-distance intelligence did not exacerbate the Cold War, but the more intrusive kinds of collection had some effects in reinforcing East–West tension. In war and similar situations security reactions to intelligence threats restrict the reactors' operational freedom of action and effectiveness, particularly the effectiveness of their communications in permanent compromises between security and user-friendliness. Similarly in conditions of prolonged conflict the counterintelligence threat to the opponent's intelligence limits its effectiveness. Most intelligence is an 'enabling' facility, helping the world of action to exercise national power and influence. But power is some-

---

[43] Winks, *Cloak and Gown*, p. 424.
[44] Lockhart, 'Intelligence: a British View', p. 42.
[45] G. Till (ed.), 'Editorial Introduction' in *Seapower: Theory and Practice* (London: Cass, 1994), p. 5 (special edition of the *Journal of Strategic Studies* vol. 17 no. 1 (March 1994)).

times described as 'power over' others;[46] and in this respect intelligence as a threat exercises some power over opponents.

These effects of intelligence are subsidiary to its main value in providing information for use (chapters 8 and 9) and in bolstering its own state's defensive security (chapter 10). But they are part of intelligence's significance in war and prolonged enmity. The relevance to international relationships in the 1990s can be examined in chapter 20.

[46] L. Freedman, 'Strategic Studies and the Problem of Power' in Freedman, P. Hayes and R. O'Neill (eds.), *War, Strategy, and International Politics* (Oxford: Clarendon Press, 1992), p. 284.

12 Intelligence cooperation

The previous chapter described intelligence's effects on its adversaries, but it also has its friends. These produce its own international cooperative system, rather like the other 'expert' intergovernmental relationships which develop on the fringes of diplomacy. Cooperation of this kind is a feature of almost all modern intelligence, overlaying the received picture of it as a secretive, exclusively 'national' entity. This chapter describes this cooperation and its international effects.

Development of the international dimension

Regular cooperation of this kind is a twentieth-century development but exchanges of some kind have a much longer history. Allies have always shared some information in war, and information exchanges have always been part of diplomacy. In secret intelligence, cipher-breaking had an international dimension in advance of its time. The British liaison with Hanover in the eighteenth century through the royal connection included exchanges of intercepted diplomatic traffic, solutions of ciphers, and decrypted messages; the Hanoverians also trained apprentices to the British organization in the art of forging seals, and may even have supplied the results of collaboration with the Danes.[1]

Yet regular peacetime exchanges did not take place until well after intelligence's nineteenth-century institutionalization. Military staff talks before the First World War required discussion of potential enemy strengths and intentions, and the war subsequently produced organized intelligence cooperation between allies at various levels; by 1916 the British and French intelligence staffs in France were exchanging information daily on German troop movements.[2] British naval Sigint was

---

[1] K. Ellis, *The Post Office in the Eighteenth Century* (Oxford: Oxford University Press, 1958), pp. 74, 76; P. S. Fritz, 'The Anti-Jacobite System of the English Ministers 1715–1745', *Historical Journal* vol. 16 (1973), p. 269.

[2] C. Andrew, *Secret Service: the Making of the British Intelligence Community* (London: Sceptre edition, 1986), p. 219.

permanently indebted to the Russians for the captured German naval codebook sent to them early in the war, and regular naval Sigint cooperation seems to have existed between Britain and Russia, and among the Allied Powers in the Mediterranean.[3] But on the whole cooperation even in this war remained rudimentary. Intelligence was still overwhelmingly a national preserve, in a war fought largely with national strategies and direction.

Some international cooperation probably took place after 1918 in connection with policing German disarmament. Bolshevism after 1917 may have had similar effects in promoting security intelligence exchanges; certainly the fear of communism and clandestine Soviet influence was a factor in promoting subsequent British Commonwealth cooperation.[4] The rise of Hitler then gave a special impetus to exchanges on the German threat.[5] Covert intelligence cooperation developed for the same reason; the head of the Czech intelligence organization claimed to have developed contacts with Switzerland, the USSR, France, the Baltic States and Britain, culminating in the removal of the nucleus of the organization to Britain just before the occupation of Prague in 1939.[6]

The most famous collaboration of this kind was French assistance to the Polish cryptanalytic attack on the German Enigma machine. A French-controlled human source provided the Poles with technical material from 1932 onwards, and subsequent Franco-Polish collaboration on the machine culminated in the important meeting in 1939 at which the results were shared with the British.[7] The British government authorized extensive (though still not complete) intelligence exchanges with France in April 1939, and in the early part of the war (up to the fall

---

[3] For naval Sigint cooperation in the First World War see P. Beesly, *Room 40: British Naval Intelligence 1914–18* (London: Hamish Hamilton, 1982), pp. 5–6, 80, 178–82. Beesly also claims (p. 13) that the French provided British Army Sigint with solutions of German military ciphers in 1914; however this has been queried (J. Ferris, 'The British Army and Signals Intelligence in the Field during the First World War', *Intelligence and National Security* vol. 3 no. 4 (October 1988), p. 47 note 26).

[4] C. Andrew, 'The Growth of the Australian Intelligence Community and the UK–US Connection', *Intelligence and National Security* vol. 4 no. 2 (April 1989), pp. 216–17.

[5] See for example W. Wark, *The Ultimate Enemy: British Intelligence and Pre-War Germany* (London: Tauris, 1985), pp. 51, 120, 216; F. H. Hinsley with E. E. Thomas, C. F. G. Ransom and R. C. Knight, *British Intelligence in the Second World War* vol. I (London: HMSO, 1979), p. 76.

[6] General F. Moravec, *Master of Spies* (London: Bodley Head, 1975), pp. 56–7, 61, 66–7, 124–5, 144, 158–63.

[7] F. H. Hinsley with E. E. Thomas, C. A. G. Simkins and C. F. G. Ransom, *British Intelligence in the Second World War* vol. III part 2 (London: HMSO, 1988), appendix 30, p. 950.

of France) this extended to technical Anglo-French collaboration on the Enigma cipher.[8]

Yet these arrangements were dwarfed by the scale and completeness of subsequent UK–US cooperation. Key features in it were the concept of combined intelligence assessments as agreed inputs to the Combined Chiefs of Staff; the establishment of some UK–US intelligence organizations and staffs; the integration of specialists from one nation within the organizations of the other (notably the attachment of Americans to work at Bletchley Park); and the idea of 'divisions of effort' whereby one country took on responsibility for selected areas and tasks on behalf of both. Contacts with the intelligence organizations of the exiled governments of conquered Europe were never so intimate as UK–US collaboration; nevertheless there was extensive cooperation in Humint and covert action which laid the basis for many post-war liaisons.

Integration and liaison were therefore powerful elements at hand for the refashioning of Western intelligence for the Cold War. Wartime UK–US cooperation became a permanent peacetime feature, particularly the complete transatlantic exchange of Sigint and the inclusion of the Old Commonwealth countries within this arrangement. Intelligence collaboration of this kind was not a complete Anglo-Saxon preserve. NATO and other alliances were underpinned by extensive peacetime exchanges and plans for wartime intelligence collaboration.[9] The FRG's post-war intelligence organization was created with US assistance.[10] The Soviet military threat promoted bilateral and multilateral cooperation throughout the Western alliance, with extensions outside Europe. Counterespionage and counterintelligence cooperation against Soviet espionage was even more widespread.

On the other side in the Cold War, the counterpart of Western cooperation was the KGB's and GRU's control of Warsaw Pact intelligence. In the Third World, intelligence cooperation and training became part of the competing aid offered by East and West. Other conflicts added new exchanges, for example on international terrorism or as part of US support for Israel. Israel itself developed many other relationships; press reports over the last twenty years have referred to liaisons with most Western European countries (including Cold War neutrals), Iran (before the Shah's fall), Morocco, various Black African countries, South Africa, Egypt, Pakistan, India, China, Japan and other East Asian countries,

---

[8] Hinsley, *British Intelligence in the Second World War* vol. I, appendix 1, pp. 488, 493.

[9] P. Stares, *Command Performance: the Neglected Dimension of European Security* (Washington D.C.: The Brookings Institution, 1991), pp. 87–100.

[10] J. T. Richelson, *Foreign Intelligence Organizations* (Cambridge, Mass.: Ballinger, 1988), pp. 133–6.

besides the US.[11] Latterly the Gulf War and subsequent events showed the scale of intelligence-sharing needed for coalition war and international sanctions and arms limitation.

This growth of international cooperation produced a mixture of *ad hoc* exchanges and permanent liaisons. Accredited intelligence representatives (still under some kind of official 'cover' for public purposes) became regular members of diplomatic missions in friendly and neutral countries; this was by no means universal, but on a similar scale to the representation of other expert departments. Close allies started to exchange specialist liaison staff for particular agencies. Intelligence became a form of international diplomacy in its own right, though still inchoate and undeveloped, rather like diplomacy itself before its seventeenth-century legitimation and codification.

The effect has been to establish regular and systematic intelligence exchanges, and a structure of alliances and agreements of varying degrees of formality. These partly reflect US pre-eminence, a hegemony matched until the end of the Cold War by Soviet intelligence with its control of its East European clients. Britain has some influence of this kind on a smaller scale, through the Old Commonwealth and its many other connections. The outlines of the UK–US and linked Old Commonwealth arrangements are well known.[12] In Sigint the collaboration is so close that the 'home' and 'foreign' contributions are often difficult to distinguish; it is an exaggeration to liken UK–US–Commonwealth Sigint to some large multinational corporation, serving its different national users through its related national operating companies, but the analogy contains a grain of truth. What is not as well recognized is the scale of other less complete exchanges that have developed with other Western countries and between them. Most intelligence agencies now conduct foreign liaison of some kind; indeed access to bigger partners may be the main justification for some agencies in small powers. National intelligence systems are not self-sufficient. Intelligence on some subjects (the USSR in the Cold War; international terrorism and nuclear proliferation now) has become a kind of international knowledge system, a partial and undeclared replica of open systems such as the World Meteorological Organization.

The result is a patchwork of bilateral and multilateral arrangements of all kinds and all degrees of intimacy. The patchwork is unusual in its secrecy, but otherwise is not unlike the intergovernmental arrangements

---

[11] Richelson, *Foreign Intelligence Organizations*, pp. 231–3.
[12] J. T. Richelson and D. Ball, *The Ties that Bind: Intelligence Cooperation between the UKUSA Countries* (London: Allen and Unwin, 1985).

that have developed in other specialized areas. Rather as in these other areas, arrangements for intelligence are modulated by states' political alignments and overseas policies, and at the same time interact with them. We can look in turn at the professional-technical factors and then at the interaction with foreign policy.

Professional-technical factors

Reasons for collaboration

One basic reason for cooperation is that there is always more information potentially available than any agency can collect by itself. The loss of the East European intelligence services is said to have reduced the effectiveness of KGB Humint by at least 30 per cent. The size of the West's Soviet and Warsaw Pact targets in the Cold War put a special premium on mutual assistance, but the need for it applies almost everywhere. The appetite for information is insatiable, and even the US superpower has to collaborate with others to meet it. For Britain and others, access to the United States' weight of resources, technology and expertise is an overwhelming attraction. The same has applied on a smaller scale to others' cooperation with the British.

But there are more specific reasons for cooperation. Most states can carry out some unique collection with unique results. Some collection for example can only be carried out by the local intelligence organization, with its physical surveillance of people and premises, its access to police records and its powers (depending on national legal provisions) to tap telephones and intercept other communications which would otherwise be inaccessible. Local access of this kind applies particularly to counter-espionage, counterintelligence and counter-terrorism, and has given these subjects a distinctive international flavour; the same now applies to intelligence on nuclear proliferation. The general run of Humint has an equally large element of liaison. Friendly Humint agencies have their own sources, or can help in recruiting new ones or conducting technical operations. They may also have other local opportunities such as access to useful groups of refugees or particular foreign equipment. There was a brisk Cold War trade in procuring specimens of Soviet military equipment through intelligence contacts in the Third World countries that had acquired them.

Local assets of this kind are linked with another major factor: the significance in Sigint and other technical collection of local geography. The geopolitical intelligence history of the Cold War has yet to be written, but a dominant theme was the US need for forward technical intelligence bases around the periphery of the USSR, and the parallel (though smaller-scale) Soviet requirement for the same kind of overseas technical facilities, as in Cuba, Vietnam, South Yemen and Nicaragua.[13] Intelligence collection was an element, though a subsidiary one, in the US military presence in Western Europe, Japan and indeed in all its forward deployment. Intelligence followed the military flag; partly as a necessary support for deployed forces, but mainly as part of the American national system for warning of Soviet activities and assessment of capabilities.

Local geography was needed for three reasons. First, intelligence collection by ships and aircraft needed airfields and port facilities near mission areas. The U-2 overflights of the USSR in the 1950s needed take-off and landing bases. The daily world-wide schedule of peripheral flights throughout the Cold War needed its similar infrastructure. Second was the Sigint requirement for ground interception sites at medium ranges (generally in hundreds of miles) from Soviet and Warsaw Pact territory. Most of the United States' allies – including the UK and Canada – could offer this geography, whereas the United States itself was too distant. Third was the need for other, closer-range access, at ranges in tens or (low) hundreds of miles, to those emissions which were not otherwise interceptable. This gave a special importance to areas like Berlin, the East–West German border and other land and sea areas adjacent to the Soviet Union and its naval and air training areas. Most of these areas provided equivalent opportunities for Soviet collection, mirror-imaging the collection posture of the West.

Most of the United States' allies could offer unique collection geography to meet one or more of these needs. Those closest to the USSR and most directly threatened usually had most to contribute; but despite its relative distance from the Soviet target Britain was a geographic asset as a collection 'platform'.[14] The importance of unique geography for technical means of intelligence collection plus the sheer size of the Soviet target also meant that the small and medium powers in the Alliance needed exchanges with each other as well as with the United States. All these factors gave focus to the other reasons for collaboration.

The result was a wide-ranging network of bilateral and multilateral arrangements, some linked with NATO and others independent of

[13] D. Ball, *Soviet Signals Intelligence (Sigint)* (Canberra: Australian National University, 1989), pp. 27–37.
[14] As acknowledged by Admiral R. R. Inman, former head of the American NSA, in an explanation of Britain's role as a Cold War base for intercepting many kinds of Soviet communications, including those from Soviet communications satellites (*Dispatches*, Channel 4 TV, 6 October 1993).

it.[15] They were mixtures of cooperative reactions to common threats and complex jigsaws of swaps and bargains. Central features were the USA's special needs as the 'distant' superpower, and the continuation of the close US–UK wartime collaboration; but these were no means the only elements.

The actual arrangements took various forms, sometimes in combination. One was to have military intelligence units as part of military 'forward basing', as in the US and British military presence in West Germany and Berlin. Others included similar arrangements for civilian facilities, or for joint operations with host countries. But the most pervasive way of exploiting geography was by exchanges of collected material and analytical conclusions with the local intelligence organizations. The Cold War provided the best examples of technical collaboration of this kind, but these geographic-technical factors apply more widely. Overseas military bases have general intelligence roles; the British Sovereign Base Areas in Cyprus for example have been acknowledged as a surveillance as well as a military base.[16]

For those who have access to it, satellite surveillance modifies this dependence on overseas geography, but does not remove the need for it completely, except for those systems that are equipped with (additionally expensive) satellite-to-satellite communications for control purposes and the relay of data to ground stations on home territory. The US (and Soviet) satellites which revolutionized imagery seem to have been designed not to depend on overseas facilities. On the other hand electronic collection from US satellites (which replaced some 'conventional', non-satellite collection, but by no means all of it) still posed some geographical requirements for overseas ground stations. The role of Australia in providing the ground 'tethers' for some US satellites originally positioned to 'see' the south and east of the USSR has been well publicized.[17]

Unique local assets and local geography merge into wider kinds of burden-sharing and joint operations. If the collaborator has the necessary technical competence, his contribution can be to assume responsibility for particular geographic areas or subjects. Or there can be burden-sharing and divisions of effort between close partners or between major powers and their clients, as illustrated by press reports at the time

---

[15] For some details see Stares, *Command Performance*, pp. 87–100.

[16] General Sir William Jackson and Lord Bramall, *The Chiefs: the Story of the United Kingdom Chiefs of Staff* (London: Brassey's, 1992), p. 379.

[17] Richelson and Ball, *The Ties that Bind*, pp. 193–4. For a list of overseas ground stations for US satellites in 1987, see P. B. Stares, *Space and National Security* (Washington D.C.: The Brookings Institution, 1987), p. 188.

that the USA was dependent on Japanese recordings of Soviet air-ground conversations for the evidence about the Soviet shooting-down of the South Korean airliner KAL 007 in September 1983.[18] Exceptionally, burden-sharing can be applied on a strategic as well as a tactical scale; thus in Sigint and in some other lines of research Britain and the United States in the Second World War had some broad (though by no means complete) divisions of intelligence effort between the European and Far Eastern theatres.[19] Joint operations between close allies are another way of economizing in resources and cutting costs, particularly for the big technical operations embarked upon under US–UK–Commonwealth arrangements. Joint funding by Italy and Spain in support of the French Helios satellite may be a similar example of load-sharing.

Apart from pooling and burden-sharing there is also the exchange of single-source ideas and interpretations, and all-source analysis and output. UK–US and Old Commonwealth exchanges are based on the Second World War pattern of large-scale exchanges on common targets, including selections of top level JIC assessments and NIEs. NATO developed arrangements for receiving national outputs of finished intelligence, and most other countries have arrangements for bilateral exchanges of some kind. There are few formal agreements for complete all-source exchanges; but most Western intelligence output is exchanged with someone. Most intelligence agencies are producing partly for an international audience of fellow-professionals, as well as for their primary national recipients.

Restraints on collaboration

These are powerful motives for international cooperation. On the other hand there are constant reasons for professional caution. International relationships cost time and effort; material received from abroad is not altogether a free good. All organizations have the usual institutional conviction that no-one else's work is as reliable as their own. Small organizations also have an instinct that cooperation with big foreign ones runs the risk of being swallowed up by them.

Above all there are the risks to sources. Every new foreign exchange is a new risk, through intelligence penetration of the foreign agency or its users, its careless handling or public leaking of the material, or its deliberate use of it in trading with its other intelligence contacts. Multi-

---

[18] Richelson, *Foreign Intelligence Organizations*, p. 267.
[19] F. H. Hinsley with E. E. Thomas, C. F. G. Ransom and R. C. Knight, *British Intelligence in the Second World War* vol. II, pp. 49–58.

lateral 'clubs' and international networks of exchanges increase these risks geometrically. Of course sources can be disguised, but professional collaborators always press for details, and make their own guesses if they are not satisfied. Security acts as a general counterweight to expansion, and is the main reason why the many *ad hoc* exchanges have a pragmatic and cautious flavour about them, limited to particular categories of material.

The result is a mixture of extrovert and introvert tendencies. Huminters on the whole live and breathe through their foreign liaisons, though they have to take special care of their human sources; Britain currently has relationships of some kind with the intelligence and security organizations of some 120 countries.[20] Defence intelligence organizations liaise with military allies, but the frequent turnover of their top uniformed people tends to limit close personal relationships. Security intelligence practitioners, brought up to sniff out treachery via counterespionage, are wary by nature, yet need their tight networks of professional overseas contacts. Technical intelligence collectors have their special UK–US–Commonwealth relationships, but otherwise mix caution with a technical freemasonry in which national loyalties merge into professional, transnational ones.

Professional forms and effects

The result is an international 'system' of great variety, from close cooperation to occasional contacts, varying between tightly held bilateral exchanges to big international conferences. This variety precludes much generalization, but some recurrent features and effects can be mentioned.

The first is the generally pragmatic, cautious but long-lasting nature of these relationships, at least in peacetime. UK–US intelligence cooperation originated as part of Churchill's concept of the English-speaking partnership, and has perhaps kept this element of vision; but other relationships develop in a step-by-step fashion, with a conscious attempt to avoid linkages with Foreign Offices and 'politics' generally. Organizational reputations for reliability count for a lot, as do personal relationships; British practitioners like to think that trustworthiness has been part of their services' international *persona*. Cooperation at its closest depends upon individuals who have grown up in their national organizations, done business against common enemies, socialized together for years and helped each other out of difficulties on the way.

---

[20] Unattributable official statement.

There is also a genuine sense of professional community. National and agency positions are defended tenaciously, but there is also a sense of common problems and the search for solutions; the Cold War sense of unity probably still continues on targets like terrorism or nuclear proliferation. Agencies in close collaboration over long periods develop a kind of bonding. One effect is to reproduce something not unlike the 'invisible colleges' which determine academic reputations and so set academic standards.[21] For photographic interpreters and Sigint practitioners, international contacts are their only chance of honing techniques and interpretations with other professionals – rather as the British and Hanoverian Black Chambers had a dialogue about their recondite art in the eighteenth century. Even in less specialized areas, overseas links provide the only source of objective professional criticism. In a secretive and insulated world, the international 'invisible colleges' are a factor in keeping national systems intellectually honest; the UK–US relationship has meant that analysts have the equivalent of academic external examiners marking their papers.[22] One of the many differences between Western and Soviet intelligence was that the Soviet system was incapable of having analytic and interpretative debates with allies.

Thus long-established liaison brings out all kinds of non-material factors. The effects of personal relationships, organizational ties and characteristic national generosity were present, for example, in US support for Britain during the Falklands War. Doing an ally a favour may produce a return which continues under its own momentum for decades; Britain's reported participation in airborne collection over the USSR (chapter 11) may well have been among the origins of vital, long-term access to US satellite imagery.

Yet there are also basic elements of bargaining, especially where collection and exchanges of material are involved, and there is always a bottom line of national self-interest. Underneath the camaraderie, the terms of trade – in information exchanged, manpower provided, analytic assistance, the provision of equipment or occasionally money – depend on who feels the greatest need. Small powers with significant assets can bargain effectively with big ones who need them badly.

Another distinctive feature is the agency-to-agency nature of these relationships, and the single-discipline nature of the various multilateral intelligence clubs. Links are between individual agencies and their

[21] See D. Crane, *Invisible Colleges: Diffusion of Knowledge in Scientific Communities* (Chicago: University of Chicago Press, 1972).
[22] Compare with the role in scientific research of published papers and networks of collaboration and criticism; see Crane, *Invisible Colleges*, pp. 41–65.

foreign opposite numbers, and not between national intelligence communities as a whole. Like talks to like, whether Huminter, Siginter, counterespionage specialist, defence intelligencer, national assessor or whatever. Sometimes a single agency is given a formal role of coordinating all external intelligence relations; usually the national Humint agencies are chosen (for example CIA and Israel's Mossad) since they tend to have the biggest overseas representation.[23] But the others do not like using them as middlemen. Trade-offs in collaboration between one specialization and another are rare. Intelligence's own 'foreign policy' is mainly the policies of its individual national agencies.

One effect of overseas connections is therefore to reinforce the centrifugal tendencies of national communities. Another is to encourage nations to imitate their bigger partners. The powerful influences of the individual US agencies rub off on the organization of their overseas collaborators. Big nations' communities consciously and unconsciously shape the intelligence structures of the smaller partners with whom they deal.

Close cooperation also depends on some degree of standardization. Divisions of effort depend on technical agreements on methods, particularly in connection with modern information technology. The future of close international exchanges lies in standardized computer-compatible formats, or in direct computer-to-computer links across national boundaries; close collaboration now requires some integration of national systems. Decisions about close intelligence collaboration now tend to turn on issues of hardware and software compatibility, in which technical issues are entwined with political ones. The wider public issue of a distinctive 'European defence identity' versus cooperation with the United States is probably being played out within intelligence in debates over forms of information technology standardization and remote access.

However one of the main practical effects of intelligence collaboration is to reinforce purely national needs for strict information security. Accepting specific security procedures laid down by the other party can be part of specific intelligence bargains. Some general uniformity of security standards is a prerequisite of serious long-term collaboration; occasionally the object of cooperation may actually be to influence the other party towards better security standards. The transatlantic and Commonwealth intelligence relationships are based on comparable national security practices supplemented by special agreements for the handling of intelligence; these include formal limitations on what can be

---

[23] For a description of US relationships and CIA's role in them, see J. T. Richelson, *The US Intelligence Community* (Cambridge, Mass.: Ballinger, 1985), chapter 10.

passed outside the UK–US–Commonwealth circle. Specific foreign concerns over national arrangements can sometimes manifest themselves; after the Prime espionage case in 1982 the British Security Commission explicitly cited US views and practices when it recommended the introduction of the polygraph for intelligence vetting, in the light of damage thought to be 'very high' to British and US Sigint operations.[24]

But the general result of this stress on security is simply to strengthen national security disciplines. National reputations for good or bad security are crucial elements in international intelligence standing. Those given access to sensitive intelligence by a foreign partner have to follow the partner's rules to the letter. The presence of foreign data complicates both the declassification of historical intelligence material and the operation of Freedom of Information legislation where this applies. If intelligence communities seem excessively secretive, this foreign security dimension is one cause.

Yet another effect of intelligence collaboration is on the targeting of cooperating countries. There is tacit professional recognition that cooperation is not necessarily a bar to continued targeting of each other's government, defence forces and the like. Sometimes there is even a purely technical need to test friends' security standards, in order to know what secrets can be entrusted to them.

Nevertheless the existence of close cooperation exercises some restraint on targeting. Professionally collaborating agencies are reluctant to target each other. The temptation to do so may be strong, as in the Pollard case already mentioned in chapter 10. But apart from other considerations the intimacy of intelligence liaison makes targeting a close collaborator too risky to be worthwhile. The savage US reaction to the Pollard case showed how far this was regarded as off limits.[25]

Cooperation rubs off on national intelligence communities in these various ways. The main effect is to make national systems more productive than they would otherwise be, with more data and the technical advantages of dialogue with others. Governments get better views of the world at cut prices. But this international dimension brings with it some problems of management. National users' requirements cease to be the only basis for intelligence priorities. Agencies also need to maximize their value to foreign partners, and may be locked into burden-

---

[24] Cmnd 8876, *Report of the Security Commission* (London: HMSO, May 1983), paragraph 1.3.

[25] W. Blitzer, *Territory of Lies* (New York: Harper and Row, 1989). Pollard was given a life sentence in spite of a 'plea-bargain' of admitting guilt in return for leniency.

sharing agreements with them that limit flexibility; conversely some national needs may be met in what is received from them. What intelligence does, and needs to do at the technical professional level, becomes even more of a mystery to its users.

Cooperating with larger partners also introduces problems of scale; the national system may have to cope with an incoming flow of foreign material geared to bigger information-handling capacities than its own. Western intelligence overload in the Cold War came mainly from the superpower scale of the US data made available, necessarily on a 'take it or leave it' basis. International influence has to be reconciled with the independence of national analytic conclusions, and the need to keep national freedom of intelligence action. Complete dependence on others is uncomfortable. In the worst case there is the risk of being provided with consciously or unconsciously rigged evidence, as may have applied to the information passed by Soviet intelligence services to Egypt that provoked the Six Days' War in 1967.[26] The strategy and tactics of intelligence collaboration seek to balance its advantages against the need for some national independence.

These characteristics create the fabric of the international intelligence system and shape its effects. National intelligence communities have a perceived 'weight', made up of their local access, general capabilities, foreign associations and national security standards; other powers have fairly precise ideas of what they have to offer in collaboration. Negotiation is rarely between exact equals. Increasing technical costs are spurs to combined efforts, yet these have the usual problems of control. Ideas discussed in recent years of multinational European satellite collection sum up both the attractions and the practical problems of ambitious intelligence collaboration.

Notwithstanding these professional and technical considerations, intelligence collaboration is also bound up with national policies at the general political level. This interaction can now be examined.

Political dimensions

Political influences on intelligence liaisons

Intelligence is influenced by foreign policy but also influences it. Quite often the political and professional–technical factors point in the same

---

[26] M. I. Handel, 'A "Runaway Deception": Soviet Disinformation and the Six-Day War, 1967' in D. A. Charters and M. J. Tugwell (eds.), *Deception Operations: Studies in the East–West Context* (London: Brassey's, 1990).

direction. Occasionally it may be so vital to plug national intelligence gaps that requests for help from foreign liaisons are put at a national political level, as when Israel asked for US intelligence during the 1973 Yom Kippur War and subsequently for immediate warnings of Scud missile launches against it in the 1991 Gulf War. Generally however the picture is of the political and professional levels operating separately, but reinforcing each other.

Thus major flows of intelligence tend to be natural corollaries of politico-military alliances, as in NATO. The same applies to international political collaboration on specific subjects such as international sanctions, the dissemination of advanced military technology, nuclear proliferation, threats of chemical and biological warfare (CW/BW), and arms control verification. In such cases intelligence collaboration follows from normal professional calculations of benefits and costs, but with some adjustment round the margins to take account of wider policy dimensions.

Within this general picture there are some special cases of intelligence cooperation across political divides; there were suggestions of East–West cooperation on international terrorism even before the end of the Cold War.[27] Though most of the stories about Western collaboration with dictatorships are exaggerated, issues like cooperation on Soviet espionage or intelligence assistance to Britain during the Falklands War can cross political boundaries. But on the whole international enemies do not cooperate, and there have to be compelling reasons for relationships with politically unpopular regimes. Generally speaking, foreign policy and national sensitivities set intelligence's general frames of reference.

Additionally intelligence liaisons can be used deliberately to further national policies. At a very general level, the cultivation of good relations at the political level tends to keep intelligence relationships in being, even when they are technically unrewarding. Diplomats on the whole tend to be wary of new liaisons as potential hostages to fortune, but are supportive of existing ones, especially where a reduction at the professional–technical level might be taken as a political signal.

More specifically, intelligence can indeed be used as signals of this kind at a policy level, and as symbols, rewards and punishments; the more so, perhaps, because of intelligence's secrecy and mystique. The Israeli requests in 1973 and 1991 had political as well as practical

---

[27] Gordievsky claims that the KGB Resident in London approached the British police on about a dozen occasions between 1980 and 1984 with information about Middle Eastern terrorism (C. Andrew and O. Gordievsky, *KGB: the Inside Story of its Foreign Operations from Lenin to Gorbachev* (London: Hodder and Stoughton, 1990), p. 532).

significance, as had the US responses, for example Kissinger's instruction in 1973 'to give them every bit of intelligence we have'.[28] In a similar way, British and Irish cross-border intelligence cooperation against the IRA is always both a practical issue and a touchstone of Dublin attitudes. Intelligence flows and relationships are available as diplomatic negotiating cards. Intelligence assistance is a useful (and relatively inexpensive) form of aid to clients, as in the British help given to the Omani government in the 1970s as part of the campaign against externally-backed subversion.[29] The contrary also applies; withdrawal of intelligence can be a diplomatic punishment, as when the Reagan Administration withdrew services to New Zealand in the early 1980s in the dispute over the denial of port facilities for US nuclear-equipped warships.

Intelligence liaisons also come into the political calculus in various other ways. Apart from their underpinning of political relationships, they have a diplomatic value simply as contacts with an influential local group; sometimes indeed with key figures in the local regime, or perhaps the next regime. Having a reputation for good intelligence is a factor in national diplomatic weight abroad; so is the reverse. States needing more intelligence for active international roles, or simply for defence against threats, may feel that international intelligence liaisons are the only way to get it. And intelligence organizations and leaders have their own institutional agenda, served by expanding into new areas of international influence or by remaining content with well-established relationships.

Many of these elements can be seen in the British attitudes to the transatlantic intelligence relationship. British foreign policy is conceived in terms of influencing groups of allies towards sensible joint policies on a more or less worldwide basis.[30] Good judgment for this policy requires good intelligence, for which the US connection is deemed essential. But the intelligence connection is itself also seen as an influence on the USA in the 'Atlantic pillar' on which Britain rests; intelligence-sharing and analytic debate contribute further by influencing US thinking and helping Britain to act as the American interpreter to Europe. Intelligence influences both British and US participation in the transatlantic dialogue. As Kissinger elegantly put it in 1982, writing of the previous decade:

---

[28] H. Kissinger, *Years of Upheaval* (London: Weidenfeld and Nicolson, 1982), p. 493.

[29] D. F. Eickelman, 'Intelligence in an Arab Gulf State' in R. Godson (ed.), *Comparing Foreign Intelligence* (London: Pergamon–Brassey's, 1988), pp. 89–114.

[30] For a description and critique of this view, see W. Wallace, 'British Foreign Policy after the Cold War', *International Affairs* vol. 68 no. 3 (July 1992), pp. 423–42.

Their [the British] way of retaining great-power status was to be so integral a part of US decision-making that the idea of not consulting them seemed a violation of the natural order of things. So able and assured were our British counterparts that they managed to convey the notion that it was they who were conferring a boon on us by sharing the experience of centuries. Nor were they quite wrong in this estimate.[31]

Maintaining this degree of intimacy in intelligence matters was a British policy objective throughout the Cold War, and probably still is.

This interaction of intelligence relationships and policy stance is particularly important to Britain, but is not unique. US intelligence relationships are grounded in US professional–technical needs, but they are also part of hegemonic influence. The Australian intelligence connection with the United States has been publicly recognized as part of Australia's contribution to Pacific security.[32] Conversely, France's relative disinterest in intelligence and intelligence relationships – until the traumatic experience of dependence on the United States in the Gulf War – reflected the somewhat disengaged French stance within the Western alliance during the Cold War.[33]

Thus foreign policy intervenes in intelligence, in both general and specific ways, despite practitioners' occasional misconceptions that their professional relationships are insulated. Politics establish the context; for instance Britain was presumably brought fully into the Polish work on the Enigma cipher in the summer of 1939 partly because of the political guarantee to Poland in March of that year. (It is interesting to speculate whether earlier British continental commitments at the political level would have produced this impetus to Enigma cryptanalysis sooner.) The UK–US relationship in intelligence is inseparable from other aspects of this relationship. Wider post-war Western intelligence cooperation owed much to the existence of NATO, directly and indirectly.

Yet intelligence relationships have their own momentum; once well established, considerable political weight is needed to disrupt them. UK–US intelligence-sharing survived the Suez crisis and other smaller UK–US disputes. Diplomats recognize intelligence's significance, but are inclined to regard it as a slightly fenced-off mystery. In this it is much like other specialist areas of government, whose

---

[31] Kissinger, *Years of Upheaval*, p. 140.
[32] Initially in P. Dibb, *Review of Australian Defence Capabilities: Report to the Minister for Defence* (Canberra: Australian Government Publishing Service, 1986); and *The Defence of Australia* (Canberra: Australian Government Publishing Service, 1987).
[33] For French intelligence reforms in reaction to France's dependence on US intelligence in the Gulf War, see P. Kemp, 'The Rise and Fall of France's Spymasters', *Intelligence and National Security* vol. 9 no. 1 (January 1994).

international contacts now form their own 'systems' – linked with traditional diplomacy, sometimes influenced by it, but operating with a degree of practical autonomy, intensified in intelligence's case by its special secrecy.

Liaisons' influence on politics

The reverse effects of the international intelligence 'system' on foreign policies are even more mixed. We have already noted that intelligence requirements can give governments an impetus towards cultivating foreign providers at a political level. But it is difficult to isolate the effects of this on national policy from the many other factors working in the same direction: for example the value attached by Britain to US support on nuclear policy, transatlantic cooperation in naval matters, and the special influence of the English-speaking countries within NATO. The same difficulty would be encountered over trying to isolate the professional–technical value to Germany of developing US–German intelligence exchanges from other factors influencing overall US–German relationships.

In the same way it is difficult to demonstrate that intelligence liaisons have such a professional–technical value to the junior partners that they can be used for effective political pressure by the senior ones. Enoch Powell was exaggerating when he said that all British Prime Ministers from 1970 onwards had been subject to (and influenced by) a tacit US threat to cut off supplies of intelligence;[34] though (rather surprisingly) the advantage of being independent of US satellite intelligence was officially cited as one reason for Britain's choice of the Trident missile system instead of terrain-following cruise missiles.[35] There was in fact an isolated (and undisclosed) top-level US attempt some years ago to use the withdrawal of some intelligence as a political signal to Britain at a time of acute political disagreement; it misfired, largely through US agencies' institutional resistance to implementation. Even New Zealand, a very junior intelligence partner, was not intimidated by the withdrawal of US supplies. This is not to deny that the intelligence provided by strong powers does not give them additional political leverage. But the actual effects have been less than might be expected. In this a significant factor has been the inertial resistance of intelligence communities to being used in this way.

---

[34] BBC broadcast 26 June 1991, in C. Andrew's programme *What If . . .*
[35] House of Commons Defence Committee 1980–1, Fourth Report, *Strategic Nuclear Weapons Policy* (London: HMSO, 1981), paragraph 11. The terrain-following guidance for cruise missiles 'could involve continual dependence on information from US satellites and this would reduce the operational independence available with an SSBN force'.

Thus the professional–technical requirements and results of intelligence liaisons affect foreign policies only at the margin. On the whole they accord with the political alignments that states have adopted for weightier reasons. Yet there is a more important though diffuse effect, underpinning political collaboration rather than shaping its direction. States guide each other towards common perceptions through intelligence exchanges and dialogues. British analysts believed that they exercised a significant influence on US Cold War perceptions; only detailed historical research will show whether they were right. Mutual education also promotes common action, just as having a common base of intelligence knowledge promotes agreed decisions. There can be little doubt that British support for the United States in the Cuban crisis and in the 1986 bombing of Libya was facilitated by intelligence-sharing and common analysis.[36] These probably had similar influences upon Australian support for British action over confrontation with Indonesia, and for the US in Vietnam. Irrespective of the merits of these decisions, they came about more easily because the intelligence underlying them was not in dispute. There are important implications for NATO and UN action which will be examined in chapter 20.

However it would be wrong to see such exchanges, not limited to collaboration on particular situations, as altruistic international education. Powers want others to share their world views, and intelligence is one of the influences. Britain in the Cold War thought that through intelligence assessment it was educating its big ally; but who most influenced whom? Perhaps Britain and the United States buttressed each other in a common set of assumptions, and the same may have been true of intelligence's effects in the Western alliance as a whole. Consciously and unconsciously intelligence is under international as well as national pressure to support established perceptions. How intelligence can cope with these pressures is a theme of the next three chapters.

Summary

Modern intelligence is a multinational activity. National intelligence power is a function not only of national capabilities but also of the foreign cooperation and product they obtain. Governments' intelligence

---

[36] According to the then Foreign Secretary (now Lord Howe), British intercepts confirmed the American view of Libyan responsibility for the attack on an American-used nightclub in Berlin that precipitated the US retaliation (G. Howe, *Conflict of Loyalty* (London: Macmillan, 1994), pp. 504–5). For a reference to shared intelligence contributing to common UK–US action over severing relations with Syria because of its support for terrorism, see p. 509.

needs are met by varying mixtures of national and foreign efforts. Investments in national intelligence organizations are, in some degree, subscriptions to the variety of specialist international clubs to which these organizations belong. For most powers – including even the US superpower – part of the national intelligence effort is the *quid pro quo* for what is received from partners and clients. Cooperation with foreign agencies is often rooted in historical links and other intangibles, but there is usually a bottom line of national professional–technical self-interest. Overseas liaisons are ultimately sets of professional bargains.

This international dimension of intelligence fits the modern patterns of increased international specialist contacts. Intelligence has considerable day-to-day independence from foreign policies and government-to-government contacts at the political level, and some longer-term insulation from them. Nevertheless the setting for its overseas arrangements is provided by international political alignments. Intelligence has some influences on these alignments, but its usual effect is to buttress and not redirect them. Conversely its relationships can be manipulated to support foreign policy objectives, though this is not easy; the professional–technical basis of long-standing intelligence relationships gives them a considerable durability. In the last resort intelligence collaboration is the servant of national political objectives, but at a strategic rather than tactical level.

Part IV

Accuracy

13   Failure and remedies

Part III (chapters 8–12) considered intelligence's effects. This Part (chapters 13–15) deals with its major task of getting things as nearly correct as possible about its targets, making accurate forecasts about them, and calibrating the reliability of its own findings. No complete account can be given of all intelligence's difficulties under these headings. These chapters illustrate them by discussing three important aspects of intelligence assessment. This chapter considers 'warning failure' and its assessment implications. Chapters 14 and 15 deal with the quality of defence intelligence and the organization of national assessment. All three concentrate on finished intelligence, but many of their conclusions apply also to the output of collection and single-source analysis.

Accuracy is a prime concern of intelligence management, but has to be combined with the pursuit of other kinds of efficiency. Being right and being efficient are closely linked, but raise slightly different problems. After the present group of chapters geared to the first, chapters 16–18 deal with the second. Good management is an amalgam of both.

Incidence of fallibility

Intelligence failure has become part of modern political vocabulary, just as have government failure and market failure, and perhaps the term has become overworked.[1] The best known variety is 'warning failure' against surprise attack, particularly in peacetime and as war initiation. The list of these failures over the last fifty years is surprisingly long, including Denmark and Norway in 1940; Pearl Harbor and the Philippines in 1941; Russia in 1941; Korea in June 1950 and the Chinese intervention later that year; the Chinese attack on India in 1962; Czechoslovakia in

---

[1] For a view of intelligence failure see M. W. Lowenthal, 'The Burdensome Concept of Failure' in A. C. Maurer, M. D. Tunstall and J. M. Keagle (eds.), *Intelligence: Policy and Process* (London: Westview, 1985). For comments on market failure and government failure see J. Le Grand, 'The Theory of Government Failure', *British Journal of Political Science* 21, pp. 423–42.

August 1968; the Yom Kippur War in 1973; the Chinese invasion of Vietnam in 1979; the Falklands in 1982; Kuwait in 1990.[2] On all these occasions skilled intelligence systems were to some extent caught by surprise. Stalin is said to have ignored eighty-four separate warnings of the 1941 invasion.[3]

Surprise attack within wars also has a record of success. The same applies to deception; for sixty-eight cases of deception between 1914 and 1968 a 91 per cent success rate has been calculated.[4] Many of these were part of tactical surprise attacks, but some were longer running, like the Allied strategic deceptions of the Second World War. Warning failures also extend to some cases of successful diplomatic surprise, like the 1939 Nazi–Soviet Pact. Outside this area of surprise action is the wider one of failing to forecast political coups and regime changes, such as the overthrow of the regime in Portugal in 1974 and of the Shah of Iran in 1978–9. Outside all these is the even wider circle of events that, although not necessarily planned around surprise, came as shocks because they had not been forecast, as in the OPEC use of the oil weapon in 1973–4.

These failures of short- and medium-term warning merge into much longer-running misjudgments. During the Cold War the US intelligence community was heavily criticized at different times, from both ends of the political spectrum, for mistakes in assessing Soviet intentions and military capabilities.[5] There were both under- and over-estimates of Soviet strategic capabilities, but the best known is the over-assessment of a Soviet ICBM threat in the late 1950s which in fact hardly existed; US analysts had not guessed that the USSR would build up their MRBM and IRBM force for use against European targets before investing in an ICBM force to attack the USA.[6] On the other hand US intelligence has recently been criticized for not forecasting Soviet economic collapse and

---

[2] For examples of warning failures see *inter alia* R. K. Betts, *Surprise Attack: Lessons for Defense Planning* (Washington D.C.: Brookings Institution, 1982), chapters 2 and 3; and E. Kam, *Surprise Attack: the Victim's Perspective* (Cambridge, Mass. and London: Harvard University Press, 1988), pp. 3–4.

[3] B. Whaley, *Codeword Barbarossa* (Cambridge, Mass.: MIT Press, 1973), chapters 3–5.

[4] B. Whaley, *Strategic Deception and Surprise in War* (Cambridge, Mass.: MIT Press, 1973), p. 164 and quoted by R. Heuer, 'Cognitive Factors in Deception and Counter-Deception, in D. C. Daniel and K. L. Herbig (eds.), *Strategic Military Deception* (New York: Pergamon, 1982), p. 60.

[5] For commentary see B. Berkowitz and A. Goodman, *Strategic Intelligence for American National Security* (Princeton: Princeton University Press, 1989), pp. 125–36. For a hawkish critique see D. S. Sullivan, 'Evaluating US Intelligence Estimates' in R. Godson (ed.), *Intelligence Requirements for the 1980s: Analysis and Estimates* (Washington D.C.: National Strategy Information Center, 1980), pp. 49–73.

[6] J. Prados, *The Soviet Estimate: US Intelligence Analysis and Soviet Strategic Forces* (Princeton: Princeton University Press, 1986 edition), chapters 5–8.

the break-up of the Soviet state. Modern Western intelligence is good at producing information on current observables, particularly through the use of US satellite imagery; but it has no magic properties in forecasting.

Intelligence fallibility has produced its own literature, based partly on official investigations. The first official British inquest into warning failure was probably the enquiry after the Dutch Fleet had sailed up the Thames in 1666; the findings about intelligence shortcomings resemble those reached by modern enquiries three centuries later.[7] In recent years the Congressional investigation of the Pearl Harbor disaster was the basis of Roberta Wohlstetter's definitive study published in 1962.[8] The official Israeli and US investigations of the Yom Kippur War encouraged further academic work on 'warning' and 'warning failure'.[9] This linked up with other investigations of surprise and deception, and with the wider study of international perception and misperception.[10]

The keynote of this literature is Wohlstetter's famous analogy between intelligence warning and the detection of radar signals from background 'noise':

The fact of surprise at Pearl Harbor has never been persuasively explained by accusing the participants, individually or in groups, of conspiracy or negligence or stupidity. What these examples illustrate is rather the very human tendency to pay attention to the signals that support current expectations about enemy behavior. If no one is listening for signals of an attack against a highly improbable target, then it is very difficult for the signals to be heard.[11]

Handel concludes that, at the strategic level, surprise and deception are likely to succeed.[12] Richard Betts has written that 'intelligence failures

---

[7] P. Frazer, *The Intelligence of the Secretaries of State and their Monopolies of Licensed News 1660–1688* (Cambridge: Cambridge University Press, 1956), p. 79.

[8] R. Wohlstetter, *Pearl Harbor: Warning and Decision* (Stanford: Stanford University Press, 1962).

[9] The literature includes Betts, *Surprise Attack*; M. I. Handel, 'Intelligence and the Problem of Strategic Surprise', *Journal of Strategic Studies* vol. 7 no. 3 (September 1984), pp. 230–81, reprinted together with his 'Overview' in his *War, Strategy and Intelligence* (London: Cass, 1989); Kam, *Surprise Attack: the Victim's Perspective*; A. Shlaim, 'Failures in National Estimates: The Case of the Yom Kippur War', *World Politics* vol. 28 no. 3 (April 1976); A. Levite, *Intelligence and Strategic Surprises* (New York: Columbia University Press, 1987).

[10] For deception see *inter alia* Whaley, *Codeword Barbarossa*; and articles in Daniel and Herbig, *Strategic Military Deception*. For a general treatment of misperception see R. Jervis, *Perception and Misperception in International Politics* (Princeton: Princeton University Press, 1976). For the problems of information in decision-taking see I. L. Janis and L. Mann, *Decision-Making* (New York/London: The Free Press, 1977).

[11] Wohlstetter, *Pearl Harbor: Warning and Decision*, p. 392.

[12] Handel, *War, Strategy and Intelligence*, pp. 18–19, 32, 36.

are not only inevitable, they are natural.'[13] Rather similar conclusions emerge about longer-term assessment. According to Robert Jervis,

Those who are right, in politics as in science, are rarely distinguished from those who are wrong by their superior ability to judge specific bits of information . . . Rather, the expectation and predisposition of those who are right have provided a closer match to the situation than those who are wrong.[14]

These are useful correctives to intelligence's claims, yet they can be taken to imply fundamental flaws in the process. All professions attract criticism when they slip on banana-skins. But errors in weather forecasts do not call meteorology into question, and the persistent forecasting failures over the British economy only lead to the employment of more economists. A first question is therefore whether there is really anything special about intelligence failure.

The idea of 'failure'

The concept of 'failure' introduces its own problems. Failure attracts more attention than success. A behavioural scientist has commented that 'focus on failure is likely to mislead by creating a distorted view of the prevalence of misfortune . . . Belaboring failures should, therefore, disproportionately enhance their perceived frequency in the past (and perhaps future).'[15] The circumstances of intelligence increase the risk of biased judgments about it. Its failure makes for good media exposure; and official enquiries always search for culpability, in a way historians are liable to inherit. Recent successes by contrast stay under security wraps, as in the way the Second World War successes remained concealed for twenty-five years. Others go almost unrecognized if their effect is to enable crises to be avoided. The British pre-emption of the Iraqi invasion of Kuwait in 1961 is much less remembered than the question whether there was adequate warning in 1990. The USA's effective use of Western intelligence on Soviet military preparations to deter Soviet action against Poland in 1980–1 has attracted less attention than the failure to judge that the Warsaw Pact preparations around Czechoslovakia in August 1968 were for a military invasion.

---

[13] R. K. Betts, 'Analysis, War and Decisions: Why Intelligence Failures are Inevitable', *World Politics* vol. 31 no. 1 (October 1978), p. 88.

[14] Jervis, *Perception and Misperception in International Politics*, p. 179.

[15] B. Fischhoff, 'For Those Condemned to Study the Past: Reflections on Historical Judgment' in R. A. Shweder and D. W. Fiske (eds.), *New Directions for Methodology of Behavioral Science: Fallible Judgment in Behavioral Research* (San Francisco: Jossey-Bass, 1980), p. 83.

Failure and success are also intermingled; as Betts puts it, the glass is either half full or half empty according to one's viewpoint,[16] and this is influenced by the outcome. The Cuban missile crisis was partly an intelligence failure, since US intelligence originally discounted the possibility that Soviet surface-to-surface missiles would be deployed on the island. Yet their subsequent detection in U-2 imagery was an intelligence triumph. Similarly the Falklands invasion in 1982 is seen as a British intelligence failure, yet the tactical warning of two or three days before the Argentine landing was probably crucial for preparing a prompt response and getting the United States diplomatically engaged; the invasion failed as the complete *fait accompli* which it could easily have been.

Components and criteria

What is labelled as intelligence failure also has its various different components. Some non-intelligence elements get included; for example the delayed warning from Washington, eventually arriving at Pearl Harbor by commercial telegram at the time of the Japanese attack, was a straightforward failure of command and communications, not intelligence. At the point where intelligence meets policy, leaders sometimes reject warnings, as when the Johnson Administration rejected CIA assessments on Vietnam. More often policy-makers are slow off the mark or deliberately delay; every intelligence warning has to force its way into governments' attention. Betts argues that policy-makers' failures to respond are more common than intelligence's failure to warn.[17]

Clearly some of these are failures of intelligence to get close enough to its users to carry conviction, or to draw enough attention to the significance of its reports; if there was a Western warning failure over the Soviet invasion of Afghanistan, it was partly through not recognizing the profound effect that the operation would have on the Carter Administration and the US–Soviet relationship. But unless everything is laid at intelligence's door, some of these failures must be classed as policy

---

16 R. K. Betts, 'Surprise, Scholasticism, and Strategy: A Review of Ariel Levite's *Intelligence and Strategic Surprises*', *International Studies Quarterly* vol. 33 no. 3 (September 1989), p. 331.

17 'The common view is that surprise occurs because intelligence services fail to warn . . . In most cases [of successful surprise attack], leaders in the victim state were warned that the enemy was marshaling the capabilities to strike, but they did not react to the warning in ways that hindsight demonstrates were necessary.' (Betts, *Surprise Attack*, pp. 16–17.) There is scope for argument about what constitutes effective warning in these cases.

responses. Stalin acted as his own assessor of the evidence, and his misjudgment in 1941 illustrates more about dictators than about intelligence.

Even over wrong conclusions there is the obvious point that intelligence cannot expect to be always right. 'Since estimating is what you do when you do not know, it is inherent in a great many situations that after reading the estimate you still do not know.'[18] States can never fully understand each other or predict others' actions, or even their own. Forecasts may themselves alter the situations they are forecasting. Even for short-term and apparently predictable events, there are all the problems of understanding the crazy logic of secretive dictators.

This unknowability applies particularly to long-term forecasts. There is Gates's distinction discussed in chapter 6 between secrets and mysteries. Though intelligence could have drawn more attention to the fissiparous forces within the Soviet state, the non-prediction of its collapse was hardly 'failure'. Intelligence can seek to find out what is planned for the reasonably near future or assess short-term intentions, but can hardly be said to 'fail' in the same way over a much longer time-scale; though it may still fail to draw attention to the degree of uncertainty surrounding any forecasts of this kind.

Finally there is the element of straight contest between intelligence and the opposing information security, designed to keep the secrets that intelligence is supposed to tease out. Assuming equal competence, intelligence might be expected to win some contests and lose others. Pearl Harbor showed good Japanese security as well as US intelligence failure. The two are relative to each other, and detailed study is needed to decide in any particular case which is the better explanation judged by the standards of the time. It has been powerfully argued that all history may be related as 'stories' with dominant themes, such as comedy, tragedy, romance or satire.[19] Arguably the accounts of 'intelligence failure' might all be rewritten as accounts of 'security success', recounting the detailed ways in which secrecy was maintained.[20]

[18] T. L. Hughes, *The Fate of Facts in the World of Men: Foreign Policy and Intelligence-making* (New York: The Foreign Policy Association Headline Series no. 233, December 1976), p. 43.
[19] I am indebted to H. Sugananu, 'A Theory of War Origins' (paper given to the British International Studies Association annual conference, 1995) for this reference to the writings of Hayden White, with whom this idea is associated.
[20] Successes in deception have been extensively narrated. But the (often prosaic) technical, bureaucratic and military details of how secrets are more often kept have received less attention.

The balance sheet

This survey softens the impression of intelligence failure. One side's intelligence failure is often the other's information security success. States are bound to misperceive each other to some extent. Failures of medium- and long-term forecasts do not stand out as surprising in themselves. Some failures to convince users are inevitable parts of government's in-built sluggishness. There is nothing very marked about intelligence failures; other modern studies of 'information failure' in events unconnected with intelligence come to roughly the same conclusions.[21] 'Wrong decisions, in my opinion, much more frequently arise from the failure to use information that was, in principle, available, than from one caused by the current limitations on human knowledge.'[22]

Yet it is puzzling that, with short-term warning of military attack such a central part of intelligence's role, the repeated failures in it are not balanced by comparable warning successes. The contests between intelligence and security over detecting surprise attack seem more one-sided than might have been expected. Short-term warning failure of this kind hits systems with high reputations, and in prolonged crises as well as when there are bolts from the blue. With hindsight, the errors seem so *obvious*, as if they are a punishment for professional hubris. The issue of warning failure merits the attention it has received, for its own sake and for clues to longer-range inaccuracies.

The literature points to multiple causes, including the politics of intelligence–user relationships. It also discusses problems of organization, data-handling and the effects of secrecy:

Collected information must pass through numerous potential bottlenecks. It must be screened at low levels to raise an initial suspicion; it must be transmitted to higher levels of the intelligence bureaucracy to be compared with data from other sources; it has then to be passed to policymakers who must judge whether the evidence warrants action.[23]

Nevertheless the literature as a whole conveys two general conclusions. First, the weak link in the process is intelligence analysis, rather than the collection of evidence; warning failure happens despite apparently adequate evidence. Second, the analytic weakness has a particular, recurrent quality; as Kissinger put it over the American failure to detect

---

[21] For cases and discussion see F. W. Horton Jr and D. Lewis (eds.), *Great Information Disasters* (London: ASLIB, 1991).

[22] L. W. Branscombe, 'Preface' in S. Dedijer and N. Jéquier (eds.), *Intelligence for Economic Development* (Oxford: Berg, 1987), pp. ix–x.

[23] Betts, *Surprise Attack*, p. 92.

the preparations for the Yom Kippur War, 'the breakdown was not administrative but intellectual'.[24] People interpret data through images, historical analogies, personal experiences and other hypotheses. There is a cognitive rigidity about the way they fit information into these patterns. They see what they expect to see; they come to conclusions too early and stick to them for too long. 'Groupthink' – in intelligence's relationship with its users, and within the intelligence community itself – reinforces these effects.

This diagnosis produces an impressive typology of analysts' errors – 'mirror-imaging' of motives and values; 'perseverance' with initial conceptions; the avoidance of discrepant information; the influence of expectations; bias and rigidity and the protection of cognitive consistency; the seductive heuristics of 'availability', 'representativeness' and 'anchoring' in the process of reaching conclusions; the overconfidence of groups compared with the views of the individuals within them; and so on.[25] A scholarly analysis of German intelligence failure over the Normandy landings discerns ten kinds of misperception and some fifty sub-elements.[26] The literature recognizes the multiplicity of factors, but the general effect is to emphasize these 'intellectual' explanations; and this is how it tends to be interpreted.[27] Moreover these features of warning failures tend to be extended as explanations of intelligence shortcomings as a whole.

Prescriptions

This emphasis on intellectual explanations is reflected in the way in which the recommendations about analysis stress the importance of individual calibre. Walter Laqueur concludes that 'the quality of analysts will remain the decisive factor in the future as it has in the past'.[28] 'The only promising way to improve intelligence performance is to select recruits who have at least some of the faculties needed, and then give

---

[24] H. Kissinger, *Years of Upheaval* (London: Weidenfeld and Nicolson, Joseph, 1982), p. 466.

[25] Summarized in Kam, *Surprise Attack*, chapters 4–6.

[26] T. L. Cubbage II, 'The German Misapprehensions Regarding Overlord: Understanding Failure in the Estimative Process' in M. I. Handel (ed.), *Strategic and Operation Deception in the Second World War* (London: Cass, 1987).

[27] As an example of the influence of these (mainly US) explanations on British thinking, see Air Chief Marshal Sir Michael Armitage, 'General Problems of Intelligence Assessment' in J. N. Merritt, R. Read and R. Weissinger-Baylon (eds.), *Crisis Decision-taking in the Atlantic Alliance: Perspectives on Deterrence* (Menlo Park, Ca.: Strategic Decisions Press, 1988), p. 6-1.

[28] W. Laqueur, *A World of Secrets: The Uses and Limits of Intelligence* (New York: Basic Books, 1985), p. 308.

them a good training.'[29] 'It may well be that intelligence genius is born, not made. But it is also true that intelligence needs only a few geniuses, and that political judgment and understanding can be taught – at least up to a point.'[30] T. L. Hughes similarly stressed the need for special skills for 'that strange but vital art form which catalyzes analysis and precipitates useful action', and adds Woodrow Wilson's unhelpful advice to the Latin Americans: 'you need to find "good men".'[31] As for organization and management, the same writer believes that 'it is the human variables that defy the jurisdictional reforms, mock the machinery of government and frustrate the organizational tinkering. These are the phenomena that help assure that no rejuggling of administrative charts can finally surmount the uneven qualities of the men who inhabit the institutions.'[32]

Other more general recommendations deal with intelligence–policy relationships and the loosening of analytic shackles. Godson describes 'the new analysis', including 'opportunity-oriented analysis' in which intelligence points up opportunities for implementing national policies.[33] Betts argues for a freer style of long-term estimate, less wedded to consensus and definitive conclusions and with more emphasis on the kind of 'net assessment' which compares 'our' capabilities with 'theirs'. Estimates should 'focus attention more forcefully on the critical uncertainties'; a 'more extensive and creative sort of NIE . . . would probably have to sacrifice concision and full coordination of agency views'; this should be encouraged by 'a more demanding agenda and a freer rein'.[34] The system should not be too purist in avoiding policy recommendation. 'It is nearly impossible to write any analysis (that is sharper and more useful than grey mush) on a controversial subject without being partial.'[35] But analysts have to have some general identification with the policies being pursued; they are not there to criticize by implication: 'Analysts are servants of policy, not merely objective observers of events and trends.'[36]

---

[29] Laqueur, *A World of Secrets*, p. 319.
[30] Laqueur, *A World of Secrets*, p. 322.
[31] Hughes, *The Fate of Facts in the World of Men*, p. 60.
[32] Hughes, *The Fate of Facts in the World of Men*, p. 60.
[33] R. Godson (ed.), *Intelligence Requirements for the 1990s* (Lexington, Mass.: Lexington Books, 1989), pp. 5–8. For an excellent case for opportunity analysis see J. Davis, *The Challenge of Opportunity Analysis* (Washington D.C.: Center for the Study of Intelligence (CIA), 1992), pp. 6–17.
[34] R. K. Betts, 'Strategic Intelligence Estimates: Let's Make Them Useful', *Parameters* (US Army War College) vol. 10 no. 4 (December 1980), pp. 25–6.
[35] R. K. Betts, 'US Strategic Intelligence: Politics, Priorities and Direction' in L. Pfaltzgraff Jr, U. Ra'anan and W. Milberg (eds.), *Intelligence Policy and National Security* (London: Macmillan, 1981), p. 263.
[36] P. Seabury, 'Analysis' in Godson, *Intelligence Requirements for the 1990s*, p. 97.

There are many other recommendations. Manning and organization are not excluded. Betts suggests the use of non-specialists to challenge conventional wisdom, especially to ensure that foreign miscalculation is taken into account.[37] Handel urges that the effects of hierarchy should be reduced: 'contact between highest level decision-makers and lower-level experts must be encouraged.'[38] Multiple advocacy and 'devil's advocate' procedures are considered as means of bringing out dissenting views.[39]

But the main conclusions are still that the important shortcomings are the intellectual ones, and that their root causes are the weaknesses of human perception and cognition. Organizational reform is less relevant, and in any case there is not much to be achieved there either. Hence the overall judgment is fairly pessimistic, not only about short-term warning but also about assessment and forecasting in general. Handel writes of 'a certain sense of futility'.[40] According to Jervis, 'The impediments to understanding our world are so great that even without organizational deformities, and politicization of the intelligence process, intelligence will often reach incorrect conclusions.'[41] Too much should not be expected of change: 'The key is to see the problem of reform as one of modest refinements rather than as systematic breakthrough.'[42] In reorganization for warning 'the United States has reached the point of diminishing returns from organizational solutions to intelligence problems'.[43] On longer-term estimates, 'Reorganization can improve intelligence production at the margins, perhaps, but it will not create breakthroughs.'[44] (There is however a dissenting opinion, that despite the limitations of organizational change, it may still be right for a particular organization at a particular time.)[45] Generally speaking, governments should accept the risk of intelligence failure and adjust their policies and precautions accordingly.

So much attention has gone into intelligence's assessment problems that nothing radically new can be added here. But comments can

---

[37] R. K. Betts, 'Warning Dilemmas: Normal Theory vs Exceptional Theory', *Orbis* (Foreign Policy Research Institute) vol. 26 no. 4 (winter 1983).

[38] M. I. Handel, 'Avoiding Surprise in the 1980s' in Godson, *Intelligence Requirements for the 1980s*, p. 104.

[39] Summarized by Handel, 'Intelligence and the Problem of Strategic Surprise', pp. 267–70; and Betts, *Surprise Attack*, pp. 288–90.

[40] Handel, 'Intelligence and the Problem of Strategic Surprise', p. 270.

[41] R. Jervis, 'What's Wrong with the Intelligence Process?', *International Journal of Intelligence and Counterintelligence* vol. 1 no. 1 (spring 1986), p. 28.

[42] Betts, 'Analysis, War and Decision', p. 84.

[43] Betts, *Surprise Attack*, p. 17.

[44] Betts, 'Strategic Intelligence Estimates', p. 26.

[45] See A. Codevilla, 'Comparative Historical Experience of Doctrine and Organization' in Godson, *Intelligence Requirements for the 1980s*, pp. 12–13.

be made on two conclusions of this extended diagnosis: the relative unimportance of collection, and the balance of intellectual and other causes of analytic failure.

Collection and failure

The roots of failure in analysis and not collection has been challenged by one of the writers on warning, in a comparison between Pearl Harbor and the Battle of Midway from which he draws the conclusion that analysis depended in each case on the quality of the evidence; the United States at Midway had decrypted Japanese naval messages which gave a window not available for Pearl Harbor.[46] The controversy it produced cannot be discussed in detail here, except as a reminder of the variations in collection and the extent to which it sets the framework within which analysis operates.[47] Knorr pointed out that the Pearl Harbor surprise would have been impossible in the age of US ocean surveillance satellites.[48] The failure to detect planning for the Falklands invasion was due partly to the lack of collection; Argentina was a low priority target. The all-weather real-time satellite imagery that appeared from the late 1980s onwards would have made a significant difference to the assessments produced on Soviet military activities before the invasions of Czechoslovakia and Afghanistan: the imagery coverage of the time had to contend with cloud cover; and was in any case delayed by the means used for recovering films. Even so there are different sources' strengths and weaknesses. The sources of observational intelligence never quite explain whether military forces are being deployed for training, political sabre-rattling or a real attack. Access to the right kind of message-like sources from military documents or decrypted messages has this potential, but is rarely available.

Thus it is worth stating the obvious: that the extent and type of collection have some bearing on success and failure. The US government's action in the Cuban crisis of October 1962 sprang from the U-2's detection of the Soviet missile sites under construction there, combined with the photographic interpreters' ability to identify the kinds of missiles being deployed by comparison with earlier imagery of such sites within the Soviet homeland. Similarly the Western Allies' intelligence superiority in the Second World War was grounded in their superior

[46] Levite, *Intelligence and Strategic Surprises*, p. 177.

[47] Betts, 'Surprise, Scholasticism, and Strategy', and Levite, '*Intelligence and Strategic Surprises* Revisited', *International Studies Quarterly* vol. 33 no. 3 (September 1989).

[48] K. Knorr, 'Avoiding Surprise in the 1980s' in Godson, *Intelligence Requirements for the 1980s*, p. 116.

single-source cipher-breaking; the intelligence staffs' insight into German military decision-taking followed the accumulation of rich evidence and did not precede it. Most of the twentieth-century intelligence failures against surprise attack came when the victims did not read the attackers' military ciphers. (Though this is not a universal rule; the German Ardennes offensive in 1944 still took the Allies by surprise, through good German security over the use of radio, mixed with Allied over-confidence.)

None of the writers quoted in this chapter have maintained that collection has not had these effects; the question is one of emphasis. There is also the less obvious aspect of modern 'collection' to be considered: the role of the collection agencies in analysing their own material. Warning failures have included failures to take sufficient note of collectors' interpretations, as well as collectors' own reluctance to speak loudly enough in situations in which assessment responsibility rests (rightly) with the all-source agencies. The chances of successful warning are influenced by collectors' own analysis and its weight within the assessment process, as well as by the fortunes of collection itself. In all, the quality of the collection effort might appear to be rather more important as a cause of intelligence failure than appears from the accumulated writing on the subject.

Components of analytic failure

Nevertheless the general conclusion about the importance of analytical failure cannot be contested. The question is how it is best described. Its discussion in terms of innate intellectual shortcomings is impressive, but something in it is reminiscent of D. H. Fischer's anatomy of historians' fallacies: fallacies of generalization, narration, causation, motivation, composition, false analogy, semantic distortion, substantive distraction, and so on.[49] This is magnificent typology; but does it explain *why* historians fall into these traps? Does the analysis of cognitive shortcomings *explain* intelligence failure, or classify it?

There is also the puzzle that these intellectual limitations should apply as much to those responsible for defensive information security as to offensive intelligence; indeed one of the biggest examples of cognitive rigidity in the Second World War was the German *security* authorities' persistent belief that the Enigma cipher could not be broken cryptanalytically. If cognitive shortcomings are inevitable in both offence and

---

[49] D. H. Fischer, *Historians' Fallacies: Towards a Logic of Historical Thought* (London: Routledge and Kegan Paul, 1971).

defence, how do they account for offensive intelligence's persistent failure over warning?

Here practitioners' own recollections about warning failures may perhaps carry some weight. Failure almost always has some organizational and procedural causes. Apart from warning's intellectual difficulties, the machinery is under pressure; 'the clock is always ticking', as Betts put it.[50] At best, distributing and evaluating new evidence takes time, as does drafting and disseminating disturbing conclusions and persuading users about them, all amid other intelligence commitments and distractions. Using interdepartmental machinery like the JIC builds in further delays, even if it works perfectly.

Apart from these built-in delays and pressures, failure reveals defects in machinery or procedures. In the Pearl Harbor disaster, warning machinery hardly existed at all; irrespective of cognitive factors, the basic reason for intelligence failure then was that there was no way of bringing disparate items of intelligence together. Even where there is proper provision for assessment, failing to arrange interdepartmental consultation early or regularly enough has been a feature of some British warning failures (though not all). Syndromes noted in the warning literature (fear of the 'cry wolf' effect of too many warnings; looking at situations in day-by-day increments and losing sight of trends; delays through waiting for positive explanations rather than reporting uncertainty) have been significant elements there and elsewhere. Even more important has been 'alert fatigue', when threats of aggression do not materialize until the warning machinery has gone off the boil about them; this has particular weight in the long-running threats of the Czechoslovakian invasion in 1968 and the Yom Kippur attack in 1973. Other warning failures have owed something to more detailed breakdowns; omissions over the distribution to the Cabinet Office of British diplomatic reports of hardening Argentine attitudes in early 1982 were said in an official investigation to have been a factor in the failure to assess the increased threat to the Falklands.

Similar points can be made about some medium-term failure. British failures to recognize German rearmament in the early years of Hitler owed something to failures in the distribution of relevant studies by the small Industrial Intelligence Centre.[51] Before the fall of the Shah the US community failed to produce anything to meet the policy-makers'

---

[50] Betts, *Surprise Attack*, p. 89.
[51] See W. Wark, 'Intelligence Predictions and Strategic Surprise: Reflections on the British Experience in the 1930s' in K. G. Robertson (ed.), *British and American Approaches to Intelligence* (London: Macmillan, 1987), pp. 91–100.

specific request for a National Intelligence Estimate on his internal prospects; a straight failure of the system's operation.[52] By contrast, UK–US warning performance over the threats to Poland in 1980–1 was better than over Soviet preparations for the invasion of Afghanistan in late 1979; in the UK this was partly because the 1979 events had caused the warning assessment machinery to be thoroughly run in.

In short, warning failure includes the effects of intelligence's equivalents of Clausewitz's 'friction', or what stops organizations from getting their acts together. Added to them are the accidents of personalities and inexperience which are never recorded in official investigations; as a US warning analyst of thirty years' experience wrote, 'All official intelligence history is inadequate, particularly that relating to analysis.'[53] From this viewpoint warning performance is related less to individual perspicacity than to collective dynamics: how the group of those involved fitted together, and with what slant from previous experience and professional attitudes. Additionally a special feature of the British system – though not the US one, except perhaps just before the Gulf War – has been to attach considerable weight to the views of ambassadors in the threatening or threatened countries; these tend to argue against the likelihood of military action, and their judgments carry special weight in a system with strong FCO representation.

These features imply a 'system-based' view of warning failure, though failure's links with organization remain to be explored in detail.[54] Experience of failure tends to focus less on innate propensities to misperception, and more on specific fallibilities in organization and direction, particularly of multi-organization operations. Of course these are really two different, complementary levels of explanation, reminiscent of A. J. P. Taylor's distinction between the general and particular causes of war.[55] Innate human frailties obviously exist; but the

[52] House of Representatives, Select Committee on Intelligence, *Staff Report. Iran: Evaluation of US Intelligence Performance Prior to November 1978* (Washington D.C.: US GPO 38-745, 1979), p. 5.
[53] C. M. Grabo, 'The Watch Committee and the National Indications Center: the Evolution of U.S. Strategic Warning 1950–75', *International Journal of Intelligence and Counterintelligence* vol. 3 no. 3 (fall 1989), p. 364.
[54] But see G. P. Halstedt, 'Organizational Foundations of Intelligence Failures' in Maurer, Tunstall and Keagle, *Intelligence: Policy and Process*.
[55] 'Wars are much like road accidents. They have a general cause and a particular one. Every road accident is caused, in the last resort, by the invention of the internal combustion engine . . . [But the police and the courts] seek a specific cause for each accident – error on the part of the driver; excessive speed; [etc.] . . . "International anarchy" makes war possible; it does not make war certain.' (A. J. P. Taylor, *The Origins of the Second World War* (London: Penguin, 1964), pp. 135–6, quoted in A. Danchev, 'The Anschluss', *Review of International Studies* vol. 20 no. 1 (January 1994).)

warning system should be devised and managed to try to insure against them, and failures occur when it has not succeeded in doing so. Implications for warning (extending into longer-term assessment) can now be considered.

Implications

Organization

The need to bring all sources of information together applies in warning just as in other all-source assessment. Effective warning therefore needs a collective effort; something like the British JIC system is needed if all relevant information is to be made available, and different (and sometimes contradictory) sources are to be properly evaluated. The strengths and weaknesses of 'collegial' assessment of this kind are discussed further in chapter 15.

But within this wider interdepartmental machinery there is also a history of special arrangements to identify warning information. For twenty-five years from 1950 the United States had its Watch Committee and National Indications Center, and this was followed in the 1970s by the National Intelligence Officer (NIO) for Warning established as part of the NIO system.[56] In the 1990s under the NIO 'each principal agency of the national Foreign Intelligence Board now has a unit that acts as its focal point for warning'.[57] After the Falklands experience Britain vested a special 'warning' responsibility in a senior member of the Assessments Staff. The Cold War also produced specialized, mainly military, warning systems geared to 'indicators', beginning as early as 1948.[58]

The merits of these various arrangements vary; clearly they have not prevented warning failures. There is some advantage in having someone with a special responsibility for guiding collection to potential warning targets, and for looking for warning evidence. But indicator systems have pitfalls, partly because they are guesses about expected rather than unexpected contingencies and partly because they take indicators out of their context. Warning is not a separable activity from other intelligence understanding.

The main organizational conclusions are that warning cannot be separated from normal current analysis; and that this in turn cannot

[56] Grabo, 'The Watch Committee and the National Indications Center'.
[57] M. McCarthy, 'The National Warning System: Striving for an Elusive Goal', *Defense Intelligence Journal* vol. 3 no. 1 (spring 1994), p. 8.
[58] Grabo, 'The Watch Committee and the National Indications Center', p. 365.

be insulated from medium- and long-term work. Warning involves bringing accurate long-term understandings to bear on current situations; its failures tend to reflect long-term misperception.[59] In the 1968 invasion of Czechoslovakia Western intelligence tracked the assembly of Warsaw Pact forces, but failed to realize how deeply the Soviet leadership felt threatened by the Prague Spring. (Now, having seen the entire system's collapse, we can understand the decision rather better.) Before the Falklands invasion Britain held it as axiomatic that any move by the Argentine Junta towards direct action would be graduated and incremental. Even though Japanese surprise at Pearl Harbor was successful largely through the absence of proper US machinery, an additional factor was the US failure to appreciate the importance in Japanese thinking of the surprise naval attack initiating the Russo-Japanese war in 1904. Current analysis should draw on long-term assumptions; conversely these need to be tested against current intelligence and updated. Thus the US assumptions in December 1941 that Japanese torpedoes could not be used in the Pearl Harbor anchorage had not kept up with recent developments; the same was true of the assumption that Japanese aircraft did not have the range to bomb airfields in the Philippines.

Thus warning and longer-term assessment are all of a piece. Short- and long-term assessment should be arranged not as separate activities but with overlaps and interchanges between them. Seeking to understand targets has to be combined with keeping an eye open for unlikely threats and atypical behaviour. This is now said to be reflected in US changes made after the Gulf War with the result that 'in a fundamental departure from past practice, the warning system no longer exists in isolation from, or parallel to, the remainder of the analytic and collection community'.[60] If this is the case it is a wise move.

People

Warning and longer-term assessment need the same qualities of analytic judgment. These have been discussed in the literature summarized in this chapter, though there is no recipe for discerning them in selecting individuals. But the emphasis here is on assessment as a group activity, and something can be said about the size and composition of its groups.

Increasing staff numbers is no insurance against intelligence failure;

[59] M. E. Herman, 'Warning: Some Practical Perspectives' in Merritt, Read and Weissinger-Baylon, *Crisis Decision-taking in the Atlantic Alliance*, p. 7-2.

[60] McCarthy, 'The National Warning System: Striving for an Elusive Goal', p. 8.

there is a positive value in keeping the numbers of assessors small. The British Joint Intelligence Staff in the Second World War and its successor the Assessments Staff have demonstrated the value of small groups without much hierarchy. But small size and flat structures put a special premium on talent and experience, and compared with the bigger US system the British one runs its risks over warning through leave, illness, gaps in previous experience, learning curves and so on. In connection with the Falklands episode, the present writer has argued that

The Cabinet Office system [of the British Assessments Staff] has the priceless assets of small size and informality . . . On the other hand these strengths are also risks. The machinery is worked hard in keeping up with world events, and there is little double-banking to cover for weaknesses or learning periods. Since so much depends on those at the centre, variations in individuals' backgrounds and aptitudes have disproportionate effects. Its small size focuses the system on 'useful' and 'relevant' output, rather than more speculative items or apparently academic contingencies . . . Few people stay in the central staff long enough to build up first-hand warning experience, and there is little institutional memory of past failures or knowledge of the academic literature about them.[61]

Questions of optimum size are therefore linked with those about assessors' background and experience. In the United States assessment is an activity mainly for intelligence professionals, predominantly in CIA. The British system on the other hand staffs its central Assessments Staff largely with people on secondment from non-intelligence work. Among them are seconded diplomats, whose profession trains them to analyse events in foreign countries, forecast outcomes and express conclusions pithily. In these respects they are ready-trained intelligence officers. But their experience does not usually include much contact with foreign military matters, or much handling of the covert intelligence that bears on them. From this comes the British tendency in warning failures to undervalue military and overrate political evidence.

Both nations' arrangements have their advantages. Warning assessment needs a professional core of all-source analysts who have done forecasting for some time, are experts on their areas and have learned from previous warning experiences, either by experiencing them at first hand or by imbibing corporate doctrine about them. Turnover in the British system is such that it is rare to have people with this experience or knowledge.

On the other hand Britain gains something on most subjects from

---

[61] M. E. Herman, 'Intelligence Warning and the Occupation of the Falklands' in A. Danchev (ed.), *International Perspectives on the Falklands Conflict* (London: Macmillan, 1992), p. 159.

drawing its assessors from varied backgrounds, sometimes including a professional background in collection and single-source analysis. The US professional assessors might be expected to be more reliable, with fewer problems of inexperience and learning curves, but they do not have a better record of warning successes in practice. Perhaps the conclusion to be drawn is that some professional assessors are needed, but with some leavening of other experience; the key is the right balance. Seconded diplomats can make an important contribution but should not dominate the system completely. In various ways the British and US systems can learn something from each other.

Supervision

Warning is part of assessment as a whole. Assessment in its normal business is always under pressure of events. In this sense intelligence is permanently at war, extended to produce its current, day-by-day and week-by-week product and its special assessments for particular reasons. There is no time for exercises like those that occupy military forces in peacetime. Yet its skill in detecting surprise military attacks is tested only at long intervals. There are immediate post-mortems after warning failures, but the lessons are forgotten after a time. For those engaged in assessment it seems more important to cope with immediate require-ments than to worry about the warnings of surprise attack they may never have to give. Unconsciously these get put into the 'not on my watch' category, to use the American description. Yet the challenges catch up with the system and find out its weak spots.

Hence someone needs an overall responsibility for the community machinery and seeking to make it better. It was in this light that, while NATO's warning in the Cold War was still a live issue, the present author wrote about its oversight that:

Because the intelligence machinery is permanently in operation, it does not lend itself as easily as other parts of the Alliance's military apparatus to training, exercises, and formal evaluation. Those in positions of responsibility tend to be more occupied with the substance of intelligence assessment than with increasing the effectiveness of the process. After major disasters, ritual organis-ational changes are made, but old habits tend to resurface with a fresh cast. Yet it is perhaps in pointing to the managerial factors that practical experience can make a distinctive contribution . . . The practitioner will remember the details that academic and official history rarely record: the faulty distribution of a particular line of papers; the inexperience of a particular desk officer who had been left to sink or swim; the effects down the line of a particular chemistry of senior prejudices; and so on. The detailed working of the warning machinery is surprisingly important, and getting it right puts a particular onus on local management. An effective warning system needs some people in its supervisory chain with the qualities of good Regimental officers, ever alert to dirty rifle-barrels or to slackness in the recesses of the cookhouse.[62]

Warning depends partly on direction and management. Someone needs to worry about improving the system's ability to give warnings which he may not be around long enough to hear. The question arises: who is responsible for intelligence's efficiency as an interdepartmental system? It arises out of warning failure; but extends to intelligence's performance as a whole. We return to it in chapter 17 below.

Summary

Intelligence can never understand foreign states completely and forecast all their actions. But there is a puzzling record of consistent failure to provide warning of surprise attack. Limitations of intelligence collection are partial explanations in some cases, as is insufficient weight given to collectors' interpretations of their material. But some evidence has usually been available pointing to an increased likelihood of attack or preparations for it. All-source analysis has failed to draw the correct conclusion.

This can be explained at one level as cognitive rigidity: the human tendency to interpret all evidence in the light of preconceptions and to resist alternative explanations. At a different level there are the effects of personal factors and organizations' failures to 'get everything together' under pressure.

Some practical recommendations can be drawn from this record. Short-term and long-term understanding of the targets are inseparable; warning needs to be linked with long-term assessment. The core assessment group should be kept small. It benefits from the continuity and experience provided by professional intelligence assessors, but there is also some advantage in the British mixing of disciplines. Warning tends to find out weaknesses in the intelligence community's arrangements which are effective enough in normal production. The question arises of responsibility for professional oversight of national intelligence and trying to improve its interdepartmental arrangements.

---

[62] Herman, 'Warning: Some Practical Perspectives', p. 7-3. A British example of old habits resurfacing can be seen in the chairmanship of the JIC. After the Falklands war and the recommendation of the Franks Committee, this became a non-departmental, Prime Ministerial appointment, filled so that a senior officer could give it something approaching his full-time attention. It has now reverted to being the part-time responsibility of a busy FCO official, combined with his heavy workload on detachment to the Cabinet Office as head of the Overseas Secretariat.

14   Problems of defence intelligence

The previous chapter discussed warning failure and its relationship with other intelligence assessment, and it cast some light on the intelligence system's problems of making correct judgments. However it did not examine a complicating factor: intelligence's external relationships with its users. The need for close intelligence–user contacts has already been discussed (chapter 6), and their role in the intelligence production process will be examined in chapter 16. But to be of any value intelligence has to be credible to its recipients; its analysts need empathy with their users, as well as their targets. Yet the user relationship may affect objectivity on particular issues, or lead to systematic institutional bias. The problem can be illustrated by considering the special position of defence intelligence and its record in the Cold War.

Defence intelligence merits consideration in its own right. On the whole it provokes relatively little interest. In Britain it tends to be regarded as being concerned mainly with specialized defence decisions. In public controversies about intelligence accountability, no one has worried about the DIS, which constitutionally is simply part of the Ministry of Defence's central staff. In the USA its equivalent organizations have always had fairly low esteem. In his written evidence to the Murphy Commission in 1974 Huizenga questioned

(1) whether serious and objective intelligence work can be done in the present organizational environment of the military estate and therefore (2) whether the military intelligence agencies should have the great, and lately increased, weight they carry in the national intelligence effort. My answer to both questions is 'no'.[1]

Subsequent US writers have continued the same line of criticism, for instance when Stansfield Turner as former DCI listed 'Help the Defense

---

[1] *Commission on the Organization of Government for the Conduct of Foreign Policy* (the Murphy Commission), *Report of the Commission* (volume 7) (Washington D.C.: US GPO, June 1975), appendix U, p. 41.

Intelligence Agency improve its analysis' as part of his agenda for improving the US community in the mid-1980s.[2] In 1993 a member of the US Department of Defense wrote that 'The most memorable thing about defense intelligence in the last dozen years is the lobbying inside and outside defense intelligence for its reorganization. Indeed four reorganizations have taken place and a fifth is under way . . . for all the lobbying, there does not seem to be much satisfaction with the organization of defense intelligence, within and without the organization.'[3] On the whole however the literature on intelligence and policy concentrates on the position of civilian assessors, like those in CIA, rather than the military ones. Defence intelligence tends to appear as something slightly apart from the mainstream of top level advice.

Yet foreign military power remains by far intelligence's biggest target. Russia is still a big nuclear and conventional military power. Related international targets including nuclear proliferation, international arms trade and widespread local conflicts add to defence intelligence's importance. In a variety of peacetime subjects defence intelligence is still the major ingredient, and has a more central position than it is often credited with. Its potential effects can be illustrated by its Cold War record on assessing Soviet military capabilities.

Defence intelligence and the Cold War

Assessments of Soviet and Warsaw Pact military capabilities – in particular, forecasts of *future* capabilities – dominated Western defence decisions, but were of wider importance. The USSR's 'massive preponderance' – in the term made public in 1955 in the annual British Defence White Paper[4] – was taken by NATO nations as an indication of its political objectives; 'appreciating the size of the Soviet Union's armed forces is not enough. We must also think critically about why the Soviets continue to devote such a large proportion of their national resources . . . to supporting this military buildup.'[5]

Successive British Defence White Papers illustrate this use of Soviet capabilities to gauge intentions. In the late 1960s and early 1970s they consistently claimed that the size of Soviet naval programmes indicated

---

[2] S. Turner, *Secrecy and Democracy* (London: Harper and Row, 1985), p. 276.
[3] W. Jajko, *The Future of Defense Intelligence* (Washington D.C.: Consortium for the Study of Intelligence, 1993), pp. 10–11.
[4] *Statement on Defence 1955* (London: HMSO, Cmnd 9391, February 1955), paragraph 22.
[5] Preface to *Soviet Military Power 1987*, issued by the US Department of Defense (Washington D.C., 1987), p. 5.

objectives of world-wide power projection.[6] Later they argued that the growing firepower and mobility of Soviet conventional forces in Central Europe demonstrated threatening intentions; these forces were 'far larger than could be necessary for defensive purposes', being 'composed, equipped and deployed in a manner which would enable them to undertake offensive operations at relatively short notice', and strengthened 'in size and quality on a scale which goes well beyond the need of any purely defensive posture'.[7] The USSR's 'enormous, and constantly expanding, military might' raised 'legitimate questions about how the Soviet Union might behave if it were not deterred by Western capability and will to resist any aggression'.[8] Similar political inferences were also drawn from the technical evidence of military exercises; the claim that Warsaw Pact exercise scenarios always started with an attack upon the West was made as further evidence of hostile intent.[9] As late as 1988 emphasis was laid on Soviet military doctrine: 'the effect of the doctrine has been to create in Eastern Europe a force that remains structured, equipped and trained for offence and surprise. The Warsaw Pact thus has a *capability* that could be used for aggressive purposes if Soviet *intentions* should change, without the necessity for any action to be taken that might signal such a change.'[10] In forecasting future Soviet military procurement it was predicted in 1986 and 1987 (though not by 1988) that 'the higher annual rate of increase in defence spending seen in recent years will be sustained at least until the end of the decade' and that 'the high priority traditionally given to defence seems unlikely to be eroded'.[11] These quotations are taken from public justifications of British defence spending; nevertheless they reflect the trend of UK–US governmental thinking and the role which military evidence played in it.

It is still too early to pronounce definitely upon these views. In many ways Western intelligence was a success. On observable, actual aspects of Soviet military capabilities it moved from great uncertainty in the 1940s and 1950s to a reasonably good picture from the 1960s onwards, much

---

[6] For example, Cmnd 4592, *Statement on the Defence Estimates 1971* (London: HMSO, 1971), paragraph 5: 'Backed by its [forces] . . . the Soviet Union is engaged in enhancing its power and influence across the world. Success in this policy will be at the expense of Western political interests; it could also put at risk important economic interests.'

[7] Cmnd 5976, *Statement on the Defence Estimates 1975* (London: HMSO, March 1975), paragraph 20; Cmnd 7099, *Statement on the Defence Estimates 1978* (London: HMSO, 1978), paragraph 121.

[8] Cm 101-I, *Statement on the Defence Estimates 1987* (London: HMSO, 1987), pp. 1, 7.

[9] This claim was made publicly by Zbigniew Brzezinski, *The Times*, 17 September 1987.

[10] Cm 344-I, *Statement on the Defence Estimates 1988* (London: HMSO, 1988), pp. 6–7.

[11] Cmnd 9763-I, *Statement on the Defence Estimates 1986* (London: HMSO, 1986), paragraph 108; and *Statement on the Defence Estimates 1987*, p. 69.

of it derived from satellite reconnaissance. The official Soviet baseline figures handed over for the SALT, START and CFE arms control agreements of the 1970s and 1980s contained few surprises. The transparency provided by Western intelligence gave reassurance during periods of tension, and played a significant part in arms control and the eventual winding down of the conflict. Considering Soviet secrecy, these were no small achievements.

On the other hand the assessment of current Soviet capabilities now seems to have contained some important early errors of fact, and the forecasts of Soviet plans to have had a fairly consistent bias. The most important factual error was the assessment made in the late 1940s, and not revised until the early 1960s, that the post-war Soviet army fielded about 175 *full-strength* divisions. It now seems that a picture of roughly one-third full strength, one-third partial strength, and one-third purely cadre formations would have been more accurate.[12] This early view of overwhelming military strength was accompanied by high forecasts of what Soviet defence production *could* attain by the mid-1950s, so that this became identified as the time of danger when the USSR would have fully equipped conventional forces, a repaired economy, and nuclear and missile capabilities.[13] In the absence of contrary evidence, these forecasts achieved credence as assessments of Soviet intentions. There can be little doubt that the overestimates of current Soviet strength and the forecasts of the maximum that the USSR could achieve later were a combination that played a major part in the scale of Western rearmament, the adoption of a nuclear doctrine to offset conventional Soviet superiority and the whole process of East–West action and reaction in developing military forces.

This error of the second half of the 1940s was followed ten years later by the US overestimate of Soviet strategic missile strength and production rates at the time of the so-called 'missile gap', followed by the

---

[12] M. A. Evangelista, 'Stalin's Postwar Army Reappraised', *International Security* vol. 7 no. 3 (winter 1982–3), p. 112, quoting an opinion of Paul Nitze. It has recently been argued that reasons for reducing the 175-Division threat were recognized in intelligence circles quite early in the 1950s, but not incorporated in governmental pronouncements. (J. S. Duffield, 'Soviet Military Threat to Western Europe', *Journal of Strategic Studies* vol. 15 no. 2 (June 1991).) On the other hand Garthoff is clear that the distinction between cadre strength, low strength and combat-ready divisions was not incorporated into US intelligence estimates until the early 1960s; incidentally Penkovsky gave the West a figure of fifty active divisions in 1961 (R. L. Garthoff, 'Estimating Soviet Military Force Levels', *International Security* vol. 14 no. 4 (spring 1990)).

[13] See 1948 British Joint Intelligence Committee paper, JIC(48)9(0) Final, 23 July 1948 (India Office Library and Records, L/WS/1/1173). For commentary upon it see P. Hennessy, *Never Again: Britain 1945–1951* (London: Vintage edition, 1993), pp. 245–72.

accelerated US ICBM programme of the following decade, the Soviet response of striving for approximate parity, and the subsequent US fears in the 1970s of being threatened by a Soviet strategic nuclear 'window of opportunity'.[14] There were underestimates as well as overestimates: thus

Intelligence underestimated the pace of the Russian ICBM buildup in the late sixties and that of Soviet SLBM construction in the 1970s. There were evidently underestimates of Soviet achievements in missile accuracy in the late seventies and it has been admitted that there was a substantial underestimate of the size of the Soviet defense budget. On the other hand there have been overestimates such as those of Soviet bomber forces and initial deployment of ICBMs in the 1950s . . . the bomber gap dispute raged for three years, the 'missile gap' overestimates for five. Intelligence underestimated the pace of Russian missile emplacement only between 1967 and 1972. During that same period there were other over-estimates: of Soviet MIRV capability; of the appearance of a mobile ICBM; of the ballistic missile defense capability of the Tallinn SAM; of the appearance of a new Soviet penetrating bomber; and of the amount of defense goods purchased by the 'defense ruble'.[15]

But on balance the strategic nuclear overestimates outweighed the underestimates. The thirty years' spiral of US–Soviet competition was sparked off by the initial US overestimates of the late 1950s.

Other defence intelligence appraisals will probably turn out to have tended towards overestimates. Western intelligence failed to detect the decline in the rate of growth of Soviet military expenditure in the second half of the 1970s; the US and NATO military build-ups during the first Reagan Presidency may well have been out of synchronization with the Soviet trend. Western defence policy over the Soviet chemical warfare (CW) threat in the late 1970s and early 1980s included crucial judgments that Soviet strategy for conventional war included the use of extensive CW stocks; its apparent omission from Soviet exercise play in the later Cold War years was never satisfactorily explained,[16] and British

---

[14] J. Prados, *The Soviet Estimate: US Intelligence Analysis and Soviet Strategic Forces* (Princeton: Princeton University Press, 1986 edition); L. Freedman, *US Intelligence and the Soviet Strategic Threat* (London: Macmillan, 1986 edition).

[15] Prados, *The Soviet Estimate*, pp. 294–5. The 'Tallinn SAM' was new SAM construction near Tallinn in Estonia, first noted in 1963 and thought for some time to be the nucleus of an ABM system.

[16] For a summary of published Western assessments of Soviet CW capabilities, see J. P. Robinson, *NATO Chemical Weapons Policy and Posture* (Armament and Disarmament Information Unit, Science Policy Research Unit, University of Sussex, 1986), pp. 17–24. For the difficulties of assessing Soviet intentions over the use of CW in conventional warfare, see J. Hemsley, *The Soviet Biochemical Threat to NATO: the Neglected Issue* (London: Macmillan, 1987), chapter 3.

estimates that stocks amounted to 300,000 tons were later heavily scaled down.[17] Massive British nuclear expenditure, first for the addition of Chevaline penetration aids to the Polaris missile and later for its replacement by Trident, drew upon intelligence assessments which affirmed the 'Moscow criterion', by which effective deterrence was held to require the ability to strike Moscow and the accuracy to destroy elements of state power in and around it, in the face of present and future anti-missile defences there.[18] In some views intelligence thereby legitimized a gold-plated British approach to deterrence.[19]

Similarly at the politico-strategic level intelligence overestimated the reliability of the Eastern European forces in Soviet eyes.[20] It was slow to accept that the rationale for Soviet naval development was initially the defence of the homeland against Western invasion and naval air attack, and later the defence of the Northern deployment areas of the ballistic missile submarines.[21] It ignored the hypothesis that the offensive Soviet military doctrine in Central Europe was contingency planning against the possibility of a conventional war, which the USSR was bound to lose to the USA's superior industrial resources unless it could expel it from Europe.[22] The size of the Soviet army obscured the way its basic function for the Soviet leadership was essentially as a training machine, for providing a huge reserve of manpower for mobilization in the event of war; what appeared to be the massive scale of Soviet equipment obscured a design philosophy based on periodic factory refurbishment rather than

---

[17] The figure subsequently accepted for the Chemical Weapons Convention was 40,000 tons (M. Dando, 'Chemical and Biological Warfare Review: Problems and Prospects in Building an Integrated Arms Control Regime', *Brassey's Defence Yearbook 1995* (London: Brassey's, 1995), p. 225).

[18] House of Commons Defence Committee 1980–1, Fourth Report, *Strategic Nuclear Weapons Policy* (London: HMSO, 1981), paragraph 8.

[19] For a recent military criticism of the scale of nuclear provision see letter from Field Marshal Sir Nigel Bagnall, *The Times*, 3 August 1994, referring *inter alia* to 'exacting and extravagantly wasteful survival and damage criteria'. David Owen claims in his autobiography that as Foreign Secretary he put the case for a 'cut-price deterrent' in 1978 (D. Owen, *Time to Declare* (London: Penguin edition, 1992), p. 381). For the same point see also D. Healey, *The Time of My Life* (London: Michael Joseph, 1989), p. 455.

[20] For a selection of views on the conventional balance in Europe, see articles by J. M. Epstein, K. R. Holmes, J. J. Mearsheimer and B. R. Posen, *International Security* vol. 12 no. 4 (spring 1988).

[21] For an account of the controversy see J. S. Breemer, 'The Soviet Navy's SSBN Bastions: Evidence, Inference and Alternative Scenarios', *RUSI Journal* vol. 130 no. 1 (March 1985); for subsequent developments, see the same author's update in vol. 132 no. 2 (June 1987).

[22] The thesis was developed in detail in M. K. MccGwire, *Military Objectives in Soviet Foreign Policy* (Washington D.C.: The Brookings Institution, 1987).

in-service maintenance.[23] It is doubtful if the West ever appreciated just how far its own early military preparations and covert action inside the Soviet Bloc were interpreted in this way by the other side, or how the US military posture of the 1970s and early 1980s appeared to take the form of a two-front US–Chinese threat. Both sides' military programmes proceeded with major elements of action and reaction. Both sides failed to see each other through the other's eyes.[24]

These are still uncertain historical judgments. From what is known of the comparable Soviet intelligence inputs to its leadership they presented far more distorted views than those in the West. Nevertheless the conclusion on present evidence is that, despite all its advances in collection, Western intelligence maximized the threats of Soviet military force. This of course was by the intelligence community as a whole, and not just by its defence components. Initially Western attitudes were formed by assumptions about worldwide communist objectives and by the way Soviet behaviour seemed to bear them out; nevertheless it was Soviet military capabilities and potential that appeared to transform this picture of hostility into a massive threat. As the Cold War progressed the Soviet strategic arsenal and conventional military superiority took a growing place in the Western world-view, particularly as world communism and Soviet support for decolonization came to be of less weight. Military targets were intelligence's highest priority and provided much of the hard information available about the USSR. Why then was there this skewing of defence intelligence and the conclusions drawn from it?

Reasons for error

Worst cases and their psychology

There was the sheer technical difficulty of obtaining information on the Soviet target; collection on it encountered formidable obstacles to

[23] I am grateful to C. N. Donnelly for these reflections on Soviet military philosophy. The significance of the training role of Soviet forces was put forward in 1980 by P. Vigor, 'Doubts and Difficulties Confronting a Would-be Soviet Attacker', *RUSI Journal* vol. 125 no. 2 (June 1980); but was not generally appreciated.

[24] The opportunity costs of overestimation in the Cold War are too complex for discussion here. But on the consequences for the British economy of large-scale rearmament in 1950–1 'there are powerful reasons for supposing our best hope for the kind of post-war economic miracle enjoyed by so many western European countries was scattered in fragments in the committee rooms of Whitehall, on the hills above the Imjin in Korea and along the Rhine in Germany as British occupation forces were rearmed in readiness for a Stalinist assault.' (Hennessy, *Never Again*, p. 415.)

producing regular high-quality message-like material from human or technical sources.[25] There was also the Western political capital invested in the Soviet threat, not just nationally but also through NATO; formal NATO 'threat' documents were drawn up annually by national intelligence representatives. But there were also special reasons associated with military matters. One was the effect of the normal military inclination towards 'worst case' planning. Intelligence needs some worst case thinking; indeed in warning it is failing if it does not look particularly for bad news. But the military inclination towards worst cases fed into the intelligence assessments of future Soviet capabilities and gave them a self-fulfilling quality.

This military inclination coincided with the difficulty for anyone in an ideological conflict of seeing the opponent in purely clinical terms. When ideology and threat provide the adrenalin there is always a temptation to dramatize the enemy's strength. After 1945 time and distance from Soviet armed forces increased the risks of this stereotyping; as already noted, few among those studying the Soviet Union were able to visit it.

This power of the 'enemy image' links with some facets of intelligence psychology. For collectors as well as analysts there is an attractive self-image of the intelligence practitioner as the warner, jolting policy-makers out of complacency and making them listen. 'Sounding the tocsin' is a proper role but carries some psychological kudos in peacetime; there is an element of macho satisfaction in an intelligence line of tough realism, free of delusions.[26] By contrast the business of cutting threats down to size has more ambivalent professional and psychological overtones.

These features apply particularly to military threats. Something of the emotional shock of war, the *effort du sang*, spills over into the assessment of potentially hostile forces; underestimation is less readily forgiven than overestimation, and the analyst in any case has his own inherited compulsions not to let the fighting men down. English-speaking agencies were deeply influenced in the Cold War by national folk-memories of the payment in blood for underestimation in the 1930s and unpreparedness before Pearl Harbor. On the whole it is more satisfying, safer professionally and easier to live with oneself and one's colleagues as a military hawk than as a wimp. In the Cold War intelligence seemed more useful when demonstrating new Soviet military capabilities and causing something to be done about them, than from studying Soviet limitations. Many of these influences applied generally; CIA was involved in defence

---

[25] For the distinction between 'observational' and 'message-like' intelligence see chapter 5.
[26] For discussion of dramatized assessment, see S. F. Wells, 'Sounding the Tocsin: NSC 68 and the Soviet Threat', *International Security* vol. 4 no. 2 (fall 1979).

estimation as heavily as DIA and the other American service agencies. But defence intelligence as the expert assessor of military power carried considerable weight and set the terms of debate.

Vested interests and staffing

In the defence intelligence agencies these inclinations were linked with the interest group pressures from the armed services and defence industry. The consequences of underestimating enemies fall directly upon the services in war, as casualties and defeat; while their peacetime conditions and equipment depend on the threat estimates around which they are designed. All departments of state have ingrained institutional attitudes. But the Foreign Office's size and emoluments do not depend on the size of foreign threats, and neither do those of others like the Treasury or Department of Trade; whereas those of the armed services emphatically do. Threat assessments have always been one of the military cards in bargaining with Treasuries. In the Cold War, defence intelligence was leaned on with unusual weight by its clients. The US Air Force's pressure towards higher estimates of Soviet missile strengths was only one example of vested interests.

These effects were all the greater since the armed forces are not just users of intelligence, but are locked into the business of producing it. Defence intelligence is an integral part of the military apparatus; and although the British and American situations differ in details there are important similarities. While much other Western intelligence is based on semi-autonomous civilian agencies, defence intelligence has consistently had members of the armed forces at its head and in the key posts. Filling these service-manned posts introduces its own problems of continuity and quality. Military intelligence is not as important to the services as the 'teeth arm' manifestations of military power; intelligence postings are unattractive to high-fliers. In Britain there are relatively few uniformed intelligence specialists, and the service officers in defence intelligence are mainly on one-off tours of duty. In the United States the size of the armed forces facilitates more intelligence specialization; but even so there is the clash between the continuity needed for high-quality top level assessment and the turnover of service life.

Hence defence assessment in the Cold War had the problems of a minority trade in getting its share of the best military brains; and keeping them on repeated tours was even harder. The rapid succession of serving officers had to learn their jobs while simultaneously coping with the intensive routine of high-level assessment and top level briefings. It was hardly surprising that those plunged into this world found it difficult to develop independence of mind in assessment.[27] For those with their careers to make there was no incentive to depart from the orthodoxy that served their 'parent' services' interests.

The civilians employed within central defence intelligence might have brought greater objectivity to assessment; but they had a basic problem of civilian credibility. Service experience is needed for credibility over military power. A former British Chief of the Defence Staff spoke from the heart about the dangers of civilians who 'have never been to the grass-roots . . . They have no idea what a Tornado really can do – or an SSBN, what its operation is. They have probably never been to Faslane. They have never visited Coltishall. They have perhaps been in the same Ministry for twenty years . . . some of them do not know the sharp end.'[28] Those comments were directed at policy-makers, not intelligence, but they illustrate the cultural divide.

Hence the civilian influence was diluted. The civilians tended to be classed as specialists, on tap rather than on top, with effects on their own recruitment and morale. Another result in Britain was that defence intelligence tended to look for its ballast to the recruitment of 'second career' retired service officers, in carefully graduated strata below the active service ones. They looked at subjects in detail and acted as the collective memories, but did not write the policy-directed assessments; their expertise was in the detail rather than the broad view. There was no stereotypical desk officer, but some years ago the present author produced a pen-portrait as follows of the group of people he greatly respected:

Picture a retired service officer aged fifty-five. As a younger man, he had had a good average service career, but a posting into intelligence was a self-confirming indication that he was not destined for the top prizes. But he liked the work, took his pension at forty-five and continued the work as a civilian. He catches a very early train to get to the office to read a large box of incoming signals to brief his office chief by 9.30, and puts in a long day.

He is a conscientious man and is comfortable in a tight hierarchy in which he and his colleagues do the detailed analysis while those higher up the line draw on it for the broad pictures. It annoys him occasionally that the young serving officers now his seniors come and go with great rapidity, seeking to cut a dash without ever knowing enough about the detail. But he comes from a disciplined background in which you don't worry about what you can't change.

---

27 For the unsatisfactory experience of being brought into intelligence at the top, see Vice Admiral Sir Louis le Bailly, *The Man Around the Engine: Life Below the Waterline* (Emsworth: Mason, 1990), chapter 15.
28 House of Commons Defence Committee, Session 1983–4, Third Report, *Ministry of Defence Reorganisation* (London: HMSO, 15 October 1984), Minutes of Evidence; evidence of Marshal of the Royal Air Force Lord Cameron of Balhousie, question 17.

In any case he is a modest man who does not claim to be a deep thinker about Soviet intentions and strategy. He enjoys getting the detailed analysis right and is respected for his expertise. He welcomes the contact with his former service. The pay and conditions of the work are unimpressive, but there is an order and a security that appeal to him. Though he would never parade it, the work satisfies deep feelings of loyalty to his former service and defence of the realm; feelings which took root as a young officer and have never quite left him. He does not slant evidence, but is not given to pulling assumptions up by the roots; service and official life have shown him that pursuing the best is the enemy of the good. If his former service borrows selectively from intelligence in its wars against Treasury cuts he is not a man to object on principle.

Intelligence depends greatly on him and his like, and for what he gives he is a bargain. The nation is conscientiously served. But he fits into a service organization not inclined to challenge military orthodoxy.[29]

In all the circumstances it is not surprising that defence intelligence in the Cold War was largely geared to updating and elaborating the details, and not to demolishing Soviet threats which broadly suited service interests. There were some revisionists of independent spirit – mainly naval – but not many of them; their results showed what might have been achieved elsewhere.[30]

Effects on analysis

In these circumstances one must praise what was achieved. It has been argued that the military personality is incompatible with open-mindedness; the anti-military tract of 'On the Psychology of Military Incompetence' leans heavily on examples from military intelligence.[31] There is indeed some conflict between the military emphasis on decisiveness and teamwork – 'better a bad decision wholeheartedly executed than no decision at all' – and intelligence's need for qualifications, shades of grey, and continuous questioning and revision. But if any generalizations about the military character are relevant then weight has to be given to the military virtues of adaptability and hard work that have served intelligence well. The ethic of officer-like behaviour provides some underpinning for integrity in the job described by a British

---

[29] Unpublished Oxford lecture 1990.

[30] For an example of a more critical attitude within defence intelligence, and the results, see M. E. Herman, 'Cold War Naval Intelligence' in K. Booth (ed.), *International Security: the Cold War and Beyond* (Cambridge: Cambridge University Press, forthcoming).

[31] There are thirty-four references to military intelligence in the index of N. F. Dixon, *On the Psychology of Military Incompetence* (London: Jonathan Cape, 1976).

Director-General of Intelligence (DGI: the head of the Defence Intelligence Staff) as telling 'all those who won't listen all the things they don't want to know'.[32]

Nevertheless the Cold War showed up the combination of pressures and vulnerabilities. On the one hand there were the powerful interests of military users; in Britain the former DGI also testified that 'the pressures on him to trim assessments either for reasons of prejudice ("We know better") or lack of understanding or, more often, plain wishful thinking, are powerful and persistent.'[33] Pressures were reinforced by practitioners' own identification with armed forces and their instinct not to let them down.

On the other hand there were the institutional vulnerabilities. Service officers in intelligence depended for their subsequent careers on reputations with their parent services. (The issue was touched on obliquely in the UK over a decision in 1984 to make the head of the DIS a serving officer post, instead of being held by a recently retired service officer as had been the custom. The House of Commons Defence Committee took the view that 'a serving officer with hopes of advancement will find it less easy to offer independent and forthright advance than an officer who is retired.')[34] Defence intelligence organizations were part of the military structure, with little institutional separation in Britain, though rather more in the United States. They did not have the continuity needed for corporate pride. Inexperience limited their ability to adopt unpopular positions.

Thus defence intelligence helped to perpetuate convenient worst case views about the Soviet military threat.[35] It did not raise its sights often enough to formulate and answer big questions. And counting numbers – essential though this was – commanded more attention than evaluating threats in qualitative terms. The Director of Net Assessment in the Office of the US Secretary of Defense commented in the 1980s that

in the U.S. at least, intelligence tends to focus most on the opponents' strengths – which is all to the good – but much less on his weaknesses. If members of the intelligence community are asked to describe enemy weaknesses, they tend to

---

[32] Vice Admiral Sir Louis le Bailly, letter to *The Times*, 3 August 1984, quoted in the House of Commons Defence Committee's report in note 28 above, p. 36.

[33] See previous note for letter of 3 August 1984.

[34] House of Commons Defence Committee, Session 1983–4, Third Report, *Ministry of Defence Reorganisation*, paragraph 74.

[35] For a former British Minister's recollection of tendentious defence intelligence, exaggerating the East–West imbalance in conventional strength, see Healey, *The Time of My Life*, p. 457.

draw up a very short list to which they often attach limited importance, compared to a much fuller enumeration of his strengths.[36]

The need to strive to see things continuously through the target's viewpoint became somewhat submerged. Speaking about arms control near the end of the Cold War, the UK Permanent Representative at NATO made the comment that

The arms control process is, in my view, going to have a direct effect on the defence side of the house in one slightly unexpected way. It will force the Alliance to think harder and more collectively than ever before about the equipment the other side has; why it has it and how good that equipment really is. It will force us to think through the consequences of the answers for our own forces. The incorporation of the outcomes in 'net' assessments may, in due course, have considerable consequences for our perception of the nature of the East/West imbalance and for military planning.[37]

After forty years in which the Soviet military threat had been the top intelligence priority this was a remarkable official admission.

There is no evidence that any of this has recurred in the very different conditions of the 1990s. Defence intelligence is not automatically wedded to worst cases. Indeed in some of the Cold War warning failures discussed in the previous chapter it subscribed to 'best case' rather than 'worst case' views of targets' intentions; in Britain the over-emphasis on political over military indicators in some of these episodes represented an out-gunning of defence intelligence representatives by those of the FCO.

Nevertheless the experience of the forty years of estimating Soviet military capabilities should not be forgotten. Defence intelligence was of central importance. It was insufficiently critical and too open to armed forces' pressures. Governments did not regard it as sufficiently important to pay it enough. Britain and the United States were both dazzled by wartime experiences and let analysis get out of balance with improvements in collection. In Washington CIA was relied on as a counterpoint to service views, with variable results. Whatever the causes, the results were somewhat weaker Cold War performances than might have been.

It is true that, as Lawrence Freedman has pointed out, 'prudence argues for not putting too much stress on the "threat" to explain and justify policy'.[38] But this does not mean that defence intelligence can be

---

[36] A. Marshall, 'Intelligence and Crisis Management' in J. N. Merritt, R. Read and R. Weissinger-Baylon (eds.), *Crisis Decision-taking in the Atlantic Alliance: Perspectives on Deterrence* (Menlo Park, Ca.: Strategic Decisions Press, 1988).

[37] Sir Michael Alexander, '1988: How Well Will The Alliance Cope?', *RUSI Journal* vol. 133 no. 1 (spring 1988), p. 11.

[38] L. Freedman, 'The Use and Abuse of Threats', *Brassey's Defence Yearbook 1995* (London: Brassey's, 1995), p. 10.

excused objectivity. The current issue of NATO's eastward expansion to include Poland and other former Soviet satellites is increasing tension between Russia and the West. Renegotiation of the CFE Agreement will be a tricky issue. There is wild talk in Russia of creating a CIS military alliance to counter a NATO expansion;[39] and some observers of the US scene fear that a renewed 'worst case' view of Russian intentions may soon emerge. In these circumstances it is again important that intelligence assessments of the Russian military capabilities – currently fragmented, in great disarray – should be objective and not again moved by 'worst case' interests. Against this background, we can consider what could be done about the Cold War lesson.

Remedies

Manning policies

Defence intelligence's key problem in the UK and US – and indeed in most Western countries – has been lack of professionalism. One solution would be increased intelligence professionalism in the armed forces, but at a time of big cuts in military manpower this seems unrealistic. In practice therefore more professionalism equates with more civilianization.

In Britain this might fit the current 'Front Line First' defence policy of economizing on military supporting arms, with its vision of troops in the front line and civilians doing the jobs behind it. The policy assumes commercial contracts as the main means of civilianization, and applying them to intelligence would pose problems over guaranteeing secrecy and expertise. But the general idea of smaller, slimmer defence intelligence, with permanent civilians taking over from ever-changing members of the services, is in tune with the current reforming spirit.

There are various reasons why civilianization is not a complete panacea. First it presupposes civilian quality, and is pointless without paying enough to attract and keep a few people of the highest ability. Defence intelligence in the USA suffers from its image as CIA's poor relation; in Britain the long-standing assumption has been that defence analysis ranks lower than the cutting edges of collection. Second there are the connections mentioned earlier between central defence

---

[39] See, for example, Conflict Studies Research Centre Sandhurst summary and comment *Advab No. 1010* (3 October 1995) on article by A. Lysako, *Komsomol'skaya Pravda* (29 September 1995) on the General Staff's draft new military doctrine, including some reliance on nuclear weapons to deter NATO expansion. (Also *Advab* No. 1017.)

intelligence and the military commands. The head of central defence intelligence needs to be head of the military intelligence community, and there should be some interchangeability between the centre and the uniformed command staffs. Developments in information technology make inter-working among this community all the more important. Third is the argument that service expertise is needed to understand foreign military power. This can be overdone; the Cold War showed the pitfalls of assessing Soviet activities in the light of Western practices. But at bottom it reflects a sound instinct about civilian limitations. Fourth is the accelerating importance in the armed services of understanding how to use intelligence. Some serving officers *en route* for their top service positions need to circulate through central defence intelligence, to learn about it as well as to bring fresh minds to it.

What is needed is still a service–civilian mixture of service 'generalists', service intelligence specialists (where they exist or can be made to exist) and civilian professionals, without a rigidity in which they all have their own fiefdoms. Nevertheless in Britain it would be right to give defence intelligence a greater civilian weight, without complete civilianization; despite recent changes this may also be true in the United States.[40] Britain is already moving in this direction but probably needs to go further. The possibility of formally expanding the DIS role to be a national as well as departmental agency will be considered in the next chapter.

The challenge of community argument

Whatever is done over its staffing, defence intelligence will still be open to pressure from service interests. Hence its findings will still need to be open to intellectual scrutiny of some kind.

This scrutiny exists in plenty in the United States. The duplication of military assessment between the DIA and the service intelligence agencies is indeed a problem needing solution; it was claimed in 1995 that there were some 13,000 military analysts, many of them duplicating others.[41] But at least this ensures competing views. Even more to the point, the analytic work of CIA provides a civilian challenge to all these service positions in the production of NIEs. The US problem throughout the Cold War was not in lack of challenge but in the system's ability

---

[40] For recent changes giving greater authority to DIA, see W. Jajko, *The Future of Defence Intelligence* (Washington D.C.: Consortium for the Study of Intelligence, 1993).

[41] J. H. Hedley, *Checklist for the Future of Intelligence* (Georgetown: Institute for the Study of Diplomacy, 1995), p. 21.

to resolve it; policy-makers had some freedom to pick the interpretations of the Soviet military threat that best suited their preconceptions. But at least the faculties for criticism of military orthodoxy are in place.

This is less the case in the British system, which has never been able to afford duplicating defence analysis as in CIA. JIC assessment originally developed in the Second World War as a forum for resolving inter-service intelligence controversies, but this lost much of its force after the three single-service staffs were merged into the DIS in 1964. The JIC developed a greater interest in political assessment than in what appeared to be purely military matters. With hindsight a surprisingly small proportion of its week-by-week attention in the Cold War was devoted to Soviet military matters and their significance. Except in the rare crises in which military activities had warning implications, they were treated mainly as a DIS speciality; and Soviet capabilities were treated largely as 'givens', meriting periodical updating rather than deep consideration by the complete community. The result was a JIC system that was Rolls-Royce in its foreign political assessments, but less deeply engaged with Soviet military power. This was especially the case on scientific–technical matters on which laymen were reluctant to argue. The same applied to the threat assessments underlying major Western defence procurement programmes.

A Cold War lesson is therefore to ensure that important defence intelligence assessments are subject to the critical community assessment process, and not regarded as the sole province of defence experts. The national assessment system needs to have a well-developed military vision, as well as a political and economic one. For the United States this is one of the arguments for maintaining the system of NIEs and not letting defence intelligence go its own way. For Britain this conclusion points to getting more professional defence intelligence expertise into the JIC process. If this does not happen the system will lack one of the safeguards it exists to provide.

Wider implications for objectivity

Intelligence has to be close to its users. It has to know what they need, and they have to believe what it says. Defence intelligence in the Cold War was in a special position. In Britain it was (and is) part of the MoD Staffs who are its most immediate users. In both Britain and America it was staffed in its influential positions – to varying degrees in the two countries – with temporary intelligence officers rather than uniformed or civilian professionals. Neither country was able to make defence intelligence a recognized centre of excellence.

This chapter has discussed the special factors that put defence intelligence in this position, and suggested lessons that it can absorb. But there is a more general conclusion to be drawn. Whatever criticisms can be made of defence intelligence's part in the Cold War, no one can say it was not close to its users or unaware of their needs. The concepts of 'opportunity analysis' and 'customer service' discussed elsewhere in this book capture features of intelligence efficiency. But the record of defence analysis brings out their pitfalls.

This chapter has indicated the main ways of avoiding them. Three of its safeguards – developing organizations with a corporate identity and professionalism; recognizing and cherishing the importance of high-quality all-source analysis as an intelligence career; and overseeing the intelligence community to ensure that investments in this work are kept in balance with collection – are implicit in the later discussion of management in chapters 16–18. The fourth safeguard mentioned here – that important departmental conclusions of any kind should be exposed to criticism and validation through a community process of some kind – leads to the discussion of national assessment in the next chapter.

Summary

Defence intelligence is the biggest all-source analytical activity, and a particularly important one. Unlike most other intelligence it has not become a professional, civilian activity, but remains closely affiliated to the armed forces which it serves. It is under unusual pressure from its military users, and is more vulnerable to it than it should be. It receives less central government attention than other parts of the intelligence community. One result in Britain and the United States was to produce and legitimize 'worst case' assessments of Soviet military strength in the Cold War and the Soviet political objectives that could be deduced from it.

Hence defence intelligence needs a stronger corporate identity and more professionalism. The practical way to improve it is to give the civilian element a more important role within it, and to provide career prospects that recruit and retain people of high quality; but mixed uniformed–civilian staffing is still essential. There needs to be a better balance in talent and resources between this all-source effort and those of collection.

15   Top level assessment

Intelligence's most important service is to top national policy-makers. The end of the previous chapter touched on the Anglo-Saxon national assessments (or 'estimates' to the Americans) that provide the all-source inputs that bear most closely on policy. The concept they embody of top level intelligence has two related features. One is that its assessment should be objective, free of the preconceptions that skew purely departmental assessment towards its users' interests in the way we have just examined in defence intelligence. The second is that assessment should be presented at this top level as interdepartmentally agreed judgment, so that disagreements within the intelligence community over interpretation and forecasting are disengaged from executive departments' differences over policy, and are resolved prior to intelligence's use in decision-taking. The principle is the same as that once declared for the British Government Statistical Service: 'to make sure that the Cabinet need never argue about statistics'.[1]

The evolution of national assessment to achieve these objectives was outlined in chapter 2, and its place as a distinct part of the intelligence process was described in chapter 3 (see figure 4). Here we need to consider in more detail what machinery is needed to make it work. For this there are British and US models. This chapter suggests conclusions that emerge from their resemblances and differences.

Top level decision-taking and desiderata

Top level decision-taking considered here is at the level of Presidents and Prime Ministers; members of the White House staff, the National Security Council (NSC), the Overseas Policy and Defence Committee of the British Cabinet and other formal and informal groups; and other senior government members, officials and service officers operating

---

[1] As set out by John Boreham: see R. Ward and E. Doggett, *Keeping Score: the First Fifty Years of the Central Statistical Office* (London: HMSO, 1991), p. 82.

collectively. These groups want considered intelligence conclusions and supporting evidence in forms easy for them to use. Producing national assessments of this kind is distinct from the more detailed desk-level analysis and research that precedes it. National assessments entail viewing their subjects broadly. They need the ability to tap government sources across departmental boundaries, to bring all relevant knowledge and opinion to the table through interdepartmental integration or community processes. These arrangements also promote objective analysis, with a discipline of scrutiny and argument to eliminate departmental biases. The product must command interdepartmental agreement to give it credibility and acceptability.

The subjects of assessment of this kind have the intellectual difficulties brought out in chapter 6's description of Kent's 'speculative knowledge' and his 'speculative-evaluative element' of analysis. Kent argued that although evidence is important it avails nothing at this level without good judgment; for accurate assessment the prerequisite is 'not the important but gross substance which can be called recorded fact; it is that subtle form of knowledge which comes from a set of well-stocked and well-ordered brain cells'.[2] Reflecting on assessments (estimates) Cline wrote that

Estimates are careful descriptions of the likelihood that certain things will exist or occur in the future. National Intelligence Estimates are papers setting forth probable situations or occurrences that would make a major difference to our national security or our foreign policy. When the answers are clear to questions about the future, there is no need for an estimate. The easy questions are never asked. An estimate tries to reduce the inevitable degree of uncertainty to a minimum in making calculations about future situations . . . It is not easy to make estimates that are well-calculated in terms of evidence and logic, carefully set forth with great objectivity, and plainly relevant to decision-taking.[3]

But the process is not purely intellectual. It entails orchestrating multiple organizations, including departmental intelligence with its primary allegiance to a single policy department; as in the way defence intelligence is subordinate to Defence Departments, with the departmental pressures just discussed. Departmental subordination of this kind also applies to the US State Department's INR and the similar intelligence units of Treasury, Energy and Commerce, and to their nearest British equivalent, the FCO's Research and Analysis Depart-

---

[2] S. Kent, *Strategic Intelligence for American World Policy* (Hamden, Conn.: Archon Books, 1965 edition), pp. 39–65, quotation from p. 65.

[3] R. S. Cline, *Secrets, Spies and Scholars: Blueprint of the Essential CIA* (Washington D.C.: Acropolis Books, 1976), p. 136.

ment. For national assessment, intelligence agencies and departmental intelligence units need to come together in some supradepartmental way along with other community members. Doing this is the organizational problem.

There is nothing unique about it. Intelligence emerged as part of organized knowledge within government: 'Between Burke and Balfour, the "expert" – a protean image of authority and rational knowledge – became a key factor in the "technique of government" that accompanied the nineteenth-century revolution in government.'[4] In the process there has been continual experiment on how to organize this expertise on something more than a purely departmental basis. A. J. P. Taylor's description of government statistics in the 1930s – 'four separate departments collected industrial statistics; five classified employers of labour; two produced rival and conflicting figures concerning overseas investment' – could well have been applied to the departmental intelligence of the time, in pre-JIC days.[5] Since then British government statistics have slowly evolved from being just parts of departments to organization around the Central Statistical Office and Government Statistical Service, in an evolution not dissimilar from intelligence's.[6]

There are no simple solutions. Most nations are in any case not greatly interested in welding together departmental intelligence outputs, or regard it as too difficult. But for those that practise community assessment there are two models available: on the one hand *interdepartmental* arrangements that enable departments to cooperate collegially, and on the other the existence of *central intelligence* to supplement the departmental system. The former is characteristic of the British JIC; the latter is epitomized in the United States by the position of the DCI and CIA's Intelligence Directorate. But in fact both systems have elements of collegiality and centralism, as emerges from an account of their evolution.

British and US experience up to 1945

We saw in chapter 2 how assessing states in the round evolved out of the need to view enemies and potential enemies in terms of national capabilities and intentions as well as traditional military yardsticks. In Britain the need was met through two routes. One was to establish

---

4 R. MacLeod (ed.), 'Introduction' in *Government and Expertise: Specialists, Administrators and Professionals, 1860–1919* (Cambridge: Cambridge University Press, 1988), p. 1.
5 A. J. P. Taylor, *English History, 1914–1945* (London: Penguin, 1970), p. 409.
6 Details in Ward and Doggett, *Keeping Score.*

non-departments, 'national', central units for analysis that fell outside departmental boundaries. The Security Service emerged between 1921 and 1931 as the non-departmental agency for internal security.[7] The important prototype of non-departmental analysis on foreign subjects was however the small Industrial Intelligence Centre (IIC) established in 1931 to study the German economy on behalf of all government users.[8] The Second World War then produced more non-departmental, inter-service units. Most of them were for dealing with collection sources – Sigint, photographic interpretation, and strategic prisoner-of-war interrogation – or with covert action and political warfare; but some were for all-source data-handling and analysis. Tri-service warfare, especially the amphibious invasions of Europe, could not be planned on a single-service basis and needed similarly integrated intelligence support. The biggest example of this kind was the Inter-Services Topographical Department, responsible *inter alia* for collecting and collating the beach intelligence needed for the Normandy landings.[9]

But non-departmental creations of this kind encountered instinctive departmental resistance, so the main line of British development was the better-known JIC one. This retained departmental organizations but superimposed interdepartmental coordinating machinery upon them. The Committee was formed in 1936 to bring together the three service intelligence departments, but only became effective from 1939 onwards when Foreign Office membership (and chairmanship) led to the integration of political, military and economic assessment.[10] The separate Situation Report Centre, established in 1939 to provide some warning machinery to evaluate the contradictory reports of short-term German intentions, was soon incorporated within it. This gave the JIC the top level responsibility which it bore throughout the war for 'the assessment and coordination of intelligence received from abroad with the object of ensuring that any Government action which might have to be taken should be based on the most suitable and carefully co-ordinated information available'.[11] A crucial addition to it was the creation in 1941 of the Joint Intelligence Staff (JIS) of departmental representatives,

---

[7] F. H. Hinsley and C. A. G. Simkins, *British Intelligence in the Second World War. Vol. IV: Security and Counterintelligence* (London: HMSO, 1990), pp. 3–9.

[8] F. H. Hinsley with E. E. Thomas, C. F. G. Ransom and R. C. Knight, *British Intelligence in the Second World War* vol. I (London: HMSO, 1979), pp. 30–1, 59–73.

[9] Hinsley, *British Intelligence in the Second World War* vol. I, pp. 161, 292; vol. II (1981), pp. 9–12.

[10] For the outline of the JIC's development see Hinsley, *British Intelligence in the Second World War* vol. I chapters 1 and 9; vol. II chapter 15.

[11] Hinsley, *British Intelligence in the Second World War* vol. I, p. 43.

originally just to act as a drafting sub-committee but in the event with a greater effect. All this was joined with the Committee's other responsibility, for the management of the intelligence system as a whole.

The US system before 1941 of separate Army and Navy intelligence plus the FBI was even more departmental than its British counterpart, and after Pearl Harbor it encountered the same need for additional machinery. Some of the wartime British bodies became combined UK–US entities or were duplicated in US versions. In addition, the Research and Analysis (R and A) Division of the US Office of Strategic Services (OSS) developed as a large, all-purpose analysis agency, competing with the services' organizations.[12] Under British influence parts of the interdepartmental JIC model were also adopted, and interlocking committees in Washington and London produced agreed intelligence inputs to the two countries' Combined Chiefs of Staffs Committee.[13]

The Second World War thus demonstrated that purely departmental intelligence was not enough. US army and naval intelligence still found it hard to collaborate, yet Pearl Harbor had burnt the lesson into American memory that some central point was needed. The Cold War needed some continuation of the wartime arrangements for community assessment. Yet in both Britain and the United States there remained an unstated – perhaps hardly understood – conflict between the two wartime models, of separate central organizations on the one hand and collegial interdepartmental machinery on the other.

Post-1945 models

In the post-war reconstruction the British moved some way towards central agencies, notably in establishing GCHQ as the national Sigint collection organization. There were moves in this direction in analysis when economic, topographical and some scientific intelligence were amalgamated in the new Joint Intelligence Bureau (JIB).[14] But the main weight for assessment was placed on continued departmental organizations with community processes added to them. Service intelligence remained single-service; the JIB's role was gap-filling and studying subjects of common interest; the JIC was confirmed as the organ of

---

12 R. Winks, *Cloak and Gown: Scholars in America's Secret War* (London: Collins, 1987), pp. 62–115.
13 Hinsley, *British Intelligence in the Second World War* vol. II, pp. 42–3.
14 Major-General Sir Kenneth Strong, *Intelligence at the Top: the Recollections of an Intelligence Officer* (London: Cassell, 1968), pp. 223–5.

community assessment, though initially with a military slant.[15] Subordinate JICs were established overseas, and the joint intelligence structure developed in Malaya became standard for counter-insurgency campaigns.[16] 'Jointery' – cooperation between the three services and other departments through committees – became the standard British solution in intelligence as in other military matters. Yet to some this seemed a concession to single-service prejudices against the logic of central analysis. R. V. Jones's verdict on the post-war structure established for scientific intelligence was that 'in six hours the experience of six years was jettisoned'.[17]

An official snapshot of the post-war JIC system was first given in the report of the Falklands Committee chaired by Lord Franks in 1983.[18] Apart from its managerial responsibilities the JIC makes 'assessments for Ministers and officials of a wide range of external situations and developments'. These are prepared by geographically-based Current Intelligence Groups (CIGs), made up of 'those in the relevant Departments with special knowledge of the area'. The groups are serviced and chaired from the Cabinet Office by members of the small Assessments Staff (perhaps about twenty people), made up mainly of seconded FCO and Ministry of Defence (MoD) civil servants and service officers. CIGs' assessments are normally (but not necessarily) considered in draft by the JIC itself, which consists of the heads of the intelligence and security agencies and representatives of the MoD and Treasury and 'other Departments, including the Home Office, as appropriate'.[19] Prior to the Franks Committee's recommendations the committee had always been chaired by a senior FCO official.

This is essentially the Second World War system, with a wider remit and a transfer to Cabinet Office control in 1957. The Assessments Staff is a more powerful successor of the wartime JIS. The CIGs are a formalized version of wartime inter-service discussions. On Franks's recommendations, the JIC Chairman became a full-time Cabinet Office official appointed by the Prime Minister. This was a novelty, though the idea had been urged in print by a retired deputy chairman some years

[15] JIC(48)21 *Charter for the Joint Intelligence Committee*, 27 February 1948 (India Office Library, London, reference L/WS/1/1051).

[16] For the Malayan structure see A. Short, *The Communist Insurrection in Malaya 1949–1960* (London: Muller, 1975), pp. 83, 134, 275, 349–63.

[17] R. V. Jones, 'Scientific Intelligence', *RUSI Journal* vol. 92 no. 567 (August 1947), p. 364.

[18] *Falkland Islands Review, Report of a Committee of Privy Counsellors* (the Franks Committee) Cmnd 8787 (London: HMSO, 1983), pp. 94–5.

[19] *Central Intelligence Machinery* (London: HMSO, 1993), p. 11.

earlier, and ignored.[20] A former FCO Permanent Under Secretary subsequently noted that 'Mrs Thatcher removed one Foreign Office chairman only to replace him by another from the same source.'[21] Subsequently the post has reverted to being the part-time responsibility of an FCO official, at present also the head of the Cabinet Office's Overseas Secretariat. The system remains collegial as a set of committees of equals.

Central intelligence made more progress in the United States with the evolution of OSS's R and A to become the basis of CIA's Directorate of Intelligence. The National Security Act of 1947 established CIA 'to correlate and evaluate intelligence relating to the national security, and provide for the dissemination of such intelligence within the Government using where appropriate existing agencies and facilities'.[22] The post of combined DCI and CIA Director was established as intelligence adviser to the President and the NSC.

However the DCI and CIA were never intended to become sole assessors. The 1947 Act charged the DCI and CIA with *coordinating* departmental intelligence for national assessment and with services of common concern. (The DCI was also given the origins of his modern managerial responsibilities, but like those of the JIC these need not be discussed in this chapter.) The subsequent emergence of CIA as a comprehensive central analysis agency was a matter of bureaucratic growth and accident, including the armed services' refusal to release sensitive material to it. From 1950 onwards NIEs were presented by the DCI as community products, produced through a JIC-like process.[23] What emerged was a mixed system; partly collegial, but with the DCI and CIA as potentially powerful central elements.[24]

There have been many subsequent adjustments to this machinery. Up to 1973 estimates were drafted by the Office of National Estimates (ONE), which coordinated them with the community before final approval by the Board of National Estimates. In 1973 ONE was

---

[20] General Strong wrote in 1970 that the JIC was 'still a long way from the ideal of an inter-departmental committee to control intelligence, with an independent chairman divorced from any department and responsible directly to the Prime Minister' (Major-General Sir Kenneth Strong, *Men of Intelligence: a Study of the Roles and Decisions of Chiefs of Intelligence from World War I to the Present Day* (London: Cassell, 1970), p. 150.

[21] D. Greenhill, *More by Accident* (York, England: Wilton 65, 1992), p. 126.

[22] *National Security Act 1947; Public Law 253*, 26 July 1947, Section 102.

[23] For origins of the NIE system see L. Freedman, *US Intelligence and the Soviet Strategic Threat* (London: Macmillan, 1986 edition), pp. 30–2; and R. L. Garthoff, *Assessing the Adversary: Estimates by the Eisenhower Administration of Soviet Intentions and Capabilities* (Washington D.C.: Brookings Institution, 1991), p. 2 (note).

[24] 'CIA' is used here to refer to its Intelligence Directorate only, not its Operations Directorate for collection and covert action.

abolished and replaced by the rather looser system of National Intelligence Officers (NIOs), with changes in the forms of approval.[25] The NIOs now have some corporate identity as the National Intelligence Council (NIC) and have been assisted by a central Analytic Group; the NIC's estimates are formally approved by the National Foreign Intelligence Board (NFIB). Despite minor changes made periodically the basic framework of national assessment through NIEs and the like has remained in place. For many years matters of urgency were covered in special NIEs, or SNIEs; these have recently been revived as Special Estimates and supplemented by President's Summaries.[26]

The creation of integrated armed service intelligence organizations in both countries (chapter 2) had rather different effects on national assessment. In the United States the DIA has tended to be just one military voice added to those of the continued single-service agencies. In Britain one result of the amalgamation of the service departments was that inter-service debates ceased to be conducted in the JIC forum, with some consequent decline in the Foreign Office's original 1939 role of inter-service mediator. However this was balanced by the consolidation within it shortly afterwards (under its new name abbreviated to the FCO) of the Commonwealth Relations Office and Colonial Office, both formerly JIC members in their own right. The effect in Britain has therefore been some polarization of military and civilian viewpoints, while in the USA the military inputs to assessment have been numerous but uncoordinated.

The two systems therefore show common origins and some divergence. Britain is more wedded to collegial procedures, committee-work and consensus-seeking; the US system is marked by the strong central institutions of the CIA and the DCI, the latter as the President's adviser on substantive intelligence as well as intelligence policy. Thus Britain produces the flow of current assessment for the Prime Minister and other Ministers through the JIC machinery of the CIGs, whereas the daily Presidential Brief is a CIA product not formally coordinated between agencies. On the other hand there are more separate flows of intelligence to the top level NSC members in the US system than to their British equivalents. The size of Washington intelligence and its users breeds diversity; thus DIA and INR produce their own departmental equiv-

---

[25] B. Berkowitz and A. Goodman, *Strategic Intelligence for American National Security* (Princeton: Princeton University Press, 1989), pp. 11–12.

[26] Details from H. P. Ford, *Estimative Intelligence: the Purposes and Problems of National Intelligence Estimating* (Lanham, Md.: University Press of America with Defense Intelligence College, 1993), chapters 5 and 6. Also G. F. Treverton, 'Estimating Beyond the Cold War', *Defense Intelligence Journal* vol. 3 no. 2 (fall 1994).

alents of CIA's daily brief. But as well as these differences of scale there is also a US toleration, even encouragement, of departmental diversity; as part of the NIE procedures, participants have had a long-standing right to 'take a footnote' of disagreement.[27] In the British system, by contrast, departmental disagreement is felt to represent a collective failure, and formal notes of dissent are almost unknown.

Both countries also have extensive informal intelligence inputs to policy-makers, not going through formal interdepartmental processes. Yet in both it is striking that the idea of formal community assessment is accepted. In Britain this goes without question. In the United States the system had its problems of political acceptability from the period of the Vietnam War to the accession of President Bush, and has suffered its internal strains between hawks and doves, usually divided on military–civilian lines. Informed insiders suggest that fewer NIEs and other interdepartmental reports are now produced than during the Cold War, and that for top level intelligence there is a greater reliance on CIA than hitherto. But the principle has not been abandoned that the formal intelligence inputs to big decisions should be community views as NIEs and similar product.

Experience elsewhere

UK–US commentators take community assessment for granted; but it seems more remarkable when compared with the situation elsewhere. After 1945 the Old Commonwealth countries followed the British example. National assessment structures were originally created as copies of the JIC but developed their own identities. Canada retained a very collegial system but has recently developed a central analysis staff. Australia moved earlier towards a more centralized system, incorporating US features; in 1977 its Office of National Assessments (ONA), later Office of National Estimates (ONE), replaced the former National Intelligence Committee completely. New Zealand steered a middle course. But all retained departmental defence intelligence and some concept of community assessment.

Elsewhere however the position remains not very different from the pre-Second World War situations in which leaders formed their own judgments from conflicting reports. Unlike the United States, the continental governments-in-exile in London during the Second World War were not much exposed to the JIC system and were in no position to imitate it when restored to their countries. Stalin surprisingly created

---

[27] Berkowitz and Goodman, *Strategic Intelligence for American National Security*, pp. 132–3.

a unified intelligence assessment office (the 'Committee of Information') in 1947 in imitation of the newly-formed CIA. It remained in existence until 1958, but it never had access to all information, always told the leadership what it wanted to hear and did not have much effect.[28] Elsewhere the West German Bundesnachrichtendienst (BND) was devised by General Gehlen after the Second World War as a centralized system in reaction to the fragmentation of intelligence under Hitler. But German assessment of foreign affairs remains a matter for conflict between the Federal Chancery and the Auswärtiges Amt, just as intelligence in France is part of the competition in top policy formation between the Quai d'Orsay, the Elysée, and the Matignon.[29] In Israel defence intelligence has had a central role, as befits a nation under threat; after the debacle of the Yom Kippur attack in 1973 there was a reappraisal, but the result was to seek plural views rather than more collegiality.

In sum the UK–US–Commonwealth system has evoked interest but not much imitation. Most foreign leaders are defeated by the intractable problem of integrating inputs from diplomatic reporting, military intelligence and covert intelligence collection. Selection and evaluation remain generally part of the policy process; by private secretaries, Ministers' *cabinets* and policy advisers, or the decision-takers themselves.

The fact is that community assessment of the UK–US–Commonwealth kind is not a simple thing to organize. The way it works depends on four matters of organization: whether central analysis is provided; the interaction of big committees and small central groups; the scale of non-intelligence 'user' participation; and the influence of the governmental environments in which intelligence is set. They can now be examined.

A central intelligence organization

The creation of CIA in 1947 was a landmark for analysis, however limited the original intent; it was the first specialist, non-departmental all-source analysis organization which evolved in peacetime to study foreign targets in full and serve any part of government. (The difference must again be stressed between the CIA model of complete, all-source analysis, with everything from day-to-day monitoring to basic research

---

[28] See V. M. Zubok, *Soviet Intelligence and the Cold War; the 'Small' Committee of Information, 1952–3* (Washington D.C.: Woodrow Wilson Center, Cold War History Project Working Paper no. 4, 1992).

[29] R. Hibbert, 'Intelligence and Policy', *Intelligence and National Security* vol. 5 no. 1 (January 1990), pp. 117–18.

and institutional memory; and a small, high-powered group like the British Assessments Staff drawing on the research and data bases of others.) Britain flirted periodically from 1918 onwards with the idea of a central agency, but settled for more limited solutions.[30] The JIB was a halfway house, and when it was amalgamated with service intelligence in 1964 there were ideas that the new DIS would have an unambiguous national role; hence its head became 'Director General of Intelligence', acting as deputy chairman of the JIC. But periodic economies have tended to cut the DIS's remit back towards defence intelligence, as was recognized when the DGI's post became 'Chief of *Defence* Intelligence' in the 1980s. Yet in practice the DIS has always been landed with important non-defence tasks, from support for Rhodesian sanctions in the 1960s onwards, simply because there is no other intelligence unit to take on detailed, day-by-day analysis of this kind.

In this tackling of foreign countries as a whole the CIA model has obvious appeal. The US system may have failed in predicting the end of the USSR because, as one of CIA's Soviet experts put it, it did not give enough attention to the Soviet Union as a complete society.[31] But at least it had in CIA an institution with the remit to try; Britain by contrast had excellent machinery for overall assessment but, with no central agency, had no institution for a detailed, holistic *study* of countries in all their political, military and economic detail. The JIC is good at pulling things together but does not direct research.

The disadvantages of CIA's central analysis are the obverse of the coin. Operational departments want intelligence units responsive to their particular needs; the US concern about intelligence–user relationships reflects CIA's position as a central agency without a captive departmental clientele. Fitting a substantial central agency into the British pattern of Ministerial responsibility would be awkward; what Minister would want to have to answer for it in Parliament when its forecasts turned out to be wrong? But the main problem for a central analysis agency is its relationship with the entrenched positions of defence intelligence, Foreign Ministries and other departmental analysis; a central agency cannot supersede the others and has to have a *modus vivendi* with them. The

---

[30] In 1918, the 1920s and 1939. See A. Wells, 'Naval Intelligence and Decision-Taking in an Era of Technical Change' in B. Ranft (ed.), *Technical Change and British Naval Policy* (London: Hodder and Stoughton, 1977), p. 135; Hinsley, *British Intelligence in the Second World War* vol. I, pp. 18–19; D. Dilks, 'Flashes of Intelligence' in C. Andrew and D. Dilks (eds.), *The Missing Dimension: Governments and Intelligence Communities in the Twentieth Century* (London: Macmillan, 1984), pp. 124–5.

[31] Senate Intelligence Committee, Gates confirmation hearings, October 1992, evidence of D. J. MacEachin (*New York Times*, 13 October 1991, p. 24).

US solution is to accept duplication and competitive assessment between CIA and departments. Smaller countries feel they cannot afford it.

Because of this duplication the question has been asked in the USA why policy-makers cannot rely on departmental work (as in the DIA for military and INR for political intelligence) and dispense with CIA analysis completely. Yet the British system is the poorer for its lack of a central analysis agency. (It must be repeated yet again that this is not to be confused with the high-level assessment function based on the Cabinet Office.) No one can split analysis of events such as those in the former Yugoslavia into separate political, military and economic segments. The voluminous overt data now available on many countries strengthens the case for central research. At a time of radical military change Britain might do well to reformulate the DIS's charter and give it explicitly dual roles – serving the MoD and the military for defence intelligence on the one hand, but acting as a national analysis agency on the other – and staff it for the job.

Big committees and small central groups

Even where there is a non-departmental, central analysis agency like CIA, departments and agencies still have to be drawn into the assessment process to ensure that they volunteer information and interpretations. Unless the whole community is engaged some information will get overlooked. Thus a JIC study in the Second World War of the possibility of a German advance from southern Russia through the Caucasus and Turkey towards the Middle East had to be re-written because the Ministry of Economic Warfare, not present at the drafting meetings, subsequently produced crucial information that Turkish coal stocks were in the wrong place to enable captured railways to be used to supply the German advance.[32]

The assessment circle particularly needs to include the collectors, especially since so much now turns on the selections and interpretations of the big technical agencies like NSA and GCHQ. Interdepartmental machinery not only pools information but also tests assumptions and conclusions; a good group, working regularly together, is better than the sum of its parts. Edward Thomas said of the wartime JIS that it 'incorporated the principle of the search for truth through the medium of

---

[32] D. McLachlan, *Room 39: Naval Intelligence in Action 1939–45* (London: Weidenfeld and Nicolson, 1968), p. 241.

the seminar – a word little heard in Britain in those days – and in their case a seminar that sat permanently'.[33] Something of the same can be said of British CIG meetings, or the interdepartmental networks operating under the US NIOs. Departmental participation also ensures the output's acceptability; without it there will be no agreed intelligence for decision-taking. National assessment needs some institutionalized collegiality. The greatest British contribution to modern intelligence is the idea that it needs committees.

Yet these have their obvious defects: the propensity towards blandness and the lowest common denominator of agreement; the search for drafting solutions that obscure real differences; stitching departmental segments together instead of looking at subjects as a whole. Committee work brings in institutional pecking orders and the oddities of group psychology. Despite the value of the interdepartmental group, good analysis at some point needs the clarity of a single mind, working in depth without sectoral commitment and bias.

Committees bring other problems. They are expensive in participants' time, and there are the practical problems of getting them together. The Franks Committee on the Falklands invasion criticized the JIC machinery as being 'too passive in operation to respond quickly and critically to a rapidly changing situation which demanded urgent attention', but the truth may well have been that those actively concerned with the situation in the FCO and DIS were too busy handling it departmentally to find time for a formal intelligence assessment.[34] Some sensitive information cannot be shared by a complete group. There is a heavy premium on chairmanship. Getting the best out of a committee is an art in itself, and distracts from a single-minded concentration on quality and impact.

Many writers have underlined these disadvantages. General Strong, the first head of the DIS, emphasized individual judgment: 'As I was constantly reminded during the Second World War, what was required of me was a *personal* judgment or recommendation, however many might have contributed their judgment on various aspects to help me forming mine.'[35] So did R. V. Jones, who was critical of the JIC in both war and peace: 'A joint report is only as effective as common agreement will allow, and – so far as interpreting intelligence evidence goes – common

[33] E. Thomas, 'The Evolution of the JIC System up to and during the Second World War' in C. Andrew and J. Noakes (eds.), *Intelligence and International Relations 1900–1945* (Exeter: Exeter University Press, 1987), p. 232.
[34] *Franks Report*, paragraph 318.
[35] Strong, *Intelligence at the Top*, p. 220.

agreement rarely goes far enough.'[36] Committees may be necessary, but no one likes them. In the US it has recently been argued that NIEs are 'time-consuming exercises in compromise' which 'have largely outlived their usefulness' and 'should be limited to a few special cases'; the President and NSC should rely principally on CIA.[37]

Hence there has always been a tension between the need for a collegial committee system and the compelling alternative of some central, élite group, drawing on the basic analysis of the community but free to make high-quality assessment, free of departmental allegiances or the need for committee endorsement. This is indeed an intelligence version of the non-intelligence world's idea of independent think-tanks, 'policy units' and similar non-departmental groups. Cline put the case for it as follows:

I firmly believe in the . . . concept of a small, capable unit with exclusive responsibility for making the difficult estimates in the light of the evidence available from all sources with no vested interest in either foreign policy or military policy and no bias except towards establishing the truth as well as it can be perceived. I believe that the ONE of my last year there (1954) was forthrightly dedicated to this process and an excellent example of what it could achieve.[38]

The question is whether these qualities of a central group can somehow be grafted on to committees to get the best of both worlds; combining the wisdom of Plato's small group of Guardians with the virtues of tapping the knowledge and instincts of a wider community. In the USA, despite the formal role of the NFIB in approving them, the production of NIEs is subject to the strong central influence of the DCI and the NIOs under him. Power rests with those who write the drafts, chair the meetings and lead with conclusions. ONE had this power until its abolition; and the NIOs who inherited it are leaders and not just coordinators. ONE was CIA-staffed, as is still largely true of the NIO system. Despite its fluctuating political fortunes, CIA is *primus inter pares.* The result has been to balance the centrifugal tendencies of US departments by a kind of central spine of the DCI and CIA which holds the system together, at the cost of military accusations in the Cold War that it was loaded towards 'soft' CIA views.

What is less obvious is that there is also a mixture of community and central forces in the British system. The JIC and its CIGs are nominally committees of equals; but in reality there is a strong central element. In

---

[36] Valedictory report on leaving the Ministry of Defence, 1954, quoted in R. V. Jones, *Reflections on Intelligence* (London: Heinemann, 1989), p. 156.

[37] J. H. Hedley, *Checklist for the Future of Intelligence* (Georgetown: Institute for the Study of Diplomacy, 1995), p. 17.

[38] Cline, *Secrets, Spies and Scholars*, p. 135.

the first place the committee benefits from the central authority of the Cabinet Office and the role of the Cabinet Secretary, with his special responsibilities for the intelligence services.[39] This central power provides the necessary carrots and sticks that ensure that departments cooperate. Like other Cabinet Office meetings, CIG meetings can be called at short notice, not negotiated with participants; middle-level officials drop everything to attend.

There is also the influence of the central Assessments Staff. Accounts of the JIC in the Second World War emphasize how the JIS became the kernel of the assessment process, and transformed it from committee consensus to high-grade assessment. Though the JIS's members represented departments' interests, they developed a corporate objectivity, authority and teamwork, partly through the influence within it of independently-minded civilians whose wartime uniforms were only skin-deep. In Thomas's description of its creation, 'This was the reform that stuck. Within a short time the JIC was issuing appreciations of a very different stamp from what had gone before.'[40] Donald McLachlan's description catches the small group flavour in words reminiscent of Cline:

Day after day of patient and protracted argument on a single question, such as their masters had no time for, took place in the JIS; and when they had achieved agreement, it still remained to persuade each Director of Intelligence in an hour or two that the joint view was correct and that if he disagreed he was probably wrong . . . As time went on, however, the Rear Admirals and Major Generals and Air Vice Marshals learned to suspend judgement until their Captains, Colonels and Group Captains had produced collective common sense. There can be no doubt that this work of joint intelligence appreciation did a great deal to reduce inter-service rivalry and create a habit of objective study and discussion of common problems . . .

and

This joint staff, in which officers of the rank of Captain, Colonel and Group Captain represented their Directors, each with a junior officer chosen for his intellectual record in civilian life, had one habit of mind . . . It set out consistently and stubbornly to see the various problems put before it exclusively from the enemy's point of view . . .

The value of this way of looking at the facts and prospects of war was considerable; not so much for its positive grasp of the enemy point of view – though

---

[39] For confirmation of this role see the letter from Lord Hunt of Tanworth and Sir Robert Armstrong, *The Times*, 30 July 1987, commenting on the obituary of Lord Trend (22 July).
[40] Thomas, 'The Evolution of the JIC System up to and during the Second World War', p. 230.

this was the main business of intelligence – as for its critical influence on the concourse of facts, ideas, political and personal influences pressing on the conduct of the war in London and Washington. 'But this is how the enemy may, or must, see it; these are his resources, his positions, the distances he has to cover, the principles of strategy he has so far followed. He *is* probably capable of this but he is certainly not capable of that'; this kind of staunch reminder, from a small body of men who gradually achieved a collective intellectual integrity which no amount of ministerial cajolery could shake, was salutary.[41]

The JIS continued in peacetime but lost some of its standing until reconstituted as the higher profile Assessments Staff in 1968.[42] This drew in additional manpower and high-flying talent, principally in the form of seconded diplomats. The result was to produce strong central leadership of the collegial process. The seminar atmosphere remains, but with 'guided collectivism' from the centre. Papers are drafted by the Assessments Staff independently of departmental positions, and some are passed direct to the Prime Minister and other top users. But those on subjects for important Cabinet decisions are still processed through, and approved by, the interdepartmental machinery; most of what Ministers receive is a genuinely collegial view, not just a central view produced after purely formal consultation.

The Assessments Staff remains quite small, dependent on others for expertise and information, and subject to community endorsement of its judgments; it is not part of a central agency like CIA or responsible to a single intelligence chief like the DCI. These apparent weaknesses are its real strength, since they bind it to the collegial system that surrounds it, and prevent it from becoming just another agency competing with others. Success comes from a delicate balance between the centre and the community. One recurrent danger is of the central staff operating as an agency in its own right, with the risk of losing its community roots; the opposite one is of not being independent enough of departmental positions. With the predominance of FCO secondees in the Assessments Staff the FCO has usually had a position as dominant in the British system as CIA's in the United States.[43] Nevertheless the overall effect is a profitable blend of strong central guidance and committee consensus.

The resulting British and US styles are rather different. The British system sets considerable store by set procedures and formal consensus;

[41] McLachlan, *Room 39*, pp. 241, 251.

[42] *Central Intelligence Machinery*, p. 11.

[43] For numbers and parent departments of Assessments Staff secondees, showing the preponderance of the FCO, see M. Lee, 'The Ethos of the Cabinet Office: a Comment on the Testimony of Officials', *Public Administration* vol. 68 no. 2 (summer 1990), pp. 238–9.

as a departmental, collegial system without a central agency like CIA it needs established interdepartmental procedures and cannot stand too much dissent. On the other hand the stronger centre of the US system enables it to tolerate more diversity, even encourage it. However much departmental dissent there may be, the President has the DCI as his intelligence adviser to provide a best judgment on disputed issues; and the DCI for his part, as CIA's director, will normally (though not inevitably) give special weight to the Agency's analysis. But despite their differences the British and US systems deal successfully, in broadly similar ways, with the problem of making a community system better than just a set of committees.

It has to be added that in recent years the US community has introduced some new interdepartmental devices. One dating from the Gulf War is the creation of numerous Joint Intelligence *Centers* (JICs) as part of inter-service 'jointery' within the defence intelligence community, providing joint-service, multi-agency organizations, not committees where independent organizations meet.[44] The other is the idea of co-located interdepartmental task forces on specific subjects, or 'Multi-Mission Single-Issue Cooperative Mechanisms' (MMSICMs). In 1992 there were five of these – the long-established Arms Control Intelligence Staff; the Counterterrorism Center; the Counternarcotics Center; the Counterintelligence Center; and the Nonproliferation Center.[45] All were located on CIA's premises and reported to the DCI.

These are examples of matrix working of the kind common in the private sector, and appear to be fruitful experiments in detailed analysis and collection guidance. They give new twists to the departmental–central balance. But they seem designed to improve operational level intelligence rather than top level assessment.

Intelligence assessors or a bigger college?

Alongside this balancing of central groups and committees there is another organizational issue: what should the assessing community actually consist of? In the United States it is formally defined, and is

---

[44] An account of the JIC established in September 1990 as part of the Iraqi Intelligence Task Force of DIA is given in J. R. Clapper Jr, 'Defense Intelligence Reorganization and Changes', *Defense Intelligence Journal* vol. 1 no. 1 (spring 1992), p. 8. It was manned from each of the services, DIA and NSA and 'operated around the clock in an all-source intelligence fusion effort never before attempted'. After the war single-service organizations were amalgamated into JICs for all the Unified US Commands.

[45] For details see P. L. Scalingi, 'Intelligence Community Cooperation: the Arms Control Model', *Journal of Intelligence and Counterintelligence* vol. 5 no. 4 (winter 1991–2), pp. 401–10.

made up of specialist intelligence organizations and the intelligence units of State Department and other executive departments; intelligence's users are not included. On the other hand the composition of the British JIC and its CIGs is described as including, besides intelligence organizations proper, the main policy and executive departments: the FCO, Treasury and 'other Departments as appropriate'.[46]

This difference lies partly in the purely semantic one that research units in these British operational departments do not call themselves 'intelligence'. These units are in any case far smaller than their US equivalents. More important, none of them has a particular role of analysing incoming covert intelligence and acting as its department's intelligence specialist. The British Foreign Office established a Political Intelligence Department in the two World Wars but never continued with it in peace;[47] its current successor, the Research and Analysis Department, participates in the collegial process but has never had special intelligence connections like those of its US opposite number the INR, or a place at the intelligence table in its own right.

The most important point, however, is that the JIC seeks FCO and similar inputs to its process from these operational organizations as a whole, and not just from their research units. These units contribute to their own departments' thinking, and sometimes attend the JIC's 'working-level' CIG meetings; but do not have distinctive voices. The head of the FCO's Research and Analysis Department does not have a seat at the JIC and does not attend it. The FCO is represented by senior policy-makers who draw on their own experience and knowledge combined with that of their colleagues, and give what is essentially a departmental view, not that of its research unit. The same applies even more to other departments like the Northern Ireland Office which have no relevant research back-up. In addition a senior civilian member of the central policy staff of MoD has a permanent seat at the main JIC, and attends or is represented when necessary, in addition to the participation of the Defence Intelligence Staff. This flexibility in JIC membership represents an attempt to tap all available specialist knowledge; thus in dealing with terrorist subjects the system adapted to having some police representation at CIGs. The main effect is however to make policy officials participants in its assessment process.

---

[46] *Central Intelligence Machinery* (London: HMSO, 1993), p. 11.
[47] E. Goldstein, 'The Foreign Office and Political Intelligence 1918–1920', *Review of International Studies* vol. 14 no. 4 (October 1988); R. Cecil, 'The Assessment and Acceptance of Intelligence: a Case-Study' in K. G. Robertson (ed.), *British and American Approaches to Intelligence* (London: Macmillan, 1987), pp. 172–3.

There is therefore a distinct difference: US meetings in the NIE process are of intelligence people, while their British JIC and CIG equivalents are mixtures of intelligence and policy-makers. The US system emphasizes the distinction between intelligence and policy, with the former an independent input to the latter. The British system is more elastic. Intelligence assessments are clearly distinct from policy papers, but their production has a mixed intelligence and policy-based cast. Besides the all-source and single-source intelligence agencies the system pulls in policy-makers *ad hoc*, plus FCO officials as permanent and important members. The system as a whole draws heavily on the FCO. One of its features is that draft assessments are frequently telegraphed abroad for the appropriate ambassadors' comments before finalization – something that does not feature in any accounts of the US system. FCO interpretations are certainly influential, and the same applies to the Treasury on economic and financial matters. The JIC and its CIGs are partly meetings of intelligence professionals, but partly also a means of 'gathering the voices' within government as a whole. Pedantry would suggest that, unlike the US system, what they produce is not strictly '*intelligence* assessment', but 'government assessment'.

This may seem a Gilbertian comedy. An FCO official attends a CIG or JIC meeting and plays his part (often a leading part, since diplomats tend to be the best informed and most articulate people around); then back in his office he changes roles and waits for the intelligence assessment to arrive as the 'objective' input to his policy recommendations and decisions. It is not surprising that foreign visitors find it hard to understand. Cynics may see it as no more than a legitimation device, part of Whitehall's trick for producing foreign policy consensus under FCO leadership. But it raises the serious question whether assessment should be the product of specialized 'intelligencers' or some wider forum.

There is no doubt that all-source finished intelligence has to suck information and expertise from non-intelligence sources. Non-governmental ones can be used by subscribing to the many commercial 'risk assessments' and other sources available, and by commissioning studies by research institutions, academics and other experts. The British system probably needs to make better use of these inputs than it has in the past.[48] There is no inherent reason why some assessments could not be contracted out, in full or for a second opinion, somewhere within the burgeoning world of commercial and academic assessors; Oxford

---

[48] For the American NIC's increased use of outside contractors to produce independent assessments, see G. F. Treverton, 'Estimating Beyond The Cold War', pp. 8–9.

Analytica is only one among many.[49] But policy-makers' own official information also has to be tapped and usually only intelligence can do it, sometimes with difficulty; gaining access to sensitive 'no distribution' telegrams may be a problem, as US intelligence found with Kissinger.[50] The same difficulty applies to tapping policy-makers' own impressions from their direct contacts; and also to operational police information on terrorist matters. But the system has to try.

What is less clear is how far this justifies engaging policy-makers in the assessment process itself. Clearly there is the danger that policy preconceptions shape assessment. In the British system the effect of diplomatic opinions on warning has already been mentioned; but in most circumstances the arrangement is more defensible than it sounds. The effect is to bring knowledge and viewpoints to the table that would not otherwise be there, and to help intelligence towards acceptance by users. The British involvement of senior policy officials is another reason why concerns about intelligence–policy relationships seem less pressing in Whitehall than Washington. If one result is that policy views carry too much weight, the remedy is presumably not to exclude them but to strike the right balance with the professional intelligence contribution.

In any case it can be suggested that British policy-makers' biases are not immune to the influence of intelligence mystique. The ritual of intelligence assessment – in special rooms, with special secrecy, as something different from normal operations – has some power in differentiating it from normal policy business. Edward Thomas's metaphor of the wartime seminar is not inappropriate for the peacetime ethos.

Assembling a varied cast, including those from policy departments, for CIGs at short notice reflects the Cabinet Office's power; the ability to do it is part of the British system's strength. Perhaps it would be impossible on the larger scale of Washington, but the US system could perhaps try. It has been claimed in the past that 'one essential feature of a national estimate is that it draws on all of the information and wisdom available to the US government',[51] but one may ask how effectively this works in

---

[49] So too could Chatham House be if it had a mind to do so, but this does not imply that experts outside government are wiser than those inside; an academic recounts with sadness that his article on the Falklands–Malvinas question was turned down for publication by Chatham House in 1981 on the grounds that the subject was insufficiently topical. But the outsiders are at least different from insiders.

[50] Cline, *Secrets, Spies and Scholars*, p. 264. For an extended treatment see the same author's 'Policy Without Intelligence', *Foreign Policy* no. 17 (winter 1974–5), pp. 121–35.

[51] Evidence from Richard Lehman, then Chairman of the NIC, to the House Committee on Foreign Affairs on 8 February 1980; quoted in Ford, *Estimative Intelligence*, p. 142.

practice. At all events these differing circles of participants constitute a significant difference between the two systems.

Constitutional and administrative context

Intelligence to some extent has its own international patterns. Different national structures have points in common, with influence and imitation operating on transnational intelligence networks. The post-1945 German system was shaped by US advice added to German professional lessons drawn from the Second World War. Similarly the JIC model was an important transnational influence – perhaps the last British constitutional export to the United States and the Old Commonwealth.

Nevertheless what has already been said shows that intelligence is by no means insulated from non-intelligence government. The British JIC and its CIGs draw strength from their status as part of the Cabinet Office's network of interdepartmental committees which translate Ministers' collective Cabinet responsibility into effective government. Within intelligence the JIC's prestige is buttressed by various factors: the authority of the Secretary of the Cabinet; the Committee's own position as part of the Cabinet Secretariat; the intimacy of what has been called 'the Whitehall village'; and the village's culture of interdepartmental give-and-take. The JIC shares and benefits from the Whitehall preoccupation with making Cabinet government work through cooperation and compromise.

This comes out in style as well as mechanisms. The JIC Chairman has traditionally been the spokesman of his committee, serving top government as a whole; the DCI by contrast speaks to the President as his chief of intelligence. The JIC uses standard Cabinet Office procedures for smoothing out departmental differences, for example in the style of committee minutes which depersonalizes discussion and emphasizes collective decisions. Assessment takes place in the Cabinet Office building, with the mystique of being close to the heart of government. Such elements oil the system and induce cooperation. If the result is to work too hard at achieving agreement instead of pointing up differences, that is no more than an echo of the standard criticisms of British civil servants.

The same applies to the element of guided collectivism provided by the Assessments Staff. Cabinet government is not pure collegiality. The Prime Minister is more than just a first among equals; the Cabinet Office is more than just an efficient secretariat. Ever since its emergence in the course of the First World War, the Cabinet Office has been a fixer, nudging policy in the right direction. Its influence within Whitehall is the more pervasive since the senior staff are all on temporary secondment from other departments.[52] These surroundings provide backing for the Assessments Staff's leadership of its groups. The JIC as a whole is a symptom of British interdepartmentalism.

Fitting the wider environment also applies in the United States. The central power of the DCI and CIA fit the Presidential style of government with only loose Cabinet responsibility. For the President and those close to him, they are one means of securing authority vis-à-vis the departments. The DCI himself is a typical figure of the Presidential system: powerful in some ways, and circumscribed in others. The intelligence mixture of central authority and departmental independence encapsulates the complexity, competition and confusion of US government; but also the richness of its diversity. Evaluating the effectiveness of assessment in both countries needs to take account of these wider contexts.

There are similar connections between intelligence and government elsewhere. JIC-like systems in the Old Commonwealth are linked with Cabinet systems derived from Westminster. The absence of agreed intelligence community assessment in France and Germany reflects national decision-taking styles.

Thus intelligence structures are shaped by the systems around them; but they may also have some influence upon this environment. The evolution of the office of British Cabinet Secretary cannot be understood without taking his intelligence responsibilities into account, with their Walsingham-like hints of secret knowledge and power. CIA has been a factor in diminishing the role of State Department; by contrast intelligence in Britain tends to be a factor in the FCO's continued influence. The NSC evolved in symbiosis with the US intelligence system, and may perhaps have been influenced by it. The service of intelligence to the Congress in recent years may be an important constitutional innovation; intelligence's role there is evolving towards servicing legislators as well as the Executive Branch, helping to increase Congressional power in foreign affairs. In such ways intelligence acts in wider constitutional and administrative settings and has some influence on how they evolve.

Summary

The biggest service intelligence can offer government is to provide objective and interdepartmentally agreed assessments as inputs to top

---

[52] For Cabinet Office influence on policy see A. Seldon, 'The Cabinet Office and Coordination', *Public Administration* vol. 68 no. 1 (spring 1990), pp. 103–21; and Lee, 'The Ethos of the Cabinet Office'.

level decision-making – and for them to be correct. Interdepartmental assessment of this kind, with some separation from policy preconceptions and disagreements, is a UK–US–Commonwealth speciality. It needs suitable organization and machinery.

Most assessment of this kind entails broad understanding of foreign countries, not limited to particular departmental sectors. One underlying question is therefore how to organize the detailed all-source analysis that precedes assessment, and on which it is based. CIA's Directorate of Intelligence is able to study foreign countries as a whole. Britain fragments this work between subject departments, and might well consider some reorientation of its DIS to be both a defence and a 'national' agency.

Irrespective of whether a national analysis centre of this kind exists, effective national assessment needs some interdepartmental participation. Community machinery is needed to get different departments and agencies to the same table; otherwise assessment will not be based on the full range of information and expertise. A balance has to be maintained between these collegial approaches on the one hand and central, élite leadership on the other. Britain emphasizes community processes and consensus, but combines this with leadership from its Assessments Staff. The United States has the central roles of the DCI and CIA, but has combined these historically with the long-established arrangements for community NIEs and scope for departmental dissent. Community participation is an essential part of both systems, but in different ways.

There are also different balances between assessment by professional intelligence practitioners and by a wider circle including policy-makers. The United States emphasizes the professional practitioners. The British model attaches more importance to wider involvement, particularly by its FCO. This practice mobilizes a wide range of inputs and knowledge, and helps to ensure intelligence's acceptance by users – at some risk that assessment may be weighted in favour of policy assumptions. It is an effective system, but is based on the intimacy of Whitehall compared with Washington.

Both the UK and US systems work, and represent major successes in making intelligence useful to top government. The different structures and balances reflect the differences between Presidential and Cabinet government. Intelligence's machinery is not divorced from the public administration environment in which it operates; and perhaps has some influence upon it in return.

Part V

Evaluation and management

Page 282 blank

16   The production process

Intelligence strains after quality, and the last three chapters have discussed its implications for the community's organization and management. In this context we have discussed top-level intelligence–user relationships: how the relatively small number of intelligence assessors need to be close to top policy-makers and know what they need, while at the same time retaining their objectivity and freedom from policy preconceptions. But modern intelligence also needs to be considered in a complementary, rather different way. Large parts of it are a kind of mass production, with production lines that include 24-hour activities scanning for targets, computers operating continuously, and some lines of product being produced virtually 'untouched by human hand'. The scale is different from that already considered.

This factory-like element looms increasingly large. British Sigint in the Second World War set a pattern for the future when its successes came not only from cipher-breaking, but also from organizing speedy exploitation and delivery of the product. Since then the big technical collectors have ceased to be cottage industries and have become high-technology enterprises. Other intelligence is moving in the same direction as data handling becomes mechanized.

This change brings with it the need for management which aims at *effectiveness* and *efficiency*, not only in the application of technology but also in motivating large numbers of people, cutting costs and delivering output to the right place at the right time.[1] Nevil Shute, the novelist-cum-engineer, wrote in 1954 that 'I would divide the senior executives of the engineering world into two categories, the starters and the runners,

---

[1] Definitions of 'effectiveness' and 'efficiency' are discussed in management literature but are regarded here as self-evident. Commentators now tend to expand two Es to three – effectiveness, efficiency and *economy*. Effectiveness and efficiency seem enough here. For discussion see N. Carter, 'Learning to Measure Performance: The Use of Indicators in Organization', *Public Administration* vol. 69 no. 1 (spring 1991), p. 90; and J. Glyn, A. Gray and B. Jenkins, 'Auditing the Three Es: The Challenge of Effectiveness', *Public Policy and Administration* vol. 7 no. 3 (winter 1992), pp. 56–70.

the men with a creative instinct who can start a new venture and the men who can run to make it show a profit.'[2] *Mutatis mutandis*, something of this duality applies with modern intelligence. One of the satisfactions to be gained as a practitioner is improving cost-effectiveness through good management, reflecting the British JIC's responsibility for 'efficiency, economy and prompt adaptation to changing requirements'.[3]

This group of chapters therefore deals with intelligence as 'production' in this sense: gearing big production lines to what is most needed, with maximum output at minimum cost. This chapter considers basic assumptions about how intelligence operates on this scale and how it can be evaluated. Chapter 17 considers managing the community as a whole, and chapter 18 the management style of the individual agency. An underlying question in all three chapters is how far intelligence can learn from business management and from the new organization and management styles being applied within the public service. Does intelligence resemble the rest of the world or is it unique?

Understanding intelligence organizations

Metaphor and intelligence doctrine

Management takes its style from its view of the organization; different ways of looking at it are encapsulated in the metaphors used to describe it. 'Many of our conventional ideas about organization and management build on a small number of taken-for-granted images.'[4] There are 'different ways of thinking about organizations' which 'can be used in a practical way to read and understand specific situations, and to shape the management and design of organization generally'.[5] Hence 'our theories and explanations of organizational life are based on metaphors that lead us to see and understand organizations in distinctive yet partial ways . . . The use of metaphor implies *a way of thinking* and *a way of seeing* . . . ' (original italics).[6]

Intelligence as a whole is pragmatic, not doctrinal. Training is mainly technical and departmental; there are no community staff colleges. Yet there are professional metaphors, and some doctrine derived from them. The dominant one is that the process is driven by user requirements and priorities, with the 'intelligence cycle' as the way in which they are

---

[2] N. Shute, *Slide Rule* (London: Pan edition, 1968), p. 219.
[3] *Central Intelligence Machinery* (London: HMSO, 1993), p. 23.
[4] G. Morgan, *Images of Organization* (London: Sage, 1986), p. 12.
[5] Morgan, *Images of Organization*, p. 321.
[6] Morgan, *Images of Organization*, p. 12.

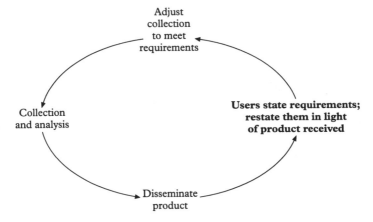

Figure 16 Military concept of the intelligence cycle

applied. There are many versions, but a typical one was given by the Congressional Church Committee in 1976 as follows:

- Those who use intelligence, the 'consumers', indicate the kind of information needed.
- These needs are translated into concrete 'requirements' by senior intelligence managers.
- The requirements are used to allocate resources to the 'collectors' and serve to guide their efforts.
- The collectors obtain the required information or 'raw intelligence'.
- The 'raw intelligence' is collated and turned into 'finished intelligence' by the 'analysts'.
- The finished intelligence is distributed to the consumer and the intelligence managers who state new needs, define new requirements, and make necessary adjustments in the intelligence programs to improve effectiveness and efficiency.[7]

This concept of reacting to specific requests becomes generalized; 'requirements' become standing guidance. Collection agencies have lists of them, often updated annually. At the community level, requirements are aggregated, 'validated', 'prioritized' and issued as formal statements

---

[7] US Senate, *Final Report of the Select Committee to Study Governmental Operations with Respect to Intelligence Activities* (The Church Committee) (Washington D.C.: US GPO, April 1976), book I, p. 18. The military version of the cycle puts rather more emphasis on leaders' own statements and restatements of requirements and less on the 'intelligence managers'.

like the US DCI's Directives, sometimes supplemented by lists of special topics or 'intelligence gaps', as in the Key Intelligence Questions (KIQs) introduced in the 1970s and its later National Intelligence Topics (NITs).[8] Requirements can also form the basis of community-wide collection planning and audits of results.

Hence they have more status than if they were just 'needs'; they have connotations of *authorization*, 'claiming and demanding by right and authority'.[9] Some brave practitioners have condemned requirements and the priorities associated with them as a wholly bureaucratic exercise.[10] But generally they have a mystique. Some of the discussion about controlling intelligence is about strict monitoring of the requirements placed upon it. The intelligence cycle for translating them into intelligence actions is less in vogue, but is accepted as an explanation, for example in CIA handouts.[11] On the whole, 'this is how most people probably believe that intelligence *should* be produced'.[12] All this draws on, and contributes to, a metaphor of intelligence as an orderly process originating in users' needs.

Evolution of the metaphor

The cycle is in fact a military creation. Thus in NATO it is described as a 'logical system of thought and action for providing the intelligence required by a commander . . . All intelligence work should be based on the commander's intelligence requirements . . . if it is to be effective and economic it must have a specific aim, and the aim is to provide the commander with what he needs.' A 'clear statement by the commander' leads to the staff's 'collection plan', selecting the appropriate source for a particular task to eliminate duplication.[13] 'The checking of productivity not only embraces the intelligence principle of continuous

---

[8] B. Berkowitz and A. Goodman, *Strategic Intelligence for American National Security* (Princeton: Princeton University Press, 1989), pp. 47–8, 174.

[9] Definition from *Longman Dictionary of the English Language* (Harlow: Longman, 1984).

[10] Requirements are 'the most over-bureaucratized aspect of intelligence management . . . The larger the requirements apparatus, the less meaningful collection guidance will be; well-trained collectors mostly know what to collect; arrangements should be made for as much direct exchange as possible between collectors and analysts.' (Comments by J. W. Huizenga in *Commission on the Organization of Government for the Conduct of Foreign Policy* (the Murphy Commission), *Report of the Commission* (volume 7) (Washington D.C.: GPO, June 1975), appendix U, p. 43.

[11] For example, *Fact Book on Intelligence* (Washington D.C.: CIA Public Affairs Agency, 1987), pp. 16–17.

[12] Berkowitz and Goodman, *Strategic Intelligence for American National Security*, p. 30.

[13] Allied Intelligence Publication No. 1 – *Intelligence Doctrine* (NATO, 1984), paragraph 401.

review but is an essential part of the activity of the intelligence cycle.'[14] This military doctrine is tacitly accepted more widely. Civilian intelligence has no formal intelligence community doctrine and has accepted the military thinking by seepage, *faute de mieux*.

But with it has been borrowed the characteristic style of military thinking: the emphasis on simplifying complex processes; standard linear sequences; and the importance of drills.[15] Disciplined mental drills are a military survival mechanism evolved to cope with the confusion of war. This military style of thought was part of the development of early twentieth-century Western 'scientific management' and thinking about organizations as a whole. Other organizational theory has now moved on to other metaphors. Intelligence – with some insulation from this other, more recent thinking – remains wedded to the military one. Contrary to critics' belief, peacetime intelligence sets considerable store by behaving 'properly' with 'proper' procedures. Hence the attraction of the military metaphors of requirements and the cycle.

The metaphor and reality

Yet critics point out the mismatch between this doctrine and what happens in practice. Their distress was classically expressed by the Church Committee when it concluded that

In reality, the pattern [of the intelligence cycle] is barely recognizable . . . intelligence requirements reflect what intelligence managers think the consumers need, and equally important, what they think their organizations can provide. Since there are many managers and little central control, each is relatively free to set his own requirements.

It quoted an earlier report that

After a year's work on intelligence requirements, we have come to realize that they are not the driving force behind the flow of information. Rather, the real push comes from the collectors themselves – particularly the operations of large, undiscriminating technical collection systems – who use national intelligence requirements to justify what they want to undertake for other reasons e.g., military readiness, redundancy, technical continuity and the like.[16]

A few years later President Carter said in the same way that 'When I became President I was concerned . . . that the intelligence community,

---

[14] NATO *Intelligence Doctrine*, Annex E, paragraph 4.
[15] For a discussion of military rationality see J. Shy, 'Jomini' in P. Paret (ed.), *Makers of Modern Strategy* (Oxford: Clarendon Press, 1986), especially pp. 184–5.
[16] *Church Committee Report*, pp. 18, 346.

itself, set its own priorities as a supplier of intelligence information.'[17] These impressions figured in the later discussion of 'managing the octopus'.[18] Recent proposals for reforming the US system have been in a similar spirit.[19] Its divergence from the requirements-led metaphor is part of its indictment.[20]

But perhaps what is wrong is not intelligence, but the metaphor. Diplomacy is also (in part) an information system, but formal requirements and priorities have never been applied to its reporting. There has never been talk of a 'diplomatic cycle'; embassies use their nous in deciding what to report, and learn from recipients' reactions. Information in the private sector defies neat patterns of requirements and cycles; organizations buy computers to meet clearly defined information needs, but find instead that they revolutionize them.[21] Even in intelligence, formal requirements and priorities do not apply at the top assessment level; producers are expected to keep in close touch with users and remain flexible. We therefore need to consider what is the real driving force behind large-scale intelligence production.

Requirements and real life

Procedural limitations

Clearly intelligence cannot do whatever it chooses; precise user needs are a major element. Commanders using air power request intelligence on targets of their choice, such as Iraqi Scud batteries in the Gulf War. Policy-makers request specific assessments, in peace as well as war. Imagery is given lists of targets, as is some Humint; KGB and GRU collection of Western technology used requirements from the Soviet military–industrial complex.[22] Precise targets of this kind are less directly translated into Sigint coverage, but they are still an important factor in it.

---

[17] L. K. Johnson, *America's Secret Power: the CIA in a Democratic Society* (Oxford: Oxford University Press, 1989), p. 81.

[18] S. Turner, *Secrecy and Democracy* (London: Harper and Row, 1985), pp. 223–85.

[19] For example, D. L. Boren, 'The Intelligence Community: How Crucial?', *Foreign Affairs* vol. 71 no. 3 (summer 1992).

[20] The defaulters at whom these criticisms were aimed were probably not the community as a whole, but the technical collectors. The criticism was largely that NSA and the NRO were not driven by all-source *analysts'* requirements; the complaint was probably on their behalf, not for the real, non-intelligence users.

[21] For discussion of these characteristics see B. Cronin and E. Davenport, *Post-Professionalism: Transforming the Information Heartland* (London: Taylor Graham, 1988), chapter 3.

[22] P. Hanson, *Soviet Industrial Espionage: Some New Information* (London: Royal Institute of International Affairs Discussion Paper no. 1, 1987), p. 18.

In short there is no argument about the role of detailed and up-to-date user requests, especially in war and warlike situations.[23] But there are limitations which need to be recognized.

Some of them are inherent in users' roles. Their interest in intelligence varies: some politicians are fascinated by it, while others find it vaguely improper. Intelligence seems vital in war, but often seems a bonus in peace, not a make-or-break factor. Secrecy and sensitivity limit users' understanding; in three small wars over the last fifty years Britain had to relearn the Second World War lesson that, to give proper support to its military users, intelligence has to be brought into the secret of its own side's forthcoming operations; probably the lesson will have to be learned again. Users do not think in broad terms about the information needs of their whole department. Most of them welcome anything that can help them immediately but are not discriminating 'requirers', especially when intelligence is only one source of information among others. 'Policy officials are more comfortable thinking in terms of outputs [i.e. their own objectives, hopes and fears] than of inputs.'[24] According to a future DCI (Gates), 'often the requirement has more to do with the last item that popped into the policy-maker's in-box or some hairbrained idea he concocted while shaving that morning.'[25] Users also make short-term assumptions; Argentina was a low priority in 1982 because no one expected the Falklands *coup de main*. Intelligence often needs to take longer views, especially in collection. Even if the user is conscientious there is the genuine problem of defining what he does not know, rather like the difficulties elsewhere in establishing requirements and priorities for scientific research.[26] Arrangements within NATO for handling military users' operational needs through the Collection Coordination Intelligence Requirements Management (CCIRM) system are a

---

[23] For the handling of operational requirements in the Gulf War, see Report of the Oversight and Investigations Subcommittee, Committee on Armed Services, House of Representatives, *Intelligence Successes and Failures in Operations Desert Shield/Storm* (Washington D.C.: US GPO, 1993), pp. 10–11. There is praise for the way in which the command 'devised a system of twenty-seven intelligence targets essential at a particular time to provide the information the combat commander would need to make a decision on the next step in the campaign'. But this was a carefully pre-planned battle. And even there 'the speed with which it evolved overtook much of the planning that went into the concept'.

[24] J. Davis, *The Challenge of Opportunity Analysis* (Washington D.C.: Center for the Study of Intelligence (CIA), 1992), p. 6.

[25] Johnson, *America's Secret Power*, p. 82.

[26] In the recurrent debate about guiding science, Britain was about to establish a 'Technology Foresight Steering Group' in 1993 to apply 'a new technique, technology foresight [sic] . . . to identify key areas for investment'. *The Times*, 27 May 1993, p. 7.

praiseworthy attempt to impose some method on the confusion of war; but they cannot cope with serendipity and the unexpected. What users feel they want is always important, but ideally it should be the basis of a provider–user dialogue that develops ideas of what could be provided and what would be genuinely useful.

Other major limitations are bureaucratic, when specific needs are subsumed into multiple users' standing requirements. Something of this kind is no doubt needed. Yet codification has been described as producing 'nearly always either a wish list or an after-the-event description of an existing capability that just needs packaging'.[27] There is also the confusion between the intra-intelligence requirements that all-source analysts place on collectors and the extra-intelligence ones which the 'real', non-intelligence users place on the intelligence as a whole. Figure 17 shows (in a greatly simplified form) how collectors receive different kinds of requirements from different kinds of recipients. With many consumers there are the problems of consensus and accommodating everyone. Western community requirements in the Cold War tended to be exhortatory *tours d'horizon*; the KGB's annual directives bore some similarity.[28] Lists of requirements and priorities are essentially intelligence writing for itself, for external legitimation.[29] Talking to users about their problems is vital; yet formal community lists of subjects and priorities lose this whiff of reality. Few of them tell intelligence anything it does not know.

The main limitation is however that, even if well founded, requirements are no more than one factor in what actually happens.[30] Collection and subsequent analysis have to be optimized between competing demands. They depend on the *opportunities* presented by opponents' weaknesses and intelligence's own technical capabilities. Operational decisions balance user needs against professional estimates of costs and yields. Exploiting low priority, soft targets may be more cost-effective

---

[27] A. Katz, 'Technical Collection in the 1980s' in R. Godson (ed.), *Intelligence Requirements for the 1980s: Clandestine Collection* (Washington D.C.: National Strategy Information Center, 1982), p. 104.

[28] For Soviet examples see C. Andrew and O. Gordievsky, *Instructions from the Centre* (London: Hodder and Stoughton, 1991).

[29] Mainly within government, but exceptionally for public information; in Canada there have been public priorities in the form of National Requirements for Security Intelligence (L. Lustgarten and I. Leigh, *In from the Cold: National Security and Parliamentary Democracy* (Oxford: Clarendon Press, 1994), p. 390).

[30] Humint sometimes responds directly to specific requests for a 'single issue' agent, with access to particular bits of information in a particular place. But other agents are sought for more general and obvious reasons: penetrate the KGB or the Soviet General Staff anywhere you can.

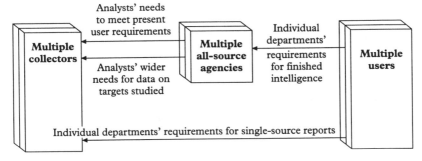

Figure 17 Complexity of 'requirements'

than tackling near-impossible, high priority ones.[31] Generalized priorities are only one factor in determining effectiveness.

There is also the technical need for indirect approaches; messages in low grade ciphers used by German dockyards and lightships in the Second World War were intercepted and exploited not for their intelligence yield but because they provided Bletchley with plain text 'cribs' for breaking into the high priority Enigma.[32] Sigint and other sources have to build up the many forms of their technical base, as an insurance against new needs. All this rules out a simplistic coupling between requirements with action, which is influenced fundamentally by what is possible.[33]

Results

The Church Committee's criticism about intelligence's nonconformity can therefore be turned on its head. The JIC argued about requirements in the Second World War, but always over specific issues of priority, as over the allocation of aerial photographic sorties. Wartime intelligence operated successfully without overarching national requirements and

---

[31] Hugh Alexander, the Bletchley Park cryptanalyst and chess player, used to explain that ciphers should not be attacked if there was zero probability *either* of technical success *or* of useful output coming from it. Imagery satellites similarly should not be programmed to take photographs of objects they cannot see or are not worth seeing.

[32] F. H. Hinsley with E. E. Thomas, C. F. G. Ransom and R. G. Knight, *British Intelligence in the Second World War* vol. I (London: HMSO, 1979), pp. 338–9.

[33] Compare with the differences in military doctrine between 'reconnaissance-push' attacks (in which the attacker follows any weaknesses he detects in attacking the enemy position) and 'command-push' ones (in which attacks take place in accordance with a tight plan). Intelligence penetrations necessarily accentuate the exploitation of weaknesses.

priorities systems;[34] the same was true of the Falklands War. Western problems after 1945 were not in choosing between different Soviet targets, but getting access to any of them.[35] The inspired US projects of U-2s and satellite collection owed nothing to formal requirements procedures,[36] and much the same applied to the Western harnessing of other technology to provide 'real-time' warning of Soviet military moves. The British intelligence community in the Cold War went at one stage for two or three years without formal requirements and priorities lists, without any discernible effects. The US system of having to quote requirements when asking for any service of intelligence added a bureaucratic layer to producer–consumer relationships. On the whole Soviet intelligence was even more requirements-driven than the West; like the rest of the Soviet state, it ran on requirements and production targets and no doubt on falsified statistics about meeting them.[37] In all, a requirements system necessarily lags behind reality and following it is no guarantee of success. 'We found no evidence that an intelligence failure could be attributed to a lack of requirements.'[38] They may still be helpful in their practical spin-offs in promoting practitioner–user discussion. But the main effects are confirmatory and legitimizing; and the use of requirements to drive the cycle is not notable in practice.[39]

This should not be a surprise; the same applies elsewhere, particularly to other information services. Everything needs machinery that seems to work 'properly'. 'Ceremonial criteria of worth and ceremonially derived production functions are useful to organizations: they legitimate

---

[34] The British JIC's overall 'Special Sub-Committee on Intelligence Priorities' was formed late in the war (May 1944), but with a view partly to post-war needs. Hinsley, *British Intelligence in the Second World War* vol. III part 1, p. 472.

[35] See requirements in R. Aldrich and M. Coleman, 'The Cold War, the JIC and British Signals Intelligence, 1948', *Intelligence and National Security* vol. 4 no. 3 (July 1989). These are comprehensive and unsurprising, as are the relative priorities between them.

[36] For the atmosphere see Berkowitz and Goodman, *Strategic Intelligence for American National Security*, pp. 51–3, and W. E. Burrows, *Deep Black: the Secrets of Space Espionage* (London: Bantam, 1988), chapters 3–4.

[37] See for example the KGB's annual directive to the London Residency in 1983, and the reports and correspondence on its work, in Andrew and Gordievsky, *Instructions from the Centre*, pp. 118–33.

[38] W. R. Harris, 'Collection in the Intelligence Process' in Godson (ed.), *Intelligence Requirements for the 1980s: Clandestine Collection*, p. 184, quoting from an official US report of 1966.

[39] See 'The Intelligence Cycle: A Checklist of What Can Go Wrong', Berkowitz and Goodman, *Strategic Intelligence for American National Security*, pp. 185–92. (But this list of failures still poses the question whether successes show any *better* correlation with the cycle.) For other criticism and reformulation of the cycle see A. S. Hulnick, 'The Intelligence Producer-Policy Consumer Linkage: A Theoretical Approach' in *Intelligence and National Security* vol. 1 no. 2 (May 1986); and his 'Controlling Intelligence Estimates' in G. P. Hastedt (ed.), *Controlling Intelligence* (London: Cass, 1991).

organizations with internal participants, stockholders, the public, and the state, as well as the Inland Revenue Service and the Securities Exchange Commission.'[40] Yet good management recognizes the risk of distancing itself from reality through formal control systems. Intelligence needs responsiveness and constant modification, and the military metaphor of the cycle brilliantly captures its need for adaptation and optimization; but not with *requirements* as the driving force. What, though, if intelligence is seen as the initiator, and the customer the reactor?

The real intelligence cycle

The cycle is a metaphor of a cybernetic system, in which a control unit 'senses' feedback and is programmed to make constant small adjustments of output, 'hunting' for the maximum desired feedback semi-automatically, without high-level decisions. The cat on the hearthrug shifts in its sleep, to get optimum stimulus from the fire, not too hot or too cold. A guided missile's sensors hunt for the radar echoes from its aircraft target, and the control unit then steers it to achieve a hit.

In the metaphor of the conventional military cycle the users are the control unit, constantly adapting their stated needs to optimize their intelligence inputs. For large-scale intelligence producers a more realistic version is as shown in figure 18; *they* are the driving force, hunting for feedback from users and using it to optimize output. An effective production unit is constantly exploring new subjects and experimenting with its forms of output in the search for what the Americans call 'tailored intelligence', geared to users' particular needs. The intelligence objective in this constant modification – akin to the cat's shifting on the hearthrug – is to maximize user satisfaction over the product received.

All this depends on feedback. User requirements may be incomplete or unreliable, but users have *reactions* (positive and negative) to what they get. They know if a report interests them or wastes their time. The remark attributed to Kissinger, that he did not know what intelligence he needed but recognized it when he saw it, sums up the position the user is often in. Intelligence seeks to provoke this feedback and develops the sensors to pick up and analyse it, rather as the missile's sensors seek and process its radar echoes.

This is the intelligence cycle adjusted, with intelligence as the controlling element and user reactions as its primary input. Seeking reactions

[40] J. W. Meyer and B. Rowan, 'Institutionalized Organizations: Formal Structure as Myth and Ceremony', *American Journal of Sociology* vol. 83 no. 2 (1977).

and optimizing them might seem to imply short-termism and 'intelligence to please', but the cycle metaphor allows for longer views. Missiles do not fly towards maximum radar returns, but are programmed to aim off to allow for the target aircraft's own movement before hitting it. Part of intelligence's imperative is to maximize user satisfaction years ahead, when long-term sources come on stream or unpopular lines of analysis turn out to be right.

To change the metaphor, this is the difference between an entrepreneurial market and a command economy driven by requirements and priorities.[41] (The entrepreneurial element is also implicit in intelligence's own jargon of 'production', 'the product' and 'the consumer'.) Intelligence in practice listens to what customers say, not to formal requirements. Its recipients are clients. Its aim is to 'sell' useful material.[42] The return is consumer satisfaction, given in return for its output. Efficient intelligence producers know their users and care about them, at all levels from desk officers upwards, in a way reminiscent of customer service in the private sector, where 'the excellent companies *really are* close to their customers . . . Other companies talk about it; the excellent companies do it.'[43] Customer contact is all-important for intelligence at every level – for its massive, desk-level outputs, just as for its special assessments at top levels.

Of course users' reactions and intelligence's search for them are not the only dynamic. Formal requirements are part of intelligence's background and establish its general territory; as such they demonstrate conformity with the legal mandate for what intelligence is authorized to do.[44] Where users have specific requirements on specific subjects these are important driving forces in their own right – if intelligence can do anything to meet them. In reality the cycle is driven by complex factors. Corporate information systems in private enterprise are said to be driven by mixtures of 'pushes' (data pushed to management by those who believe it will be useful to them) and 'pulls' (data requested by

---

[41] For the essence of markets see R. E. Lane, *The Market Experience* (Cambridge: Cambridge University Press, 1991), pp. 11–15.

[42] This aim of 'selling' knowledge applies mainly to foreign intelligence. Security intelligence, concerned with *detecting* espionage, subversion and terrorism, has different dynamics.

[43] For examples see T. J. Peters and R. H. Waterman, *In Search of Excellence* (New York: Harper and Row, 1982), chapter 6 ('Close to the Customer'), pp. 156–99.

[44] For example the new British Parliamentary Intelligence and Security Committee, examining the 'expenditure, administration and policy' of the intelligence and security agencies, is to be given access to the annual UK guidance on 'intelligence requirements'. (Lustgarten and Leigh, *In from the Cold*, p. 513.) The requirements are also submitted for approval by the Ministerial Committee on Intelligence Services.

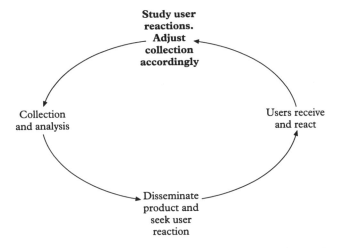

Figure 18 Intelligence cycle with intelligence as the driving force

managements themselves).[45] By analogy, there is the same mixture in the intelligence cycle.

Nevertheless, where large-scale intelligence production is involved, the 'push' factor has to be emphasized, together with the importance of seeking reactions rather than 'pulls'. Good intelligence agencies – especially the big ones – have many of the characteristics of entrepreneurs, 'pushing' to customers in ways that seek to optimize demand and approval from them. In this they are like CNN and Reuters.[46] Customers are reactors to masses of intelligence they receive, rather than simply 'requesters' of individual intelligence from scratch. This applies to the services of large-scale outputs from collection agencies to all-source analysts, as well as to their services to (non-intelligence) users proper. It would be tidier if all intelligence production were more precisely driven by users, but this is not how any knowledge system works. Monitoring formal lists of requirements may be necessary to demonstrate intelligence's legitimacy. But it is not the secret of effectiveness and efficiency.

As in other things, this does not make intelligence unique in public service. A 'market' for public bureaucracy as a whole was presented in W. A. Niskanen's writing in the 1970s about the relationship of non-profit-making 'Bureaus' (government agencies) and 'Sponsors'

---

[45] H. S. Rowen, *Reforming Intelligence: a Market Approach* (Washington D.C.: Consortium for the Study of Intelligence, 1993), pp. 7–8. For further reference to this 'market approach' see the following chapter.
[46] The analogy was suggested by Rowen, *Reforming Intelligence*, p. 8.

(customer departments), in a bilateral monopoly in which activity and output are offered in exchange for annual budgets. Sponsors depend on bureaus for the services they make available, and bureaus depend on sponsors for finance through annual appropriations or grants. Bureaus seek bigger budgets to improve services and grow, with the rewards of better careers, professional satisfaction, improved morale and ease of management. They have superior information and more incentive to expand than their sponsors have for reducing them. From this came a theory of public service over-supply.[47]

The argument is contentious, but has been influential in attitudes to other parts of the public sector; and it provides a disconcertingly plausible explanation for intelligence's growth over the last half-century. Intelligence's entrepreneurial dynamic keeps the system basically healthy, but arguably it also causes the problem of intelligence over-supply, particularly in single-source material on military subjects; a lesson drawn from the Gulf War was that 'without this distinction [between raw data and analysis of the adversary's intentions] the recipient will often be deluged with information that cannot usefully be employed'.[48] Customers rarely ask for these inputs to be cut off.

Hence large-scale intelligence needs an additional discipline for testing effectiveness and efficiency. The question thus arises whether it lends itself to the evaluation that would be applied to other production processes, particularly through the measurement of the product's cost and utility. This can now be considered.

Measurement

Intelligence's 'externals'

Management in the rest of modern society constantly seeks quantification. There are of course other, qualitative values, but these are 'soft' ones, difficult to measure ('the measurement of quantities and changes in quantities is easy compared with measurement of qualities');[49] hence the search for numbers. The modern approach to the public sector constantly emphasizes quantification and quantified targets, typically in 'value for money' studies of cost-effectiveness and cost-benefit. (Cost-effectiveness analysis measures inputs in money terms and outputs in

---

[47] W. A. Niskanen, *Bureaucracy and Representative Government* (Chicago: Aldine Atherton, 1971).

[48] J. McCausland, *The Gulf Conflict: a Military Analysis* (*Adelphi Paper* 282) (London: IISS/Brassey's, 1993), p. 57.

[49] M. Carley, *Rational Techniques in Policy Analysis* (London: Heinemann, 1980), p. 72.

'natural units'; full cost-benefit analysis measures both inputs and outputs in money terms.)[50]

Intelligence is in some ways well placed to respond. It has led in the use of computers in government, and one of the side-products is the scope they offer for quantitative information on the processes they serve. Computers in large-scale production processes generate their own statistics for immediate 'flow management' purposes. Intelligence outputs can be counted in units of individual reports, or pages, words, letters, 'groupage' in signals, electronic bits in computers and so on. Input resources of people, money and equipment are also measurable, and computers can collect and correlate data on inputs and outputs in more complex ways than were ever possible by old means. The management system of an imagery satellite, for example, can easily produce figures on images taken, those scanned by interpreters and final reports produced. Computers also produce statistics on subjects, since computer-countable 'tags' of subject-matter are added by report producers.[51] Electronic delivery times can be recorded. Intelligence agencies are in varied stages of computerization; but in principle they now have the information society's option of cheap and almost unlimited data about processes and output. Most important of all, individual outputs or lines of output can be costed.

Thus intelligence can be mapped in quantitative terms, and separate strands within it can be modelled like lines of factory inputs and outputs. It thus lends itself to 'information management', or 'the formal representation or modelling of information resources, events and flows', to evaluate its efficiency.[52] Investments in different parts of the process have always had to be kept in balance; at one time in the Korean War this was not done, and the effectiveness of a large tactical photo-reconnaissance collection effort was determined by the throughput of the four junior interpreters who were all that were available to analyse what it produced.[53] Modern technology makes the optimization of investments easier, enables productivity to be more easily measured, and makes it possible to compare items and lines of output for cost-

[50] S. Roberts and C. Pollitt, 'Audit or Evaluation: A National Audit Office VFM Study', *Public Administration* vol. 72 no. 4, p. 541.

[51] These 'tags' resemble the subject classifications that now appear in the 'Cataloguing in Publication' data at the beginning of books.

[52] B. Cronin, 'The Management of Intellectual Capital: From Texts to Markets' in B. Cronin (ed.), *Information Management: From Strategies to Action 2* (London: ASLIB, 1992), p. 3.

[53] A. Katz, 'Technical Collection in the 1980s' in Godson, *Intelligence Requirements for the 1980s: Clandestine Collection*, p. 105.

effectiveness. In translation, for example, costs can be established in total and per item, as can the effects of investing in computer support for translators' productivity.

These measurable outputs are intelligence's '*externals*'; for instance the numbers of photographs from an imagery satellite but not the information derived from them. Even as externals these have their limitations. Tracing the many separate strands of input to a substantial all-source report is like unravelling a cat's cradle of wool. Each form of intelligence generates its own individual units; there is no standard form of intelligence report to act as a standard unit. The totals of reports from source A cannot usefully be compared with those from source B of a different kind on a different subject. Some statistics are less precise than they look; for example the reports' subject tags have the vagueness about intelligence subjects discussed in chapter 3, and can produce statistics without much value. Statistics in any case just provide snapshots of the present with no allowance for the future.

Yet these limitations on externals resemble many production measurements elsewhere; there is never a perfect system of accountancy. Apportioning private sector costs between different products and common services is usually a matter of convention and argument. Measurement is never complete. All figures have systematic biases, but this does not stop managers from learning by comparing like with like. All firms have to guess about the future as well as measure the present. Processes like cultivating prospective agents or breaking ciphers have long lead times and uncertain prospects of success, but there is nothing unusual about this; pharmaceutical companies take ten years from initial research to marketing, and lose most of their products on the way. None of this invalidates intelligence's measurable externals *if* they provide some valid indicator of what is actually being produced, open to systematic evaluation.

Measuring content and effects

The real problems are twofold. In the first place intelligence's value to users obviously comes from its 'internals' or content and not from the measurable 'externals'; measurements are of the packages, not the contents. Counts of bits of data, numbers of words or totals of reports do not reflect the density or quality of information content; all intelligence involves gradations of 'rich' and 'poor' information. In the example already given, figures of translators' productivity are misleading without reference to their translations' quality.

Secondly there is the difficulty already discussed in chapter 8 of tying particular intelligence to particular governmental actions; effects are mainly through accretions and their general influence on preconceptions. Most intelligence effects are on users' frames of mind rather than on identifiable actions. Even where particular intelligence outputs can be correlated with use there is usually no obvious way of measuring effects on outcomes.

In these ways intelligence also has the characteristics of all information. 'Firstly, there is no agreed *quantum* or unit of information; it is not measured in gallons, pounds, or whatever . . . Secondly, there is no accepted performance standard (mpg: cups per pound).'[54] Information cannot be measured like the volume, chemical constituents and purity of oil. Where it is known to have been used it is difficult to be precise about cause-and-effect. Value in scientific research is sometimes assessed by 'citation analysis', or counting how many times a publication is cited in subsequent work by others. But even this (very rough) measure is not available in government, where policy papers do not systematically cite the intelligence reports that influence them.

This picture of imprecision can be modified for rather simple kinds of information and its effects. Information theory indeed measures the transmission of information and its distinction from noise. A recent study of battlefield information measures its effects: thus

The advantages of information manifest themselves rather abruptly. There is a threshold effect . . . Far below the threshold, changes in information production have little influence . . . The same is true far above the threshold. However, in the narrow region around the threshold, small increases in the information production rate cause major improvements in the exchange ratio [in attrition between two opposed forces] and in other measures of effectiveness.[55]

Quantified statements of this kind can sometimes be made about intelligence and outcomes. In the Second World War DF bearings on radio transmissions from U-boats in the Battle of the Atlantic were able to establish their locations with various areas of probability. The more bearings, the smaller the area in which the enemy had to be sought, the fewer aircraft and ships needed for search and the greater the probability of engagement. Here the intelligence might be quantified (as numbers and quality of bearings taken), as can the force-multiplication for users. Similarly one of the most effective but inconspicuous uses of Enigma decrypts was in enabling the RAF mining effort to be concentrated on the

---

[54] Cronin and Davenport, *Post-Professionalism: Transforming the Information Heartland*, p. 93.
[55] B. Conolly and J. G. Pierce, *Information Mechanics: Transformation of Information in Management, Control and Communication* (Chichester: Ellis Horwood, 1988), p. 164.

Germans' shipping channels, perhaps with a roughly calculable improvement to lethality compared with laying mines at random.[56]

But these are very limited treatments. Quantification in information theory applies only 'relative to some firmly circumscribed situations' like the difference between information and noise in electronic communications, or the bytes in computer memories.[57] The mathematical model just quoted of information's battlefield effects is built around relatively simple situations, and makes no allowances for varying kinds and qualities of intelligence content.

Thus information seems radically different from a measurable and consumable commodity like oil, with its quantifiable quality, output and consumption. 'Informatics' argues that information is 'slippery', hard to measure, and with revolutionary effects not captured in traditional cost-benefit analysis.[58] Van Crevald's study of military command reached a similar conclusion from the opposite direction; the formal hierarchy of US command in Vietnam had so much information going everywhere that it effectively throttled itself.[59] The importance of intelligence's forecasting compounds the difficulties. As for its use, no one ever really knows what difference information makes; 'the relationship between information and government has in recent years provided the focus for considerable debate.'[60] There is 'a rich diversity, both in the impact, and the sociopolitical implications, of information use'.[61]

Intelligence is therefore in a situation common within information services. A growing body of data of 'external' kinds is available about it, but the content defies systematic quantification. So do its use and effects. Yet for its large-scale, expensive production decisions managers search for something more than rule-of-thumb judgments.

---

[56] Hinsley, *British Intelligence in the Second World War* vol. II, pp. 196–9, 537–8.

[57] W. V. Quine, *Quiddities: An Intermittently Philosophical Dictionary* (London: Penguin, 1990), p. 103: 'How much information, true or false, novel or trite, have you gleaned since breakfast? Or since opening this book? The question is meaningless; we have defined no measure. Relative to some firmly circumscribed situations, however, Claud Shannon and Warren Weaver did define a measure of something they called information; such is their information theory. It has been prized by Bell Labs for its utility in communication projects.'

[58] For discussion see Cronin and Davenport, *Post-Professionalism: Transforming the Information Heartland*, 'Value Accounting', pp. 93–172.

[59] M. Van Crevald, *Command in War* (Cambridge, Mass.: Harvard University Press, 1985), pp. 232–60.

[60] R. Davidson and P. White (eds.), *Information and Government: Studies in the Dynamics of Policy-Making* (Edinburgh: Edinburgh University Press, 1988), Introduction, p. 1.

[61] Davidson and White, *Information and Government*, Introduction, p. 11.

Practical conclusions

Intelligence is bound to be influenced by the public administration setting in which it operates, and in which there have been extensive changes in English-speaking countries over the last fifteen years towards a style of a 'New Public Management' (NPM). Central assumptions there are that performance can be driven by targets and measured by quantified indicators; hence the bevy of British management audits, 'financial management initiatives', devolved agencies, simulated markets, 'market testing', privatization, performance pay for civil servants and so on.[62] The essence of the change is the belief that public administration can be seen as measurable provisions of goods or services. There is some academic scepticism about the whole concept; 'performance is a complex and contestable subject'.[63] Nevertheless countable costs, outputs and outcomes have become potent measures of governmental activity, even if incomplete ones.

Against this background some things can be emphasized about intelligence. First, it can in principle be costed, not merely in total but also individual lines of product. Modern intelligence has always had to think in terms of capital costs for new technical equipment, but was slower to cost particular activities and individual lines of output, particularly individuals' *time*. Costing of this kind brings a new dimension to intelligence's traditional decision-taking. With the rest of the public service thinking more systematically about costings, there is every reason for intelligence to move in the same direction.

Second, 'external' data about its outputs can provide some useful management information, even though the central issues of content and quality defy quantification. Counting the different categories of intelligence output provides some information about them. Many lines of reports are fairly stereotyped; changes in the volumes produced or resources involved are indicators of production successes or failures. Some features of effectiveness and efficiency can also be usefully expressed in terms of externals rather than content; thus timeliness of production and delivery can be measured precisely. Similarly investigating 'intelligence overload' starts with quantitative studies of the volumes being distributed and users' ability to cope with them.

---

[62] For accounts of NPM see R. A. W. Rhodes (ed.), 'The New Public Management', *Public Administration* vol. 69 no. 1 (spring 1991); and G. Drewy and T. Butcher, *The Civil Service Today* (Oxford: Blackwell, 1991 edition), chapters 10–12. It is discussed as a global trend in C. Hood, 'Contemporary Public Management: A New Global Paradigm?', *Public Policy and Administration* vol. 10 no. 2 (summer 1995).

[63] Carter, 'Learning to Measure Performance', p. 99.

The scope for quantification on peripheral and supporting activities is even greater than on central production. Comparative costing of supporting functions between different organizations has been one of the more illuminating tools in the pursuit of public service efficiency elsewhere; indeed a civil servant's book about waste in defence-supporting services was a catalyst for Civil Service reform in Britain.[64] Intelligence's support – the cost of the personnel branch or the car pool – lends itself to the same measurement and comparison as elsewhere.

Third, users can be encouraged to react in quantitative terms where they can. Annual reviews of intelligence budgets can seek quantified outcomes, however rough and illustrative, of intelligence's success and failure or even simply the cost of the government operations on which it has a bearing. National pay-offs from good negotiating intelligence can sometimes be expressed in cost-benefit terms, of 'saving the nation so-much a year' through helping to get advantageous terms. The direct and indirect costs of terrorism in Northern Ireland were estimated in the region of £3 billion annually, plus mainland costs; these figures gave some background to deciding what was worth spending on relevant intelligence projects.[65] Other, non-financial measures of use may sometimes be available. If indeed, as was claimed by the Director-General of the British Security Service in 1994, 'in Northern Ireland the security forces prevent four out of five terrorist attacks which are attempted', then there is a basis for a cost-effectiveness calculation about what intelligence 'bought' in those circumstances.[66] Intelligence failure can sometimes also be quantified; the 'failure' to provide warning of the Falklands invasion led to the cost of a new airfield and a permanent garrison, quite apart from the cost of the war itself.[67] Quantified relationships of these kinds between intelligence outputs and users' outcomes are bound to be

---

[64] L. Chapman, *Your Disobedient Servant* (London: Chatto and Windus, 1978).

[65] For example *The Independent*, 19 September 1994. Figures were quoted in 1992 as £650 million and £1 billion annually for the cost to the UK of garrisoning and policing Northern Ireland against terrorism. (N. Lydon, 'Ulster: An Issue Suppressed', *The Independent*, 4 March 1992.) A complete costing of the IRA campaign would also include compensation for damage in Northern Ireland and on the mainland, and extra mainland security costs.

[66] S. Rimington, *Security and Democracy – Is There a Conflict?* (Richard Dimbleby Lecture 1994) (London: BBC Educational Developments, 1994), p. 9. It has been suggested that in other public investments some rules of thumb have to be used about what it is worth spending to save a life. According to a London Underground safety specialist, up to £500,000 is spent without question to avoid even a small risk of a fatality; £2 million does not justify it automatically; between the two figures decisions depend on the circumstances and the risks (BBC broadcast, 27 October 1992).

[67] The capital costs arising out of the Falklands War were £2.6 billion by the end of financial year 1986–7, excluding the running costs of maintaining the garrison there (*The Times*, 28 January 1987).

rough; but they give some additional information on intelligence's order of importance.[68]

This is simply to suggest that seeking quantitative approaches – particularly costings – should be part of modern intelligence culture. But it is something to be developed inside it, not imposed ready-made from outside. To adapt Admiral Turner's metaphor of managing the intelligence octopus, the problem is encouraging the octopus to develop its own conscience about effectiveness and efficiency, seeking to deal in specific figures to test generalities. The answer lies in developing what Wildavsky described some years ago as the 'self-evaluative organization' whose spirit was 'infused with the evaluative ethic'.[69] In this context quantification has a part to play; though the attempt to travel in its direction is probably more important than arriving.

This will still leave intelligence hard to evaluate. Judgments about it as an activity will still be largely unquantifiable. This may be unsatisfactory if disciplines are sought for it comparable to those applied to other parts of public service, and it may therefore be tempting to impose a more radical solution. If large-scale intelligence has an entrepreneurial character, should investments in it not be determined simply by an 'intelligence market', similarly to those that have featured elsewhere in NPM? This possibility can be examined in the next chapter.

Summary

Much modern intelligence is a large-scale production machine. In parallel with the search for quality, it needs 'production' management, as for a high-technology factory. In the direction of this effort individual user 'requirements' are valuable, but have limitations; while generalized requirements as formal, community-wide directives are largely legitimation devices. The metaphor of the 'intelligence cycle' helps to explain the system's search for effectiveness, provided that the professional initiative of the intelligence unit is recognized as the critical factor. Rather than simply responding to requirements, effective intelligence actively seeks users' reactions to current services, adjusts coverage and forms of

---

[68] For an operational research study of British anti-drug smuggling operations, including the role of 'drug intelligence' within them, see J. A. Clark and C. J. Sanctuary, 'Anti-Drug Smuggling Operational Research in HM Customs and Excise', *Public Administration* vol. 70 no. 4. The conclusion is that 'performance measurement [of intelligence] is rather more difficult . . . However these problems can be overstated; it is generally possible to identify cases whose success is dependent on intelligence.' (pp. 587–8.)

[69] A. Wildavsky, 'The Self-Evaluative Organization', *Public Administration Review* 32 (September/October 1972), p. 511.

output accordingly, and plans its own strategy for the future. Large-scale intelligence has the entrepreneurial quality of directing production to maximize user satisfaction – in the future as well as the present

In seeking efficiency to this end much of intelligence's product can be costed, and its 'external' features quantified. But the 'internal' information content generally defies measurement, as do its effects upon users' action. There is no 'scientific' way of assessing intelligence's value. Nevertheless costings and quantified data about externals provide some information with a bearing on efficiency within intelligence itself. Furthermore users can sometimes quote orders of cost for intelligence's effects (and its failures), or for the scale of the policy problems on which it bears.

17   Managing the community

The last chapter considered what drives intelligence and how far it lends itself to measurement, and suggests some general assumptions for managers seeking its effectiveness and efficiency. This chapter discusses management at the level of the intelligence community as a whole. Chapter 18 looks at management at the individual agency level.

The community has already been discussed (chapter 15) as the means of producing interdepartmental assessments. But it also produces problems of resource allocation, common standards and community projects, the orchestration of different kinds of collection on the same targets, developing responses to new community-wide problems and projects, and so on. In addition governments need to decide on overall intelligence budgets. How to provide strategies, direction and advice to government on such issues is the subject of this chapter.

The problem is orchestrating intelligence's fairly loose communities. Two approaches are considered. One is to introduce 'market-like' disciplines, so that problems of strategy and resource allocation are solved by 'user choice'. The other is to increase central authority, preferably linked with budget processes.

The consensus community

The community is charged not only with assessment but also with the responsibility already quoted for 'the organization and working of British intelligence activity as a whole at home and overseas in order to ensure efficiency, economy and prompt adaptation to changing requirements' – words little changed from the Committee's pre-Second World War foundations.[1] The DCI has a similar formal role within the US community, including budgetary responsibility for the National Foreign Intelligence Program.[2]

---

[1] *Central Intelligence Machinery* (London: HMSO, 1993), p. 23.
[2] See for example Presidential Executive Order 12333, 4 December 1981, 1.5(g).

But the community is still a loose one managerially. Earlier we noted its fuzzy boundaries and tactical offshoots. Even the main, central community is far from being a monolith. Its membership is more like an association of independents than the sub-units of a single national intelligence service. The important entity is the individual department or agency. We noted for example how these usually conduct overseas relationships direct with foreign opposite numbers, not through any central machinery. The centre has only intermittent influence on what goes on in the outfield.

This might seem at variance with the success of the UK–US–Commonwealth communities in producing national assessments, yet is in fact consistent with it. Despite central leadership, interdepartmental assessments are made by equal participants, as recognized in US departments' ability to 'take a footnote' and the British search for consensus. Since producing assessments has been the community's most constant activity it is not surprising that its management role is influenced by its negotiating, consensus-seeking nature.

The results are reflected partly in agencies' attitudes of mind but also in the limits on central institutional power. Admittedly the DCI has a nominal Presidential-like authority over the US community; but in practice his authority is circumscribed by the Department of Defense (DoD)'s responsibility for five out of every six dollars spent on intelligence, particularly on the big Sigint and imagery collectors.[3] 'The DCI continues to be essentially a titular leader of the twelve large and several smaller agencies that make up "the community".'[4] The DCI's roles as the President's chief intelligence assessor and Director of CIA also distract him from community management. William Colby, writing with frankness of his time in the post, emphasized the office-holder's need 'to be able to speak with conviction not only when he presents the opening intelligence assessment at NSC meetings . . . but also when he has to defend it against a Kissinger or a Schlesinger challenge in the ensuing discussion.'[5] Colby described the challenge: ' . . . what I saw as the most important job ahead of me, becoming confident that I, as DCI, was the best informed intelligence officer in the government about every one of the major substantive problems that confronted the policy officers I was supposed to assist.'[6] Hence current events, briefings, reading and substantive assessment are major preoccupations, and management is

---

[3] J. H. Hedley, *Checklist for the Future of Intelligence* (Georgetown: Institute for the Study of Diplomacy, 1995), p. 3.

[4] L. K. Johnson, 'Smart Intelligence', *Foreign Policy* no. 89 (winter 1992–3), p. 65.

[5] W. Colby, *Honourable Men* (London: Hutchinson, 1978), p. 373.

[6] Colby, *Honourable Men*, p. 352.

secondary. Colby says that the substantive intelligence commitment 'requires that he [the DCI] be helped by having as many as possible of his remaining jobs done by deputies and other subordinates'.[7] The DCI is 'a juggler of many different things at one time . . . But my main point is that his responsibility for substantive intelligence is the most important thing he is charged with.'[8]

These limitations on central power also apply in Britain. The JIC's managerial responsibilities are those of a committee, a corporate body managing itself under a chairman. Foreign Office chairmanship was instituted in 1939, but without any financial responsibilities – which are what really count in peacetime, though not in war. We saw in chapter 2 that, despite the remit in 1939 to consider 'any further measures . . . to improve the efficient working of the intelligence organization of the country as a whole', the wartime view was that, as a sub-committee of the military Chiefs of Staff, the JIC should not sort out the problems of the civilian agencies; and something of this view was carried over into peacetime. The Chairman has taken responsibility for proper intelligence assessment of all the available data, but not to the same extent for managing the machine that collects it. The Intelligence Coordinator, whose post was instituted on a part-time basis in 1968, 'advises the Secretary of the Cabinet on the co-ordination of the intelligence machinery and its resources and programmes. He has particular responsibility for reviewing the United Kingdom's intelligence require-ments and for advising on the allocation of resources to enable the Agencies to meet them.'[9] Coordination and advice loom large in his responsibilities.[10] Secretaries of the Cabinet have often taken a special interest in intelligence matters, but no one in Britain has ever had even the DCI's titular position of intelligence supremo. The independence of US military intelligence also now has an echo in the position of British defence intelligence. The DIS is managed as 'an integrated part of the Ministry of Defence' rather than by any community authority, with only the loosest integration into the overall intelligence budget; and the same applies to MoD-controlled collection, particularly to the important imagery interpretation at JARIC.[11]

Yet effective intelligence is an inter-agency business. Collectors and all-source analysts need each other. Even in collection, Humint helps Sigint to acquire cryptanalytic knowledge, and close access bugging and

---

[7] Colby, *Honourable Men*, p. 372.
[8] Colby, *Honourable Men*, p. 372.
[9] *Central Intelligence Machinery*, p. 12.
[10] Now, it is reported, with a status and pay-scale below that of some Heads of Agencies.
[11] *Central Intelligence Machinery*, pp. 17, 21.

eavesdropping is a tangle of overlapping jurisdictions. US satellite collection similarly overlaps Sigint and imagery compartments, while the reports of Cold War cable-tapping imply a mixture of underwater, clandestine and Sigint disciplines. Considering the individual agency's need to fight its own corner, the surprising thing is not inter-agency rivalry and friction, but the extent of cooperation across organizational boundaries.

This is by no means unique. Studies of public administration for big undertakings such as education and health describe the way in which independent institutions cooperate to provide complex public services. Professional cultures mix cooperation with rivalry. Institutions work together with tacit understandings about keeping off each others' turf and forming common cause against outsiders.[12]

Thus loose communities do not necessarily mean ineffectiveness. The divided power in the US system between the DCI and the DoD reflects intelligence's inherent duality between military and non-military elements.[13] The JIC reflects the British culture of committee government. Both systems have infinitely more cooperation within them than existed within or between the apparently more unitary KGB and GRU. The intense inter-agency competition of US intelligence did not preclude – and may indeed have assisted – its technical achievements during the Cold War. 'Turf fights' between front offices coexist with unspectacular backroom cooperation.

But this is not quite enough. The community needs its overall strategies; if individual agencies need ten-year forward plans, so should the community. Even in shorter terms, resource allocation needs to be optimized between the community's separate parts; a system that just reacts to agencies' bids favours big and powerful activities against new or weak ones. Hence the greater attention in the Cold War to resources for collection than for all-source analysis; Britain does not have machinery for optimizing the allocation of resources between the secret agencies on the one hand and the all-source DIS on the other. Other big problems cut across institutional boundaries and need a community-wide perspective. IRA terrorism from 1969 onwards presented long-standing organizational problems for the British community, and it took twenty years from the first bomb in Britain to resolve (in 1992) the divided

---

[12] For a discussion of the combination of close working connections with organizational fragmentation in mental health and education, see J. W. Meyer, 'Institutional and Organizational Rationalization in the Mental Health System', *American Behavioural Scientist* vol. 28 no. 5 (May/June 1985).

[13] E. R. May, 'Intelligence: Backing into the Future', *Foreign Affairs* vol. 71 no. 3 (summer 1992).

responsibilities of the Security Service and the Metropolitan Police Special Branch for coordinating intelligence on IRA threats on the mainland.[14] Even after that aspect of intelligence on the IRA had been settled a former Prime Minister advocated the need for a more centralized effort; 'there is not one EC country that has succeeded in defeating terrorism without first establishing a proper, national central agency.'[15] His solution may not have been the right one, but it pointed to the need for a continual, dispassionate review of the machinery from above. Sometimes the centre needs to recognize and solve problems by something more than community consensus.

This applies particularly where new technology cuts across established boundaries. Getting an efficient information handling system so that computers in different agencies can be linked with each other needs supra-agency planning and direction, not just a club of agencies looking after their own immediate interests. On a larger scale, European powers wrestled throughout the 1980s with deciding whether to have intelligence satellites, independently or in collaboration, and of what kind. Britain had its schemes for a purely national Sigint satellite, subsequently cancelled according to the then Chancellor of the Exchequer on grounds of inordinate expense.[16] France opted for its own imagery vehicle; Germany originally decided against joining the French programme but may recently have joined in a new venture of some kind.[17] All needed (and need) educated central views for these issues; the choices were (and are) too big to be based just on agency bids.

Loose communities are not good at tackling these difficult, cross-agency issues. The British Intelligence Coordinator's position has echoes of an Oxford Head of College: a determined and knowledgeable incumbent has considerable influence and can achieve a lot, but the *modus operandi* tends to require carrying independent-minded colleagues with him. Perhaps the same applies to the DCI's relationship with the DoD agencies. Something needs to be added; but what?

---

[14] S. Rimington, Richard Dimbleby Lecture, *Security and Democracy* (London: BBC Educational Developments, 1994), p. 8.

[15] Sir Edward Heath, 'Outflank the IRA Bombers', *The Times*, 10 June 1993.

[16] N. Lawson, *The View from No. 11: Memoirs of a Tory Radical* (London: Corgi edition, 1993), p. 314. A report in P. Chilton, O. Nassauer, D. Plesch, J. Patten (Whitaker), *NATO, Peacekeeping, and the United Nations* (London: British–American Security Information Council, 1994), p. 55, gives details of current French developments and claims that Germany has now agreed to pay up to 20 per cent of the cost of a Helios 2 system. France is also said to be procuring a signals intelligence satellite; at the time of the first generation Helios launch it was reported that an accompanying satellite would 'monitor radio transmissions' (*The Times*, 8 July 1995).

[17] P. Chilton, 'French Policy on Peacekeeping', *Brassey's Defence Yearbook 1995* (London: Brassey's, 1995), p. 149.

An intelligence market

One solution might be to build on the cost consciousness just advocated and create a genuine 'intelligence market', in which user feedback and demand would shape resource allocation directly through the allocation of money. There is the right-wing view that central planning is always wrong; better leave things to the market. An intelligence market would supersede the need for central planning. Espionage agencies have always paid agents and informers, sometimes as a symbol of the relationship but often as a genuine monetary transaction between buyer and seller; why not generalize the habit and arrange for intelligence customers to pay for what they eventually receive? Agencies seek user satisfaction; users in a market would indicate this through specific financial transfers to 'buy' intelligence supplies. The best output, greatest efficiency and most attractive plans would get the rewards of the market-place, and customers would for the first time have to think deeply about their needs now and in the future. This is how services of area studies, risk assessments and weather forecasts are organized for the private sector, and there is no *a priori* reason why it should not apply to government intelligence.

Indeed NPM has a spectrum of devices for introducing these private sector disciplines to the public sector. At the 'hard' end is complete privatization. Not far from it is the mandatory contracting-out of particular functions from within departments, as in the 1993–4 British 'market testing' exercise to contract out significant Civil Service segments. Another variant is converting departments into official trading entities, encouraged to sell their output to private buyers, with genuine profits and losses.[18] The 'soft' end includes the drive for more general use of external contractors, 'performance pay' and contracts within the public service, and delegated financial responsibility; thus even British Armed Forces' units now have substantial local budgets and delegated authority to spend them.[19] These soft end devices involve less direct marketization. Nevertheless across the spectrum there are the common themes of breaking producer–user monopolies and encouraging users to make market-like decisions. If these can be made to apply to other bits of government, why not to intelligence?

The application of the extremes can be disposed of briefly. At the hard

---

[18] On the pattern established some years ago for the Royal Mint, and an objective for other departments in the British 'Next Steps' initiative.

[19] D. Omand, 'Towards a New Management Strategy for Defence', *RUSI Journal* vol. 134 no. 3 (August 1989).

end, complete privatization of intelligence would have bizarre and unacceptable results. Sensitive operations need political accountability and supervision, and governments would not sell off their espionage agencies to private buyers, or even to management buy-outs by their employees. Agencies with public trading status, obliged to market their product to private users – or even foreign states – seem almost as unlikely, though CIA now publishes unclassified work. International intelligence collaboration is indeed based on bargains, but not with agencies acting as free enterprise mercenaries.

As for the less extreme devices, intelligence has long used external contractors for some purposes. US contractors operate important facilities and make extensive inputs to analysis; while everywhere (including Britain) intelligence depends on industry for much of its technological hardware and software. Despite security constraints, Britain is now reported to be making more use of contracting-out. There may also be things to be learned from NPM's trends in contract employment, though intelligence still needs a stable workforce (see next chapter). But this 'soft' marketization is imitating markets, not creating them.

We therefore concentrate on the most plausible variant of a proper market: a simulated one between official intelligence providers and receivers, using the data on output that can be captured through intelligence's electronic dissemination. Users would 'pay' for the lines of output received and contract to get lines in the future. These contracts would be funded out of users' own (expanded) budgets and would form the basis of intelligence's financial provision. Intelligence output would have this (simulated) financial value. Out of what was available, users would get what they really wanted. The demand for intelligence would compete with other ways of spending the money. Intelligence would cease to be a free good.

A simulated market of this kind now operates in supplier–user contracts throughout the British National Health Service (NHS) in which it has been said that 'money follows the patients'.[20] Other parts of British government service have similar 'markets' for official providers and users of such diverse services as recruitment, training and the provision of stationery.[21] None of this has yet been applied to intelligence,

---

[20] For a critique see M. Moran, 'Explaining Change in the National Health Service', *Public Policy and Administration* vol. 10 no. 2 (summer 1995).

[21] For a closer parallel with intelligence, see the British Meteorological Office's 1990 report; there was to be a study of making the cost of Ministry of Defence user requirements (for the armed forces) into a direct charge against users' budgets. (*Meteorological Office Executive Agency Framework Document*, April 1990; Ministry of Defence issue.)

though the idea has occasionally been aired by US commentators.[22] If it can be applied elsewhere, why not there as well?

Two applications can be distinguished. One would be to provide better, demand-driven cutting of the cake between agencies within an overall intelligence budget. The NHS market does not determine the total budget, but distributes it, rewarding successful institutions and penalizing failure. The other would be to use the market to solve the different problem of what to spend on intelligence in total. In Britain the PSIS already 'scrutinises the Agencies' expenditure forecasts and management plans as part of the Public Expenditure Survey arrangements'.[23] But a market would make both the cutting of the cake and the overall total far more directly user-driven. We concentrate here on a market for determining the overall intelligence budget. Applying it to cake-cutting raises the same issues on different scales.

Markets' limitations

The whole idea of simulated markets can be criticized; a British Chancellor of the Exchequer described them in the 1980s as 'playing at shops'.[24] They lack the bottom lines of real markets, and it can be argued that the accountancy developed to simulate them multiplies the complexity of the command economy they are trying to avoid. For intelligence, we have already seen the special problems of measuring content and use, but there are similar problems about measuring numbers of users. An intelligence report is not a discrete item of service given only once to a single unique user. Most intelligence has wide distributions, with multiple primary and secondary recipients, all of whom would presumably 'pay' varying amounts for it. Some recipients themselves reproduce and disseminate the intelligence they receive; a logical consequence of a market might be a recipients' black market.

There is also the overlapping of producers and users. Single-source collectors have producer–customer relationships with the all-source agencies they supply, yet the latter exist to produce finished intelligence for the real, non-intelligence users. Logically 'payments' would cascade

---

[22] W. R. Harris, 'Collection in the Intelligence Process' in R. Godson (ed.), *Intelligence Requirements for the 1980s: Clandestine Collection* (Washington D.C.: National Strategy Information Center, 1982), pp. 161–95; and H. S. Rowen, *Reforming Intelligence: a Market Approach* (Washington D.C.: Consortium for the Study of Intelligence, 1993).

[23] *Central Intelligence Machinery*, p. 17.

[24] Private occasion. For a more general criticism see B. J. O'Toole, 'The Loss of Purity: the Corruption of Public Service in Britain', *Public Policy and Administration* vol. 8 no. 2 (summer 1993).

down from these ultimate users to the all-source agencies, who would then 'pay' collectors after taking their cut. But the market would also have to provide for collectors' direct services to the 'real' users and their lateral services to each other. There would be the further problem of apportioning credits for interdepartmental assessments (such as NIEs and JIC output) among the many sources contributing to them. Apart from being an accountants' bonanza, the system would probably end up as a mass of costing conventions that negated the vitality of a true market.

There are other more fundamental problems. What intelligence collection can provide depends on its contest with its targets' defensive measures; the element of unpredictability does not lend itself to contracts to provide particular lines of information. As for users' market decisions, the previous chapter discussed their variabilities over recognizing their information needs. If money was involved departments might think harder but would seek to get others to pay; no one who has seen British departments arguing about how the costs of the BBC Monitoring Service should be split between them has much faith in an information market. In any case proper user decisions between intelligence and other information would logically mean costing these other sources; the Diplomatic Service's telegrams would need to be provided on the same market basis as similar political intelligence obtained by covert means.

The general peacetime effect would probably be for users to take short-term views, economizing on the insurance offered by intelligence warning. Crises and war by contrast would dramatically increase demand, giving intelligence a boom-and-bust quality resembling oil futures in the Gulf War. The main peacetime effect would be an uneven relationship; users might feel they could get by without intelligence, while intelligence could not survive at all without them.

Intelligence effects

It would thus be an imperfect, volatile market. The most likely effect would be a depressed intelligence economy, in which short-term considerations would tell against long-term ones. Warning surveillance and the capability for wartime use would tend to be squeezed out; in peacetime the armed forces still tend to prefer guns to classified data. The market would make it even harder for the community to operate *qua* community than now. 'Market failure' might come to be added to the other causes of intelligence failure.

And yet: intelligence suffers from being a free good. Paradoxically this produces a need to 'empower users' as has been cogently argued by the recent US advocate of market-like approaches.[25] Empowerment in this sense would make for more involved and discriminating consumers, better at discussing their needs with providers and making better use of what they get.[26] It would also check the over-supply of single-source material. Intelligence's own search for feedback concentrates attention on highlights and away from the low value material that clogs the system; without a market there is more incentive to increase services than to prune them. A market would raise consumers' thresholds. All-source analysts would be encouraged to use commercial data bases and open sources in a better balance with secret ones. A more rational investment strategy might result in more support for the valuable activities of the BBC Monitoring Service and its US equivalent. Despite political controversy about the pseudo-market in the British NHS, few would deny that it has had invigorating effects.

Nevertheless the practical effect of an intelligence market would be to create a bureaucratic monstrosity. Probably the most that can be done is to ensure that annual scrutiny of intelligence budgets is supported by statements of the quantities of reports received by users and their unit costs. As concluded in the last chapter, quantification of such kinds provides useful additional information. But decisions about how much to spend on intelligence are bound to be the same as other spending decisions: in the last resort, matters of informed guesswork.

Central management

Thus strategy cannot be left to a market; some supervision is needed. There is scope for stronger user representation in the official management boards that exist for some kinds of intelligence. The United States has had a variety of advisory boards from the President's Foreign Intelligence Board downwards. Britain had a nominal supervisory body (the Secret Service Committee) in the 1920s, presumably the ancestor of the modern Permanent Secretaries' Committee on the Intelligence Services (PSIS) which annually scrutinizes intelligence budgets.[27] Below the community-wide level, the Second World War saw reasonably successful

---

[25] Rowen, *Reforming Intelligence*, p. 11.

[26] Including better use of modern IT within their departments. A comment by a British FCO official in 1991 on his department's management – that 'The main blot is IT. Our approach appears antediluvian. We are being left behind' – was particularly relevant to its handling of intelligence material (R. Tomkys, 'The Financial Management Initiative in the FCO', *Public Administration* vol. 69 no. 2 (summer 1991), p. 263).

[27] Hinsley, *British Intelligence in the Second World War* vol. I, pp. 17–19, 50; (with Simkins) vol. IV (London: HMSO, 1990), pp. 6–9.

arrangements for inter-service control of Sigint (the 'Y Board', generally outside the JIC's purview) and imagery.[28] But a separate committee for the coordination of the Security Service and SIS (the Secret Service Co-ordinating Committee) established in 1942 was ineffectual and lapsed.[29] And there is a general peacetime tendency for intelligence boards of management to become formal, rubber-stamping bodies.

Thus the key to supervision lies in central intelligence machinery rather than in individual boards. Central management needs power with some influence through budgets and patronage. Some of this is already in place. The DCI's titular responsibilities are considerable, even though they are difficult to exercise *vis-à-vis* the DoD-controlled and financed agencies since he 'controls only a fraction of its [the community's] budget and appoints none of the chiefs of the agencies that comprise it'.[30] Within the British community the Intelligence Coordinator has the influence already described, and also conducts preliminary scrutinies of intelligence budgets for the PSIS.[31] Yet in both countries the question remains: who is managerially responsible for intelligence as a whole or for the effectiveness of inter-agency working? The problems of managing the community are a microcosm of managing defence, and lessons can be learned from a digression on central power there.

Central management in defence

Edmonds has written that central defence machinery and overall defence budgeting are 'a relatively new phenomenon in the experience of modern government'.[32] Nevertheless armed force has gradually come to be perceived as a unity, rather than separate land, maritime and air power. The emergence of British and US machinery for overall defence policy in the Second World War has already been mentioned in chapter 2's account of the origins of the JIC and other national assessment. The search for adequate defence arrangements continued after 1945. One issue was the right balance between single-service organization and more integrated defence; another was whether integration should be sought through inter-service cooperation and committees, or through the position of individuals.

---

[28] For the control of Sigint see Hinsley, *British Intelligence in the Second World War* vol. I, pp. 267–74; and imagery, vol. I, pp. 279–82, and vol. II, pp. 34–9.

[29] Hinsley and Simkins, *British Intelligence in the Second World War* vol. IV, pp. 174–5, 187.

[30] Hedley, *Checklist for the Future of Intelligence*, p. 2.

[31] *Central Intelligence Machinery*, p. 17.

[32] M. Edmonds, *Armed Services and Society* (Leicester: Leicester University Press, 1988), p. 173.

In Britain there was general agreement about inter-service 'jointery', as expressed in the foundation of the Joint Services Staff College 'to nourish and to disseminate among the higher commanders of all services and their staffs that mutual understanding and inter-service comradeship in arms which, in war, were the very basis of our success'.[33] 'Jointery' took a committee style derived from the top; the Chiefs of Staff were still a committee of equals supported mainly by single-service staffs. But critics saw joint-service committees as a means of striking bargains between single-service interests, and from the 1960s onwards there was a trend towards central machinery driven by individuals, not committees. In Britain the powers of the Secretary of State for Defence and the professional Chief of Defence Staff (CDS) grew, at the expense of the Chiefs of Staffs' Committee and its members' position as professional heads of service. In this the Mountbatten reorganization of 1964 was a landmark, as were the further ones of 1982 and 1985. Despite the British liking for committees, power shifted towards central individuals and staffs reporting only to them. 'CDS was to be the principal military adviser to the Government in his own right, and not just as Chairman of the Chiefs of Staff Committee.'[34]

US power evolved in the same direction. After the independence of the individual services came the growing power of the DoD and the Joint Chiefs of Staff (JCS) collectively. Chairmanship of the JCS evolved from a position of *primus inter pares* to become the personal link between professional forces and political leadership, as demonstrated by the role of General Powell in the Gulf War; General Schwarzkopf wrote that he was 'virtually my sole point of contact with the Administration'.[35] Less is now said in both countries about defence 'coordination' and 'collective advice', and more about personal roles and responsibility.

Making these institutional changes work has depended partly on modifying the single-service culture. Single-service tribalism in Britain was modified by inter-service training and postings; exposure to other services became part of the curriculum vitae for making it to the top.[36] Despite greater inter-service rivalry, something of the same has happened

---

[33] Chiefs of Staff message on its foundation in 1947; in General Sir William Jackson and Lord Bramall, *The Chiefs: the Story of the United Kingdom Chiefs of Staff* (London: Brassey's, 1992), p. 462.

[34] The history of the British evolution is set out in Jackson and Bramall, *The Chiefs*; quotation from p. 400.

[35] H. N. Schwarzkopf, *It Doesn't Take a Hero* (London: Bantam, 1992), p. 325.

[36] For an endorsement of 'jointery' in defence see (for example) the Ismay–Jacob report of 1962 (Jackson and Bramall, *The Chiefs*, p. 338).

in the United States.[37] But change has owed most to the creation of effective central staffs taking over single-service functions, a development turning *au fond* on motivation and rewards. People will not perform 'nationally' in central staffs if their career prospects still depend on their parent services.[38] Central staffs have had to become metaphorically 'purple-suited', discarding their mental uniforms, and the most important factor in progress towards this has been 'the centre's' recent influence in senior promotions. Below the very top level, services have had to accustom themselves to tri-service commanders; the British commander in the Gulf War has noted that 'tri-service command is a peculiar art, difficult to manage until one is used to it' and needs 'a combination of tact and firmness'.[39]

Parallels with intelligence

The intelligence community is in rather the same situation as defence was about thirty years ago. The DCI is like the JCS Chairmen who could not effectively override individual services. In the British case, the JIC has a distinguished history in collective assessment. But in its managerial role it resembles the US Chiefs of Staff thirty years ago, not obtruding regularly on single-agency autonomy. Effective central management needs more than a committee. Arguably Britain needs someone on managerial intelligence issues who is in the position of defence's modern CDS, advised by a committee but with personal responsibility. At a lower, regional level an effective single chief of intelligence is sometimes needed, for example for anti-terrorist intelligence in Northern Ireland, or as was the practice in the British decolonization campaigns overseas.

There may therefore be some scope for institutional changes along the lines of those in defence. Congressional proposals were put forward in

---

[37] For Schwarzkopf's appointment to the (largely naval) Pacific Command and contact with the Navy in the invasion of Grenada, see *It Doesn't Take a Hero*, pp. 217–21, 246–58. (The encounters were not particularly amicable, but seem to have advanced his career.)

[38] As expressed by Marshal of the Royal Air Force Lord Cameron in talking of advice from central staffs: 'I think some of these people will be looking over their shoulders knowing that they will be returning to the Royal Air Force one day and they will be waiting for the sort of "terrible fate" which is likely to befall them if they have "spoken badly" (to use a Foreign Office expression) against their own service.' (House of Commons, Third Report of Defence Committee 1983–4, *Ministry of Defence Reorganisation*, evidence 19 July 1984, question 41.) For the establishment of a central Senior Appointments Committee, see Jackson and Bramall, *The Chiefs*, p. 400.

[39] Sir Peter de la Billière, *Storm Command: a Personal Account of the Gulf War* (London: HarperCollins, 1993), p. 57.

1992 for making the DCI a genuine overlord, no longer tied to his departmental base as Director of CIA.[40] In Britain it is possible – and has indeed once occurred, with considerable success – for the Intelligence Coordinator to be combined with JIC Chairmanship. But permanent changes of this sort would create problems as well as solving them. If the DCI were made an overlord, and no longer also Director of CIA, he would lack a power base. It is difficult to see the US system breaking the budgetary link between the DoD and the big collection agencies. Permanently combining the roles of JIC Chairman and Coordinator in Britain would reproduce the DCI's problem of being simultaneously chief intelligence assessor and chief manager. In both democracies there are instinctive aversions to over-powerful Chiefs of Intelligence.

The immediately practical course may be to learn defence's lesson about the importance of central staffs. In their different ways both the US DCI and the British Coordinator depend for effectiveness on adequate staff support. Only an intelligence staff of the right size and competence can provide them with independent central fact-finding and evaluation for big and contentious issues of management, particularly the complex, high technology projects. In the United States there was recurrent criticism of the central Intelligence Community Staff and its ability to take on the agencies, and a new Community Management Staff was created in its place.[41] The British Coordinator has never had more than a tiny staff, even though his influence depends on the amount of information available to him. On their very different scales both communities could ensure that the central staffs match the need for central management. This does not point to creating an intelligence equivalent of the Soviet General Staff, but to some modest central increases, at least in Britain.

This provision of more staff support for central management could be combined with strengthening the community's cohesion in another way: through an increased 'community' approach to intelligence careers. Peacetime intelligence practitioners are now career people in their own agencies, rather as military people used to spend all their time in their own services. The Americans and British both lack community career planning that would give promising officers the experience of working in

---

[40] Described in D. L. Boren, 'The Intelligence Community: How Crucial', *Foreign Affairs* vol. 71 no. 3 (summer 1992).

[41] 'The evolution of the Intelligence Community Staff . . . had reflected a series of lost battles between the Director of Central Intelligence and the Secretary of Defence.' (B. D. Berkowitz and A. E. Goodman, *Strategic Intelligence for American National Security* (Princeton: Princeton University Press, 1989), p. 44.)

other agencies. (Britain's DIS gives its officers some experience of non-intelligence appointments, but interchanges with the collectors would be equally profitable, perhaps more so.) There is a similar absence of community training. The United States has large-scale training at the Joint Military Intelligence College and in CIA's Center for the Study of Intelligence, but it has no *community* institution; one of the best US investments for the future might be to create a genuine community staff college, combining the two and bringing civilians and military together. British intelligence is too small for training on that scale, but it could afford some systematic cross-postings.

This point bears on producing agency leaders as well as members of central staffs. Half a century of professional intelligence in peacetime has produced sets of agencies without much inside knowledge of each other. The community would benefit from some provision for future leaders at agency level with multi-agency experience. This need for broader professionalism applies even more to the central top management posts. In the USA it is now some time since the DCI post was filled by an intelligence professional, and indeed it has recently seemed difficult to fill the position at all. In Britain one of the arguments against a unified British intelligence service in the 1920s was that it would be difficult to find anyone capable of running it,[42] and there is still no system for preparing future central managers. Nothing was more impressive in the Congressional hearings on Gates's appointment as DCI than Admiral Inman's testimony that, when Deputy DCI, 'I became persuaded that there was a major responsibility to spot talent and move it fast along to provide leadership for the Intelligence Community', instead of leaving the succession to the whims of the US political system.[43] But this community-oriented view of career planning and professionalism seems exceptional.

Clearly the centre must not seek to do too much. The analogy with defence can be extended to a recent comment about the British CDS's current authority: though he 'must rightly have the ultimate responsibility for advising the Government on military policy', he 'is not there to ride roughshod over them [his professional colleagues], but rather to provide the central dynamic'.[44] Welding all intelligence into a unified national intelligence agency is no more a feasible objective than the idea of a single defence force, discredited by the unsuccessful Canadian

---

[42] Hinsley, *British Intelligence in the Second World War* vol. I, p. 19.
[43] Senate Select Committee on Intelligence *Hearings on Nomination of Robert M. Gates to be DCI* vol. I (Washington D.C.: US GPO, 1992), p. 926.
[44] Jackson and Bramall, *The Chiefs*, pp. 447, 449.

example. As in large business conglomerates, a delicate balance is needed between the independence of operating units and the need for some corporate strategy and planning. Successful firms go to great lengths to combat over-centralization.

The suggestions made here for central staff support and career planning may therefore be practical and unspectacular (though slow) ways of building up the intelligence equivalent of the 'central dynamic' in defence, without centralizing too much. But there is still the question whether they go far enough. Despite the many diverse activities encompassed within the intelligence community, modern intelligence power has a unitary quality resembling that of military power. Another analogy can be drawn with large business enterprises: however extensive, complex and dispersed these may be, ultimate responsibility for success and failure is vested somewhere at the top of the organization. It is difficult to see why the same should not apply to intelligence. Both Britain and the United States, in their different ways, may need to acclimatize themselves to the concept of an intelligence Chief Executive.

Summary

The intelligence community is attuned to seeking consensus; though this is right for assessment, it is not enough for community management. In the United States the DCI has nominal power, but only limited actual control over the DoD-funded agencies which make up most of the community; in any case his primary commitment is as the President's chief intelligence officer. In Britain the Intelligence Coordinator works in the committee ambience of the JIC, through influence rather than executive responsibility. For big questions of interdepartmental strategy (such as satellite policy or integrated IT) something more is needed.

It is tempting to create an intelligence market to determine resources and resource allocations. Something can be done to focus attention on quantities and unit costs of output, as background to intelligence's budgetary process; users could be encouraged to decide whether they were getting too much intelligence or too little, especially by comparison with what is available from modern non-intelligence sources. But a comprehensive market would be far too complicated; and would do nothing to create community strategy.

Some strengthening of central management is therefore needed. In both Britain and the United States practical steps would be to strengthen the staff support for the Coordinator and the DCI, and at the same time to promote 'community-mindedness' through programmes of inter-agency exchanges, training and career development. But both countries may need to go further, and recognize the question about the professional direction of the community as a whole: in managerial terms, who's in charge?

18   The agency manager

Important as the centre is, success and failure still depend mainly on how individual agencies are managed. Modern management theory tends to emphasize 'informal', 'organic' styles and structures, and points to questions of 'organizational culture' and management 'style'. Some of it also takes a 'contingency' view of organization and management: that the optimum form depends on the nature of the job, the workforce, the environment and the organizational culture.[1] This chapter first considers these factors in intelligence, and whether they pose special challenges and point to particular solutions. It then discusses the implications for management and offers some conclusions.

Obviously these are generalizations about diverse operations. More weight is given here to big, technical collection and processing than to what are still the smaller activities. But the impact of technology is increasing the 'production' element. In any case intelligence as a whole has some distinctive characteristics, and conclusions drawn from the big organizations apply in some degree to all of it.

Work and skills

Large-scale processing was discussed earlier. Bletchley's production line built up around cipher-breaking machines set a pattern. The Second World War also saw the introduction of large-scale data-handling and indexing, applying *en masse* the techniques of individual scholarship.[2] Subsequently the power of computers has given a further impetus towards man–machine interaction. Intelligence resources now need to be described in terms of computer power as well as staff numbers.

This has not reduced individual skills. Intelligence has always had its special aptitudes and techniques: the flair and linguistic skill of

---

[1] For summary see G. Morgan, *Images of Organization* (London: Sage, 1986), pp. 54–69.
[2] For Yale-inspired indexing in OSS, see R. Winks, *Cloak and Gown: Scholars in America's Secret War* (London: Collins, 1987), pp. 96–110.

eighteenth-century decipherers, the dissimulation of spies, the relentless-ness of interrogators. The First World War brought the new crafts of radio interception, traffic analysis and photo interpretation but did not supersede the old ones. In a 1947 lecture R. V. Jones described the variety of Second World War collection as follows:

There were thousands of them [sources]: secret agents at Peenemünde, in the German night-fighter control rooms and on the flying bomb sites; photographic reconnaissance pilots travelling thousands of miles alone above Germany or diving down for a perilous oblique; girls in remote huts listening to German night-fighter radio-telephony; photographic interpreters ruining their eyesight through poring over photographs; aircrews in radio reconnaissance aircraft patrolling alone in the German night-fighter belt; technical officers sieving the earth around crashed German bombers trying to read the vital clue and trying to read the burnt documents; and many others.[3]

The responsibility resting on individuals is illustrated in his cautionary tale of misidentifying German missiles as sludge pumps, 'a theory perhaps coloured by the [photo] interpreter's previous experience as an engineer with a river Catchment Board'.[4]

Modern intelligence production still needs individuals' problem-solving skills plus flair, as in some radio operators' knack of identifying weak signals and plucking them out of the ether. Moreover there is a need for constant adaptability. Intelligence has to follow its targets' activities, security measures and technical changes. It is reactive and opportunistic; it has to run hard to keep up.

Despite all this change, it also has its elements of regular, stable intelligence production, for example when substantial resources are employed to monitor military targets in peacetime as precautions against surprise attack. The lower parts of the organizational hierarchy have large elements of routine. Handling large-scale, low-grade evidence depends on *method*; as said in an earlier chapter, a good sign of an office's quality is the state of its indexes. Surveillance needs patience and reliability; the escape of German battleships up the English Channel in February 1942 came from fallible British surveillance routines.[5] The intelligence–security war is one of discipline and attrition, as well as blitzkriegs based on initiatives and breakthroughs.

Thus individual skills are important but set within a teamwork typical

[3] R. V. Jones, 'Scientific Intelligence', *RUSI Journal* vol. 92 no. 567 (August 1947), pp. 352–69.
[4] R.V. Jones, *Most Secret War: British Scientific Intelligence 1939–1945* (London: Hamish Hamilton, 1978), pp. 339–40. See also pp. 132–4, 189–90.
[5] Details in F. H. Hinsley with E. E. Thomas, C. F. G. Ransom and R. C. Knight, *British Intelligence in the Second World War* vol. II (London: HMSO, 1981), pp. 185–7.

of the information society. 'It is not enough for the knowledge worker to apply his or her knowledge. The knowledge must be applied so that it redounds to joint performance . . . By itself, specialized knowledge has no results unless it focuses on the needs and goals of the entire organization.'[6] Likewise intelligence depends on motivation, organization and management.

People

Intelligence's diversity of skills is matched by the diversity of its employees' abilities and rewards. Agencies need their top-class brains, but also many more journeymen and supporters. They have ceased to have just the two Edwardian classes of 'officers' and 'clerks', and are broad-based pyramids. At all levels there is the normal quota of those rising and those at their ceilings, and of saints and sinners. The human texture on which management operates is generally unremarkable.

The great change after 1945 was for intelligence to become both a large-scale and a lifetime employer. Technical collection's special skills have come to be developed by early recruitment and subsequent apprenticeship, no longer by the use of gifted amateurs or those on short-term secondments. Even Humint – the least technological form of collection – now has its highly developed tradecraft; accounts of the thorough KGB training reflect the career professionalism of both sides.[7] Skills have been diversified with the growing importance of scientists, engineers, systems analysis and computer programmers, and the need for maintainers of technical equipment, computer operators, printing shop operators, secretaries, filing clerks, security guards and the other trades and supporting staff typical of large organizations. Agencies have their own hierarchies for particular specialist skills, and their elaborate codifications of pay and conditions of service. Intelligence has acquired the characteristics of large Weberian bureaucracies, modified but not submerged by the growth of computerization.[8]

This makes for the workforce's stability as single-agency employees; even in the United States there is less mobility than might be expected, either between intelligence agencies or in and out of other professions. The most specialized trades have no transferability, and even the practitioners with marketable technological or linguistic skills tend to have long-term intelligence careers. Agencies need stable workforces

---

[6] P. F. Drucker, *The New Realities* (London: Mandarin edition, 1990), pp. 90–1.
[7] For example, V. Kuzichkin, *Inside the KGB: Myth and Reality* (London: Deutsch, 1990).
[8] For Weber and theories of bureaucracy, see Morgan, *Images of Organization*, pp. 24–5.

to develop what management jargon would call their 'firm-specific competences': 'the ability to do useful and difficult things better than their competitors.'[9] Turnover also increases security risks and the costs of security vetting and specialized training. People feel that secrecy makes it hard for them to compete elsewhere, even with apparently transferable skills; most of them feel themselves to have become intelligence specialists of some kind. Even by the traditional standards of public bureaucracies, there is little interchange with other intelligence agencies or non-intelligence departments.

Of course there is still the turnover usual in junior grades everywhere; there are 'second career' people like retired servicemen; and the military components have their own secondments and shorter-term engagements. Intelligence is not completely insulated from the labour market, particularly when 'system management' and other computer skills are in demand elsewhere. Nevertheless it is an unusually long-term, single-agency occupation, and a lifetime placement for key civilians. It has little of the mobility said to be part of modern knowledge work. 'Knowledge now has become the real capital of a developed economy. Knowledge workers know that their knowledge . . . gives them the freedom to move.'[10] 'For all these people, the institution they work in is not primary; their knowledge, their craft is.'[11] In intelligence the reverse applies, with the important factor being the institution. Once variegated and colourful bunches brought together temporarily by war-work, its practitioners now form permanent, closely-knit groups of specialists. In Britain the attempts to reduce the permanency of Civil Service employment have not yet had much effect on the intelligence agencies.

Occupational stability of this kind does something to shape a characteristic professional temperament. Practitioners are normal people living normal lives. Professor Watt's verdict that 'It is the nature of intelligence work to attract men of unusual strength of personal convictions, exceptionally resistant to the normal pressures of social and political conformism and governed by their own highly personal sets of hates, abhorrences and taboos' is surely coloured by wartime and immediate post-war experience.[12] Peacetime reality is less colourful.

But his picture is not altogether unrecognizable, though reality has

---

[9] K. Pavitt, 'Key Characteristics of the Large Innovating Firm', *British Journal of Management* vol. 2 no. 1 (1991), p. 42.

[10] Drucker, *The New Realities*, p. 174.

[11] Drucker, *The New Realities*, p. 175.

[12] D. C. Watt, *How War Came: the Immediate Origins of the Second World War, 1938–1939* (New York: Pantheon, 1989), p. 104.

softer colours. Natural talent for the skills of collecting information, solving puzzles and analysing data puts some emphasis on perfectionism, a certain propensity to argue, a degree of stubborn individualism and an occasional disregard for practicality. In those devoting themselves to understanding their targets and their information defences there has to be some of what C. P. Snow described as good scientists' 'trace of the obsessional'.[13] The stereotype of the researcher seems less out of place in intelligence than among public service's decision-takers and executive agencies.

Environment

Targets and events provide constant change, though with some stable elements. Competition between the agency and other intelligence and non-intelligence sources is a further stimulus to flexibility. But the wider environment of the public service as a whole emphasizes stability. Being a part of government bureaucracy has put premiums on intelligence's order and predictability. Treasury controls over spending impose widespread constraints: being found departing from proper financial procedures is particularly bad news for intelligence, with its inherited reputation for uncontrolled expenditure on secret projects. The same applies to the control of politically sensitive activities. Intelligence's safeguards against political disasters like the affair of Commander Crabb are clear procedures and hierarchies of authorization, and clear accountability if things go wrong.[14]

There is also the pervasive influence of security defences against the hostile intelligence penetration discussed in chapter 10. Personnel security has its set definitions of the conduct and character that constitute 'security risks', and its procedures for vetting, recruitment and investigation; and there are all the other features of secrecy. Current espionage threats – or the need to guard against them in the future – are likely to stay part of intelligence's external environment. As a whole, then, security reinforces formal organization against loose structures and easy information flows.

---

[13] See C. P. Snow, *Science and Government* (London: Oxford University Press, 1961), p. 72.

[14] Crabb was lost while diving under a Soviet cruiser in Portsmouth in 1956. A Prime Ministerial statement of 4 May recorded that 'what was done was without the authority or the knowledge of Her Majesty's Ministers. Appropriate disciplinary steps are being taken.' (N. West, *The Friends: Britain's Post-War Secret Intelligence Operations* (London: Coronet, 1990), pp. 109–18.)

Organizational culture

'Organizations are mini-societies that have their own distinctive patterns of culture and subculture.'[15] These are the set of important under- standings (often unstated) that members share. The factors just described help to produce intelligence's organizational culture. Agencies have their own self-images and characteristic ways of presenting them- selves to the world. Some also contain their own subcultures, particularly those 'in the field', or at 'outstations' away from headquarters. Military intelligence has the wider general-purpose military ethos. We saw earlier that security intelligence has some traits of detecting and policing. With all these differences, there is no homogeneous intelligence culture. But three complementary features can be identified in most of the community.

One is a greater-than-usual sense of *difference* from other walks of life. Intelligence's identity is based on its separation from decision-taking and action. Lifetime careers institutionalize the gap. Intelligence feels itself in a constant struggle to be appreciated by 'the outside world', sometimes with some embattlement – typically in a common sentiment that 'if only "they" would stop interfering and take more notice of the intelligence we send them.'

The sense of difference is partly in pursuing knowledge, not action. The biblical 'And Ye shall know the truth and the truth shall make you free' on the CIA building sums up part of the ethos, as does the common dictum of 'telling the truth as it is'. Agencies' folk-memories are rich in accounts of practitioners who stood out against prevailing wisdom, to be proved right eventually.

Enacted myths also include heroic intellectual efforts with a touch of academic eccentricity. The description of a US cryptanalyst in the run-up to the Battle of Midway typifies part of the puzzle-solver's role model:

Under his arm was his old lunch box. His uniform looked as though he had slept in it for three days. He had. He was unshaven and his hair looked as though it had not been cut for a month. It had not. His eyes were bloodshot from lack of sleep, and his gait betrayed how close he was to utter exhaustion.[16]

'Difference' comes out similarly in Churchill's often-repeated comment on visiting wartime Bletchley: 'I told you to leave no stone unturned in

---

[15] Morgan, *Images of Organization*, p. 121.
[16] R. Lewis, *The American Magic: Codes, Ciphers and the Defeat of Japan* (London: Penguin, 1983), p. 107.

finding the staff you needed, but did not expect you to take me so literally' – probably myth, but still repeated with a relish that reveals something of the Bletchley legacy to its successors' self-image. In the same way the Security Commission's report in 1983 on Prime's espionage in GCHQ noted that his oddities did not attract suspicion there, since 'because of the nature of GCHQ's work and their need for staff with esoteric specialisms, they attracted many odd and eccentric characters'.[17]

A second recurrent feature is the sense of *mission*. This comes partly from the record of wartime success, perpetuated by the crucial role of intelligence in the Cold War, counter-terrorism and elsewhere. Wartime memories have a deep influence and intensify professional enthusiasm.[18] The intelligence psyche has powerful images of giving warnings and saving lives (though not of killing opponents). Love of country has been a powerful driving force; the memoir of a much-respected British intelligence leader brings out 'a sturdy, if unobtrusive patriotism'.[19] Feelings about 'serving the country' in national security matters run deeper than if intelligence were just the production of useful knowledge such as domestic national statistics, however important these are. The most impressive thing about US technical practitioners in the Cold War was that they really felt that the safety of the free world depended on them. Patriotism nowadays merges into wider ideas of public service, and serving international justice, peace and order.[20] Practitioners feel that, whatever the merits of particular national policies, their role in producing accurate intelligence on the whole makes for a better world.

But feelings of difference and mission are not unique to intelligence. Organizations everywhere prize (and exaggerate) their own individuality and achievements. Feelings of working for the public good are common to most of government. Intelligence's third and most special feature is that difference and mission are multiplied by *secrecy*. This gives an extra dimension to being 'special', in the eyes of both intelligence and the

---

[17] Cmnd 8876, *Report of the Security Commission May 1983* (London: HMSO, 1983), paragraph 6.14.

[18] Speaking on the insatiable appetite for intelligence and the size of the Soviet targets, a Sigint briefer during the Cold War commented to a visiting diplomat that 'Of course in an ideal world we would have unlimited resources.' 'Is that really your idea of an ideal world?' asked the diplomat.

[19] R. Deacon, *'C': a Biography of Sir Maurice Oldfield* (London: Futura, 1985), p. 261.

[20] For the public service ethos, see B. J. O'Toole, 'T. H. Green and the Ethics of Senior Officials in British Central Government', *Public Administration* vol. 68 no. 3 (autumn 1990), p. 345; and R. A. Chapman, 'The Role of the Civil Service: a Traditional View in a Period of Change', *Public Policy and Administration* vol. 10 no. 2 (summer 1995).

public. Most other professions have secrecy about specific cases. Intelligence on the other hand has habitually concealed everything about itself, including overall numbers, organization, funding and sometimes its existence. The newcomer goes through his novitiate in a secret society, with its secret knowledge and special rituals and obligations. He joins a world of special 'indoctrinations' and codewords, and knowledge compartments within compartments. Communications are by special, secure networks. The office is guarded, sometimes literally as well as figuratively 'behind the wire'. Rooms are 'swept' for electronic devices, and the newcomer is forbidden to discuss classified matters at lunchtime, off-duty or on the open phone. There are strict end-of-day routines of locking up papers and destroying waste paper.

These are all institutionalized barriers between the secret society and what it sometimes calls the 'outside world'; this half-conscious prison metaphor reflects a wry professional pride in secrecy. A retired senior civil servant, writing of the anonymity of normal Whitehall work, described the 'thrill of non-recognition, a particular instance of the general feeling that it is better to be a grey eminence than no eminence at all'.[21] Secrecy raises this to the greater power of *mystery*.

Mystery reinforces security disciplines, but is also a psychological defence against the secret society's frustrations. The work has to be kept from families and friends, as sometimes has the mere fact of intelligence duties. Practitioners develop habits of social reticence. There are standards of private conduct and belief, reinforced by investigations during periodic security clearances. Spouses may be held to be security risks, as may friends. There is an obligation to note and report unusual behaviour by colleagues, and there are limitations on individuals' privacy such as exit searches, restrictions on foreign holidays and notification of visits to psychiatrists. No work can be taken home – not an unmitigated disadvantage, but an unusual one. Some obligations are lifelong, not lapsing with retirement.

None of this is unique. The public sector has many other secrets, and private organizations now have to take their own precautions against industrial espionage, bugging and computer fraud, hacking and viruses. The modern information economy increases the importance of secrecy. Intelligence's social conformity has parallels in William Whyte's description thirty-five years ago of Organization Man in large corporations.[22]

[21] D. Johnstone, *The Middle of Whitehall* (Bath: Bath University Centre for Fiscal Studies, 1984), p. 24.
[22] W. H. Whyte, *The Organization Man* (New York: Simon and Schuster, 1956).

Some theorists use metaphors of all human organizations as 'psychic prisons' and instruments of domination.[23]

Intelligence's secrecy also has fewer practical effects than one might expect; human nature – and the urge to get jobs done well, despite security regulations – is resilient and resourceful. Information defies the bulkheads designed to prevent it flowing around the organization; office grapevines are particularly active since practitioners are expert at drawing big inferences from small details. As a group they are not notably inhibited or straitlaced; they and their families usually take secrecy in its stride. The Cold War practitioner was indeed obscurely flattered to know that he was the KGB's highest priority target.

Nevertheless there is something special about secrecy's intensity and duration, and its strain does sometimes manifest itself, typically in the newly-joined or nervous. Intelligence's mystique may therefore have therapeutic functions through the group bonding it provides. The German sociologist Georg Simmel described the thrill of shared secrets, compensating for secret society's effect of distancing its members from the rest of society. 'The secret society compensates for the separating factor inherent in every secret by the single fact that it is a *society*.'[24] Rituals of entry add to the intensity. 'The strongly emphasized exclusion of all outsiders makes for a correspondingly strong feeling of possession.'[25] Mutual dependence 'ties every single member with incomparable closeness to the group'.[26]

Simmel's analysis rings true for intelligence. Secrecy adds a cachet to the necessity of being different. Americans who have passed the polygraph examination report the emancipating feeling of becoming full members of the group. Policy-makers regard covert intelligence as a faintly disreputable activity but nevertheless one that merits curiosity and respect. Practitioners hint at deep mysteries beneath sober exteriors, and are supported in this by spy fiction and media attention to intelligence, intensified by governments' own emphasis on its special status.

Simmel's analysis also brings out the power of the group. The priesthood of those 'in the club' – the intelligence jargon – derives from the organization. In return they show a greater-than-usual personal commitment to it. Despite everyday grumbling, practitioners are believers in the organization and what it does. They also bring Weberian ideals of fairness and predictability to their expectations of how it will treat them.

[23] Morgan, *Images of Organization*, pp. 199–231, 273–319.
[24] K. H. Wolfe (ed.), *The Sociology of Georg Simmel* (Glencoe, Ill.: The Free Press, 1950), p. 356.
[25] Wolfe, *The Sociology of Georg Simmel*, p. 332.
[26] Wolfe, *The Sociology of Georg Simmel*, p. 351.

In this way the organizational culture gives management a credit balance of high morale. Its actions can multiply the account, or cause it to run dramatically into the red.

Management in action

This then is the distinctive context of jobs, people, environment and organizational culture in which agency management has to work. The picture has rather greater implications for management than R. V. Jones's minimalist view of it in the Second World War: 'intelligence depends more than anything on individual minds and on individual courage, and your organization should only provide a smooth background on which they can operate.'[27] Perhaps management was always rather more than that; certainly it is now more proactive in the big modern agencies. Managing them is much like managing other organizations of comparable size and composition, and most of the doctrine about good practice applies as much to intelligence as elsewhere. Nevertheless, management style needs to reflect its distinctive features. The implications can be considered here.

Forms of organization

Where responding to change is crucial, success needs forms of organization that promote information flow. Private sector firms in rapidly changing environments succeed because they are better at learning and applying information than their competitors. They have such features as 'flat' structures, project teams, matrix responsibilities, and fluidity and apparent untidiness. 'Horizontal communications, across-functional boundaries, flexibility in the definition of tasks, links with outside sources of expertise and with users, and with the authority and experience of responsible managers, are all factors that influence a successful implementation, in addition to the quality and competence of R and D and related technological activities.'[28] On the other hand more formal, functionally-based structures suit large-scale production, with stable markets and technology and emphasis on service and cost-cutting.

Intelligence's environment has its large element of change; coping with constant modifications in its targets' defences is rather like dealing with competition and market changes in a volatile private sector. The need for

---

[27] Jones, 'Scientific Intelligence', p. 365.
[28] Pavitt, 'Key Characteristics of the Large Innovating Firm', p. 43, summarizing the research of the 1960s and 1970s.

flexibility, opportunism and entrepreneurial drive would seem to point it towards 'open', 'informal' organization and the features that go with it. But there is the security requirement for limiting, not encouraging, the spread of information inside the organization; and there are also operational pulls in the formal, hierarchical direction. The attack on German machine ciphers in the Second World War had to be carried out centrally, with tight control of radio interception by many hundreds of radio operators at widely dispersed locations. There is frequent criticism of the peacetime habit of checking draft intelligence reports at successive layers of management, each re-editing and 'improving' them, but there is a well-founded urge to maintain high standards. Political sensitivity likewise requires tight control over some kinds of operation. In the private sector it may be true that 'the management task becomes one of nurturing good tries, allowing modest failures, labelling experiments after the fact as successes, leading the cheers, and quietly guiding the diffusion process.'[29] But intelligence has a deep professional perfectionism and fear of failure, and rightly so.

So there are varied pressures on its forms of organization, as is not unusual; no organization can be fashioned from a single template. The innovative firm needs 'organizational forms that reconcile both the decentralization required for effective implementation, and the centralization required for the exploitation of core technologies'.[30] One knack of management is to know what to devolve and what to control; Peters and Waterman describe this as a 'loose–tight' feature of successful private sector managements.[31] Intelligence needs the same. Bletchley Park in the Second World War managed to combine organizational fluidity and an apparently anarchic disregard for hierarchy with success in getting its key areas under firm control.[32]

Nevertheless intelligence needs a general organizational philosophy of some kind. Its military origins and influence, its bureaucratic setting and the effects of security have inclined it in peacetime to favour formal

---

[29] T. J. Peters and R. H. Waterman, *The Pursuit of Excellence* (New York: Harper and Row, 1982), pp. 149–50.
[30] Pavitt, 'Key Characteristics of the Large Innovating Firm', p. 48.
[31] Peters and Waterman, *The Pursuit of Excellence*, pp. 318–25.
[32] As was illustrated by the achievements of Eric Jones (later Sir Eric Jones, Director GCHQ) as Head of Hut 3, in getting a grip on the direction of its operations. (W. Millward, 'Life In and Out of Hut 3' in F. H. Hinsley and A. Stripp, *Codebreakers: the Inside Story of Bletchley Park* (Oxford: Oxford University Press, 1993), p. 26. For tributes to Jones in other authors' recollections see pp. 31, 72, 96.) For a general discussion of strong administration and creative anarchy at Bletchley, see F. H. Hinsley with E. E. Thomas, C. F. G. Ransom and R. C. Knight, *British Intelligence in the Second World War* vol. I (London: HMSO, 1979), pp. 273–4.

styles. Yet there is the critical importance of reacting to opportunities and change, and welding diverse skills together into 'horizontal', project-like strands of innovation and production. Britain also has its own particular challenge of bridging the gaps between arts and science education in an increasingly technological business. For all these reasons management should probably give the benefit of the doubt to informal and fluid organization rather than traditional formality, in the same spirit as the trend elsewhere in public administration. Secret agencies need some organizational restlessness.

The self-critical organization

Compared with other public institutions intelligence is insulated from external criticism. Its production processes have no clear yardsticks of efficiency (though close relationships with foreign opposite numbers sometimes provide very useful comparisons). Its organizational culture produces high morale, but with it the danger of collective self-satisfaction; the feeling of being 'special' is liable to produce the 'not invented here' reaction to ideas from outside. Intelligence's need to sell itself to its clients brings the risk that it persuades itself about its own virtues. What Snow called the 'euphoria of secrecy' can produce a 'can do' optimism about its ability to carry things through.[33]

This is not unique to intelligence. Advocating greater openness within British industry as the antidote to complacency, Sir John Harvey-Jones remarked that

Argument will only actually grow in a large organization if it is actually encouraged, and if the example is given from the top of courteous listening and praise for differences of view . . . We have to have a far greater tolerance of difference and a far greater respect for differences of view. It is not easy in a country as hierarchically inclined as ours to continually question authority in a constructive way. It requires a lot of faith to believe that such questioning will actually be recognized, liked and rewarded.[34]

Secrecy increases the risk of pulling up the mental drawbridge. Hence a corollary of the secret environment is that intelligence organizations have

---

[33] For 'euphoria of secrecy' see Snow, *Science and Government*, pp. 68, 72. See also G. Howe, *Conflict of Loyalty* (London: Macmillan, 1994), pp. 338–48 for his reflections about planning the ban on national trade unions at GCHQ without prior consultation. 'This was our fundamental mistake . . . We had got used to thinking it in secret, because we had been dealing with a topic where secrecy had been, quite properly, the habit' (pp. 343–4).

[34] J. Harvey-Jones, *Making It Happen: Reflections on Leadership* (London: Collins, 1988), pp. 88–9.

to work quite hard at absorbing new ideas from outside, and creating open, constructively critical atmospheres inside themselves.

Management and 'human relations'

The 'human relations' school became in vogue in management theory some thirty years ago, and is still widely quoted.[35] All managements still use the cliché that 'people are our greatest resource'. Excellent private sector managements 'create environments in which people can blossom, develop self-esteem, and otherwise be excited participants in business and society as a whole'.[36]

Intelligence's people are central to its success and failure. Despite high technology, most of its money still goes on salaries. Human factors can produce dramatic increases in its productivity or make operations almost completely unproductive. It can absorb current thinking about the human factor, but with some modifications.

Thus since the 1960s the then prevalent ideas of 'human relations' in management have undergone some criticism, and have moved into a no-nonsense phase, typified by Robert Townsend's early recommendation in *Up the Organisation* that the route to business efficiency was to 'fire the whole personnel department'.[37] 'Value for money' has been the watch-word of British governments' reform of public administration in the 1980s and 1990s. This emphasizes individual targets and performance pay, with a shift away from what a Director-General of the Royal Institute of Public Administration described – perhaps unfairly – as 'a soft and sentimental view of "people management" in the civil service, rampant in the extravagant 'seventies'.[38] 'Safe', 'cushioned' public service jobs have been seen as the enemy of efficiency. 'Empowerment' of individuals to make their maximum contributions is now the watch-word, with performance pay and other carrots and sticks brought in from the private sector. There is a difference between these values and those in the older, more paternalistic style of managerial doctrine.

Clearly intelligence can learn something from the modern trend; but there are some factors in it which point to respect for the old style of being a 'good employer', the phrase used in the past for standards in the British public service. Intelligence has to be concerned with care for its

---

[35] For a summary (and criticism) see C. Perrow, *Complex Organizations: a Critical Essay* (Glenview, Ill.: Scott, Foresman and Co., 1972), chapter 4.

[36] Peters and Waterman, *The Pursuit of Excellence*, p. 86.

[37] R. Townsend, *Up the Organisation* (London: Michael Joseph, 1970), p. 134.

[38] W. Plowden, 'What Prospects for the Civil Service?', *Public Administration* vol. 63 no. 4 (winter 1985), p. 409.

staff, and not just the encouragement of talent. It is committed to having a long-term, permanent workforce, without much hiring and firing. Secrecy promotes high morale but adds a degree of intensity and fragility to it. In the slightly hot-house atmosphere of secret organizations, intelligence practitioners tend to expect idealized behaviour from their managements, and reality can produce strong reactions.[39] Unlike occupations with more mobility, intelligence is committed to keeping most of its problem cases and taking care of them.

This springs not only from common humanity but also from its special vulnerability. The classic target for agent recruitment during the Cold War was the discontented intelligence employee.[40] Restless employees in the private sector can always try their luck with the competitors, and even within other parts of the public service there is usually some mobility for changing scene; but for intelligence staff there are fewer escape routes. Hence management in the Cold War always had to have at the back of its mind the threat of betrayal from inside. Peter Wright's book about his career in the British Security Service showed how, even well short of espionage, an embittered former employee can wreak considerable revenge as a whistle-blower.[41] Even though the espionage threat has now declined (though not disappeared), there is still the media industry of seeking leaks and disclosures. As far as can be foreseen intelligence will have to maintain some special secrecy to protect its sources and methods.

This has some implications for its management style. The serious Security Service case of Bettaney's attempt as a counterespionage officer to offer his services to the KGB provoked quite savage criticism by the Security Commission of that service's management.[42] The Commission stressed the need for open management styles; 'the very fact of the Service's comparative isolation makes it all the more important that those responsible at the higher levels of management should maintain a self-critical attitude and be constantly alert to the need to keep the Service's organization, practices and procedures under review.'[43] There has

---

[39] Feelings of injustice about his pension were a significant element in Peter Wright's publication of *Spycatcher*; see note 41 below. For the unexpected reaction of some specialists to the banning of national trade unions at GCHQ in 1984, see M. E. Herman, 'GCHQ De-Unionisation 1984', *Public Policy and Administration* vol. 8 no. 2 (summer 1993), p. 78.

[40] Like Prime, whose offer to spy for the USSR while in the RAF was precipitated by a mixture of ideology and resentment.

[41] P. Wright, *Spycatcher: the Candid Autobiography of a Senior Intelligence Officer* (New York: Viking, 1987).

[42] Cmnd 9514, *Report of the Security Commission May 1985* (London: HMSO, 1985), paragraphs 5.1 to 8.11.

[43] *Report of the Security Commission*, paragraph 8.2.

been even more serious US censure of CIA's failure to observe Ames's lifestyle as a well-paid Soviet agent within it. Whatever the facts of these particular cases, they bring out intelligence managements' need for an unusual surveillance of their staff. In Western societies this is only tolerable if combined with a genuine humane concern. The morale and circumstances of individuals and of staff as a whole need to carry special weight in the managerial style.

This therefore produces a limitation on intelligence's application of the brisk, results-oriented management now generally in vogue. Intelligence can benefit from modern governments' enthusiasm for judging the public service by measurable performance. But all organizations depend on the great majority of average people, not outstanding ones, and have their proportion of difficult cases. Good management involves care as well as stimulation. Secrecy gives intelligence special reasons for being more than usually interested in its employees and more than usually caring – old-fashioned though this emphasis now sounds.

Management's values

Management's most important role is communicating values: 'clarifying the value system and breathing life into it are the greatest contributions a leader can make.'[44] On the private sector it has been commented that 'There is a value set – and it is a value set for all seasons . . . However it is executed by attention to mundane, nitty-gritty details. Every minute, every hour, every day is an opportunity to act in support of overarching themes.'[45] The same is true everywhere. There are therefore the questions: what particular values should intelligence emphasize? What metaphors about the organization should it enact to convey them?

It needs a combination of three: the public bureaucracy of which it is necessarily a part; the entrepreneurial characteristics needed for change and customer relations; and the scholarly ethos of seeking and disseminating the truth. Thus it has to think of itself as part of public administration, with an extra formality made necessary by political sensitivity and security procedures; after interviews with security intelligence organizations in Britain, Canada and Australia, Leigh and Lustgarten concluded that 'above all, security officials are bureaucrats. They live by rules and paper, and function by committee'.[46] Yet

---

[44] Peters and Waterman, *The Pursuit of Excellence*, p. 291.
[45] Peters and Waterman, *The Pursuit of Excellence*, p. 324. For examples of management themes see pp. 283–5.
[46] L. Lustgarten and I. Leigh, *In from the Cold: National Security and Parliamentary Democracy* (Oxford: Clarendon Press, 1994), p. 411.

intelligence also has to set great store by being quick on its feet and customer-oriented; it stands or falls by its credibility with policy-makers, and has never had another constituency to support it (except to the extent that its oversight by the US Congress is developing Congressional customers for substantive intelligence briefings). And together with these requirements it has to prize seeking truth and telling it as it is.

Thus there is some strain between the various corporate values that it falls to management to set and nourish. Managements have to strike balances between bureaucratic and entrepreneurial values as best they can. Perhaps the more important strain is between truth-seeking and the need for close relations with policy-makers, already discussed in chapter 6 and in the subsequent chapters on intelligence's accuracy.

The conflicting demands between the two were vividly brought out in the Senate hearings in 1991 about the appointment of Gates as DCI, when charges were made that he had slanted the presentation of CIA analysts' conclusions on the USSR to accommodate the agency to the preconceptions of the first Reagan Administration and Casey as DCI. Whatever the rights and wrongs of this CIA blood-letting, the hearings brought out the conflict of values. On the one hand Western intelligence is part of the government of the day, operating to maximize user approval by being as useful as possible within a fairly short time-scale; on the other it operates as an institution with a commitment on objectivity whose value may be long delayed.[47]

At a US seminar on intelligence and policy, a former Presidential assistant asked a retired CIA officer: 'Don't any of your people think they work for the President of the United States?' Answer: 'Some think they work for the National Interest, some for Truth, some for the Policymaking Process – but few really think they work for the President.'[48] The most important of intelligence's value-sets is conveyed in that answer. The President (and the British Prime Minister) are the most important customers, but intelligence has wider obligations. Without management's value-setting in this direction intelligence loses its point.

Summary

The most important management is still at the individual agency level. The intelligence agency has become a substantial employer, and its staff

---

[47] Senate Select Committee on Intelligence, *Hearings on the Nomination of Robert M. Gates as DCI*, September–October 1991, vols. I–III, S. Hrg 102-799 (Washington D.C.: US GPO, 1992).

[48] J. Davis, *Analysis and Policy: Evaluating Intelligence in an Era of Downsizing* (paper given at International Studies Association convention (Atlanta, Ga., March 1992), p. 4).

have a great variety of skills at many different levels. It necessarily has many bureaucratic features but needs to combine them with a capacity for rapid reaction. The insulation of secrecy makes it rather harder for it to be self-critical and adopt ideas from outside; this puts some premium upon 'open', 'informal', fluid organizations of the modern style. In structure and style, as in other things, the agency can learn something from the business virtues espoused in Britain as part of the New Public Management.

But there are some special factors bearing on its staff relations. It has a long-term workforce, in which there is some emphasis on puzzle-solving, research aptitudes and the attitudes that go with them. The characteristic feature of its organizational culture is the effect of secrecy: intelligence's 'mystery' strengthens the sense of belonging to a special group. The effect of this intense 'belonging' is towards high but somewhat brittle morale.

The needs of security combine with this background to make it important for the agency to be a particularly caring employer. Staff will be subject to special security restrictions and investigations as long as intelligence remains unusually secret. These are tolerable and effective only if known to be combined with managerial humanity.

As elsewhere, management's most important role is conveying values to the organization. Intelligence has to combine those of public bureaucracy with entrepreneurial and scholarly ones. The most important is the third, in environments in which intelligence is inevitably pressed to conform to views acceptable to the users it serves.

Part VI

The 1990s and beyond

19   National importance

Modern intelligence got its peacetime form through the Cold War. The Soviet target (and its substantial Warsaw Pact allies) dominated most Western efforts. 'It is difficult to exaggerate how thoroughly the gathering of information on the Soviet Union, and especially its military power, dominated US intelligence operations since the Cold War began.'[1] Since it ended intelligence has suffered some cuts as its contribution to the 'peace dividend'; in 1995 there were said to be only between a half to two-thirds of the US satellites in orbit that had been operating during the Gulf War.[2] At the beginning of 1995 CIA was in the throes of a post-Cold War reduction quoted officially as 23 per cent, and the US General Defense Intelligence Program was said to be losing 6,000 posts within two years.[3] The British intelligence budget is currently declining at 3 per cent per annum.[4]

But the general scale of these reductions is still rather less than in the armed forces. Intelligence's position in national decision-making has been unaffected; there is no sign anywhere that it is reverting to the small scale and peripheral status of the 1930s. Indeed France, never a heavy investor in it during the Cold War, provided its own idiosyncratic pointer to intelligence's future by announcing a greatly increased programme for it after the shock of having to depend so completely on the USA in the Gulf War.[5]

Commentators have also been generally supportive. US writing up to now has shown a consensus about the continued need for intelligence.

---

[1] S. Turner, 'Intelligence for a New World Order', *Foreign Affairs* vol. 70 no. 4 (autumn 1991), p. 150.

[2] J. H. Hedley, *Checklist for the Future of Intelligence* (Georgetown: Institute for the Study of Diplomacy, 1995), p. 28.

[3] CIA figure from *Congressional Quarterly* vol. 53 no. 1 (January 1995), p. 43. GDIP reductions, including 1,000 posts in DIA, reported in S. D. Breckenridge, 'Post-Cold War Intelligence', *World Intelligence Review* vol. 13 no. 4 (1994).

[4] Unattributable official statement 1995.

[5] P. Kemp, 'The Rise and Fall of France's Spymasters', *Intelligence and National Security* vol. 9 no. 1 (January 1994), pp. 15-16.

'As the world becomes multipolar, more complex and no longer under-standable through the prism of Soviet competition, more intelligence – not less – will be needed.'[6] A British Ministerial statement over the introduction of the new Parliamentary Intelligence and Security Committee upheld 'the continued need, in this ever turbulent and unpredictable world, for the intelligence services to be able to operate effectively' and referred to their 'crucial part in countering the dangers that threaten the safety of our citizens and of this nation's interests around the world'.[7] There has been little recent description of intelli-gence in terms like the 'silent conspiracy'.[8] Perhaps even those most critical of it now accept that it has some place in the modern state.

Nevertheless it still represents significant national investments, and its scale and purpose are likely to come under further review as the Cold War recedes further. A major Presidential and Congressional investi-gation was put into motion in late 1994 into the US community's objectives and organization. In Britain the signs are that further intelli-gence cuts will follow reduced expenditure on defence and the public services as a whole. So there are still open questions: how important is intelligence power in the post-Cold War world, and how should it develop in the future?

Chapter 3 speculated about allocations of intelligence effort in the mid-1990s between various categories of target. This chapter carries the discussion further by considering national needs and intelligence's value to those defending and promoting national interests. Chapter 20 discusses its implications for international security. In these chapters, as elsewhere, what is said applies particularly to the British and US com-munities, generally to Western intelligence as a whole, and in some degree to intelligence systems worldwide. Chapter 21 then summarizes conclusions from the earlier chapters on intelligence's nature and the principles on which it should be organized and managed.

Intelligence and national situations

There is no simple link between nations' situations and intelligence's importance; they have their own varying experiences and expectations of it. The Pearl Harbor disaster produced a lasting US preoccupation with warning against surprise attack. Codebreaking's part in fighting Hitler is

---

6 D. L. Boren, 'The Intelligence Community: How Crucial?', *Foreign Affairs* vol. 71 no. 3 (summer 1992), p. 54.

7 Lord MacKay, House of Lords, 9 December 1993, *Hansard* cols. 1024, 1026.

8 As in S. Dorril, *The Silent Conspiracy: Inside the Intelligence Services in the 1990s* (London: Heinemann, 1993).

similarly part of British folk-memory; intelligence contests are things which Britain expects to win, not lose. Intelligence support has been tacitly assumed as a prop for the position that 'British foreign policy since the war has seen successive governments attempting to maintain international responsibilities without the [material] resources necessary to meet them.'[9] In Germany and Japan, by contrast, intelligence has no special place in national memory, and receives lower national expectations; perhaps since 1945 these countries' foreign policies have also needed it less than Britain and the United States.

Governments inherit a particular intelligence status and are accustomed to it: 'Britain plays with the hand it has been dealt; intelligence is one of the strong cards.'[10] Intelligence competences are developed over long periods and cannot be created on demand; neither can close intelligence alliances. If capabilities and alliances are jettisoned the decisions are often irreversible.

Nevertheless there are some broad correlations with national circumstances. One of these is the effort that needs to be devoted to national security, in its narrowest sense of preserving the state from major challenges or disaster: surprise attack, foreign domination, dissolution or violent political change. Intelligence's special position in the Cold War was defined by the Soviet threat. Similarly the record of IRA terrorism – not least its two attempts to murder the Cabinet – has been significant in maintaining support for intelligence in Britain.

Intelligence's importance in this narrow context depends upon threats and vulnerabilities and national perceptions of them. Those states with the biggest threats, internal or external, have the biggest reasons for taking intelligence seriously; hence Israel's seriousness about it as a relatively small power in a long-running confrontation with numerous enemies. Weakness is a powerful reason for intelligence investments. Thus the Polish effort to break the Enigma cipher from the 1920s onwards was a rational reaction to Germany by a weaker and threatened neighbour; similarly the remarkable Swedish breaking of the German telegraphic cipher early in the Second World War reflected the hope that intelligence might help to safeguard a small state's neutrality.[11] Wartime

---

[9] C. Tugendhat and W. Wallace, *Options for British Foreign Policy in the 1990s* (London: RIIA/Routledge, 1988), p. 118.

[10] As put, for example, by Sir Percy Cradock, BBC TV programme *Panorama*, 22 November 1993.

[11] For the Polish contribution to Enigma cryptanalysis, see F. H. Hinsley with E. E. Thomas, C. A. G. Simkins and C. F. G. Ransom, *British Intelligence in the Second World War* vol. III part 2 (London: HMSO, 1988), appendix 30. For Swedish cipher-breaking see C. G. McKay, *From Information to Intrigue: Studies in Secret Service Based on the Swedish Experience 1939–45* (London: Cass, 1993), p. 27.

intelligence achieves a special priority through disasters; the military disasters of 1940 and 1941 stimulated the drafting of British talent to Bletchley Park and the operational use of the results. Something of the same has recently applied to intelligence on terrorism. Threats and vulnerabilities are the most potent reasons for taking intelligence seriously.

But defending national security in this narrowest sense is only one of intelligence's rationales. The security element in national policy extends to defending overseas possessions, protecting nationals and property abroad and reacting to threats and conflicts between others. This merges in turn into foreign policies' much wider elements of national interests (including economic and other ones), commitments and traditions. States have their varying international responsibilities, problems and habits. They give varied degrees of support for their private sectors' international trade and protection to their overseas citizens. Active foreign policies of any kind increase the role of intelligence, for much the same reasons as influence the size of diplomatic services; indeed the information-providing functions of the two overlap. By contrast intelligence (and diplomacy) count for less in states that have relatively passive international stances.

Thus the United States as a still active superpower seeks world class intelligence with worldwide coverage, despite the absence after the Cold War of any significant international threats and vulnerabilities (though terrorism against US forces and civilians overseas provides specific reasons for extensive US intelligence against terrorist targets). Satellites and the intelligence that flows from them are spectacular elements of American power, influence and ability to assist friends;[12] increasing national reluctance to send troops abroad may make the provision of intelligence an even more characteristic US contribution overseas. British intelligence supports the claim that the country punches above its weight in the international community. Its 'top second class' status in the intelligence league table, with some continued 'world reach', is justified partly by the need to support active diplomacy and world-wide participation in international affairs, including membership of the Security Council; and partly by the part intelligence plays in the political relationship with the United States, with dividends in turn for Britain's international standing. By contrast the scale of Japanese intelligence does not match its status as an economic Great Power, but fits its relatively

---

[12] A typical example was the provision of satellite intelligence to assist the Indian government in rescuing Western hostages in Kashmir (*The Times*, 21 August 1995).

low-key participation in international affairs.[13] Intelligence's importance depends partly on governments' international roles and how they see them.

However there is another factor: the particularly close relationship with military power. Most intelligence is defence intelligence, including the detailed information needed to meet professional military needs. Military forces need peacetime intelligence to make them effective, as well as provision for intelligence support in wartime. The scale of national intelligence is related to the scale of military forces – and even more to the extent to which nations take them seriously, and are prepared to use them. The deployment of national forces in NATO and UN operations has underlined the continued need for strategic and tactical defence intelligence, from platoon level upwards – including the *minutiae* of targeting intelligence and geographical information. Intelligence support on a quasi-wartime scale has been needed for the planning and prosecution of alliance operations, and for the safety of the national forces deployed in them.

Linked with all these factors is the relationship discussed in chapter 10 between offensive intelligence collection and national standards of defensive information security. This applies particularly to the support for military forces in action, but is also a touchstone of wider national attitudes. Neither Britain nor America takes easily to the idea of successful foreign espionage against it, and each would react even more sharply to any evidence that its national ciphers were being regularly broken.

These considerations combine to negate any idea of 'natural' ratios of intelligence to GNP, defence or other objective national measures. Britain has the sixth largest industrial economy in the world and is the fifth largest trading nation, but has a rather higher level of intelligence spending.[14] States have intelligence expectations bound up with past experiences, external and internal threats and vulnerabilities, foreign policy orientations and defence investments. Nevertheless some generalizations can be made about how the changed world of the 1990s has altered ways in which intelligence counts.

---

[13] Japanese economic 'intelligence' through its MITI and JETRO organizations (mainly from open sources) is much respected; but it is not matched by heavyweight intelligence on other subjects. (J. T. Richelson, *Foreign Intelligence Organizations* (Cambridge, Mass.: Ballinger, 1988), pp. 249–71.)

[14] Economic figures quoted by Sir David Gillmore, 'Representing Britain Overseas', *RUSI Journal* vol. 138 no. 6 (December 1993), pp. 15–16.

Needs in the 1990s and beyond

It should be remembered, first, that the Cold War was never intelligence's sole focus. Substantial targets existed outside the Soviet Bloc, and many of them have continued. Extensive Western requirements continue on the Middle East and the Gulf, not least on Iraq, Iran and Israel's position *vis-à-vis* the Arab world. China is still opaque, and the British withdrawal from Hong Kong may produce a period of tension, or at least of heightened interest. Dictatorships continue to limit diplomatic and media information-gathering; North Korea remains the archetypal secret state. The West continues to be concerned about the risk of Indo-Pakistan conflict and the possible use of nuclear weapons. International terrorism has been a major target (for the agencies collecting foreign intelligence, as well as for their security intelligence colleagues) for well over twenty years, as have its associations with rogue states. Aspects of Islamic fundamentalism and its conflict with existing regimes are now expanding the range of terrorist threats and targets, and terrorists' use of poison gas in Japan has raised the spectre of nuclear terrorism and other new methods. Hostage-taking which posed high-priority intelligence targets for a decade has not been eliminated and its scale may increase again.

Secondly, some elements of the former Soviet target retain high importance; Russia remains a strategic nuclear power, still with large conventional forces; their tendency towards fragmentation and local control has in some ways complicated intelligence coverage. New aspects of the Russian target have emerged: the uncertainty about its future political orientation, the large areas of internal and surrounding instability, and its own political and military action in its 'near abroad'. There are still special Western interests in Russian nuclear weapons and the control exercised over them, and in arms exports and the implementation of arms control agreements. For such reasons Russia and the USSR's former area still merit extensive Western attention.

In the third place the end of the Cold War has been followed by a new world instability – some of it in the Russian and CIS area, some outside it – with ethno-national conflicts, religious strife and state breakdown as causes and symptoms. Bosnia has been the archetypal case of instability requiring extensive intelligence coverage. Conventional arms transfers provide an increasing target worldwide, as does the evasion of international sanctions, as for instance on Iraq.

Lastly there are the other effects of the shrinking world and the global market, and the technology which produces them. The communications age has produced its revolution in the pace and complexity of international affairs and the speed and depth of information needed. More has to be spent on making intelligence quicker. Expanded diplomatic and other inter-state contacts increase the scope for intelligence support for negotiation and the execution of policy, as well as for background use in policy formation. Governments also need to be informed about increasing numbers of foreign non-state actors, both political and economic. Demands for economic intelligence are increasing, particularly on activities with covert or semi-covert aspects. Even more demanding in resource terms is the new power of information in modern military technology; the Gulf War demonstrated the power of information-gathering for precision weaponry and the importance of dominating the electromagnetic spectrum through Electronic Warfare. Warfare is becoming 'information warfare'; 'war begins and ends with intelligence'; for the military 'we must routinely make our intelligence people respond to a wartime role even during peacetime'.[15] Information is a critical resource in war, and the same applies increasingly to international competition in peace.

Nevertheless, despite these developments, the intelligence needs of the 1990s have contracted significantly in scale. In the Cold War the intelligence–security conflict was waged on both sides with efforts of almost wartime intensity. The central point for the West was the sheer size of the Soviet military targets, plus the need for expensive 'near real time' intelligence on them for surveillance and warning purposes. Every detail of Soviet movements, capabilities and order of battle seemed important and of near-immediate significance. The same applied to the detail of Soviet activities in the Third World. The East–West counter-espionage contest had a similar seriousness, in something of a war to the death between the two intelligence systems.

Intelligence is no longer driven by the risk of world war and the scale that sprang from it. Russia may still be a significant target, but without constituting anything like the former threat. Its forces are now remnants of their former selves. The Warsaw Pact has disappeared, along with Soviet forces in Eastern Europe and other 'forward' areas, and Soviet presences and influences in the Middle East and Third World have retreated. Russian espionage continues, but the threat is a conjectural, future one, rather than of current damage. There are still fears that nuclear weapons and material may get out of control, or be passed into the hands of rogue states or terrorist groups; but these lack the Cold War's underlying East–West hostility.

---

[15] General C. Horner, 'Offensive Air Operations: Lessons for the Future', *RUSI Journal* vol. 138 no. 6 (December 1993), p. 22.

Hence for intelligence requirements there are some contradictory trends. The concentration and intensity of the Cold War have undergone a seismic change, reducing requirements and the scale on which they need to be met, particularly in the detailed surveillance of military activities. Yet some other non-Cold War targets continue substantially unaffected, and merge into the many important aspects of the new Russia and its neighbours, and the world's new and widespread instability. As put from a British viewpoint, 'although the big threat has gone, the second order threats are proliferating. The chances of a second order threat turning nasty will be greater . . . Usually there will be no direct threat to Britain or the West, but not always . . . Technology, communications, the media have transformed the world over the last fifty years.'[16] The general effect is to widen the needs for intelligence, but to suggest that the system to meet them should be more flexible and variegated than during the Cold War, and in important ways less detailed and labour-intensive. It may indeed now be more useful; instead of being in part a precaution against an unlikely East–West War, intelligence can now help governments on the challenges of an unstable world.

But to get beyond these generalizations the essential thing is to distinguish between the main intelligence components: the special case of security intelligence; the small proportion of foreign intelligence (10 per cent or so) invested in all-source analysis; and the vastly greater resources assigned to the single-source agencies. Changed circumstances affect these parts of the system in different ways.

Security intelligence

We saw earlier that security intelligence comprised both collection and all-source analysis for internal security purposes. It has now come to be dominated by terrorist targets. By 1994 half the effort of the British Security Service was devoted to Irish terrorism and another quarter to international terrorism.[17] The future of this first half seemed unclear after the 1994 terrorist 'ceasefire', but presumably the threat will continue as a long-term one. For the West as a whole, and perhaps in most other countries, the threat of international terrorism remains, as does international political crime such as assassinations of *émigrés* on foreign soil. The growth of international travel has increased the scale of these threats, and the risks of foreign connections with domestic terrorism.

---

[16] Gillmore, 'Representing Britain Overseas', p. 14.
[17] S. Rimington, Richard Dimbleby Lecture *Security and Democracy* (London: BBC Educational Developments, 1994), pp. 7–8.

As for the other security intelligence targets, the need for counter-espionage is reduced but not eliminated; the Ames case has given it a new salience. Presumably subversion threats are now minimal; but subversion, espionage and terrorism have tended historically to have some connections, although this is not necessarily so.[18] Other factors bearing on security intelligence can be summarized as follows.

First, most states will wish to retain some ability to monitor covert foreign influence. The same applies to foreign information-gathering even when it is not classical espionage; the reported Iraqi attempts to acquire expertise on nuclear technology through the education of students abroad illustrates the modern variety. Giving advice to business outside government on defending trade secrets and other technology against foreign espionage may become increasingly important. Second, some permanent security intelligence capability is needed for the event of wartime needs, including those in small wars. Though the British media was critical of the way some Iraqis were expelled during the Gulf War, the need for some precautions against terrorist action can hardly be denied; there is still no evidence to show whether the absence of Iraqi terrorism directed against the West during the war was a success for preventive security or a quirk of Saddam Hussein's tactics.[19] Third is its special contribution to personnel security and other protective information defences. Fourth, there are connections and overlaps with law enforcement. The scope is growing for intelligence assistance to law enforcement on serious crime, particularly when it crosses international boundaries. Narcotics targets provide long-standing precedents for contributions of this kind, from Sigint and Humint agencies as well as from security intelligence.

This fourth factor has been the subject of considerable discussion in Britain. The government announced in November 1995 that the Security Service's legal mandate would be extended to include assistance with the detection of serious crime. Commentators ascribed this change to the Security Service's search for new commitments in the light of reduced Irish terrorist threats. But it needs to be related to more extensive developments in law enforcement. 'Organized crime' is said to be a major growth area, and one of its features is large-scale operation

---

[18] It is interesting to note that, after the Ames spy case, a separate 'counterintelligence' organization has been proposed in the United States, similar to the British Security Service but presumably without responsibilities for work on international terrorism. (J. H. Hedley, *Checklist for the Future of Intelligence*, p. 6.)

[19] For a sample of this criticism see P. Gill, *Policing Politics: Security Intelligence and the Liberal Democratic State* (London: Cass, 1994), pp. 99–100.

across national borders. Part of the response is the development of organized 'intelligence' in police forces and other law enforcement bodies such as customs and immigration services. Intelligence in this context involves some special efforts at collection but is related mainly to the coordination and study of information in depth from all sources; it 'targets the criminal rather than the crime'. Its output is assessments and forecasts geared to assist action at all law-enforcement levels, from the pursuit of particular cases to strategic decisions about the deployment of law enforcement effort.

Organized law enforcement intelligence of this kind is therefore becoming a parallel to the government intelligence system that is the subject here. Developing the new system has become a watchword for policemen and politicians, and growth is envisaged comparable with that of the national intelligence communities during the Cold War. Indeed in Britain the new coordinating structure being advocated by professional policemen is an almost exact replica of the JIC model as it evolved in the Second World War and later. Moreover the transnational character of much organized crime is giving a boost to the international law-enforcement intelligence networks of Interpol and Europol. Here again, law enforcement follows older intelligence; its international networks are developing to cope with international crime on the same lines as the intelligence communities' transnational cooperation evolved to meet the threats of Soviet military power and espionage and international terrorism.[20]

The question therefore arises whether there should be a merger of the new law enforcement intelligence with the older intelligence communities. There is indeed ample history of targets that straddle the two. In 'exceptional crime' like the domestic bomb attack on US government offices in Oklahoma City in April 1995 it is difficult to distinguish the work of unbalanced individuals from systematic politically-inspired threats to internal security. Some terrorism has long-standing connections with crime; IRA activities have been financed partly by extortion and protection rackets, and the RUC's criminal investigation of these activities has been closely connected with its Special Branch coverage of terrorism. Similarly the international narcotics trade has implications for foreign policy as well as international law enforcement; while some intelligence collected for foreign policy or defence reasons (for example

---

[20] Law enforcement intelligence as described here and subsequently is based on evidence in House of Commons Select Committee on Home Affairs 1994–5, *Report: Organized Crime* HC 18 I (London: HMSO, 1995) and *Minutes of Evidence and Memoranda* HC 18 II (London: HMSO, 1994).

on 'sanctions-busting') has law-enforcement connections or consequences, as with British intelligence on firms exporting to Iraq.

This overlapping of targets is already reflected in cooperation between
the two types of intelligence. We have already seen that security intelligence has close links with police forces, and that British police Special
Branches have responsibilities to both. British and US intelligence
communities have made long-standing contributions on narcotics
subjects. Assistance to law enforcement by the SIS as well as the
Security Service was acknowledged in Britain in 1994, and the Prime
Minister referred to GCHQ's contribution the following year.[21]

Two points seem central to working out the relationship between these
old and new intelligence communities. The first is the distinction
between the two kinds of targets. Organized crime has financial objectives; 'its primary purpose [is] the generation of profits.'[22] Despite
overlaps, the foreign and internal security targets of older intelligence fall
outside this description. However criminal it may be, terrorism is the use
of violence for political and not for other purposes. Broadly speaking
there are different interests and objectives in both targets and the
intelligence coverage of them.

The second is the basic distinction emphasized throughout this book
between collection and the responsibility of all-source evaluation. This
applies equally to law enforcement as to other intelligence. Thus the
intelligence agencies may be able to collect in ways for which law
enforcement has not got resources, skills or special access, especially in
organized crime's transnational dimension. International money laundering for example depends on electronic transnational money transfers,
on which national Sigint has the monitoring and selection facilities which
could be duplicated by law enforcement agencies only at great expense.
The same may well apply to the other means of professional intelligence
collection. It may be sensible for the national collection agencies to
collect some targets regularly on behalf of law enforcement customers, in
the same way as they meet the needs of foreign offices, armed forces and
their other long-standing users.

But this is not the same as assuming responsibility for all-source
analysis and evaluation. In principle it would seem sensible for distinct
law enforcement intelligence organizations to keep this responsibility on
crime. The 1995 announcement about revising the Security Service's

---

[21] *Organized Crime, Minutes of Evidence and Memoranda*, p. 45 (question 256). For the
reference to GCHQ's contribution see Mr Major's speech to the Conservative Party
Conference on 13 October 1995, reported on 14th.

[22] Home Office Memorandum, Select Committee on Home Affairs, *Organized Crime,
Minutes of Evidence and Memoranda*, p. 77.

role was in terms of providing 'assistance' to law enforcement, and it may well be that, besides special kinds of collection, that Service can now provide greater analytic competence than is available in some law enforcement units. At least in Britain, exchanges of information within the multifarious law enforcement community are still in a fairly rudimentary state; and there may still be a reluctance to consider having professional intelligence officers, reminiscent of the armed services' prejudices mentioned in chapter 14 about careers in defence intelligence.[23] But these factors should not justify a permanent transfer of responsibility. In principle it would seem better for law enforcement to build up its own all-source intelligence to do what is needed than to export work permanently to the older intelligence community.

Thus security intelligence should not have a reoriented role, but will still be needed for terrorism and its other long-standing targets. Continued assistance from the Humint and Sigint collection agencies will be needed; indeed the distinctions within internal security between foreign and domestic targets may become even more blurred than in the past. But security intelligence should remain a separate entity, with a size related to present internal security threats and the need to keep a capability for dealing with future ones. Organizationally it can be the responsibility of either a discrete agency, as in Britain and the Old Commonwealth, or a specialized branch of a single national police authority (where this exists), as in the US FBI. The choice between the two is a matter of national traditions and inclinations.[24] In both cases security intelligence needs to remain part of the traditional intelligence community.

All-source foreign intelligence

Governments need all-source analysis and assessment on a wide range of subjects and countries; the Soviet target never dominated it to quite the same extent as it dominated covert collection. They are likely to need analysis and assessment on all the foreign areas just discussed, and they probably now need more studies of Russian policies and prospects than they did on the USSR. The end of the Cold War must have released

---

[23] It has been said that the police service 'viewed with suspicion the idea of individuals having a full career in intelligence'. (Select Committee on Home Affairs 1994–5, *Report: Organized Crime*, p. 106.)
[24] For discussion of the alternatives see L. Lustgarten and I. Leigh, *In from the Cold: National Security and Parliamentary Democracy* (Oxford: Clarendon Press, 1994), pp. 368–71; and Gill, *Policing Politics*, pp. 319–22.

considerable effort from analysing the details of the Soviet target, but this is probably balanced by the new needs elsewhere. The total top level demand for finished intelligence has probably increased as compared with the decades of frozen East–West relations. Below the top level detailed military intelligence is still needed for current operations, contingency planning and training. Military procurement still needs to be based on threat assessments, although these must now be more speculative (and wide-ranging) than when geared to the Cold War opponent.

This is the likely pattern for finished intelligence on subjects with national security implications. Chapter 7 discussed whether it should now expand to become government's expert assessor on other subjects, particularly international economic, financial and trade matters. All-source analysis has to be broad in what it studies. But the conclusion reached there was that its contribution to policy-making should still be centred on subjects with some bearing on national security. The close study of economic matters is a necessary part of all-source analysis; for instance forecasts of Saddam Hussein's intentions in summer 1990 depended on understanding the condition of the Iraqi economy. But the results should be seen as contributions to political and military policy-making rather than technical economic decisions. Covert collection will of course continue to make useful contributions on the details of economic and many other subjects, but as single-source inputs and not as authoritative analysis and forecasts. Governments are unlikely to request intelligence assessments as key inputs to British economic decisions such as putting up interest rates or deciding whether to join the European Monetary Union; and they should not be pressed to do so.

Even if finished intelligence does not become authoritative in these economic decisions and others which have been outside its purview in the past, governments will continue to require it on its usual subjects on at least the present scale. This top level assessment needs adequate support from the detailed all-source analysis that should precede it. The greatly increased availability of commercially-provided data services opens up a new dimension for this work: assessing and evaluating multiple data bases of this kind and integrating their material (including the 'grey' material mentioned in chapter 6) with covert intelligence and other official information.

To do this, all-source analysis must be adequately staffed. Even in the Cold War the all-source effort was under-funded compared with collection. It is now all the more necessary to ensure that it can exploit the increased volume of information at its disposal. In practice the cuts made in the first half of the 1990s have affected it *pro rata* with the rest of intelligence. This has happened in a world in which powerful all-source work is more needed, and not less.

Collection

The biggest decisions for the future will be over the biggest activity: collection (and the related single-source processing and exploitation) on foreign targets. The contraction or disappearance of Soviet military targets and those of their Warsaw Pact allies has drastically reduced the collection resources needed. However diverse, the new targets of the 1990s are smaller in aggregate than those of the Cold War; and somewhat easier to tackle, without the old Soviet Union's pervasive secrecy. On the other hand Western armed forces continue to need adequate peacetime and wartime support, and arguably the reductions taking place in them strengthens the case for continued intelligence investments. Meeting their modern needs for an 'information war' does not turn entirely on resources classified as 'intelligence' (see chapter 7), but a considerable part of it does.

However the future scale of collection also depends on its technical prospects and costs, and on the availability of cheaper, non-intelligence information. These can now be discussed.

Yield and cost of collection sources

The distinction was made in chapter 5 between observational sources (typically observing and measuring military equipment through imagery) and message-like collection (as by obtaining documents and exploiting communications). Over the last thirty years the power of the observational sources has outstripped the ability of camouflage and concealment to defeat them. The observational revolution which began with the imagery satellites of the early 1960s has by no means run its course, and the same is true of the Elint satellites capable of measuring and locating radars and similar emissions. Even for nations without satellites, technology has multiplied the performance of observation in war, or in peacetime situations in which aircraft can be used. The Gulf War was an 'imagery war'. Eventually the development of 'stealth' and 'signature reduction' for military hardware may win back some defensive ground, but there is no great sign of it yet.

On message-like sources the balance between attack and defence is not so clear. The explosive growth of electronic communications provides commensurate opportunities for technical collection, from terrestrial sources as well as satellites. Intelligence of this kind on private firms engaged in arms transfers, sanctions evasion and the like has attracted some attention as an example.[25] On the other hand technology has also strengthened textual encryption and computer security. A survey of official US collaboration with industry to enhance information protection concluded that 'encryption is a primary weapon in combating network-level security problems . . . Today, using computers and government algorithms, industry is supplying the government with high-tech encryption devices that are practically impenetrable.'[26] Over ten years ago one American commentator suggested that 'on codebreaking and cryptanalysis we have a closing window of accessibility . . . The countries whose codes we can now read, which are essentially Third World countries, are gradually depriving us of this ability . . . [through] the spread of technology to Third World nations.'[27] The information society is concerned with safeguarding information as well as disseminating it.

Varied trends are affecting collection costs. Computers are taking over many kinds of data-handling and analysis, thereby reducing staff numbers; the use of computers for simple imagery interpretation is one example. On the other hand the technology needed in Sigint to keep up with its foreign targets and their Comsec defences has ever-rising capital costs. For observational intelligence, expensive satellites will remain the prerequisite of worldwide surveillance in peacetime. Technical trends point to intelligence communities that are slimmer (in staff totals), but not cheaper.

The general effect will be to accentuate still further the difference between those near the top of the international intelligence league and the also-rans. For Britain to keep its 'world reach' and professional relationships with the United States there will be further prices to pay. Despite the France-led programme for limited imagery satellite collection, the general European position may be increasing dependence on the United States for top class intelligence in an unstable world – always assuming that the superpower, in its changing relationship with Europe, remains prepared to be a supplier.

---

[25] L. K. Johnson and A. Fletcher, 'CIA and the Collection of Economic Intelligence', *World Intelligence Review* vol. 13 no. 5 (1994). For the definitional problems over 'economic intelligence' see chapter 3.

[26] D. T. Gehly, 'Fixing the Leaks', *Journal of Electronic Defense* vol. 14 no. 1 (January 1991), p. 26.

[27] D. Kahn, 'Technical Collection: Discussion' in R. Godson (ed.), *Intelligence Requirements for the 1980s: Clandestine Collection* (Washington D.C.: National Strategy Information Center, 1982), pp. 120–1.

Effects of a more open world

However the biggest factor affecting decisions on intelligence collection is the increased availability of information from non-intelligence sources. On the former Soviet target there has been the transition from a closed to a relatively open society. The scope for overseas journalistic coverage and televised reporting has increased immensely, and foreign governments' official sources now include extensive data exchanges for arms control verification and international confidence-building. There is less need than before to use intelligence sledgehammers to crack information nuts. If the West still wants to know more about Russian or Ukrainian missiles it can look at them under arms control arrangements instead of using expensive satellite coverage. Covert intelligence throughout the area of the former USSR has ceased to be the sole information source and has become one among many. The percentage of US intelligence resources devoted to the former Soviet Union was said in 1995 to have been reduced to 15 per cent from 60 per cent fifteen years before, presumably reflecting not only the contraction of the target and requirements on it but also the availability of these other sources.[28]

This revolution in Cold War secrecy is linked with less abrupt but similar changes elsewhere. The growth of televised news-gathering and national television broadcasting has made most of the world instantaneously accessible. John Simpson's reporting from Baghdad during the Gulf War epitomized television's technical power, even in Saddam Hussein's secretive regime.[29] For 'real time' information the war was in some respects CNN's war, as in its dramatic public warnings that Iraqi Scud missiles were in flight towards Israel and Saudi Arabia.[30] Television apart, there are the effects already mentioned of on-line access to commercial data bases and forecasting services – what has been christened in the United States the 'open source intelligence revolution'.[31]

---

[28] Hedley, *Checklist for the Future of Intelligence*, p. 27. (This 15 per cent sounds a low figure, but presumably much depends on how satellite coverage is allocated for this calculation.) Half of US *collection* resources were officially said in 1984 to be devoted to the Soviet target. (R. M. Gates, remarks at Conference on US Intelligence, 11 June 1984, quoted by L. K. Johnson, *America's Secret Power: the CIA in a Democratic Society* (Oxford: Oxford University Press, 1989), p. 80.)

[29] J. Simpson, *From the House of War* (London: Arrow, 1991).

[30] The British Ambassador in Riyadh during the Gulf War received real time warning of Scud attacks from his daughter in London, who saw launches flashed on to the television news and phoned him to say they were on their way. (Sir Peter de la Billière, *Storm Command: a Personal Account of the Gulf War* (London: HarperCollins, 1993), p. 210 (footnote).)

[31] R. D. Steele in *OSS Notices* (the journal of Open Source Solutions Group), Washington D.C., 31 March 1995, p. 3.

Openness comes not only from these new non-governmental sources, but also from the changes in official access. Diplomats in most countries can travel more widely than before, and national leaders and home-based officials are international travellers. Defence attachés – if properly trained linguistically – can once again become the main authorities on the foreign forces to which they are accredited. The number of deeply protected state secrets is decreasing, even where regimes would still like to safeguard them. This is not to suggest complete openness but to point to the trend.

These developments do not invalidate the need for sizeable covert collection. States are far from being completely transparent, and regimes like Libya, Iraq and Iran remain deeply secretive. Diplomacy still benefits from intelligence support; armed forces have their classified information; secret services and clandestine action remain secret. Official and public sources can be deceived, and intelligence collection has the capacity to check. It makes special contributions even on apparently transparent events; information from US Sigint collection is said to have been used to support Yeltsin's position during the attempted Soviet coup of August 1991.[32] For military operations such as those in the former Yugoslavia, imagery retains its special power for detecting observable activity over wide areas, and other forms of collection are needed. Similarly, intelligence remains the principal source on secret non-state and quasi-state targets. Terrorism is essentially covert, requiring Humint sources for its penetration. Covert collection plays a particular part in covering aspects of ethnic insurrection, the international arms trade, and the concealed acquisition of materials and technology.

Yet the problems in assessing unstable situations now seem to be confusion and unpredictability, rather than secretive planning and direction. Covert collection still provides unique information but the proportion of this must be smaller than before. Collection's task may increasingly be to supplement public sources and advise all-source analysts on what to believe in them. It is probably losing some uniqueness and taking on a verifying and supplementing function, as one source among several.

Importance and balance

The question posed at the beginning of this chapter was of intelligence's national importance in the post-Cold War world. The answer varies between its different components.

---

[32] W. Pincus, *International Herald Tribune*, 16 May 1994. It is also claimed that an earlier US warning had been conveyed to Gorbachev.

Internal security threats (including terrorism) are essentially covert, or have large covert elements; every state needs some security intelligence capability for detecting and monitoring them. The lesson from the Soviet recruitment of agents in the 1930s and the Second World War is the need to avoid purely short-term views of what may be threats in the future. With the difficulty of this task and the political sensitivity needed for it, it needs to be done competently if it is done at all; the varied penalties of incompetence are quite high. The practical problem for security intelligence after the Cold War is to maintain quality while scaling down resources to levels commensurate with reduced threats.

Such savings in security intelligence will however be small parts of total intelligence budgets. The position of foreign intelligence is rather different. It is the major part of the total community, and a high proportion of it was geared to the Soviet threat in the Cold War and the need to avoid war triggered by surprise or misperception. Historians can argue about Soviet aims and the risk of nuclear war; but by the perceptions of the time there was no doubt about how much intelligence mattered. Both sides saw it as 'vital' in this way; and the word encapsulates the way the Cold War was seen as an intelligence war, fought *inter alia* to reduce the risks of hot war.

No foreign intelligence now seems vital in quite that way. It caters not for first order threats of the Cold War kind but for the new second order ones which merge into supporting national interests and influence. It is harder than formerly to regard effective peacetime intelligence as essential for national survival. Most of it is useful rather than vital. It can still be valuable, as in maximizing national weight and influence and getting good international bargains; at varying removes it contributes to national prosperity and to national 'feel good' satisfaction with policies overseas. But the circumstances of the 1990s increases the need to think about these results in terms of cost-effectiveness, cost-benefit and opportunity costs, and rather less in the language of national imperatives. The fact that intelligence's usefulness can never be precisely evaluated does not alter the desirability of now viewing it in utilitarian and less emotive terms. From this viewpoint it is to foreign affairs as the (British) Government Statistical Service is to domestic ones: conducive to good government, but not the stuff of great national dramas.

It is healthy and necessary to re-evaluate intelligence in this way; but it must be seen as essentially a peacetime view, and an incomplete one at that. Large sections of intelligence are still related to defence, with results that can ultimately be tested in military effectiveness; the quality of peacetime intelligence provision to armed forces and wartime support to them contributes to winning wars and losing them. Even when armed forces are operationally deployed in peacekeeping or limited intensity conflicts that are less than all-out war, intelligence's successes and failures are reflected in casualty rates: the oft-quoted body-bag count. Similar considerations apply to intelligence for counter-terrorism. Some peacetime warning arrangements against surprise attack are still needed; this may now seem unlikely, but so did the invasion of the Falklands and the crucial requirements for intelligence that followed it. Second order threats can change into first order ones. Foreign intelligence is a capability for national risk assessment in the future. More widely it bears on international security as well as national interests, as will be discussed in the next chapter.

But despite all these qualifications intelligence's order of importance has changed greatly with the end of the Cold War. The paradox is that in a sense it is probably more useful now than it was then. Intelligence's role was then to lessen the risks of nuclear holocaust; now it helps governments in more immediate but less highly charged terms.

It therefore cannot claim exemption from current cuts in government expenditure on foreign policy and defence. The way to absorb reductions is fairly clear. They should fall not on the relatively small (and cheap) all-source stage but on the far bigger collection efforts. The aim should be to safeguard all-source analysis through a changed single-source/all-source balance. The decisive factor for a higher all-source proportion of shrinking overall resources is the growth of non-intelligence sources of material in an increasingly open world. The all-source effort is even more important than before, while the relative importance of covert collection is somewhat reduced – unique as it remains on some targets. Intelligence can become a slightly more open and less secret part of government; in fact reverting some way towards the non-covert Victorian–Edwardian concept of intelligence which was used as late as 1918 in the Haldane Committee's recommendations for the encouragement of national science and 'intelligence'.[33]

This approach suggests that any overall reduction should cater for a modest alteration in the Cold War's 90:10 ratio of collection to all-source expenditure on foreign targets, but it does not point to radical recasting. Extensive covert collection is still needed, both for its material's peacetime usefulness and for its position at the core of defence intelligence and support to military power. Collection agencies' single-source analysis is an important contributor to all-source work and produces many reports

---

[33] P. Gummett, *Scientists in Whitehall* (Manchester: Manchester University Press, 1980), p. 25.

sent direct to policy-makers. The high-technology collection needed to keep up with targets' developments is increasingly expensive, even if manpower can be slimmed down and running costs reduced. There is the influence of alliance relationships; those who want to be members of high-quality international clubs (particularly in relationships with the United States) have to pay their subscriptions in collection effort. Above all there is the challenge posed by satellite collection and the value it offers; for modern Western powers, access to its results can almost be seen as a *sine qua non* for meeting current aspirations that armed forces should not be called upon to fight without the benefit of state-of-the-art technology. For all these reasons collection, even if significantly scaled down, will remain intelligence's biggest component.

Summary

Nations have varying expectations and experience of intelligence. Its importance to them is related to internal and external threats and vulnerabilities, national interests and other aspects of their international stance, and attitudes to their armed forces. The end of the Cold War has brought great changes to intelligence requirements. One is the much smaller scale of the successors of the former Soviet targets; another is the emergence of a more unstable world, and an increased international diffusion of armaments. The general pattern is now of greater variety and flexibility, and less detailed intensity and concentration than before.

A security intelligence effort will continue to be needed against internal threats, on a scale commensurate with the threats (including in Britain the threat of Irish terrorism). For foreign intelligence the massive Soviet threat that made it vital to national security no longer exists. In that sense intelligence is of reduced importance, but it is probably of more actual use now than before. National investments in it need to be evaluated largely in terms of peacetime usefulness; but its national security and precautionary roles cannot be discounted, particularly its provision of warning and its support for armed forces and counter-terrorism.

Some further reductions in intelligence budgets seem inevitable. Governments want finished intelligence on an unchanged and perhaps even increased scale. But in a more open world the uniqueness of intelligence collection is decreasing overall, irreplaceable though it is on some subjects. The balance between spending on collection and all-source activities needs adjustment. Much more information is available from public and other non-intelligence sources, and intelligence can become a slightly more open part of government. Collection will remain by far its most expensive activity, and high technology will continue to increase the cost. Access to the results of satellite collection has become almost a necessity for Western warfare on any significant scale. But cuts in collection are preferable to reductions at the all-source stage.

20 International dimensions

The last chapter reviewed intelligence's purely national importance in the present and future, but its international significance also needs to be considered. Chapter 9 outlined specific contributions from national intelligence to international security, and chapter 11 discussed effects of intelligence as threats. Here we draw on these chapters to consider wider questions. Does intelligence make for a more secure world or a more dangerous one – still in the restricted sense of avoiding wars or limiting them? Does the answer suggest ways in which intelligence's security-enhancing effects can be increased?

We have already seen how national intelligence can be used for mediation and conflict resolution, including such means as its provision to potential antagonists as a stabilizing measure; its use in international cooperation on counter-terrorism and limiting international arms transfers; and the verification of arms control and other international agreements. But these are still applications of national intelligence to serve national interests when these are identified with promoting international security. When this is not the case, then national intelligence support for this international end is not forthcoming. One question is therefore whether arrangements for international action could have permanent intelligence machinery embodied in them, so that they are not subject to national initiatives over inputs or to national intelligence biases incorporated in them. Even if practicable, such arrangements would still be supplementary to national intelligence, and not replacements for it. Hence there is the further question whether national intelligence itself should be developed in 'security-friendly' directions.

International action and intelligence support

United Nations' and other international action in, around and over the former Yugoslavia has demonstrated the need for intelligence and machinery for handling it. An ideal UN model would indeed provide for a service of common intelligence to those engaged in its operations and all the governments supporting and directing them. It is therefore instructive to consider how UN intelligence has worked in practice. The shift of the focus of action on Bosnia to NATO in late 1995 has perhaps drawn attention away from the UN's needs; but this does not signify any complete and permanent change in them, in Bosnia or for UN operations elsewhere.

In practice some of the required information may always be available from the media and from UN forces' own observation and contacts with local inhabitants; both are rough equivalents of the battlefield 'combat information' distinguished from intelligence collection in chapter 7. Even for this information the UN needs some machinery for handling and dissemination. Of the actual position in 1992–3 a British brigadier has written that 'UNPROFOR [in former Yugoslavia] . . . was operating the traditional UN system of reporting occurrences with no active collection, little if any collation or filtration and seldom any analysis.'[1] In early 1994 a French general commented that 'I have asked for numerous reforms in the structure of the UN in Yugoslavia, especially in the use of information, the capacity to analyse and reflect.'[2] According to a commentator on UN affairs 'the systematic collection and analysis of information by means of ground-reconnaissance, aerial-surveillance and information-processing systems has been a neglected area of UN activity . . . it is the *ad hoc* process of ground reconnaissance currently in place which has largely contributed to critical delays in the deployment of troops, inefficient allocation of supplies and "tactical surprises" in the early stages of an operation.'[3]

The UN is developing its information handling and assessment; by early 1994 it had a Situation Centre, and a US-donated 'Joint Deployable Intelligence Support System' for receiving and disseminating some US intelligence for operations in Somalia.[4] Even with this progress in information handling, its own local sources will still be incomplete on their own. Where there is fighting around them, UN commanders and officials need the extra information available only from intelligence sources: imagery, Sigint and even Humint. This raises the possibility of

[1] G. Messervy-Whiting, 'The Peace Conference on Former Yugoslavia: the Politico-Military Interface', *Brassey's Defence Yearbook 1994* (London: Brassey's, 1994), pp 183–4.

[2] Article by C. Bellamy, *Independent*, 31 January 1994.

[3] M. R. Berdal, *Whither UN Peacekeeping?* (*Adelphi Paper* 281) (London: IISS/Brassey's, 1993), p. 65. See also the same author's 'Peacekeeping in Europe' in *European Security after the Cold War* (*Adelphi Paper* 284) (London: IISS/Brassey's, 1994), pp. 69–71.

[4] Berdal, 'Peacekeeping in Europe', p. 67.

having this need met by some collection under UN control, distinct from national sources.

There has indeed been some talk of UN-owned or UN-controlled intelligence collection. Desultory attention has been paid since 1978 to the ideas of a UN imagery satellite, *inter alia* to give UN participants an alternative to relying on the United States, and of UN use of photography from commercial satellites.[5] (Similarly the Western European Union has also toyed with ideas of a European satellite or the use of commercial ones, and now has a permanent imagery interpretation centre in Spain.)[6] In actual practice the UN Special Inspection Commission set up to identify and destroy Iraqi capabilities for mass destruction after the Gulf War used a US U-2 aircraft and US support in photographic interpretation.[7] But there are no UN-owned intelligence collection assets, or national resources regularly at its disposal.

NATO's own Cold War experience provides some pointers to an international organization's ability to collect and handle intelligence. The NATO system included multinational intelligence staffs, but always had the insoluble problem of protecting fragile intelligence sources in a multinational environment. Hence it never had NATO-owned or NATO-controlled intelligence collectors, and relied as a matter of policy on national inputs to its intelligence staffs.[8] There were elaborate procedures for these inputs, but a fact of NATO life was that its nations judged their most important national intelligence to be too sensitive to be put into NATO in this 'official' way. NATO managed nevertheless to make effective use of much of this intelligence because its official machinery for getting national inputs was supplemented by a second, elaborate, but unofficial system of national cells nicknamed as

---

[5] Summarized in W. H. Dorn, *Peace-Keeping Satellites: the Case for International Surveillance and Verification* (Dundas, Canada: Peace Research Institute (Dundas), 1989 edition).

[6] VERTIC, *Trust and Verify* no. 24, November 1991; the conversion to a permanent WEU facility was announced in 1995 in connection with the new WEU rapid reaction force in the Mediterranean area (*The Times*, 16 May 1995). For examples of WEU studies of satellite possibilities, see WEU Proceedings 36th session part I, June 1990 (WEU Paris), pp. 215–30; and *Trust and Verify*, nos. 4 and 9, October 1989 and April 1990.

[7] Berdal, *Whither UN Peacekeeping?*, pp. 66–7, and D. Kay, 'Arms Inspections in Iraq: Lessons for Arms Control', *Bulletin of Arms Control* (London: Council for Arms Control/ Centre for Defence Studies) no. 7, August 1992. A similar use of US aircraft with UN markings was apparently intended for inspection of the Soviet withdrawal of missiles from Cuba after the 1962 crisis, but rejected by Cuba. (A. James, *Peacekeeping in International Politics* (London: Macmillan, 1990), p. 300.)

[8] NATO's Airborne Warning and Control (AWACS) aircraft are primarily for early warning and battle management ('combat information' in the sense used in this book), though they probably supply some intelligence as a by-product. Plans for some multi-national tactical intelligence collection systems were abandoned early in NATO's career.

existing 'behind green baize doors' to give private briefings. This usually ensured that the alliance obtained high-quality intelligence, fed selectively but effectively into its bloodstream. This apparently untidy position applied even though NATO was then a closely-knit alliance against a common enemy and had had many years to work out intelligence procedures and security regulations.[9]

This suggests conclusions for the far looser and heterogeneous UN in its conflict resolution mode. It needs its own arrangements for collating information, and may be able to ask nations for particular services of intelligence, and even to have national aerial reconnaissance assets put at its disposal *ad hoc*.[10] But the idea of permanently UN-owned secret collection seems visionary; and even the temporary control of national collection will be politically fraught where the UN stance is neutral. Just as the UN relies on national forces, it will have to rely on national intelligence-gathering and national inputs to top up the observations of its own forces. Since it is not designed to keep secrets, it will be even more dependent than NATO on these national 'green baize door' inputs to particular individuals.

The same applies to the WEU as an alliance for promoting international stability. A WEU satellite does not seem a complete impossibility, particularly if it were designed to collect imagery and not Sigint;[11] but the odds against it as a genuine alliance project still seem quite high. Indeed WEU shows little sign of developing its own intelligence identity; its Planning Cell has recently emphasized how much it 'needs access to NATO and national intelligence including secret material if its work is to be taken seriously'.[12]

The same need for national inputs applies to the inspection activities of the UN-sponsored International Atomic Energy Authority (IAEA) and the new Inspectorate of the Organization for the Prevention of Chemical Weapons established by the 1993 CW Convention. It has been argued that in investigating clandestine nuclear programmes IAEA needs better regular access to 'the findings of national intelligence systems that

---

[9] For NATO intelligence see P. B. Stares, *Command Performance: the Neglected Dimension of European Security* (Washington D.C.: Brookings Institution, 1991), pp. 87–100.

[10] For a case for UN-owned aerial surveillance in peacekeeping, see M. Krepon and J. P. Tracy, ' "Open Skies" and UN peace-keeping', *Survival* vol. 32 no. 3 (May/June 1990), pp. 251–63.

[11] For a case for a WEU satellite see P. B. Stares and J. D. Steinbruner, 'Cooperative Security in the New Europe' in P. B. Stares (ed.), *The New Germany and the New Europe* (Washington D.C.: Brookings Institution, 1992), pp. 237–8.

[12] Quotation from WEU-Doc 1421, Paris (May 1994) in P. Chilton, 'French Policy on Peacekeeping', *Brassey's Defence Yearbook 1995* (London: Brassey's, 1995), p. 149.

are targeted on suspect nuclear activities'.[13] International institutions of this kind should not be completely self-standing.

In short, the prospects of genuinely 'international' intelligence collection seem bleak. International security institutions will continue to depend on national inputs. Thus national intelligence now has a developing role of supporting them. It will also continue to be a deterrent to any 'cheating' of treaty provisions for nuclear, chemical and biological weapons. Far from developing its own self-sufficient 'international intelligence', the UN's more active role in crisis management now makes it more dependent on national intelligence support; and the same applies to international verification arrangements. National intelligence's support for nuclear limitation seems particularly important; if there are moves to a non-nuclear world they will need the same support for verification from NTMs as the SALT and ABM agreements received in the 1970s.

National intelligence may have instinctive resistance to this new role; so too may those who do not want international organizations corrupted by back-door intelligence contacts. According to a US Congressman, Gates as DCI had to overrule strong objections to passing satellite photography on North Korean nuclear facilities to the IAEA, and CIA analysts made new attempts to prevent it once he had left his post.[14] An inspection team leader for the UN Special Commission in Iraq wrote of national fears that it would compromise national intelligence sources and methods, and UN/IAEA anxieties that 'their moral purity would be ruined' if the Commission had this access.[15] But on the actual experience of coupling national intelligence to an international inspectorate, he enthusiastically recorded his conclusion that 'In the face of the highly efficient Iraqi deception, the inspection could not have gone forward without accurate intelligence.'[16]

The United States has now committed itself to a situation in which 'to the extent prudent, US intelligence today is . . . being used in dramatically new ways, such as assisting the international organizations

[13] D. A. V. Fischer, 'The Future of the IAEA', *PPNN Issue Reviews* (Mountbatten Centre for International Studies, University of Southampton, UK) no. 2 (December 1993). While inspecting the Iraqi nuclear effort after the Gulf War, the IAEA was 'provided with detailed information on the location of nuclear installations from national satellite and other intelligence information to which it would not normally have access'. (J. Simpson and D. Howlett, 'Nuclear Non-Proliferation: the Way Forward', *Survival* vol. 33 no. 6 (November–December 1991), p. 492.)

[14] D. McCurdy, 'Glasnost for the CIA', *Foreign Affairs* vol. 73 no. 1 (January/February 1994), p. 135.

[15] D. Kay, 'Arms Inspections in Iraq: Lessons for Arms Control', *Bulletin of Arms Control* (London: Council for Arms Control/Centre for Defence Studies) no. 7 (August 1992), p. 6.

[16] Kay, 'Arms Inspections in Iraq: Lessons for Arms Control', pp. 6–7.

like the United Nations . . . We will share information and assets that strengthen peaceful relationships and aid in building confidence.'[17] Other nations can contribute in the same way. It is potentially an important service to international security.

The same applies to the synergy described in chapter 9 between intelligence and the inspection arrangements in arms control treaties. These intelligence contributions will continue to be relevant to arms control in Europe and will apply if similar reductions and CSBM agreements are reached outside the CSCE/OSCE area. Middle East and India–Pakistan security structures are said to be under periodic consideration.[18] If agreement is reached about them the parties' national intelligence can buttress verification.

Thus national intelligence arrangements of diverse kinds can make up for what is likely to be the permanent impracticability of organizing genuinely 'international' intelligence collection. National intelligence communities can make these contributions to intelligence security and should take them seriously. But it has to be recognized that in most circumstances the important contribution is that of the United States, particularly from its satellite imagery. Inputs of this kind represent a practicable and relatively inexpensive expression of US intelligence power and a willingness to use it for international security purposes.

In this limited sense there may already be an international system of a kind. Worldwide US satellite surveillance is accepted as a feature of the modern world, and there seem to be no protests about it or systematic attempts to conceal activities from it. In an unformulated way it is perhaps acquiring an expanded version of the legitimacy it originally had from the Cold War agreement legitimizing US and Soviet NTMs. The ideas of former US DCIs were mentioned earlier: that some aspects of intelligence should become an 'international good', and not a resource that is just available nationally.[19] Perhaps US satellite imagery is evolving in that direction – though very gradually, with strict limitations to particular cases. To that extent it may already be edging towards an

---

[17] *National Security Strategy of the United States* (Washington D.C.: White House, January 1993), p. 18, quoted by H. Smith, 'Intelligence and UN Peacekeeping', *Survival* vol. 36 no. 3 (autumn 1994), p. 184.

[18] P. Jones and K. Krasznai, 'Open Skies: Achievements and Prospects' in J. B. Poole and R. Guthrie (eds.), *Verification Report 1992*, pp. 53–5; V. Kunzendorf, *Verification of Conventional Arms Control (Adelphi Papers* 245) (London: IISS/Brassey's, 1989), p. 18 for the Sinai arrangement; J. Adams, *Sunday Times*, 20 February 1994, on the possibility of Middle East and India–Pakistan regional security structures, and M. Isphanani, *Pakistan: Dimensions of Security (Adelphi Papers* 246) (London: IISS/Brassey's, winter 1989–90), pp. 39–40, for tentative beginnings.

[19] See chapter 7, note 13.

international intelligence system. But it is still basically a national system, an intelligence expression of US hegemony; and it is still as subject to the pressures and uncertainties of national interests as any other aspect of US power.[20]

Intelligence and international behaviour

Hence it is impracticable to think of genuinely international intelligence; the intelligence described in this book serves national ends, even though these may sometimes coincide with international security. Questions therefore need to be asked about intelligence's basic effects on national behaviour, and whether the system that evolved in the Cold War needs modification to meet the needs of international security in the world of the 1990s and beyond. To answer them we need to distinguish clearly between the effects of intelligence product and those of its activities.

Intelligence as product

Intelligence as knowledge does not necessarily encourage states towards peaceful rather than aggressive policies. We saw in earlier chapters that it seeks to provide warnings against surprise attack (though without a record of great success), but can also assist attackers. It might be expected to assist the weak against the strong, but the evidence discussed in chapter 8 suggests that the reverse can be true. Good intelligence helps any kind of rational, objective policy-making, whether the policies enhance international security or detract from it.

However, there are important elements of subjectivity and misconception in most foreign policies. 'People act and react according to their images of the environment'; there is 'the distortion of reality caused by attitudes, values and beliefs', and 'the distinction between psychological environment or definition of the situation and physical environment or "reality"'; 'the discrepancy between image and reality is partly a result of physical impediments to the flow of information owing to lack of time, faulty communications, censorship or lack of competent advisers or

---

[20] In analysing developments in international finance, Professor Strange concluded that the major problem for international relations was 'to persuade people and politicians in the United States to use the hegemonic, structural power they still have in a more enlightened and consistent way.' (S. Strange, 'Finance, Information and Power', *Review of International Studies* vol. 16 no. 3 (July 1990) p. 274.) On its smaller scale, the same might be applied to the use of US intelligence power to support measures of international security.

intelligence sources.'[21] Sir Michael Howard has argued that 'wars begin with conscious and reasoned decisions based on the calculation, made by both parties, that they can achieve more by going to war than by remaining at peace'.[22] But these decisions are often based on bad information; it has been claimed that, 'during the half-century from 1914 to 1964, the decisions of major powers to go to war or to expand a war involved major errors of fact of other powers' capabilities in perhaps more than 50 per cent of cases.'[23] 'The natural structure of the system tends to enhance misunderstanding . . . International relations cannot be compared to a chess game.'[24] Wars start for many reasons, but their origins include 'war-conducive' acts of contributory negligence, insensitive acts, thoughtless acts and reckless acts, in contexts of deteriorating international circumstances.[25] Misperception is a significant factor in these various origins. Even where war does not eventuate, misperception's predominant effect is to reduce international security.

If so, intelligence as considered here provides some antidote to misperception-induced insecurity between states. It may indeed bring systematic bias to its judgments; chapter 14 discussed its tendency to overestimate Soviet threats. But in this it was reflecting policy preconceptions and not creating them. Despite all its fallibilities, Western intelligence has preserved a professional ethic of objectivity, with some effect in limiting the extent of policy-makers' misconceptions. Gaddis summarized intelligence's Cold War effects as guarding against surprise, assessing adversary forces, monitoring arms control agreements and keeping track of third party crises.[26] In these areas the improvements in Western intelligence knowledge did something to anchor its 'enemy images' to reality; and intelligence warning systems had some stabilizing effects on both sides. The US discovery of Soviet missile sites in Cuba in October 1962 discouraged further Soviet adventures directly affecting the balance with the West. When the full history of the Cold War is written, the record of CIA's Directorate of Intelligence in assessing the USSR may well emerge with some credit.

---

[21] Quotations from K. J. Holsti, *International Politics: a Framework for Analysis* (Englewood Cliffs, N.J.: Prentice-Hall, 1983 edition), pp. 319–20.

[22] M. Howard, *The Causes of Wars* (London: Unwin Paperbacks, 1984), p. 22.

[23] K. W. Deutsch, *The Analysis of International Relations* (New York: Prentice-Hall, 1968), pp. 51–2.

[24] B. Buzan, *People, States and Fear: the National Security Problem in International Relations* (Brighton: Wheatsheaf, 1983), p. 230.

[25] H. Suganami, 'A Theory of War Origins' (paper given to the British International Studies Association annual conference, 1995), p. 16.

[26] J. L. Gaddis, *The Long Peace: Inquiries into the History of the Cold War* (Oxford: Oxford University Press, 1987), pp. 207–8.

When intelligence is accurate it does not remove genuine threats to international security, but improves the chances of sensible and timely responses; and it deflates non-existent threats. Understanding foreign countries gives policy-making a sense of proportion. Leaders are likely to behave more sensibly and consistently when they value intelligence than when they ignore it or do not have it. Intelligence's objectivity and effect depends on the regime it serves. In the USSR 'both Stalin and his successors actively discouraged forecasting: only the leader could see the future. Also, men at the top regarded their exclusive purpose to be an examination of the whole picture.'[27] Leaders get the quality and depth of intelligence they deserve. But any knowledge is better than ignorance; and the emergence since 1945 of all-source intelligence assessment machinery encourages governments' rationality and consistency – if this machinery exists and is coupled with an intelligence ethic, and leaders that are prepared to pay attention to it.

Intelligence as collection

This contribution of intelligence knowledge to international security does not apply in the same way to intelligence as an activity. Its collection represents conflict, or at least competition, without much amelioration by international rules. Foreign intelligence is collected by definition *against* other nations or their citizens. The US–Soviet agreement to legitimize each other's NTMs for arms control purposes and to assist them by not enciphering telemetry remains unique. There are no other inter-state agreements to send signals in plain language.

In practice most collection as an activity has no effect on international relationships. Opponents know that they target each other. Armed forces assume that other countries seek information about them, and politicians and diplomats accept some foreign intelligence coverage of them as part of the trade. David Kahn has commented that 'Nobody goes around making a big fuss if it is somehow disclosed that their codes are broken. They simply change their codes, and don't go around crying "foul" and saying that people shouldn't be doing this.'[28] The existence of long-distance technical facilities does not usually show that they have any particular national targets. The same applies to intelligence satellites. We saw in chapter 11 that even in the Cold War long-distance intelligence

[27] V. Zubok, 'Soviet Intelligence in the Cold War: the "Small" Committee of Information', *Diplomatic History* vol. 19 no. 3, pp. 471–2.

[28] D. Kahn, 'Technical Collection: Discussion' in R. Godson (ed.), *Intelligence Requirements for the 1980s: Clandestine Collection* (Washington D.C.: National Strategy Information Center, 1982), pp. 119–20.

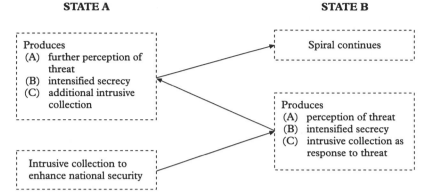

Figure 19 Intelligence–security spiral of threat perceptions

activities did not add to perceptions of threat. A nineteenth-century British argument for intelligence that 'the pursuit of intelligence has not, like swollen armaments, any tendency to bring about war' still has a lot to be said for it.[29]

Yet we also saw in that chapter that the more internationally intrusive kinds of collection – espionage, the position of embassies as espionage bases (and targets), and overflights and air and maritime technical collection entailing close access – have effects of this kind. Kahn also referred to Kant's view of spying as 'a kind of crime against the international order because if discovered it causes international difficulties'.[30] Hence there is the possibility of intelligence's version of military power's 'security dilemma': the 'structural notion in which the self-help attempts of states to look after their security needs tend automatically (i.e. regardless of intention) to lead to rising insecurity for others as each interprets its own measures as defensive, and the measures of the others as potentially threatening.'[31] Intelligence has the makings of the same paradox. Intrusive collection may be intended to increase national security, but may produce its own spiral of increased threat perceptions among its targets, leading to more secrecy and more intrusive collection as illustrated in figure 19.

Presumably the concentrated Western airborne and seaborne collection on Soviet frontiers is now largely a thing of the past (though perhaps

[29] Major C. B. Brackenbury, 'The Intelligence Duties of the Staff Abroad and at Home', *RUSI Journal* vol. 19 no. 80 (1875), p. 265.
[30] Ascribed to Kant's *Perpetual Peace* (Kahn, 'Technical Collection', p. 120).
[31] Buzan, *People, States and Fear*, p. 3.

not entirely; the Russians claim to have forced down an American aircraft over Kamchatka in 1994).[32] But espionage and suspicion of it may still have some effects, as has its association with embassies. Anglo-Soviet relations were set back temporarily in 1989 after the expulsion of some Soviet intelligence officers from London, despite Mrs Thatcher's efforts to minimize the damage.[33] In 1993 and 1994 Russia, the United States and Britain were joined in a renewed round of espionage cases and diplomatic expulsions and counter-expulsions. The Ames spy case inside CIA has been taken by some US commentators as evidence of continuing Russian hostility (although penetrating an opponent's intelligence collection is, as we saw in chapter 10, one of the more defensive kinds of intrusion). For its part the new Russian Counterintelligence Service has recently made allegations that intelligence in the West is recruiting Russian students studying there.[34] In other relationships there are recent reports of intensive French intelligence collection directed against American technology, and of a French expulsion of CIA officers from Paris.[35] China's expulsion of some US officers for examining military installations has now added a Chinese dimension to the inventory of perceived threats.[36]

Some intrusive collection is accepted as a natural part of the international scene; recent French espionage against the United States is resented by moderate opinion as an affront to national dignity rather than as a serious threat to national security. Nevertheless it is worth remembering how intrusion exacerbated Cold War tensions. Soviet espionage and secrecy were at an unprecedented peacetime scale, and so too were Western close access operations around Soviet borders and coastlines. Less of them are now needed. Treaty provisions for arms control inspection and other confidence-building measures (such as the Open Skies agreement) have resulted in increased transparency; more military collection can now be left to defence attachés and inspection teams, or undertaken by long-distance, non-intrusive intelligence

---

[32] FBIS–SOV–95–019 of 30 January 1995.

[33] For the expulsion of Soviet intelligence officers from London in 1989 and its effects on Anglo-Soviet relations, see G. Howe, *Conflict of Loyalty* (London: Macmillan, 1994), pp. 562–5.

[34] See article by E. M. Holoboff, *International Herald Tribune*, 9 March 1995 and FBIS–SOV–95–020–S, pp. 9–13 of 30 January 1995 for examples of Russian accusations. They include statements that George Soros and American academic foundations are engaged in 'subversive-intelligence' activity including 'organizing a brain drain', 'creating positions of influence' and gathering secret information or information of scientific value.

[35] *The Times*, 24 February 1995.

[36] *The Times*, 3 August 1995.

means; and there are all the public and commercial sources on the more open world already discussed. The gung-ho determination with which some Western close access operations were mounted in the Cold War was praiseworthy in many ways; but in the new world it needs to be tempered by weighing the political consequences.

Clearly intrusion continues to be needed, for present needs and insurance against an unpredictable future; human sources for example are essential for intelligence about secretive and rogue regimes, and on terrorism and its state support. Other Humint is a natural extension of confidential diplomatic sources, and some counterintelligence is needed to defend against it. Armed forces have to have technical close access resources for use in war. In any case no one suggests that the threats perceived in intelligence intrusion are the world's greatest problem.

Nevertheless three suggestions can be made for keeping them under control. In the first place, governments should exercise adequate control and take authorization seriously. This is nothing new in the West. With relatively few exceptions, sensitive UK and US operations in the Cold War had political approval; for example the U-2 flights over the USSR received explicit Presidential authorization.[37] Balancing the value of intelligence against the political effects of collecting it was done by Western governments, not by intelligence services acting out of control. But there is something to be said for getting the idea of political responsibility more widely accepted, particularly by modern Russian leaders.

Secondly, governments should encourage each other to keep provocative intrusion within reasonable limits, with some proportionality between its scale and the threats on which it collects. Intelligence intrusion became the Cold War's Great Game through the cumulative effects of its intensity. Now intelligence satellites – for those who have them, or access to the results – make many close-range air and naval approaches less important than before. The international development of patent law might be a forum for seeking to limit governments' scientific, technical and industrial espionage for national economic advantage.

Thirdly, there may be scope for some international understanding that commitments to increased openness can be linked with reductions in intrusion. In discussions in the 1980s on military capabilities the USSR tabled ideas of 'reasonable sufficiency', and perhaps intelligence needed something of the same.[38] Commenting late in the Cold War on the

---

[37] C. Andrew, *For the President's Eyes Only* (London: HarperCollins, 1995), chapter 6 (for example p. 239).

[38] S. Shenfield, *The Nuclear Predicament* (London: RIIA/Routledge, 1987); for examples see pp. 85–90.

tit-for-tat of espionage-induced diplomatic expulsions and their effects, Hibbert took the analogy of arms control negotiations and wondered about an intelligence equivalent of the Mutual and Balanced Force Reductions on military forces. 'This is not said entirely in jest. If confrontation between East and West is slowly reduced and arms control begins to become a reality . . . would it not be healthy to try to manoeuvre secret intelligence agencies a little more to the margin of affairs?'[39]

Agreements to limit intelligence intrusion sound wildly improbable; but perhaps no more so than the US–Soviet agreement not to encipher telemetry, or the US–Russian and UK–Russian agreements in 1994 not to target each other with nuclear missiles. There is a common international interest that diplomacy should be valued as 'the communication system of the international society',[40] and not just as cover for intelligence collection or as a ready-made target for intelligence attacks.

Perhaps the financial pressures of the 1990s will suffice to keep intrusion within reasonable limits. The new American DCI in 1995 has stated his intention of reducing CIA's Humint collection 'all the way down to the bare bones'.[41] There are now said to be some professional contacts between Russian and Western intelligence agencies over terrorism, policing illicit arms traffic, drug trafficking and major international crime. These may provide scope for quiet dialogues on intrusion. Astonishingly, the KGB's successor organization is said to have handed over details of the bugging of the new US embassy building in Moscow in December 1991.[42]

Some understandings might emerge to extend the existing tacit assumption that close friends do not spy on or bug each other. In a much longer term some international law might develop about states' information-gathering, particularly where it is linked with diplomacy. This may seem unlikely. But as Best has commented 'much international law of the contemporary age . . . is "normative". Normative means standard-setting; adding to established State practice, the aspirational concept of State practice as it is expected, intended, or hoped to become at some

---

[39] R. Hibbert, 'Intelligence and Policy', *Intelligence and National Security* vol. 5 no. 1 (January 1990), p. 126.

[40] A. James, 'Diplomacy', *Review of International Studies* vol. 19 no. 1 (January 1993), p. 95.

[41] Statement by J. M. Deutch at Congressional hearings on his appointment as DCI and Director CIA (*International Herald Tribune*, 28 April 1995). This intended 'purge' was probably related to the Ames case, but suggests a smaller Humint organization.

[42] D. Nelson and J. Koenen-Grant, 'A Case of Bureaucracy in Action', *International Journal of Intelligence and Counterintelligence* vol. 6 no. 3 (fall 1993), p. 314.

future date.'[43] In a recent article a US naval officer has argued that, although intelligence collection is a recognized feature of international life, there are limits of behaviour which 'create definable customary international norms . . . To those who must work with these subjects, the norms are real, the boundaries tangible, and the consequences of exceeding them unacceptable – personally and professionally, nationally and internationally.'[44] The problems are defining the norms, and achieving the reciprocity that helps them to acquire some legal status.

There is no complete escape from the paradox that intelligence's knowledge tends to contribute to international security, while some of its collection is liable to detract from it. Governments everywhere have increasing appetites for information. We saw in the previous chapter that intelligence as a whole will become rather more open, and less dependent on its own means of collection. But these will continue to be needed on a considerable scale. Most collection is conducted at long ranges and is not inimical to climates of international security. But some of it is intrusive and may exacerbate peacetime threats.

The essential thing is to keep the scale of these intrusions under control, and restrict them to important needs and reasonable limits. Opportunities may present themselves for pre-empting any competitive revival of intrusion on a Cold War scale. Taking them may be of some significance in the new picture of international relationships as a whole. 'Since the end of the Cold War a universal international system has come into existence marked by the unprecedented situation in which almost all states are in diplomatic relations with other states.'[45] In an international society now consisting of 185 independent states it will be regrettable if conducting extensive espionage and close-range technical collection comes to be seen as a badge of mature statehood.

Summary

Most governments identify their interests with some aspects of international security, and national intelligence support is given to international security mechanisms in a variety of ways. This support is given only when nations choose to do it, and the idea of 'international' intelligence collection, conducted by the UN or other international institutions, is therefore attractive. But it is impracticable. International

---

[43] G. Best, *War and Law Since 1945* (Oxford: Clarendon Press, 1944), p. 7.

[44] M. E. Bowman, 'Intelligence and International Law', *International Journal of Intelligence and Counterintelligence* vol. 8 no. 3 (fall 1995), p. 330.

[45] R. Cohen, *Diplomacy 2000 B.C.–2000 A.D.* (paper delivered to the British International Studies Association annual conference, 1995), p. 1.

operations and verification will continue to need national inputs. Services of material from the United States as the intelligence super-power will remain crucial, particularly the worldwide surveillance available from its imagery satellites.

Accurate intelligence knowledge lessens national misperception, and tends on the whole to make individual states behave as 'better' members of international society. Most of the intelligence collection contributing to this knowledge operates at long ranges, and is not perceived by its targets as a threat. On the other hand espionage and short-range technical collection can be seen as intrusive and threatening, and can exacerbate inter-state tension.

In the long term states may develop international norms for acceptable intelligence activities. Additionally chapter 19 suggested that peacetime intelligence will draw increasingly on open sources of information, with rather smaller covert elements. In the meantime governments should seek to keep the more threatening intelligence operations within reason-able limits, particularly those linked with diplomacy. The world needs to avoid imitations of the Cold War's armaments race in intrusive collection.

Part VII

Summary

21   Modern intelligence power

It may be helpful to summarize here the main conclusions about the institutions, activity and output of the government intelligence model examined here: the UK–US (and Commonwealth) community, which also illuminates many features of Western intelligence and some aspects of modern intelligence power everywhere.

The system

Intelligence developed slowly as a permanent institution from the mid-nineteenth century to the beginning of the First World War, with more rapid growth thereafter, culminating in the satellite surveillance and increased power of electronic collection in the last quarter-century. This development has been matched by the growth of other organized government knowledge, such as government statistics and law enforcement intelligence. Like these other institutions, the government intelligence discussed here is a system of organized information-gathering, analysis and forecasting; like them, it serves government's executive functions but with an all-important institutional separation from policy-making and decision-taking. Thus peacetime intelligence is separate from diplomacy; similarly wartime intelligence is organizationally distinct from Electronic Warfare and other 'combat information' collected and used as integral parts of military operations.

Intelligence's broad subjects are foreign targets of all kinds and internal security threats (including terrorism), with much overlap between the two. In resource terms 'foreign intelligence' on the first group of targets is considerably larger than 'security intelligence' on the second. Within intelligence as a whole there are two other, separable components. The first is information collection, operating without its targets' cooperation or knowledge, usually by special means designed to penetrate secrecy. It is expert on particular techniques. By contrast the second, 'all-source' component is expert on particular subjects, to which the collection effort contributes.

Most intelligence resources are invested in collection, particularly in the modern Sigint agencies and (in those countries with intelligence satellites or access to their results) in those developed for imagery collection and interpretation. These technical agencies combine collection with processing, and disseminate some important single-source intelligence direct to users. This single-source service applies particularly to direct support of diplomatic negotiations, irrespective of subject.

Collection as a whole has two broad categories of output: 'observational' intelligence on 'things'; and 'message-like' intelligence derived from access to human communication of some kind, typically through securing documents, eavesdropping on conversations or deciphering communications. Most collection, especially the message-like material, is vulnerable to countermeasures. The consequent need for special secrecy pervades the whole intelligence process.

Predominant as collection is, definitive intelligence inputs to users are from the second (much smaller) stage of all-source analysis and assessment. Modern collection agencies are skilled in interpreting their own material, but the all-source stage has to weigh and finally assess multiple intelligence sources, along with material of non-intelligence origin such as diplomatic reporting, the media and contact with the enemy in war. Exploiting the many kinds of 'open' data bases now becoming available on a commercial basis adds to this importance of the all-source stage. One of the strengths of the UK–US–Commonwealth system is that the specialist collectors of secret intelligence do not normally have final responsibility for assessing the significance of their own material. The all-source melding of all available evidence provides a much broader concept of intelligence than the Soviet idea that it was essentially the product of secret collection.[1] All-source intelligence assessment can cover a wide variety of overseas subjects, and is not just dealing in others' secrets. But its authority with governments is greatest where there is some connection with national security, and a need to cope with organized foreign concealment or deception.

Purposes

Intelligence targets range widely, but a feature of the overall effort is the considerable investment devoted to defence intelligence on foreign armed forces and armaments in their widest aspects, including the international arms trade and foreign insurrection and civil war. One of

---

[1] Soviet battlefield intelligence (*razvedka*) was of course based on normal military all-source principles

intelligence's largest if normally unspectacular commitments is meeting the peacetime needs of its own state's armed forces and being able to support them in war.

On these and other subjects intelligence's main purpose is to assist its users' actions, but how this happens is almost infinitely variable. Some intelligence is used immediately, while more of it has cumulative effects, or educational or psychological values which influence action indirectly. Some warning coverage is a precaution against threats which never materialize. Much output of all kinds has no discernible use at all. Intelligence shares with all other information these characteristics of apparent waste, unpredictable value and serendipity.

Nevertheless the general effect is to optimize national strength and international influence in peacetime and promote the effective use of force in war and other conflict. It is part of the state's defences against internal threats. In both war and peace the main impact is cumulative and undramatic; though intelligence can sometimes determine the way in which wartime campaigns are fought, and can be a major factor in counter-terrorism.

There are also secondary effects. National intelligence is used for international security as well as narrowly national purposes. It also supports national information security, through counterespionage, counterintelligence and defensive advice and standards-setting; the standard required by national governments for their defensive information protection is a factor to be considered in determining how much to spend on sophisticated offensive collection. In the Cold War the fact of espionage and other intrusive collection reinforced East–West threat perceptions. In war intelligence also operates as a threat, inhibiting targets' freedom of action and the efficiency of their command, control and communications systems.

Furthermore there is a long-running technical contest between offensive intelligence and the security defences of its targets. A small breach in the defences can lead to the 'expanding torrent' of offensive intelligence success, which in turn has effects of strengthening its own side's defensive security. Between long-standing antagonists this intelligence–security contest is supported by an even more specialized counterintelligence campaign in which intelligence seeks to disable or capture its professional opponents. Intelligence has to fight some protracted contests of these kinds at its own technical, professional level, and part of its peacetime resources are employed in this way in maintaining 'technical continuity' on its targets and a counterintelligence capability.

Along with these adversarial effects and contests, intelligence also has its networks of international cooperation. National investments buy more than purely national outputs. The forms of cooperation are influenced by states' overarching political relationships, but also have some influence on them. Intelligence cooperation tends to be based on professional considerations, particularly the assessment of partners' information security standards; but it can also be provided or withheld as a means of diplomatic leverage. In close relationships intelligence communities believe they are influencing each other's national views; the general effect is perhaps to strengthen common perceptions.

Quality

These varied national and international effects are still subsidiary to intelligence's main purpose: to make its own government's action better than it would be without it. Its primary concern is therefore with its accuracy, combined with its credibility with its users and relevance to them; it has to be close to them without sacrificing objectivity.

Three sets of conclusions can be suggested to these ends. First, 'warning failure' against surprise attack tends to reflect basic misperceptions about targets, as well as failures in the operation of the community machinery. Warning should not be separated from long-term assessment; the numbers engaged in both should be kept small. A nucleus of experienced professional assessors is needed. Some supervision of the interdepartmental machinery is needed to spot weaknesses before they are found out by intelligence failure. These conclusions over 'warning' have implications for assessment as a whole.

Second, the problem of users' preconceptions has particular salience for defence intelligence, whose organizations are large and influential parts of the intelligence community. They have never been regarded as one of its strong points. In the Cold War a lack of independence and professional quality made them unduly influenced by armed forces' and defence industries' vested interests in the Soviet threat. The antidote is more corporate identity and professionalism, and greater national esteem. At least in Britain, this means recognizing that all-source analysts warrant the same pay and promotion prospects as the professional collectors.

Third, there is great value in the UK–US–Commonwealth device of interdepartmental national assessment which tests departmental assumptions and provides policy-makers with agreed intelligence inputs. The machinery for it depends on a delicate balance between collegial participation by the intelligence community and leadership from a central assessment group. The composition of the central group needs a balance between professional assessors and those with wider experience. There is also the question whether the interdepartmental assessment 'college' should include representatives of policy-making departments (as in the influence of the Foreign and Commonwealth Office within the British system), or be limited to genuine intelligence organizations: whether national assessment is a process of 'intelligence assessment', or of 'government assessment' which engages all government knowledge and opinion. A final question is how the detailed all-source analysis needed to underpin national assessment should be organized. Arguably the US structure, in which CIA's Directorate of Intelligence can study foreign targets as single entities, has advantages over the British arrangements which divide them organizationally into separate political, military and economic segments.

Management

The intelligence community has moved in the direction of sizeable, high-technology production plants. Its management needs to evaluate effectiveness and efficiency, as well as quality of output. One conclusion for management is that the 'intelligence cycle' is a useful cybernetic metaphor, provided that emphasis is placed on intelligence's initiative; the driving force is intelligence's search for users' reactions to the service provided to them, rather than reacting only to users' 'requirements'. Intelligence has entrepreneurial instincts for maximizing user satisfaction, and these need to be given scope.

Another conclusion is that, although intelligence processes can be costed in some detail, the 'internal' information content of output cannot be quantified in any consistently helpful way. The same applies to the use made of it. Yet many 'externals' of intelligence production and supporting activities can be counted and costed, and they provide additional, useful management information.

Finally, an intelligence 'market' between producers and users would not be an effective way for deciding intelligence investments and resource allocation. The complexity of the community and the short-termism likely in a market combine to make it seem both impracticable and undesirable. Yet users must be encouraged to think more seriously about the costs of what they are asking for and receiving.

These assumptions suggest that intelligence can usefully absorb some of the cost-conscious, results-oriented culture being encouraged throughout the modern public service, but without devising any special management 'system' to embody it. At the community-wide level the main management problems are indeed of a different kind. Intelligence communities are diffuse, and some issues are too big to be resolved merely through single-agency bids or inter-agency consensus. Both the British and the US communities need stronger strategy and planning to enable intelligence to be handled as a national resource. Modest measures towards a more effective community in this respect would be some strengthening of central staffs, and the creation of greater 'community consciousness' through planned inter-agency exchanges for career development. Though excessive centralization must be avoided, both nations may also have to face up to vesting effective managerial responsibility for the community in one place.

Within agencies the normal principles of good management apply. Intelligence employs ordinary people, in large numbers and with wide varieties of skills and expectations. There is still a high proportion of lifetime careers in single organizations. The most distinctive feature of the organizational culture is intelligence's secrecy and the sense of difference and mystique it produces. Secrecy combines with long-term employment to produce high but slightly brittle morale.

The insulation caused by secrecy makes it important for intelligence to seek ideas from 'outside' and to draw on modern management practices of 'informal' organization, though there are valid reasons for preserving some aspects of tight control and formal delineation of responsibility. The main bearing of secrecy is however on the application to intelligence of the modern public service-wide style of results-oriented management, in which institutions have been enjoined by government to emphasize contracts, targets and monetary incentives rather than commitment. As long as espionage (or whistle-blowing) is a genuine threat to intelligence sources, management has to take a special interest in its staff, and exercise an unusual degree of surveillance of their official and private lives. Intelligence is particularly vulnerable to discontented employees, and the necessary surveillance of its staff is tolerable only if combined with fairness and humanity. More than most organizations, intelligence has to be a genuinely caring employer.

1990s and beyond

Chapters 19 and 20 suggested national and international needs and a strategy to meet them. Intelligence has to be judged increasingly by its peacetime usefulness; though it is also a necessary support for armed forces, a precautionary warning system, and a national capability that can be expanded in these and other unforeseeable directions. The search for measures of cost-effectiveness and cost-benefit fits the increased test of peacetime usefulness, even though the search will never be completely successful. Reductions in expenditure should be arranged so that, apart from any cuts in security intelligence, the impact falls on collection and not all-source analysis. Analysis needs more attention than it has had. The priority is the relatively inexpensive one of improving its quality, and equipping it to keep pace with the 'open source' opportunities now open to it.

Nevertheless collection will continue to be the main intelligence investment. Even with a reduced workforce, major capital investments will continue to be needed to keep pace with targets and grasp opportunities – particularly those open to satellite collection. Apart from meeting narrowly national needs, collection now has the additional role of providing intelligence for the support of UN operations and other aspects of international security. There is a growing onus upon the United States and other effective intelligence powers to develop this international role.

The general effect of intelligence knowledge is also to incline national governments to behave better, in international security terms, than they would without it. Most of the intelligence collection that contributes to this knowledge operates over long distances and is unspecific in its targets. Intelligence as a whole tends to improve international society and does not introduce new tensions within it; it is an unprovocative form of national power.

But part of its collection – admittedly a small part – is more intrusive on its target states, and is liable to contribute thereby to the spectrum of inter-state threats. Extensive Humint attacks on foreign states (not on terrorist or similar organizations) can be perceived as threats of this kind; so too can extensive close-access technical operations, and operations under diplomatic cover or attacking diplomatic premises. Threat perceptions are related mainly to the intensity of these intrusions. States could usefully work towards an international climate that moderates collection of these kinds, restricting it to reasonable limits and genuine needs.

Suggestions for further reading

This is not a complete bibliography but an introductory guide to 'intelligence studies'. It lists the main specialist intelligence periodicals but not the articles in them, apart from a few of special importance. The titles below are grouped roughly in accordance with the book's plan, preceded by some items in a 'general' category.

GENERAL WORKS

Of those shown below, Shulsky's book has been widely praised as a short introduction to intelligence as a whole. Berkowitz and Goodman produced a perceptive account of American problems, strengths and weaknesses. Laqueur's treatment is more general, with an emphasis on the intelligence–policy relationship. Godson's series produced from 1979 onwards was a *tour de force*, as one of the first attempts to describe and analyse all the different intelligence components and synthesize the results. All these works deal explicitly or implicitly with the US system and Cold War preoccupations, but are useful introductions. Richelson's recently published account of twentieth-century intelligence ranges rather more widely, and is a good introduction to modern intelligence history.

Also listed under this 'General' heading are the volumes of the British Official History of the Second World War intelligence by Sir Harry Hinsley and his collaborators (or, for the volume at IV below on deception, Sir Michael Howard). This is of course wartime intelligence history, and incomplete as such; the war against Japan is omitted, as is the contribution of secret intelligence to wartime British diplomacy. The quip attributed to a Head of SIS, that the Official History 'is a book written by a committee, about committees, for committees', has stuck. But it is a magisterial account of wartime intelligence sources, organization and effects on decision-taking. It is the most comprehensive account ever published of national intelligence in action, and no conclusions about intelligence and military power are complete without some reference to it. A shortened version is available in a single volume, which concentrates on intelligence's effects on wartime decisions and omits technical detail.

The main specialist periodicals are *Intelligence and National Security* and the *International Journal of Intelligence and Counterintelligence*. These quarterly journals are the best indication of the current scope of academic intelligence studies. They both date back to 1986 and contain rich selections of historical articles along with some on current intelligence problems and 'intelligence theory'. CIA's unclassified *Studies in Intelligence* is now also available. The *Defense Intelligence Journal* is a useful defence-orientated complement to other publications. *World Intelligence Review* contains book reviews and useful lists of international press references.

Berkowitz, B. and Goodman, A. *Strategic Intelligence for American National Security* (Princeton: Princeton University Press, 1989)

Godson, R. (ed.) series title *Intelligence Requirements for the 1980s* (published by the National Strategy Informations Center, Washington D.C.), with the individual titles *Elements of Intelligence* (1979), *Analysis and Estimates* (1980), *Counterintelligence* (1980), *Covert Action* (1981), *Clandestine Collection* (1982), *Domestic Intelligence* (1986) and *Intelligence and Policy* (1986); and *Intelligence Requirements for the 1990s: Collection, Analysis, Counterintelligence and Covert Action* (1989)

Hinsley, F. H. (with others) *British Intelligence in the Second World War* (4 vols) (London: HMSO, 1979–90)

Hinsley, F. H. *British Intelligence in the Second World War: Abridged Edition* (London: HMSO, 1993)

Laqueur, W. *A World of Secrets: the Uses and Limits of Intelligence* (New York: Basic Books, 1985)

Richelson, J. T. *A Century of Spies: Intelligence in the Twentieth Century* (Oxford: Oxford University Press, 1995)

Shulsky, A. N. *Silent Warfare: Understanding the World of Intelligence* (London: Brassey's, 1991)

JOURNALS

Defense Intelligence Journal (6723 Whittier Ave, Suite 303A, McLean, Va. 22101)

Intelligence and National Security (Cass, London)

International Journal of Intelligence and Counterintelligence (Intel Publishing Group, PO Box 188, Stroudsburg, Penn. 18360)

Studies in Intelligence (Center for the Study of Intelligence, CIA, Washington D.C. 20505)

World Intelligence Review (Heldref Publications, 1319 Eighteenth St NW, Washington D.C. 200036-1802)

I EVOLUTION AND OUTLINE (CHAPTERS 1–3)

Andrew's *Secret Service* is the standard historical account of British intelligence. There are a number of specialist historical studies of early periods; those by Black and Prestwich are interesting examples. Early military intelligence and subsequent Victorian developments are covered in Fergusson, Gudgin and Parritt. The continental background and the evolution of military staffs are described in Van Crevald's book on military command, though intelligence is not its primary concern.

Some accounts of twentieth-century intelligence are given in the 'general' books mentioned above; thus Hinsley's Official History vol. I begins with two chapters on pre-1939 developments. Good accounts of major powers' intelligence arrangements in 1914 and 1939 can be found in May's book, although the authors' main concern is evaluating the accuracy of these pre-war perceptions; the editor's masterly 'Conclusions: Capabilities and Proclivities' is relevant to IV below. For intelligence in the First and Second World Wars see III below. Breckenridge, Johnson and Jeffreys-Jones give accounts of the post-1945 US system, concentrating on CIA. Hopple and Watson provide a useful, though now dated, account of the US military community and balance the other civilian-oriented books; the article by General Clapper provides an updating. The KGB and its antecedents are covered by Andrew and Gordievsky; another excellent book is by Amy Knight. There is less about the GRU, though Suvorov's book gives impressions. Richelson's three books provide factual accounts of US, Soviet and other national systems (including the UK's); on classified matters they have a proportion of error, but are generally reliable.

For the parallels between intelligence developments and the evolution of other governmental intelligence from the late nineteenth century onwards I have drawn on essays edited by MacLeod and by Davidson and White. For comparisons between 'intelligence' and developments in the information society and 'informatics' see books by Cronin and Davenport, and Dedijer and Jéquier.

Andrew, C. *Secret Service: the Making of the British Intelligence Community* (London: Heinemann, 1985)

Andrew, C. and Gordievsky, O. *KGB: the Inside Story of its Foreign Operations from Lenin to Gorbachev* (London: Hodder and Stoughton, 1990)

Black, J. 'British Intelligence in the Mid-Eighteenth Century Crisis', *Intelligence and National Security* vol. 2 no. 2 (April 1987)

Breckenridge, S. D. *The CIA and the US Intelligence System* (Boulder and London: Westview, 1986)

Clapper, Lt Gen. J. R. 'Reorganization of DIA and Defense Intelligence Activities', *American Intelligence Journal* (autumn/winter 1993)

Cronin, B. and Davenport, E. *Post-Professionalism: Transforming the Information Heartland* (London: Taylor Graham, 1988)

Davidson, R. and White, P. (eds.) *Information and Government* (Edinburgh: Edinburgh University Press, 1988)

Dedijer, S. and Jéquier, N. (eds.) *Intelligence for Economic Development: an Inquiry into the Role of the Knowledge Industry* (Oxford: Berg, 1987)

Fergusson, T. G. *British Military Intelligence 1870–1914* (London: Arms and Armour Press, 1984)

Gudgin, P. *Military Intelligence: the British Story* (London: Arms and Armour Press, 1989)

Hopple, G. W. and Watson, B. W. (eds.) *The Military Intelligence Community* (Boulder and London: Westview, 1986)

Jeffreys-Jones, R. *The CIA and American Democracy* (London: Yale University Press, 1989)

Johnson, L. K. *America's Secret Power: the CIA in a Democratic Society* (Oxford: Oxford University Press, 1989)

Knight, A. W. *The KGB: Police and Politics in the Soviet Union* (London: Unwin Hyman, 1988)

MacLeod, R. (ed.) *Government and Expertise* (Cambridge: Cambridge University Press, 1988)

May, E. R. (ed.) *Knowing One's Enemies: Intelligence Assessment before the Two World Wars* (Princeton: Princeton University Press, 1986)

Parritt, B. A. H. *The Intelligencers: the Story of British Military Intelligence up to 1914* (Ashford, Kent: Intelligence Corps Association, 1983)

Prestwich, J. O. 'Military Intelligence under the Norman and Angevin Kings' in G. Garnett and J. Hudson (eds.), *Law and Government in Medieval England and Normandy: Essays in Honour of Sir James Holt* (Cambridge: Cambridge University Press, 1994)

Richelson, J. T. *Sword and Shield: Soviet Intelligence and Security Apparatus* (Cambridge, Mass.: Ballinger, 1986)

The US Intelligence Community (Boulder: Westview, 3rd edn, 1995)

Foreign Intelligence Organizations (Cambridge, Mass.: Ballinger, 1988)

Suvorov, V. *Inside Soviet Military Intelligence* (London: Macmillan, 1984)

Van Crevald, M. *Command in War* (Cambridge, Mass.: Harvard University Press, 1985)

II COMPONENTS AND BOUNDARIES (CHAPTERS 4–7)

Despite the many books about spies it is difficult to find one which captures the essence of Humint and Humint agencies. Gordievsky's autobiography is one of the better accounts by defectors. Brook-Shepherd gives a selection of cases. Philby's and Blake's accounts of their own treachery are interesting and plausible but there is no means of knowing how much of them to believe. Blitzer recounts the unusual case of espionage within US intelligence by its Israeli ally.

For technical collection, the standard work on the history of Sigint is Kahn's *Codebreakers*. His *Seizing the Enigma* provides a more complete account of British naval Sigint in the Second World War. Ball has written widely on Soviet Sigint and dispels the idea that Soviet intelligence collection was mainly Humint. The specialist American periodical *Cryptologia* combines technical articles on cryptology and cryptanalysis with some historical ones.

Imagery's early origins are summarized by Mead. Burrows gives a very readable account of the U-2 programme and satellite imagery and Sigint. The routine of detailed all-source analysis in peacetime does not get much description in print (but see III below for wartime accounts, especially R. V. Jones's account of putting different sources of evidence together). Cline captures very well the problems and responsibility of assessment for top level readers.

For the boundary issues discussed in chapter 7 see Kent for a 'broad' view of intelligence's role, and Shulsky ('General' above) and Robertson for 'narrower' ones. (For a portrait of Kent and an account of his ideas see the relevant parts of Winks's study of intelligence connections with Yale.) There is little public discussion of distinctions between institutionalized intelligence and other kinds of battlefield information. Electronic Warfare is described by Devereux, but he does not point to its boundaries with Sigint.

Ball, D. 'Soviet Signals Intelligence: Vehicular Systems and Operations' and 'Soviet Signals Intelligence: Organization and Management', *Intelligence and National Security* vol. 4 no. 1 (January 1989) and vol. 4 no. 4 (October 1989) (with R. Windrem)

Blake, G. *No Other Choice* (London: Cape, 1990)

Blitzer, W. *Territory of Lies* (London: Harper and Row, 1989)

Brook-Shepherd, G. *The Storm Birds: Soviet Post-War Defectors* (London: Weidenfeld and Nicolson, 1988)

Burrows, W. E. *Deep Black: the Secrets of Space Espionage* (London: Bantam, 1988)

Cline, R. *The CIA: Reality vs Myth* (Washington D.C.: Acropolis Books, 1982). *Secrets, Spies and Scholars: Blueprint of the Essential CIA* (Washington D.C.: Acropolis Books, 1976) was an earlier version.

Devereux, T. *Messenger Gods of Battle. Radio, Radar, Sonar: the Story of Electronics in War* (London: Brassey's, 1991)

Gordievsky, O. *Next Stop Execution* (London: Macmillan, 1995)

Kahn, D. *The Codebreakers* (New York: Macmillan, 1973; paperback, Weidenfeld and Nicolson, 1973)
   Seizing the Enigma: the Race to Break the U-Boat Codes (London: Souvenir, 1992)

Kent, S. *Strategic Intelligence for US World Policy* (Hamden, Conn.: Archon Books, 1965 edition; first published by Princeton, 1949)

Mead, P. *The Eye in the Air: History of Air Observation and Reconnaissance for the Army 1785–1945* (London: HMSO, 1983)

Philby, K. *My Secret War* (MacGibbon and Kee, 1968; paperback, New York: Ballantine Books, 1983)

Robertson, K. G. 'Intelligence, Terrorism and Civil Liberties', *Conflict Quarterly* (University of New Brunswick), vol. 7 no. 2 (spring 1987)

Winks, R. *Cloak and Gown: Scholars in America's Secret War* (London: Collins, 1987)

III EFFECTS (CHAPTERS 8–12)

There are many books on wartime intelligence. First World War intelligence still awaits its official or unofficial historian, but British naval intelligence (and the use of the Zimmerman telegram) are well summarized by Beesly; and Ferris has recently published an important reassessment of British military Sigint. For the Second World War, in addition to the Hinsley histories, Bennett provides a good summary of the Western Allies' intelligence in *Behind the Battle*, including maritime and air intelligence. His other books deal in more detail with Sigint in the Mediterranean and continental campaigns. The flavour of naval intelligence is well described by McLachlan; he wrote before the breaking of the German Enigma could be revealed explicitly, but this helps him to bring out the multiplicity and interdependence of sources. The Battle of the Atlantic is covered by Winton and summarized by Rohwer, but the article by Milner is a notable attempt to disentangle the effects of Sigint from developments in weaponry and other factors. R. V. Jones gives an outstanding personal account of scientific intelligence and its effects, mainly on the air war.

Intelligence in the Pacific War has no equivalent of the Hinsley history, but Lewin produced a readable summary of Allied Sigint there; as more recently has Winton. MacArthur's use of it has been studied in more detail by Drea. Chapman provides a penetrating short account of Japanese intelligence.

As for intelligence's peacetime effects, the detailed literature on the Cold War is discussed in IV below. Andrew's *For the President's Eyes Only* describes and evaluates American intelligence's top level effects, and is also a comprehensive historical account of the American intelligence community's evolution. Other studies of peacetime use tend to appear as articles in the periodicals already described. However the historical essays edited by Andrew and Dilks give good examples, mainly of support for diplomacy. The collection by Andrew and Noakes provides similar peacetime studies as well as some wartime ones. May's book (I above) provides ample material on assessing military capabilities in peacetime; Wark provides a definitive account of assessing German rearmament. The Cuban crisis of 1962 has been extensively described; Garthoff gives a brief account of intelligence and central decision-taking, while Brugioni brings out the intelligence processes involved. Handel's *War, Strategy and Intelligence* includes an analysis of diplomatic surprise. Hibbert's important article gives a diplomat's view of intelligence; my own article the following year qualified some points.

For counterespionage and counterintelligence in the Second World War see Masterman's account, and volume IV of the British Official History (see 'General' category above) by Hinsley and Simkins. Godson's *Counterintelligence* (also see 'General' above) deals very well with these subjects, though using American definitions. Little has been written about passive defensive security. The same applies to peacetime intelligence alliances, but Richelson and Ball describe US–UK–Commonwealth arrangements.

There is as yet no comprehensive theory about the effects of intelligence, and 'intelligence warfare' or the interaction between its various roles discussed in Part III here. But important contributions include those by Ferris and Handel, especially their joint article published in 1995. Hinsley provides an estimate of how much difference intelligence made in the Second World War, in his article in Andrew and Noakes.

Andrew, C. *For the President's Eyes Only: Secret Intelligence and the American Presidency from Washington to Bush* (London: HarperCollins, 1995)

Andrew, C. and Dilks, D. (eds.) *The Missing Dimension: Governments and Intelligence Communities in the Twentieth Century* (London: Macmillan, 1984)

Andrew, C. and Noakes, J. (eds.) *Intelligence and International Relations 1900–45* (Exeter: Exeter University, 1987)

Beesly, P. *Room 40: British Naval Intelligence 1914–18* (London: Hamish Hamilton, 1982)

Bennett, R. *Behind the Battle: Intelligence in the War with Germany, 1939–45* (London: Sinclair-Stevenson, 1994)

Ultra and Mediterranean Strategy 1941–1945 (London: Hamish Hamilton, 1989)

Ultra in the West: the Normandy Campaign (London: Hutchinson, 1979)

Brugioni, D. *Eyeball to Eyeball: the Inside Story of the Cuban Missile Crisis* (New York: Random, 1991)

Chapman, J. W. M. 'Japanese Intelligence 1919–1945: a Suitable Case for Treatment' in Andrew and Noakes (see above)

Drea, E. J. *MacArthur's ULTRA: Codebreaking and the War against Japan* (Lawrence: University Press of Kansas, 1992)

Ferris, J. *The British Army and Signals Intelligence during the First World War* (Stroud, Glos.: Sutton for Army Records Society, 1992)

'The British Army and Signals Intelligence in the Field during the First World War', *Intelligence and National Security* vol. 3 no. 4 (October 1988)

'The British Army, Signals and Security in the Desert Campaign 1940–42' in Handel (ed.), *Intelligence and Military Operations*

'The Intelligence–Deception Complex: an Anatomy', *Intelligence and National Security* vol. 4 no. 4 (October 1989)

'Ralph Bennett and the Study of Ultra', *Intelligence and National Security* vol. 6 no. 2 (April 1991)

Ferris, J. and Handel, M. I. 'Clausewitz, Intelligence, Uncertainty and the Art of Command in Military Operations', *Intelligence and National Security* vol. 10 no. 1 (January 1995)

Garthoff, R. L. *Reflections on the Cuban Missile Crisis* (Washington D.C.: Brookings Institution, 1989)

Handel, M. I. *War, Strategy and Intelligence* (London: Cass, 1989)

(ed.) *Leaders and Intelligence* (London: Cass, 1989)

(ed.) *Intelligence and Military Operations* (London: Cass, 1990)

Herman, M. E. 'Intelligence and Policy: a Comment', *Intelligence and National Security* vol. 6 no. 1 (January 1991)

Hibbert, R. 'Intelligence and Policy', *Intelligence and National Security* vol. 5 no. 1 (January 1990)

Hinsley, F. H. 'British Intelligence in the Second World War' in Andrew and Noakes (see above)

Jones, R. V. *Most Secret War: British Scientific Intelligence 1939–1945* (London: Hamish Hamilton, 1978)

Lewin, R. *The American Magic: Codes, Ciphers and the Defeat of Japan* (London: Penguin, 1983)

Masterman, J. *The Double Cross System in the War of 1939–45* (New Haven, Conn.: Yale University Press, 1972)

McLachlan, D. *Room 39: Naval Intelligence in Action 1939–45* (London: Weidenfeld and Nicolson, 1968)

Milner, M. 'The Battle of the Atlantic' in J. Gooch (ed.), *Decisive Campaigns of the Second World War* (London: Cass, 1990)

Richelson, J. T. and Ball, D. *The Ties That Bind: Intelligence Cooperation between the UKUSA Countries* (Boston: Allen and Unwin, 1985)

Rohwer, J. 'The Operational Use of Ultra in the Battle of the Atlantic' in Andrew and Noakes (see above)

Wark, W. *The Ultimate Enemy: British Intelligence and Pre-War Germany* (London: Tauris, 1985)

Winton, J. *Ultra at Sea* (London: Cooper, 1988)

Ultra in the Pacific: How Breaking Japanese Codes and Ciphers Affected Naval Operations Against Japan 1941–1945 (London: Cooper, 1993)

IV ACCURACY (CHAPTERS 13–15)

For an introduction to the large literature on warning failure I recommend Wohlstetter's classic study of Pearl Harbor, and Betts, Kam and Handel for general conclusions. Exchanges between Betts and Levite in the *International Studies Quarterly* illuminate the role of collection. Handel deals with the closely related subject of deception, as do Daniel and Herbig, Michael Howard (as part of the Second World War's Official History) and Whaley (for the Soviet invasion of Germany).

Broader reflections on intelligence's problems in 'getting things right' have been much influenced by the writings of Jervis. Producer–user relations are also discussed by Cline (see II above) and Betts; Gazit discusses Israeli experience (in Handel's *Leaders and Intelligence*, III above). Ford provides an admirable short summary of the problems of assessment and what can be done to reduce them.

The problems of defence intelligence (chapter 14) are illustrated largely from assessments of Soviet military capabilities. New evidence appearing in both the United States and Russia may alter historical judgments, but at present the most important works on strategic nuclear forces are those by Freedman and Prados. Garthoff adds to the picture, as have Hoffman and Steiner. On the assessment of Soviet conventional forces see articles by Evangelista and Duffield; an extensive study is still needed.

The discussion of arrangements for national assessment (chapter 15) draws upon Berkowitz and Goodman ('General' above), and upon Thomas's article on the British wartime JIC – quite the most important insight into this subject – and relevant passages in McLachlan (III above).

Betts, R. K. *Surprise Attack: Lessons for Defense Planning* (Washington D.C.: Brookings Institution, 1982)
  'Policy-makers and Intelligence Analysts', *Intelligence and National Security* vol. 3 no. 1 (January 1988)
  'Surprise, Scholasticism, and Strategy: a Review of Ariel Levite's *Intelligence and Strategic Surprises*' (and rejoinder by Levite, *'Intelligence and Strategic Surprises* Revisited: a Response to Richard K. Betts's "Surprise, Scholasticism, and Strategy"'), *International Studies Quarterly* vol. 33 no. 3 (September 1989)
Daniel, D. C. and Herbig, K. L. (eds.) *Strategic Military Deception* (New York: Pergamon, 1982)
Duffield, J. S. 'Soviet Military Threat to Western Europe', *Journal of Strategic Studies* vol. 15 no. 2 (1992)
Evangelista, A. 'Stalin's Postwar Army Reappraised', *International Security* vol. 7 no. 3 (winter 1982–3)
Ford, H. P. *Estimative Intelligence* (Lanham, Md./London: University Press of America, 1993)
Freedman, L. *US Intelligence and the Soviet Strategic Threat* (London: Macmillan, 1977 and 1986)
Garthoff, R. L. *Assessing the Adversary: Estimates by the Eisenhower Administration of Soviet Intentions and Capabilities* (Washington D.C.: Brookings, 1991)

Gazit, S. 'Intelligence Estimates and the Decision-Maker', *Intelligence and National Security* vol. 3 no. 3 (July 1988). (Also in Handel's *Leaders and Intelligence*, in III above.)

Handel, M. I. 'Intelligence and the Problem of Strategic Surprise', *Journal of Strategic Studies* vol. 7 no. 3 (September 1984)

Strategic and Operational Deception in the Second World War (London: Cass, 1987)

Hoffman, P. 'The Making of National Estimates during the Period of the Missile Gap', *Intelligence and National Security* vol. 1 no. 3 (September 1986)

Howard, M. *British Intelligence in the Second World War. Vol. V: Strategic Deception* (London: HMSO, 1990)

Jervis, R. 'Intelligence and Foreign Policy', *International Security* vol. 11 (winter 1986–7)

'Strategic Intelligence and Effective Policy' in Farson, A. S., Stafford, D., Wark, W. K. (eds.) *Security and Intelligence in a Changing World: New Perspectives for the 1990s* (London: Cass, 1991)

'What's Wrong with the Intelligence Process', *International Journal of Intelligence and Counterintelligence* vol. 1 no. 1 (spring 1986)

Kam, E. *Surprise Attack: the Victim's Perspective* (Cambridge, Mass., and London: Harvard University Press, 1988)

Levite, A. *Intelligence and Strategic Surprises* (New York: Columbia University Press, 1987)

Prados, J. *The Soviet Estimate: US Intelligence Analysis and Soviet Strategic Forces* (Princeton: Princeton University Press, 1982 and 1986)

Steiner, B. H. 'American Intelligence and the Soviet ICBM Build-Up: Another Look', *Intelligence and National Security* vol. 8 no. 2 (April 1993)

Thomas, E. 'The Evolution of the JIC System up to and during World War II' in Andrew and Noakes (section III above)

Whaley, B. *Codeword Barbarossa* (Cambridge, Mass.: MIT Press, 1973)

Wohlstetter, R. *Pearl Harbor: Warning and Decision* (Stanford: Stanford University Press, 1962)

V MANAGEMENT AND VALUE (CHAPTERS 16–18)

Memoirs by Strong, Colby and Turner give impressions of management at the top level. Outside intelligence literature this Part has been influenced by Morgan's powerful *Images of Organization*, particularly his chapters on metaphors of organizations as machines and brains. Steinbruner provides an introduction to cybernetics; for a critique of the cybernetic 'intelligence cycle' by an ex-practitioner, see Hulnick's article. The problems of measuring intelligence and evaluating it by cost-effectiveness and cost-benefit analysis are illuminated by the writing on 'informatics' and 'information science' by Cronin and Davenport (I above); Arrow (who contributed to advanced modern theory on the 'economics of information'); the Vickerys' book; and essays edited by Varlejs. The discussion of intelligence and markets draws on academic writing about recent developments in the British public service; the collection edited by Rhodes is a good specimen. On the 'culture' of intelligence organizations, Simmel's earlier work provides insights into the general effects of secrecy, but there are as yet no studies of secret intelligence organizations by behavioural scientists. Former practitioners' contributions to the recent collection by Hinsley and Stripp provide some evidence, as wartime memories recollected in tranquillity.

Arrow, K. J. *The Economics of Information* (Vol. IV of *Collected Papers*) (London: Harvard University Press, 1984)

Colby, W. *Honourable Men* (London: Hutchinson, 1978)

Cronin, B. (ed.) *Information Management: From Strategies to Action 2* (London: Aslib, 1992)

Hinsley, F. H. and Stripp, A. *Codebreakers: the Inside Story of Bletchley Park* (Oxford: Oxford University Press, 1993)

Hulnick, A. S. 'The Intelligence Producer–Policy Consumer Linkage', *Intelligence and National Security* vol. 1 no. 2 (May 1986)

Morgan, G. *Images of Organization* (London: Sage 1986)

Niskanen, W. A. *Bureaucracy and Representative Government* (Chicago: Aldine Atherton, 1971)

Rhodes, R. A. W. (ed.) 'The New Public Management', *Public Administration* (special edition), vol. 69 no. 1 (spring 1991)

Steinbruner, J. *The Cybernetic Theory of Decision* (Princeton: Princeton University Press, 1974)

Strong, Major-General Sir Kenneth, *Intelligence at the Top: the Recollections of an Intelligence Officer* (London: Cassell, 1968)

Turner, S. *Secrecy and Democracy: the CIA in Transition* (London: Harper and Row, 1985)

Varlejs, J. (ed.) *The Economics of Information* (London: McFarland, 1982)

Vickery, B. and A. *Information Science in Theory and Practice* (London: Butterworths, 1987)

Wolfe, K. H. (ed.) *The Sociology of Georg Simmel* (Glencoe, Ill.: The Free Press, 1950)

VI THE 1990S AND BEYOND (CHAPTERS 19 AND 20)

Writing on the post-Cold War value of intelligence is mainly American, or American-based, much of it in international relations and intelligence periodicals. Those by Boren, Carver, Goodman and Berkowitz, Johnson, May and Ott (below) pose many of the issues, including the role of economic intelligence. In book form, Codevilla provides a balanced 'great power' view; and Adams deals with the British as well as the American system, with good official interviews. A recent book edited by Godson, May and Schmitt explores US issues in depth. Generally speaking this literature does not distinguish sharply between single-source and all-source intelligence, as is the main theme here.

On intelligence's international effects, Gaddis and Steinberg describe and discuss the record of American and Soviet use of intelligence for arms control verification during the Cold War. The agreements about NTMs are recounted by Strobe Talbot. Intelligence collection's position in international law remains largely unexplored, except for the few incidental references given in notes to chapter 20.

Adams, J. *The New Spies: Exploring the Frontiers of Espionage* (London: Hutchinson, 1994)

Boren, D. L. 'The Intelligence Community: How Crucial?', *Foreign Affairs* vol. 71 no. 3 (summer 1992)

Carver, G. 'Intelligence in the Age of Glasnost', *Foreign Affairs* vol. 69 no. 3 (summer 1990)

Codevilla, A. *Informing Statecraft: Intelligence for a New Century* (New York: Free Press, 1992)

Gaddis, J. L. 'Learning to Live with Transparency: the Emergence of a Reconnaissance Satellite Regime' in his *The Long Peace: Inquiries into the History of the Cold War* (New York: Oxford University Press, 1987)

Godson, R., May, E. R. and Schmitt, G. (eds.) *US Intelligence at the Crossroads: Agendas for Reform* (Washington D.C./London: Brassey's, 1995)

Goodman, A. E. and Berkowitz, B. D. 'Intelligence without the Cold War', *Intelligence and National Security* vol. 9 no. 2 (April 1994)

Johnson, L. K. 'Smart Intelligence', *Foreign Policy* no. 89 (winter 1992–3)

May, E. R. 'Intelligence: Backing into the Future', *Foreign Affairs* vol. 71 no. 3 (summer 1992)

Ott, M. 'Shaking Up the CIA', *Foreign Policy* (winter 1993–4)

Steinberg, G. M. *Satellite Reconnaissance: the Role of Informal Bargaining* (Westport, Conn.: Praeger, 1983)

Talbot, S. *Deadly Gambits: the Reagan Administration and the Stalemate in Nuclear Arms Control* (London: Pan Books, 1984)

Endgame: the Inside Story of SALT II (London: Harper and Row, 1979)

'Scrambling and Spying in SALT II', *International Security* vol. 4 no. 2 (fall 1979)

Turner, S. 'Intelligence for a New World Order', *Foreign Affairs* vol. 70 no. 4 (fall 1991)

Index

Michael Herman served as an intelligence officer at
Government Communications Headquarters at
Cheltenham between 1952 and 1987. In this period
he had spells at the Joint Services Staff College and
in the Cabinet Office and Defence Intelligence
Staff. Between 1972 and 1975 he was Secretary of
the Joint Intelligence Committee. Since retirement
he has been a Gwilym Gibbon Research Fellow at
Nuffield College Oxford and an Honorary Research
Fellow at Keele University. He has taught at King's
College London and lectured at universities and
military colleges in Britain and the United States,
and has published journal articles on intelligence
and national security.